GEORGE F. WALKER has written more than twenty plays, winning six Chalmers Awards and four Dora Mavor Moore Awards and twice winning the Governor General's Award for Drama. His plays have been widely produced in Canada, the United States, Britain and Australia and translated into German, French, Turkish, Polish and Czech. He was born in Toronto in 1947. His career as a playwright began in 1970 when he wrote his first play in response to a lamp-post bill soliciting scripts for Toronto's Factory Theatre Lab, then a fledgling, shoe-string operation housed in a former candle-factory. He spent the next five years as playwright-in-residence at the Factory Theatre, where he wrote *Beyond Mozambique* which premiered there in 1974. In 1977, Walker began a three-year affiliation with Toronto Free Theatre, which premiered *Zastrozzi: The Master of Discipline*. He served as playwright-in-residence at the New York Shakespeare Festival in 1981. Walker had directed his first production in 1976; over the next decade he would direct the premieres of *Theatre of the Film Noir, The Art of War*, and *Criminals in Love*, all produced by the Factory. *Better Living* premiered in 1986 at the St. Lawrence Centre in Toronto and Walker won the Governor General's Award for *Criminals in Love;* in 1989, he won his second Governor General's Award, for *Nothing Sacred*. In 1991, *Escape from Happiness* premiered at Vassar College in a production by New York Film and Stage Co. at The Powerhouse Theater; the following year Walker directed the Canadian premiere of the play for the Factory. Most recently he has written *Tough!*, which premiered at Vancouver's Green Thumb Theatre for Young People in 1993. In 1994, he was awarded the Toronto Arts Award for Drama.

SHARED ANXIETY

Selected Plays

GEORGE F. WALKER

Coach House Press
Toronto

These plays are fully protected under the copyright laws of Canada and all other countries of the Copyright Union and are subject to royalty. Changes to the script are expressly forbidden without written consent of the author. Rights to produce, film, record in whole or in part, in any medium or in any language, by any group, *amateur or professional,* are retained by the author. Interested persons are requested to apply for permission and terms to:

Great North Artists Management, Inc.
350 Dupont St.
Toronto, Ontario, Canada M5R 1V9

The punctuation of these plays carefully adheres to the author's instructions.

FIRST EDITION
Printed in Canada
1 3 5 7 9 8 6 4 2

Published with the assistance of the Canada Council, the Ontario Arts Council, the Department of Canadian Heritage and the Ontario Publishing Centre.

Canadian Cataloguing in Publication Data

Walker, George F., 1947-
Shared Anxiety

ISBN 0-88910-472-7

I. Title.
PS8595.A55S53 1994   C812'.54   C94-931745-4
PR9199.3.W35S53 1994

CONTENTS

PREFACE

In the spring of 1993, a small group of Toronto theatre stalwarts joined George F. Walker to produce his *Theatre of the Film Noir*, which had not been seen in the city since its premiere in 1981. To present this new, pared-down production, the collective chose the Factory Theatre's Studio Café, a venue both inexpensive and appropriate. Since producing Walker's first play in 1970, the Factory has provided him with consistent encouragement and support, for which the theatre has been amply rewarded. In 1989, Walker's *Love and Anger* was an enormous success; in 1991, the Factory's production of his *Escape from Happiness* was another monster hit. What better place, then, for an independent group of artists to test the turbulent waters of commercial theatre during the recessionary nineties with a remount of *Theatre of the Film Noir?*

Theatre of the Film Noir opened to rave reviews, then played for four months to sold-out houses, which can lead one to forget that its producers worked with meager resources far beneath their needs. Though homey, the Factory's Studio is shaped like a bowling alley. To transform its narrow austerity into a suitable environment for Walker's play—a surreal comedy set in Paris at the end of World War II—would intimidate even the boldest entrepreneur, let alone to do it on a shoe-string budget. The collective acknowledged its daring with an ironic gesture characteristic of Walker's intrepid heroes: they named their co-operative Shared Anxiety.

The title of this book, *Shared Anxiety,* offers a small but sincere tribute to the actors, designers and technicians whose talent and tenacity have sustained Canadian playwriting through the last 25 years. All of them are cultural pioneers; together they have created a professional theatre almost from scratch. The term, cultural pioneer, certainly applies to George F. Walker, an artist who continues to envisage new theatrical projects, seemingly blind to the odds against them. One could say that Walker is always ready to gamble on a vision, except, as he has indicated in many interviews, he feels he has no alternative: he is compelled to pursue theatre that both signifies and structures his view of the world. For Stephen Haff, the results are tantamount to sharing anxiety in public, an idea that Haff develops in the introduction that follows.

I felt no anxiety about proposing this volume to Coach House Press, despite its being the first of its kind to be published in English-speaking Canada. Walker's achievement is widely recognized; it is substantial and consistent. Since Coach House first published three of Walker's plays in 1978, interest in his work has generated more books and increased sales. Now, as the Press begins to distribute extensively in the United States, Walker's reputation precedes us: the playwright is as well known south of the border as he is at home. Indeed, American productions of Walker's plays far exceed the number they receive in Canada—(which is not surprising given the greater range of American theatres and the larger market they serve.)

To select the plays for this volume, I talked with George on a number of occasions and happily gave him final control over the list of plays to be included. We disagreed about little, although he agreed to include one of his early plays only after he acknowledged that publishing all five of the so-called East End plays was unwieldy in a volume restricted to eight scripts. Thus *Beyond Mozambique* (1974), one of my personal favourites, serves to represent 'early' Walker in this collection. And it reveals Walker exploring the mania of obsession at full throttle. While *Zastrozzi: The Master of Discipline* (1977) already enlivens two other anthologies, Walker wanted it here chiefly because this metaphysical melodrama is widely produced and taught. We both wanted to include *Theatre of the Film Noir* because, aside from the souvenir edition printed during the run of the 1993 production in Toronto, the play has not been published. And we both picked *The Art of War* (1982), the last of Walker's *Power Plays*, to represent this popular trilogy depicting the antics of the hapless T.M. Power, journalist-turned-sleuth, who is, for me, the apotheosis of the detective figure who appears frequently throughout Walker's work.

Many people, Walker included, consider *Criminals in Love* (1984) a landmark in his career. Besides winning him his first Governor General's Award for Drama, the play signals a shift in the focus of his vision and a concomitant refinement of his comic techniques. We both consider it essential to this collection. With the exception of *Nothing Sacred* (Walker's 1988 reworking of Turgenev's *Fathers and Sons*), all of the plays that Walker has written since *Criminals* centre on the social and domestic interactions of individuals and groups living in working-class, urban settings. Indeed, *Criminals in Love* introduces characters who reappear in *Better Living* (1986), *Beautiful City* (1987) and *Escape from Happiness*. *Love and Anger*, though utilizing an entirely different cast of characters, inhabits the same social and political terrain as these other East End plays and, I suggest, works within their aesthetic parameters as well. All are constructed as emotional epics (Haff calls them Spoken Opera) in which the character's desperate manoeuvres career into the high-octane physicality that frequently is as anguished as it is funny in Walker's wild and wicked world.

The text of *Criminals in Love* included in this volume differs from the one published by Playwrights Canada in 1984. Walker explains that this new, shortened version allows a director to stage the play without an intermission, should this be desired. The other two plays from the East End cycle offered here also differ from earlier versions. *Better Living* has been rewritten so extensively that Walker considers it almost a new play; and *Escape from Happiness* is shortened from three acts to two. The final play in the volume, *Tough!* (1993), Walker's shortest play to date, is published here for the first time.

When I publish plays, I try to provide as much contextual material as possible. Usually this is limited to information about the premiere production of a script and an introduction by the director of the show or someone central to it. Because the plays in this volume document the evolution of Walker's career as well as individual productions, I have included more background than usual. Along with the credits of the plays' premiere productions, and Stephen Haff's Introduction, I have added a career chronology and two bibliographies at the end of the text. These are intended to help readers (especially teachers and students) to research more fully the social and historical contexts of Walker's work and its reception. This material is by no means comprehensive; nevertheless, it offers a useful resource with which to develop approaches to both the creation of the plays and their impact on audiences.

Having edited and published much of Walker's work during the last 15 years, I have found it especially satisfying to bring these eight plays together in one volume that captures the originality and substance of Walker's work to date. Even more satisfying is my sense that this book represents only the first half of Walker's career, and my anticipation of yet another collection still to come.

Robert Wallace, Toronto, September 1994

THE BRAVE COMEDY OF BIG EMOTIONS
An Introduction

I first met George F. Walker, by chance, on a train heading west from Sackville, New Brunswick, to Toronto. He bought me a sandwich and a beer.

At the time, I was a college student well versed in Walker's work, acquainted with the many critical accolades he'd received, the prizes he'd won, the box-office records of his plays and the trace biography recited by his chroniclers. I boarded that train in Sackville thinking I knew who George F. Walker was.

But then he bought me food, and we had a conversation, just a *real conversation,* and all of a sudden "Walker" became simply "George". I've spent the seven years since that encounter directing, writing about and promoting George's work with evangelical zeal because I find the plays, like the beer and the sandwich, life-sustaining in a basic way. It has always mattered very much to me that these plays were written by someone who's more a citizen of the world than a citizen of art. George's plays feed a need as fundamental as hunger: the need to feel connected to other human beings.

Walker's theatre crawls on its belly, arms outstretched, fingers straining to reach the audience. Nobody needs to decode a Walker play because his characters say what they mean and mean what they say. They speak with astonishing directness, telling us everything we need to know: who they are, who others are, what the situation is, how the world works, what they want, what's inside them, and how mixed up it all is.

> Am I all right. Am I all right ... No. No. I'm not
> all right. Definitely not. I'm scared shitless. [*gets*

up, starts to pace] Come on. Come on, get a hold
of yourself, Bobby. Come on, man. [stops suddenly]
Shit. That's right. You're right. I'm a coward. Holy
fuck. How'd you know that. She told you didn't
she. Jill told you. And she's right. I'm a fucking
coward. Holy fuck. I don't even care about you I'm
so scared. I want to. I want to care about you. But
really I don't. Holy fuck. I'm scum!
—BOBBY, *Tough!*

In these plays speech is thinking out loud, and it's desperately
matter of fact. Nothing is decorative, oblique, circuitous, hinted at,
hidden, subtextual or vague. In this absence of clutter, speech is
relentless, a rush of crucial word upon crucial word, revelation
revising revelation, a terrifying and exuberant momentum of
essential things spoken without preparation or regard for
consequences. Be it a solitary word, a rapid exchange of epigrams
or a dam-burst of an aria, there's no wasted space in this speech; no
pockets of relaxation for retreat; no leisure time. The characters
speak with volcanic abandon, yet they are clearly committed to
every utterance.

The words are spoken to clarify and thereby to achieve some
kind of control in a big, messy, upsetting world. Every word
matters in the characters' struggle to understand *something;* to
identify, define, simplify, make sense, find the truth, get to the
bottom of things; to figure out what's going on inside themselves
and all around them. They name things and produce spontaneous
axioms. They speak in declarations, lists, equations, contrasts and
repetitions: basic structures for basic organizing tasks. They survive
the great uncertain by speaking about it. Here, there's no such
thing as mere conversation; rather, there's revelation, rapture, the
confession of ardent hearts. This is compulsive expression: a deep
need to expose, to share, to get things out of the head and the heart
and onto the stage where, maybe, the speaker can understand those
things by sharing them.

Words also work to engage other people, to penetrate the

poisonous fog of confusion and grab hold of another human being, then to hang on for dear life. When the characters speak to each other, they use their exchanges to open each other up, to turn each other inside out. They speak with the intense and obvious purpose of communication; clear, unmistakeable truth creates a desperate, kinetic poetry of directness. The characters' need to reach each other, to get through, to connect, is so powerful that it changes their language into energy.

> You are a big stupid shit-spewing asshole. One of the world's truly pathetic empty spaces. An enormous nothingness on legs. A total waste of time. Vomit. If I had a gun I'd shoot you.
> —WILLIAM, *Criminals in Love*

Walker puts his speakers into a primal relationship with language so that everyday words are suddenly re-discovered and applied to shape the world with intense, almost physical, power. Because his words are active—searching, seizing, beating, tearing open, hanging on—the body of the speaker must speak too. The characters' acts of communication—of speaking and of listening—are so urgent that they demand the engagement of the entire person. Walker's language tells the actor: listen with your whole body; never take your eyes off the person you're speaking with; breathe each other's air; need every word the other speaks as if it were a vital drop of desert rain and let it come alive in you. His language issues directions: speak to *send* words out; send the energy through, *past* the end of the lines, so that the lines give *outward;* expel the words from the very soles of your feet. What results is Spoken Opera in which the actor must turn him or herself inside out as the characters do.

The bodies of the characters are as honest, exposed, striving and risk-taking as their speech. As a result, there's a brutal, violent physical life in these plays that complements the verbal war against confusion. There also are strong, tender gestures, such as those in *Criminals in Love* when Gail and Junior embrace to defy the world, to say, as Gail does say, "The hell with them".

Still, despite all their energy, the words and bodies of Walker's characters are merely servants of the heart, harnessed to share emotions. Walker's plays construct a place where human feelings are extended to extremes in order to respond to the high-stakes struggle for survival that is both confusing and upsetting.

> I'm worried. About my future. I'm worried that my past didn't prepare me for any future. I'm worried about a basic failure to understand how the world operates. I'm worried that I won't bring my baby up right. That I can't teach her how the world operates. I'm worried about the world. Even though I don't understand it entirely I'm worried that something is deeply wrong with it. With life in general. I'm worried that there's a general lack of faith and security in the world and in life. It's too much. Maybe it's all too much. I don't understand it but maybe that because it's too much, too complicated. Yeah. Money. Love. Responsibility. Family. Work. Crime. Food. God. Children. Insanity. Friends. Sickness. Death. Shopping. Traffic. Teeth. Pollution. War. Poverty. Oil. Infidelity. Ignorance. Fear. Shoes. Hats. Nuclear power. Cats. Winter. Sex. Elevators. I worry about all those things and more. All the time. It's awful, really.
>
> —MARY ANN, *Better Living*

The characters' need to share is so vast and insatiable that, were it not funny, it might embarrass, disgust or even frighten those who are reluctant to acknowledge that need in their daily lives. Walker's characters repeatedly expose and use their emotions to connect with each other. Their words and bodies convey a rapturous, unapologetic honesty that generates comedy as it thrills at the danger of total exposure, for it is perilous to speak with no cloak, no armour of coolness or shame.

George doesn't send anything up or put anything down with his comedy: rather he uses it to propel the audience to the heart of an all-out, last-ditch fight for survival. At a performance of his plays, the people in the room—both on stage and in the house—can publicly share the same emotional terrain, for his comedy knows no shame or fear, even when it expresses fear and shame. Thus it recognizes and facilitates a *community of emotion* in which anybody who feels anxiety, sadness, rage, uncertainty, obsession, hope—whatever—can become a member.

People who assail the outer limits of feeling can be funny, perhaps because they're unusual and surprising, perhaps because they express what others feel. But what's even funnier about Walker's characters is what activates their emotions in the first place: Walker's characters are true believers. Most of them share what's inside them because they believe that doing so can help them understand things; help them live better lives, overcome lies and disease, fix neighbourhoods, confront injustice, heal each other. Of course, their belief runs smack against reality: their own shortcomings, the size of the world. This collision provides the humane irony of the work. Walker's compassionate awareness of the painful disparity between aspiration and fact is an irony that, in its living compassion, begets invigorating, defiant humour. Although life won't make sense for most of these characters, the damage and anguish they suffer as a result makes them willingly and heroically try harder, even if they don't know exactly why, even if they run the risk of appearing ridiculous.

> JUNIOR Gotta get off the floor. Why. Why off the floor.
> NORA Because you're alive. You're not dead. The floor is for dying. You have to avoid that floor. Defeat that floor. Rise above that floor! Get up!
> JUNIOR Okay. [*staggers to his feet weakly*] Okay, I'm up. What now.
> —*Escape from Happiness*

There's no moral to Walker's work, no hidden meaning, no parallel universe. There's just a struggle to understand, to connect with others, to hang on, to survive. This is an open, endless fight, an emotionally widening experience that is at once liberating and encouraging. The fact that in Walker's world this struggle requires exposure means that conventional ideas of strength are subverted, particularly the idea that strength results from concealing pain, from denying that terror exists. Indeed Walker suggests that strength can arise from naked vulnerability, from steadfast engagement with life in all its awesome disarray.

To perform in a Walker play is to enact a brave exposure, to participate in a generous sharing of emotion. His plays are built on a rapid succession of revelations in which life begins anew again and again in a rhythm of perpetual crisis, of sudden, total reversals and drastic jump-shifts. Walker writes high-stakes jazz, a life-and-death jam session, an instinctive struggle that lives in the present tense. Everything, even a memory, is used to negotiate a present need. Never for a second do the characters leave the *now*. When rehearsing a Walker play, it's useful to raise the stakes higher than you imagine they could be and to increase constantly and mercilessly the size of the obstacles to understanding and communication among the actors. The more awesome the barrier, the greater the energy released to smash it and the more complete and desperate the emotional exposure. Intensify the desperation even more by removing cool intellect, by doing everything you can to nourish an instinctive response to the moment; free-fall through the words, do the unexpected, surprise each other, never let the bodies be a safe distance apart; make them too close or too far, but never leave them safe or settled. Discover by attempt, by ceaseless, active, breathless attempt. Do a scene over and over and over and over without pause until you work yourself into a thoughtless, lucid, present-tense fever, so that understanding comes from the gut, from living with the plays where *they* live, trusting to their extremity, taking a leap of faith across a bottomless emotional canyon, a leap justified by experience on the other side, experience inaccessible by creeping, incremental analysis. Set a punishingly swift pace and make the progress buoyant. Otherwise, the speech becomes considered, the bodies take a nap, the emotions hide away, the bravery is no more.

In the audience, when I laugh, I'm not only expressing surprise and thrill at revelation and acknowledging my membership in the community of anxiety, I'm also voting, telling the actors to *keep on* taking risks, keep exposing, never to give up; I'm encouraging their resilience, their never-say-die persistence, their bravery in a perilous, chaotic stage life. I'm asking them to *embrace* terror, as the characters embrace theirs, so that I might embrace mine. The characters are always so fervently willing to feel out loud that they're funny in the darkest circumstances, and I love them for that. Bravery is the buoyant soul of Walker's comedy and each laugh is a laugh against despair.

Wherever they are—an unspecified jungle, a crumbling prison in turn-of-the-century Italy, a graveyard in the Paris of 1945, a cliff in Nova Scotia, an alley, a kitchen, a park—Walker's characters are in our world because they give us their mighty effort to survive in words full, direct and present, with bodies active, devoted and here. Their behaviour turns the theatre into a public forum where we can try to understand difficult feelings that are often kept damagingly private. Walker's theatre offers a place where we can begin to acknowledge a community of emotion, where we can start to be brave *together*, to share life's struggle, its anxiety, its heartbeat.

Stephen Haff, New York City, September 1994

BEYOND MOZAMBIQUE

Beyond Mozambique was first produced at the Factory Theatre Lab in Toronto on May 11, 1974 with the following cast:

ROCCO Donald Davis
TOMAS Marc Connors
OLGA Frances Hyland
RITA Wendy Thatcher
CORPORAL Dean Hawes
LIDUC David Bolt

Director: Eric Steiner
Set Designer: Doug Robinson
Lighting Designer: John Stammers
Costume Designer: Marti Wright

Persons

ROCCO

TOMAS

OLGA

RITA

CORPORAL

LIDUC

SCENE ONE

Late evening
The porch and surrounding area of an old, poorly maintained colonial
house. Surrounded by jungle. Cluttered with discarded things: old tires,
machine parts, magazines and newspapers strewn all around. To one
side of the steps, a large picnic table. To the other side, DOCTOR
ROCCO'*s operating table. It has an umbrella attached to one end.*
Leaning against the roof of the house, a battered telephone pole, wires
hanging to the ground
A whistle from the jungle. ROCCO *rushes out of the house in a lab coat,*
carrying his medical bag. He looks around. Another whistle. ROCCO
goes off into the jungle towards it. Whisperings. Commotion. Branches
breaking. Muttering. Muffled drums
TOMAS *comes out of the jungle. His head is bandaged, a trace of blood*
can be seen. Over his shoulder he is carrying a corpse covered by
sackcloth. ROCCO *follows him*

TOMAS Thélo ná nikyáso éna aftokínito.
ROCCO Who cares. Just keep going. Wait. I hear something. I said.
Wait.
TOMAS O Kafés?
ROCCO Shut up. Were you followed. No. You're too shrewd. Wait. No.
Nothing. Get going.
[*He pushes* TOMAS]
Get going.
[*They start off.* ROCCO *looks under the corpse's sackcloth*]
Stop.
[*He grabs* TOMAS]
This corpse. It's Old Joseph. I saw him yesterday. In good health.
Put him down.
[TOMAS *puts the corpse on the picnic table*]
I told you. Only dead ones. Out of graves. Graves, stupid. You
murdered him, didn't you.
[TOMAS *produces a switchblade. Runs it across his own throat. Smiles*]
No. The knife was only for cutting open the corpses' sacks. To

check for decomposition. You've murdered Old Joseph. Look at him lying there. I taught that old man how to play dominoes. Oh God, he's missing a foot. Where's his foot.

[TOMAS *shrugs.* ROCCO *points to his own*]

Foot. Where's Old Joseph's foot.

[TOMAS *nods. Undoes his coat. The foot is strung around his neck*]

TOMAS Good luck.

ROCCO What's wrong with you.

[*He yanks the foot off*]

Have you no respect for human life.

[*He throws the foot into the bushes*]

I'm very sad.

TOMAS Foot.

ROCCO How many more of them have you murdered. Never mind. I don't want to know. What's done is done. At least it's for a worthy cause. He was a man of some wisdom. He might have understood. What's done is done. Off to the lab. Pick him up.

TOMAS [*stomps his foot petulantly*] Foot!

ROCCO Forget it! It's sickening. I'm sad. No. I must maintain my obsession. One day they will place a huge tablet in the foyer of the city hall in Naples. 'To Doctor Enrico Rocco, a native son. A man who had the courage lacking in all other scientists of his age. It was not that he thought that human life was cheap but that he believed that the advancement of medical science was divine.'

[TOMAS *puts his hand on* ROCCO*'s shoulder*]

Oh, yes. And a smaller plaque hidden in a corner. 'In memory of his clueless assistant. Tomas. Who was a scummy bastard of the first order.'

TOMAS [*smiles*] Tomas.

[OLGA *comes out of the house, carrying linen and a basket full of silverware, plates, etc.*]

OLGA Oh, Enrico. I have to set that table for breakfast. Please remove the patient.

ROCCO We were just leaving. [*to* TOMAS] Pick him up.

[TOMAS *throws the corpse over his shoulder. They start off*]

OLGA Don't be out late, dear. The monsoons are coming.

6

[ROCCO *and* TOMAS *disappear around the back of the house*]
Ah. The monsoon season. A trying time. A trying time indeed.
[OLGA *begins to set the table, humming the 'Polovtsian Dances.' The
sound of an approaching car is heard, screeching to a halt. The porch is
flooded with light. Sound of door opening. Door closing.* OLGA *is
oblivious, going about her business.* RITA *comes on, carrying a
shopping bag. Her hands and arms are covered with blood. The rest of
the scene is dealt with in the most casual of manners*]

RITA Where's the Doctor.

OLGA Out.

RITA Goddammit. [*sits on the steps. Fingers her hair back*]

OLGA Not so much activity please. You'll stir up the mosquitoes.

RITA Goddammit. Have you seen the Corporal. I can't find him
anywhere.

OLGA No. What's that you're covered with.

RITA Blood.

OLGA From where.

RITA His head.

OLGA Whose head.

RITA The priest. Father Ricci. Someone took an axe to him. I found
his head outside my tent. It's in this bag. And I don't know what
I'm supposed to do with it. I mean I can't carry it around forever.
It's stupid.

OLGA This joke is in poor taste, Shirley.

RITA The name's Rita. Not Shirley. Rita. And it's no joke. Look.
[*She drops the head from the bag*]

OLGA Yes. That's Father Ricci all right. I recognize the disapproving
look. Oh. Before I forget. You're invited to breakfast tomorrow
morning. It's a formal affair. In honour of my homeland. Will you
come? [*returns to setting the table*]

RITA I'll see. I have some business to tend to.

OLGA Well, if you can make it.

RITA Yeah.
[*Pause*]
Doesn't this scare you. [*pointing to the head*] This.

OLGA My dreams are much worse. Much worse. When I see blood in one of my dreams it's like comic relief. Does it scare you.

RITA Well, it doesn't seem real. I mean, no more real than the movies. [*looks at her arms*] Stage blood looks the same way. That's not what bothers me. What bothers me is why it was put outside my tent. I don't need the action. Question is, who's the one that thinks I do. [*The* CORPORAL *steps out of the bushes. Old Joseph's foot is tied around the blade of his machete*]

CORPORAL The question is this. Does that head have anything to do with this foot.

OLGA Lance. Have you been lurking around my bedroom window again. You know Enrico doesn't like it.

[*The* CORPORAL *goes to the head. Kneels*]

CORPORAL Different people. My guess is that the foot belongs to one of the sub species.

RITA Oh, I get it. Two murders.

CORPORAL Three murders. The guy who Father Ricci replaced. Father what's-his-face.

RITA Carson.

OLGA Oh, yes. I remember. The one who ran away.

CORPORAL Wrong. I found his body deep in the jungle this afternoon. Nailed to a tree.

RITA A priest killer. Oh, that's really bizarre.

OLGA Lance, you're invited to breakfast tomorrow. And will you please dress.

CORPORAL Uh-huh. This foot. This foot doesn't fit in. And I don't like that. No. I just don't like this foot. [*thinks*] Right. One thing at a time.

[*He throws foot into the jungle. There is mumbling from the bushes. They all react. The* CORPORAL *draws his gun, walks into the bushes. We hear thrashing. Screaming. And finally two gunshots.* OLGA *and* RITA *are looking at each other, slightly confused, slightly disgusted. The* CORPORAL *casually returns, wiping blood from the blade of his machete*]

Subversives.

[*Everyone nods*]

That keeps them away.

[*The ladies nod. They giggle just a bit*]
Relax. You're in good hands.
[*They all look at each other. They all smile.* OLGA *backs into the house.* RITA *begins to laugh loudly. The* CORPORAL *begins to laugh boyishly, starting towards* RITA]
[*Blackout*]

SCENE TWO

Morning
Waiting for the guests. The table is set lavishly. ROCCO, *pacing back and forth on the ground in front of the porch, is wearing an old tuxedo* OLGA *is sitting in her chair on the porch, reading a letter. She is wearing a full-length black dress with a collar*

ROCCO Like a boulder crushing my skull. Twenty-five years spent thrashing about in the wilderness. And then I wake up one day like a baby in its crib. Sucking my thumb and pissing my pants. Another wasted night. Twenty-five years long. Where are we?!

OLGA I didn't say anything.

ROCCO Neither did I.

OLGA Masha writes such good letters. Social enough to satisfy the mind. Bittersweet enough to appease the memory.

ROCCO Here. Really here. I don't believe it. And then there's the wasted time. The interruptions.

OLGA London agrees with her. She writes her letters in English now. But somehow they still have a Russian accent.

ROCCO Interruptions.

OLGA Do you know how much I miss her.

ROCCO Interruptions. Caring for the sick. Why for once can't the sick care for themselves. Don't they know I'm busy. Where am I. I'm not at the place I came to. The place I came to is somewhere else. It's quieter there. A man gets work done there without worrying about his conscience. My god. My poor conscience.

OLGA Enrico.

ROCCO [*to* OLGA] Woman. Why are you pestering me. What harm have I done you lately. Do I complain that you hum the 'Polovtsian Dances' in your sleep. No, I grant you your oblivion. And all I ask in return is that you bow completely out of the picture until my work is finished.

OLGA You were raving.
[*Pause*]

ROCCO Tell me I am a genius. There's no one around. Olga, tell me.

That if I had been born two centuries earlier and lived three times as long as anyone else I would have discovered all the cures now known to modern medicine. I don't ask much, Olga. But a mind like mine has a great appetite. It even needs flattery. Tell me. Am I amazing.

OLGA Of course.

ROCCO Somehow it doesn't seem like enough. Olga, I have something to tell you. No. Forget it.

OLGA Would you like to read my sister's letter.

ROCCO No. I can't stomach the way she manages to swoon even on a piece of paper.

OLGA She misses Moscow.

ROCCO Everyone misses Moscow. I miss it occasionally myself. And I've never been there.

OLGA The letter contains good news.
[ROCCO *gestures for her to continue*]
Your friend Livarno has won the Nobel Prize.

ROCCO [*groans lightly. Bites his knuckles*] I know. We saw it in the newspaper last month. His picture covered the entire front page. Large vacant eyes. And a smile like a sheep. He didn't exist in Naples and even now, covering the entire front page of a newspaper, he does not really exist. His Nobel Prize for Science is a bad joke.

OLGA You're jealous.

ROCCO Stupidity fits you sometimes like a glove.

OLGA [*getting up*] It's time for my nap.

ROCCO Livarno is a mediocre mind. His accomplishments seem important only because he is surrounded by apes.

OLGA Then maybe you should consider going back. You could always disguise yourself. And as for me—

ROCCO And as for you, what. You have all you need.

OLGA I don't know what I need. I do know what I have.

ROCCO What do you have.

OLGA My marriage. My history. And my original Renoir.

ROCCO Exactly. Everything you need. The question is answered in the best way possible. By evasion. We stay here.

OLGA For how long.

ROCCO The world and I will collide at the proper moment. Everything
in time.

OLGA I don't like that expression! I blinked my eyes once and half a
century passed. I found myself in a square in St. Petersburg
surrounded by young men and women all looking exactly alike. I
was wearing a ball gown and everyone thought I was about to
perform an historical drama. Immediately I gave up.

ROCCO I've always wondered what happened to your passion.

OLGA What was left I gave to you.

ROCCO Thank you.

OLGA Not at all. I scarcely miss it now.
[*The* CORPORAL *comes on in full RCMP dress uniform. Without
speaking, he goes to the table. Takes his seat*]

ROCCO What in God's name is that outfit all about.

OLGA Lance was with the RCMP before he came to work here.

ROCCO What's the RCMP.

OLGA I'll explain later.

ROCCO How'd he get here. I didn't hear his motorcycle.

OLGA Some of the locals dismantled it. And Lance doesn't know how
to put it back together.

ROCCO The man is a clown. The only policeman in the area is a full-
fledged clown. That is the most ridiculous uniform I have ever seen
in my life.

OLGA Shush. He's very insecure.
[*She goes to the* CORPORAL]
Good morning, Lance. Nice of you to attend.

CORPORAL Sure. [*quietly*] Am I over-dressed. It's the only formal thing
I've got.

OLGA No. You look fine. Almost dashing.

ROCCO [*approaching them*] Come on now. Let's get this over with.

CORPORAL Good morning, Doctor.

ROCCO Is it. [*sits*]

OLGA [*sitting*] Where is Tomas.

ROCCO Sleeping.

OLGA Well, who gave him permission to do that.

ROCCO I did. I need him well rested.

OLGA Unfair. The agreement was that I have him during the day and you have him during the night. Who is going to serve breakfast.

ROCCO I don't know. Improvise.

CORPORAL [*stands*] What do you and your boy do during the night anyway, Doctor.

ROCCO [*stands*] We make house calls. Now take off your hat. My wife has gone to a great deal of trouble to create the proper atmosphere. [*sits*]

CORPORAL [*removes his hat*] Sorry.

[*He sits. Pause*]

OLGA Enrico. The breakfast.

ROCCO Be patient.

OLGA But—

ROCCO Be patient.

CORPORAL Well now—

ROCCO That goes for you too.

[*Long pause.* OLGA *sits, restless; the* CORPORAL, *embarrassed;* ROCCO, *patient*]

OLGA Excuse me.

[*They all stand.* OLGA *smiles. Goes into the house.* ROCCO *and the* CORPORAL *sit. Long pause.* ROCCO *is looking the* CORPORAL *over*]

ROCCO How's your malaria.

CORPORAL Comes and goes.

ROCCO How often.

CORPORAL More often all the time. I think I almost died last week from the fever. I was having visions of wheat.

ROCCO Are you getting your transfer.

CORPORAL My superiors say I have to prove myself here first. And with all these murders going on and that bunch of subversives running around blowing things up, well, it doesn't make me look very good. Why are you smiling.

ROCCO I give you two months. Unless you can escape this climate. Two months at the most.

CORPORAL You're joking.

ROCCO I joke with friends. To people like you I dish out the ruthless truth. You're a dead man.

CORPORAL Then cure me.

ROCCO No.

CORPORAL It's because I did your wife, isn't it. Don't hold it against me forever, for chrissake. I mean goddammit, man. She came to me.

[ROCCO *produces a switchblade with incredible speed and efficiency. Puts the blade under the* CORPORAL's *chin*]

ROCCO I am not an impotent man, you son of a bitch. There are plenty of men who can't do their wives who aren't impotent. They just can't do their wives. For reasons none of your business. For reasons no one knows.

CORPORAL Put the knife away, Doctor. I've got something to tell you.

ROCCO Be careful, Corporal.

CORPORAL I talked to Father Ricci the night before he was killed. He'd been doing a little investigating of his own. Seems he found out about this Italian doctor who was so good at his job that he became top dog in one of those fancy Nazi hospitals. They're still looking for him.

ROCCO You repeat that once. To anyone. And I'll slice you up.

CORPORAL Listen, Rocco. You can get away with robbing graves here. It's a petty crime. Just like the little bribes you all know I take. But anything more will upset the balance. Don't do anything to upset the balance. Understand?

[*They stare at each other*]

ROCCO [*chuckles, puts the knife away*] Ah, mother of Jesus. I am only a simple country doctor. Leave me to my business in peace and you'll be fine.

[OLGA *comes out with four glasses of orange juice on a tray*]

OLGA I see that Shirley still hasn't arrived. A typical display of rudeness.

ROCCO Rita will be late. She had a business meeting.

[OLGA *is serving the juice*]

CORPORAL What kind of business.

ROCCO Ask *her.*

OLGA Is it true that she's making pornographic movies with the natives.

CORPORAL That's news to me.

OLGA Well, perhaps it's just a malicious rumour. I hear so many.

ROCCO From whom.

OLGA Many different sources, Enrico. [*raises her glass*] To dear Russia.

[ROCCO *stands. The* CORPORAL *knocks his glass over*]

What's wrong, Lance.

CORPORAL Sorry.

ROCCO The Corporal is having trouble coping with imaginary problems.

[ROCCO *and the* CORPORAL *are staring hard at each other*]

CORPORAL Two murders. Possibly three. People mucking about with government property. Strange comings. Strange goings. Mysterious sounds in the night. Add all that up and tell me what it sounds like to you.

OLGA 'Les Misérables' by Victor Hugo.

[*They look at her*]

Excuse me.

[*She stands. The* CORPORAL *and* ROCCO *stand.* OLGA *smiles, goes into the house*]

CORPORAL Victor Hugo my bassoon. It sounds like anarchy. It sounds like insurrection.

ROCCO Why are you telling me all this.

CORPORAL You were seen at three o'clock this morning sitting cross-legged in the jungle behind your house. Wearing an old army helmet and cradling a carbine in your lap.

ROCCO What were you doing sneaking around my house at that hour.

CORPORAL Subversives do their best work before dawn.

ROCCO Ah. Are you a subversive.

CORPORAL Just answer the question. What were you doing out there.

ROCCO Maybe I was out there asleep. But I haven't slept for years. Maybe I was awake and can't remember. But that is unlikely. Or maybe I was mistaken for another. Which is probably too far-fetched. All right. I was really out there like you say. Wide awake. Suspiciously dressed. And armed to the teeth.

CORPORAL Why.

ROCCO [*standing*] None of your business.

CORPORAL [*standing*] Now get this, you motherfucker. My life is on the line and no stupid wop quack is gonna ball it up for me.

ROCCO Va fungu! [*producing his switchblade*]
CORPORAL The same to you! [*drawing his gun*]
[OLGA *comes out, carrying cups and a coffee pot on a tray*]
OLGA Coffee?
CORPORAL Sure.
ROCCO Why not.
[OLGA *pours the coffee. The weapons are put away*]
OLGA Things aren't going well, are they. But then again they never do. If only Tomas was operating with all his faculties. I tried to wake him but he wouldn't budge. Enrico, where did he get that teddy bear he's sleeping with.
ROCCO Rita gave it to him.
OLGA Are they having an affair.
ROCCO Anything's possible.
OLGA Rumour has it that they are. But how many rumours can one believe. Very few. Very few indeed.
CORPORAL [*opening his collar*] I don't feel so good. [*staggers a bit*]
OLGA [*raises her cup*] Forever remembered. Forever lost. Those brittle Russian nights.
[*They drink. The* CORPORAL *spits his out*]
Well, if you'd said so earlier, Lance, I would have served you tea.
CORPORAL [*tears open his tunic*] Fever!
[*The* CORPORAL *falls on the ground, groaning, pulling at his hair*]
OLGA Goodness. It does come on suddenly, doesn't it. [*to* ROCCO] Help him.
ROCCO What's that.
OLGA Help him. It's his malaria.
ROCCO So it is. So it is. [*pours himself another cup of coffee*]
OLGA [*starting towards the house*] I'll go get him a cold towel.
ROCCO Get me my flask while you're in there, will you.
[LIDUC *comes out of the jungle, carrying a valise, covered with mud up to his chest. He is casually dressed in a windbreaker and slacks*]
LIDUC Excuse me. Can you direct me to the mission? [*smiles*]
[*They all turn towards him*]
CORPORAL [*pointing hysterically*] Assassin! Oh Jesus, an assassin!
[*He rushes at* LIDUC *screaming 'Assassin, assassin.' Throws him up*]

against ROCCO's *operating table. Turns him around. Frisks him*]

LIDUC Please.

CORPORAL Don't move.

LIDUC [*to* ROCCO] Is this a mistake.

ROCCO Corporal, what are you doing.

CORPORAL [*to* LIDUC] All right. Strip.

LIDUC I beg your pardon.

CORPORAL Off with your clothes. I wanna see you naked.

[LIDUC *undoes his jacket. The audience sees his collar and his crucifix*]

OLGA Oh, Lance. He's a priest.

CORPORAL He ain't white. He's one of them. A mulatto or something.

LIDUC No. Chinese. Half Chinese.

CORPORAL Shut up.

LIDUC I'll show you some identification. [*produces a small card*] My name is LiDuc. Father LiDuc.

[*He hands the* CORPORAL *the card*]

CORPORAL You're a goddamn chink! Goddamn—

[*He falls all over* LIDUC]

Fever.

LIDUC Oh my God. I mean. Oh. That is. This is. Oh.

[*He frees himself from the* CORPORAL's *grasp*]

OLGA Here Father. Some coffee.

LIDUC Yes. Thank you. [*takes it. Trembling*]

OLGA Please excuse the Corporal. He suffers from several viruses.

[LIDUC *nods. Hands coffee to the* CORPORAL]

Oh. How nice. Won't you sit down.

LIDUC Yes. Thank you. [*sits somewhere*] Thank you.

OLGA [*to* ROCCO] Breakfast is a disaster. I should have expected it. Actually I did expect it. But I was hoping to be surprised.

ROCCO [*to* LIDUC] Difficult journey? [*no response*] The mud! On your clothes!

LIDUC Yes. I stepped into a quagmire. I'm a bit myopic, you see. And I lost my glasses in a brief encounter with a wild pig.

ROCCO People don't usually get out of quicksand once they're in.

LIDUC No. Well, I wouldn't have either, I suspect. I spent two entire days clinging to a vine. And then this native gentleman came along and pulled me out.

OLGA You must be very hungry.

LIDUC No, the native gentleman took me to his home and fed me.

ROCCO Did you talk to him.

[LIDUC *stands. Turns towards the* CORPORAL]

LIDUC I would like an apology from you. I think it is only fair.

[*The* CORPORAL *waves stupidly*]

ROCCO I said, did you talk to him.

[LIDUC *turns slowly back towards* ROCCO]

LIDUC Yes. Not much though. He was a bit reticent.

ROCCO What did he tell you.

LIDUC I don't understand.

ROCCO What do you know.

LIDUC Oh. I know that Father Ricci is dead. I was to have been his
assistant, you see. And I know that he is a policeman. And that you
are a doctor. He made no mention of the lady, though.

OLGA I keep a low profile.

ROCCO My wife, Olga.

OLGA My husband, Enrico Rocco, M.D.

LIDUC Good. Introductions. [*shaking everyone's hand*] I am Father
LiDuc. Until they send Father Ricci's replacement I will be in
charge of the mission.

[OLGA *grabs* ROCCO's *sleeve. Directs his attention outward*]

ROCCO [*smiles*] Oh, I'm afraid not.

LIDUC What's that.

ROCCO [*points*] Look.

[*They are all staring off towards the audience*]

LIDUC A fire.

[*The* CORPORAL *has recovered sufficiently to express delight*]

CORPORAL [*chuckling*] Ah. Too bad.

OLGA [*to* LIDUC] Your mission.

CORPORAL Well, I guess I better get over there. [*chuckles again*]

LIDUC I'll come too. Doctor?

ROCCO What.

LIDUC Are you coming. Someone might be injured.

ROCCO Impossible. No one ever goes near the place anymore.

[LIDUC *starts out towards us*]

CORPORAL Not that way. Too dangerous. Follow me.

[*The* CORPORAL *is deciding which is the longest, most pleasant route. Finally he slaps* LIDUC *jovially on the back. Gestures for him to follow and starts off*]

LIDUC [*backing off*] It was nice meeting you.

OLGA Yes. Come again soon. And you can look at my original Renoir. It's superb. Like a dove in orgasm.

[OLGA *waves. The* CORPORAL *and* LIDUC *are gone*]

He seems so innocent.

ROCCO Eh. Sure.

OLGA Enrico. Who set that fire.

ROCCO I don't know. Honestly.

OLGA Thank goodness for that at least.

ROCCO [*chuckles*] You're still standing guard over my soul, woman.

OLGA Habit. I'm going in for a nap.

ROCCO Send Tomas out to me.

OLGA If I can wake him up.

ROCCO The secret is to apply pressure to his head. At the point where the blood stain is the brightest.

[OLGA *nods. Goes inside.* ROCCO *produces a notebook and pen. Writes something*]

Who'd expect to find so many social obligations in the midst of such desolation.

[*A scream from the house*]

Tomas!

[*Muttering from the house*]

Tomas! Get out here!

[TOMAS *rushes out of the house, wearing an oversized lab coat, rubbing his bandaged head. There is more blood showing.* ROCCO *hands him a piece of paper and his knife*]

I need what is written on that paper by tonight.

TOMAS O'Ponokéfalos.

ROCCO That's Greek. You're regressing.

TOMAS Yais. My haid.

ROCCO What.

TOMAS O'Ponokéfalos.

ROCCO Headache?

TOMAS Yais. My brain. Kséhasis. Forget. I forget.

ROCCO Of course you do. But stop worrying. You're lucky to be alive. You had a severe wound in your brain. You understand?

TOMAS Sometimes.

ROCCO Almost totally destroyed. I have fixed. Maybe all. Maybe just some. A great miracle nevertheless. Don't worry. Here. Aspirin.

TOMAS [*suspiciously*] Efharisto.

ROCCO Now go about my business. You are not my only concern. Be careful. Get going!

[ROCCO *points to paper and knife. Gives* TOMAS *a push.* TOMAS *takes three or four quick paces, almost running. Grasps his head. Groans. Falls into a dead faint*]

Basta! Basta! No! You don't understand. No one understands. Existence is thrust. You get sick. You get cured. There is no room for relapse. Never mind.

[*He grabs the paper from* TOMAS' *hand*]

I'll do it myself.

[*Takes off his coat. Produces a nylon stocking from his pants' pocket. Puts it over his head. Picks up his knife. Rushes off.* TOMAS *sits up. Looks around. Drops the aspirin on the ground. Muffled drums*]

[*Blackout*]

SCENE THREE

Evening
RITA *and* TOMAS *sitting on the steps. Both have their chins in their palms. A long silence.* RITA *blows down into her blouse*

RITA I'll never get used to this heat. It just whacks me out.
[TOMAS *produces a small fold-out fan from inside his shirt. Fans* RITA *slowly*]
Ah, thanks. Hey. What's wrong with you anyway. Are you in a funk.
TOMAS Funk. Sad.
RITA I know. I know. It's not easy. Ah, you're bleeding again.
[*She touches his wound. He groans*]
I'm sorry.
TOMAS Funk.
RITA Yeah. Me too. I miss my man. Did I ever tell you about him. A winner. A six-foot smile. The only genuine winner I've ever known in my life.
TOMAS Rub.
RITA Sure thing.
[*She massages the back of his neck*] pink
He's the guy who is going to make my movie. Not porn. I did porn in New York. This one is going to be a classic. It'll have sex. But it'll be sex with class. No pubics. That's what I'm doing here, you know. Research. I'm immersing myself in the place. Digging in. You know. So that when we make the movie I'll come across super real. I play a stupid slut who has always wanted to be an actress. It's a great script. It needs rewrites but basically it's a great script. I know I've told you all this before, but it's just that if I don't keep saying it I'll forget it's the truth.
TOMAS Rub.
RITA Yeah. Sure.
[*She continues his massage*]
Anyway, the Doctor thinks it's a joke. You know, 'cause I've been here for years, one year, and Chad, that's my man's name, still

21

hasn't shown up. The Doctor's an asshole sometimes. He has no idea how much dough you need to make a film. I mean as soon as Chad gets outta prison he's going to get right back to work on raising the money. God I miss him. He never was much of a letter writer.

[*Pause. She looks around*]

This place has nice sunsets. You know that? Sometimes I just pour myself a stiff gin and lean against that big tree outside my tent and just let that sun sink slowly down into the ground while I shake the ice cubes around in the glass. And when I do that I get so deeply into Rita Hayworth I could just about die.

[TOMAS *sighs as he slowly rubs his crotch*]

You and the Doctor are the only ones who know. I play the role for the rest of them. It's a defence mechanism. My mother taught me all about it. When you're dealing with men, do it like you got two balls and you'll be one up on most of them. [*laughs*] It works too. I've never been raped or exploited. And I couldn't stand either.

[*Voices from the jungle*]

All right! All right! Cut the crap! I'm coming!

[*Silence*]

[*to* TOMAS] See what I mean. Be right back.

[*She goes into the jungle.* OLGA *comes out in her nightgown*]

OLGA I heard voices. What was it.

[TOMAS *just stares at her*]

I don't like the way you look at me. Some day I'm going to tell my husband.

[*She hands* TOMAS *a letter*]

Mail that for me tomorrow. Don't forget. Someone somewhere might be contemplating suicide. And that letter could save a life.

[OLGA *goes back in.* TOMAS *rips up the letter. Throws the pieces up in the air.* RITA *returns, adjusting her clothing*]

RITA They're lunatics. I don't trust them. No way do I trust them. They drink too much and they're always wiped on this weird extract they get from the root of some fruit tree. But they've got money. And they pay me well.

TOMAS Sex?

RITA No. That's stupid gossip. Part of my false image. I smuggle for them. Just so I can help Chad get the money for our movie.

TOMAS Poso?

RITA You know I don't understand Greek. Listen. How'd you like to do me a favour.

TOMAS Poso?

RITA I want you to cross the border for me. I'd do it myself but I've been across too many times lately and my nerves are a little jangled. Whatya say.

TOMAS Your eyes. I love them. Like sky at night above Athens. We live in Hilton. You pay. I am always horny. Get it?

RITA Come on. We've been through this already. That gigolo stuff must be in your past or something. What's wrong, are you hallucinating.

TOMAS Sick.

[*Drums, very quietly*]

RITA Bloody Doctor. Mucking around with your head. Do me a favour and I'll get him to lay off you.

[*She hands him an envelope*]

Here's their money. Take it. Cross the border. Give it to the man waiting in the yellow Citroen. He'll take you to a warehouse and give you a large crate. Hire a truck and put the crate in the back under some sacks of flour. When you're driving back over the border wink at the guard and say, 'The lady from Illinois has legs.'

TOMAS [*who has been repeating odd words*] Legs.

RITA Then drive the truck to the ruins of the mission and leave it there.

[TOMAS *is ogling the money in his hands.* RITA *stands. Helps* TOMAS *up. Kisses him on the forehead*]

Thanks, sweet baby.

TOMAS Sex?

RITA No. We did it once. Because I liked your smile. More than once is infidelity. And I could never look Chad in the eye. Besides we're friends. We've got the only real friendship around here. Let's not screw it up, eh.

[TOMAS *smiles. Kisses her on the cheek*]

Thanks. Now shoo.

[*She gives him a little push. He leaves. She watches him go. Lights a cigarette. Takes a couple of puffs*]

[*to the jungle*] Okay, boys. You can pick them up at the ruins of the mission. Anytime after midnight.

[*Voices from the jungle.* RITA *counts her money. The voices annoy her*]

Is it worth it.

[*Silence.* ROCCO *comes on, a corpse over his shoulder. Sees* RITA. *Drops the corpse. Walks to her. Produces a wad of bills. Hands them to her*]

ROCCO This is for forgetting that you saw this. Put it away. It's a great deal of money.

[*She puts the money in her blouse. Snuffs out her cigarette*]

Excuse me.

[*He is dragging the corpse around the back of the house*]

I have to get to sleep. Tomorrow is clinic day and I am expecting many patients. The fever is with us again.

[ROCCO *starts to go around the back.* RITA *turns back towards the audience. Stares silently off for a moment. The* CORPORAL *is waiting for* ROCCO. *He snaps his fingers.* ROCCO *sighs. Gives the* CORPORAL *some money. Disappears. The* CORPORAL *is counting the money.* RITA *is smoking and thinking. Eventually the* CORPORAL *comes around the front, still counting. Sees* RITA. *Smiles. Puts the money in his pocket nonchalantly. Starts to circle* RITA, *sizing her up. Stops. Stands there making a rude clicking noise with his tongue.* RITA *looks at him, sizing him up. Circles him. Stops. Stomps out her cigarette. They stare at each other for a while. It is a late-evening, contemptuous conversation*]

CORPORAL I've got a problem.

RITA I'm sure you do.

CORPORAL I'm all alone.

RITA I know.

CORPORAL And I need a woman.

RITA That's too bad.

CORPORAL Lie down for me.

RITA Not a chance.

CORPORAL I'll pay the going rate.

RITA There is no going rate, mister.

CORPORAL You're a whore.

RITA You're an asshole.

CORPORAL I could force you.

RITA No you couldn't.

    [*Long pause*]

CORPORAL I've just come into a lot of money.

RITA I know. So have I.

CORPORAL Enough to make your movie?

RITA Not nearly.

CORPORAL You could be charged as an accessory.

RITA So could you.

CORPORAL I'm immune.

RITA So am I.

CORPORAL How's that.

RITA I talked to Father Ricci the night before he was killed.

CORPORAL Me too.

RITA What did he tell you.

CORPORAL What did he tell *you*.

RITA It's a secret.

CORPORAL Then tell me the secret. I could force you.

RITA No you couldn't!

CORPORAL Is it why you killed him.

RITA No, but it might be why you killed him.

    [*Long pause*]

CORPORAL Maybe it's why the Doctor killed him.

RITA Maybe.

    [*Pause*]

CORPORAL Hot, isn't it.

RITA I don't know. I never really notice it.

    [*Pause. The* CORPORAL *takes out his money. Waves it at her*]

CORPORAL Can you use this.

    [RITA *takes out a card. Waves it at him*]

RITA Can you use this.

CORPORAL What is it.

RITA A girl. Her name and where to find her.

CORPORAL What are you. Her pimp or something.

RITA Her agent.

CORPORAL Same thing.

RITA Yeah. I guess it is.

CORPORAL Is she good.

RITA She has one very intriguing asset.

CORPORAL What is it.

RITA She's only eleven years old.

CORPORAL I'll take her. Give me that paper.

RITA You first.

[*Slowly he hands her the wad of bills*]

[*counting*] Try to be gentle. She's a close friend.

CORPORAL [*grabbing the paper*] Oh, sure. [*starts off. Stops*] I want you to forget this.

[*He leaves*]

RITA I'll try.

[RITA *stuffs the money into her blouse. She looks out towards the audience*]

[*with style*] I'll try.

[*Five or six strong drum beats*]

[*Blackout*]

SCENE FOUR

Morning

Bird noises. The odd very unusual one. LIDUC *is standing by the operating table. He appears to be blessing it*

ROCCO *comes on. Abruptly throws a pail of hot water on the table. Begins to scrub it down with a brush. He is just a bit drunk.* LIDUC *steps back a bit*

ROCCO Where did they go.

LIDUC The native lady took her child to be buried.

ROCCO It was hopeless. What are you doing.

LIDUC Praying for your other patients.

ROCCO Hopeless. The fever. That child is just one of many.

LIDUC You would give them a better chance if you were sober.

ROCCO If I was sober I couldn't even look at them.

[*Pause*]

LIDUC The mother left you that tire as payment.

ROCCO [*chuckles*] That belongs to the Corporal's motorcycle. Look around. Tires. Old magazines. All this debris. The booty of my practice. Sad, eh.

LIDUC Well, if they ever take your licence away you can open up a junkyard. [*smiles*]

ROCCO European wit. Where did you pick it up. Never mind. Save it for my wife. She'll relish it.

[LIDUC *goes to the porch. Sits on the steps, his Bible held to his chest*]

LIDUC I'm sorry if my staying with you causes inconvenience.

ROCCO Just don't get in the way of my work and you'll be tolerated.

LIDUC Yes. What work is that.

ROCCO My experiments. I'm searching for the cure for cancer.

LIDUC Which one.

ROCCO All of them.

LIDUC It seems like an impossible goal.

ROCCO That's why I chose it.

[LIDUC *closes his eyes. Sways gently back and forth. There is a bottle and a glass on the floor of the porch.* ROCCO *picks them up. Pours*

himself a long drink. Leans against the porch. Drinks]
How can I love with such hell in my heart. And worse knowing
that the hell is what keeps me going. Knowing that when I was of
the age when men make those kinds of decisions I decided to steep
myself in corruption. Because corruption was the only powerful
force around. And now because the age of passion is dead there is
no energy to reverse the decision. My baseness is my strength. The
farther down I go the safer I am.
[*Pause. Drinks*]
Ah. But how to explain that I cannot love. [*turns to* LIDUC] There
is a tower growing in the jungle. It is the power of light and the
shrewd mind of darkness. It is the culmination of all history and
civilization. And it is turning my mind into soup.
[*They stare at each other. Long pause*]

LIDUC You need a psychiatrist.

ROCCO There's no psychiatrist alive who could cope with me. I am the
absence of God.

LIDUC I feel obliged to answer that.

ROCCO Ah, I'm not listening to you. Where was the Church when I
needed her. I'll tell you. The world was being torn apart. Mothers
walked around grinning foolishly at their children's graves.
Compromise was ruining good men forever. Chronology and
reason were being shot to hell. And the Church was locked up
inside an old stone palace hiding under a gigantic mahogany desk
with His Eminence. Do you drink.

LIDUC I have a glass of wine each Christmas eve. A tradition.

ROCCO A family tradition?

LIDUC No. A tradition of my order.

ROCCO Difficult things. Family traditions. Especially for a man in your
situation. What do you do to keep the Chinese half of you loyal to
tradition.

LIDUC Nothing.

ROCCO The Chinese are great gamblers. I knew one in medical school.
He was killed in that Zeppelin crash. Do you ever gamble.

LIDUC Never.

ROCCO No. Well, Father LiDuc, I'm afraid this is the end of our relationship. I'm a busy man. I have to rely on first impressions. Obviously you have nothing to offer me.

LIDUC I'm sorry. Perhaps your wife and I will find more in common.

ROCCO Go easily with her. My wife is classically deluded. Are you familiar with 'The Three Sisters' by Chekhov.

LIDUC Of course.

ROCCO My wife believes that she is a character from that play. Her namesake. The eldest sister.

LIDUC How does she reconcile this belief with reality.

ROCCO Which reality.

LIDUC I understand.

ROCCO Do you.

LIDUC No.

ROCCO No. The only way to understand it is to become part of it. I write letters. I send them to a friend in London. He posts them for me. She thinks they're from her sister. That's a secret. Do you like secrets.

LIDUC No. But sometimes they're necessary.

ROCCO Wisdom. Glib wisdom. But it's better than nothing. Maybe you'll save us all in spite of the odds.

LIDUC I'm too young.

ROCCO And I'm drunk. Tell my wife not to wait up. I have to disappear for a while.

[ROCCO *starts off taking the bottle with him*]

LIDUC May I ask where to.

ROCCO No! Yes. I'm having an illicit affair with a leopard. Three trees due east of the quagmire. Beware the cobra. Ask for Zelda.

[ROCCO *leaves.* LIDUC *sits. Closes his eyes. Leans back. The sound of an approaching automobile. Screeches to a halt. Door opens. Door slams shut. Footsteps. Eventually* RITA *appears. She is wearing a decorated bathrobe*]

RITA The new priest.

LIDUC Yes.

RITA You don't look Chinese. They told me you were Chinese.

LIDUC Who told you.

RITA Them. The guys in the bushes.

[LIDUC *looks around nervously*]

Don't worry. They're harmless. They just follow me around 'cause they haven't got anything better to do.

[*Muttering from the bushes. She turns*]

You guys are getting pretty paranoid. You know that? Keep it down or you'll give yourselves a bad name.

[*Silence*]

Well, are you or aren't you.

LIDUC What.

RITA Chinese.

LIDUC Half.

RITA No kiddin'. Why are you shaking.

LIDUC Nerves. This is my first mission. I mean I have—

RITA Stage fright. Yeah. Where's the Doctor.

LIDUC He went for a walk.

RITA I'll bet he did.

LIDUC I don't like the innuendo. Say what you mean.

RITA Forget it.

[*She hands* LIDUC *a wad of bills*]

Here. Give him this for me, will ya. Tell him I don't need the action. Tell him he's worse than shit. Never mind. Just give him the money. I'll tell him he's worse than shit myself next time I see him.

LIDUC All right.

RITA Do you like my bathrobe. I painted it myself. Do you like the glitter.

LIDUC It's very …

RITA Crass. Yeah. It's crass. But I had no choice. It was either do it up vulgar or blend in with the scenery. I mean everyone else is so weird you know. Well, I was the last one to get here and all the other styles were taken. So I got left with 'vulgar.'

LIDUC That's too bad.

RITA I'm getting used to it. Yeah. You know, I was thinking about that on the way over. I haven't got much to do while I'm waiting for Chad, so sometimes I just think. I was thinking how much I've come to like this place. It used to bore the bejesus outta me. But now, well, I guess it's just been a good change of pace for me. Like

I'm on top of things. And back home it was always things being on top of me. Not that the money wasn't good. But the hours were lousy and my body was taking a real beating. And my flicks weren't good enough to be considered art so I was getting to feel kinda cheap. You know what this place is? I just thought of this. This place is my Virgin Father, Father. The one we all want.

LIDUC I've never heard of anyone wanting a Virgin Father before. That's interesting.

RITA Nah. It's hype. But at least it matches my clothes. Gotta run. [*starts off*]

LIDUC Bye-bye.

RITA Wait. [*stops*] You must have testicles. You know that? Staying here after what's happened. I mean Father Ricci was just a nosy son of a bitch and that one before him. Father what's-his-face.

LIDUC Carson.

RITA Yeah. He was a meddling mother too. But you seem different. You got testicles. And you look like the kinda man who'll mind his own business.

LIDUC Is that a suggestion.

RITA Could be. Gotta run. [*starts off. Stops*] Oh, tell the Doc I understand, but that maybe some other people won't.

LIDUC And what does that mean.

RITA Don't worry about what it means. Just tell him. Bye for now.

LIDUC And who can I say was calling.

RITA [*leaving*] Just tell him Rita was here.

[*Laughs. Leaves, humming 'Heat Wave.'* LIDUC *waves. Notices that his hand is trembling. Produces an envelope from a pocket. Sits on the steps. Pours some powder from it on to the back of his hand. Sniffs it. Closes his eyes. Sways gently for a while*]

LIDUC Personality is a dangerous illusion. [*falls back on the porch*]
[*Blackout*]
[*And the sound of some strange people in the distance singing 'Stand up for Jesus'*]

SCENE FIVE

Late evening paranoia
We hear the CORPORAL *laughing. Lights come up. The* CORPORAL *is startled and frightened. He staggers back. Sits, staring at us in fear*
LIDUC *is sitting on the picnic table, underlining passages in his Bible*
OLGA *comes briskly through the door, fresh and bright, carrying a parasol and a book*

OLGA I've decided to make a comeback. First things first. I'm going for a walk.
[*She comes down the steps. Takes several confident steps straight ahead. Stops. Turns. A few paces to the left. Stops. Turns. Looks right*]
It's all the same. Foreign. Uninviting. Blandness in one direction. Danger in the other. Why bother choosing.
[*She returns to her chair on the porch*]
[*to no one in particular*] It's like this, I think. One cannot afford to be a romantic. In this time. At this place. It's just too dangerous. Emotion is apt to be mistaken for weakness and weakness as an invitation to manipulate.
[*Pause*]
Yes. Good. I am thinking again. I'm going to be all right . [*sits*]
Good morning.
LIDUC Good morning.
CORPORAL [*directly outward*] And further more! [*looks around. Whimpers*] Where was I.
LIDUC You were describing the murders in all their gory detail.
CORPORAL Yeah. Yeah, right. Are you feeling better. Not gonna vomit after all, eh.
LIDUC No.
CORPORAL Okay. Post scriptum to all that. [*with great emphasis and delight*] Both victims were found without clothing. Conclusion. The murderer has a fetish or two. Even Ricci's various pieces and parts were all found unclad. This brings into question sexual abuse, homosexuality, sodomy, obscene sexual abuse and necrophobia!
[*falls to his knees*]

OLGA [*writhing from his descriptions*] Lunch!

LIDUC Necrophilia.

CORPORAL Yeah. Right.

OLGA [*recovering*] Lunch?

LIDUC I haven't had breakfast yet.

OLGA Good idea. Neither have I. Tomas!

[LIDUC *begins to underline in his Bible again. The* CORPORAL *recovers. Closes in on* LIDUC]

CORPORAL Do I have your undivided attention, Father.

LIDUC Not really.

CORPORAL Why not?!

LIDUC [*nervously*] You see, Doctor and Mrs. Rocco are allowing me to give my lessons here. I've called the first one for this afternoon. And I'm not very well prepared. Perhaps we could talk later.

CORPORAL Whatya mean later, man. You might not last the day.

OLGA Tomas!

CORPORAL Will you shut up!

OLGA Shut up yourself, Lance! This is my house!

CORPORAL So what!

[*The* CORPORAL *and* OLGA *stare at each other until* LIDUC *is overtaken by the silence*]

LIDUC All right, Corporal. Out with it. All this talk was in order to frighten me into doing what.

CORPORAL Nothing. Don't go anywhere. And don't do nothin'. Just stay here where you're safe. I've got my hands full. There's rebellion in the air and we're surrounded by unpredictable primitives. And I don't need another dead priest.

[*He grabs* LIDUC's *ears*]

Do you understand me.

LIDUC Yes.

CORPORAL [*shaking* LIDUC] I hope so. I hope so, mister. 'Cause if I catch you out running around unprotected I'm going to have to toss your ass in jail. And you know what that means. That means embarrassment. For both of us. Do you understand me.

LIDUC [*crying*] I said yes.

CORPORAL Okay. Okay. [*to* OLGA] Call me on the radio at the first sign of trouble.

OLGA Of course.

CORPORAL [*to* LIDUC. *Pointing a finger*] Okay.

[*The* CORPORAL *leaves*]

OLGA He's worried about his job.

LIDUC He's a fascist.

OLGA Oh. You don't care much for fascists.

LIDUC Who does.

OLGA Other fascists, I suppose.

[*Pause*]

I mean they're still human beings, aren't they. Aren't they.

[TOMAS *comes out. Dressed in wonderful and fancy new clothes,
strutting, smiling*]

Tomas. You are getting arrogant. In the future when I call you,
come out immediately and humbly like the lackey you really are.
Now go prepare tea and heat the croissants. We are breakfasting en
retard upon the terrace.

TOMAS Kali thiaskéthasi.

OLGA Just get the tea.

[TOMAS *nods. Hands* OLGA *a letter. Goes back into the house*]

LIDUC Where did he get the clothes.

OLGA I don't know. He just came home one day wearing them. And he
had an entire new wardrobe as well. I don't know where he got the
money.

LIDUC Why don't you ask him.

OLGA Enrico doesn't allow me to say anything to him except to give
him the simplest domestic commands. He says it might cause a
hemorrhage. You see, we found him in the desert surrounded by a
platoon of dead soldiers. He was wearing an apron. And he had a
bullet in his brain. It was like a godsend to both of us. I needed a
servant and Enrico needed someone on whom to test this new
neurosurgical procedure.

LIDUC Which procedure is this.

OLGA I can't tell you. It's illegal.

LIDUC I was afraid it might be.

OLGA It's a secret. All right?

LIDUC I'll have to think about it.

OLGA Oh, no. I only told you because I thought I could trust you. If anyone finds out they'll send Enrico away and I'll have to go too. And I have a feeling I wouldn't much like it out there.

LIDUC Out where.

OLGA Anywhere.

LIDUC All right. I won't tell anyone.

OLGA Good.

LIDUC I hope so.

[*Pause*]

OLGA Another letter from Masha. My sister. A good creature with an unfortunate past.

LIDUC I know.

OLGA What's that.

LIDUC Nothing. Your sister. Is she your only relative.

OLGA No. I have another sister. But she's too young and happy to be of any importance. And I had a brother too. But that's a long story.

LIDUC Olga.

[*He goes to her. Touches her shoulder*]

I think I can help you.

[*She reacts violently. Pushes him away*]

OLGA What nonsense is that. I don't need any help. I gave myself to Christ back in Russia and he promised he would take care of me. But if you have any spare time on your hands, I mean when you're not teaching the native people, you might see what you can do for my husband. He's 'haunted.' And Lance. He's 'haunted' too.

LIDUC The Corporal's 'haunted'? How do you know.

OLGA We had a brief affair. Enrico said he wouldn't mind as long as I didn't enjoy it too much. It was in the middle of the monsoon season. I became restless. [*sighs*] It's all right. I confessed to Father Ricci and he beat me unconscious to help me repent. [*sighs again*] Anyway Lance talks in his sleep. I found out that he was drummed out of the RCMP for shooting a farmer's cows. It seems that the expression in their eyes made him feel they were in 'eternal misery.' He can't stand seeing 'eternal misery.' He calls it 'evil whining misery.' Under all that bravado, he's really just a frightened boy.

LIDUC [*looks around. Sits*] Does he still kill things that he thinks are in eternal misery.

OLGA I don't know. That's a good question. You should ask him. But be careful how you do it. Because he's 'haunted.' Why are you shaking.
[LIDUC *takes out his envelope. Sniffs some of his powder*]
What's that.

LIDUC A dangerous drug.

OLGA [*backs away*] How nice. You know I wonder if our conversation has been good for me. It seems I decided to forget all these things a while ago. Of course I can't forget my family because Masha keeps writing me these damn letters. But I do try and forget about Lance. And especially my husband.

LIDUC I'm sorry. I thought some information about everyone might help me adjust.

OLGA Well. We're simple people, really.
[TOMAS *brings out the tea and biscuits on a tray. Sets them down on a small table near* OLGA's *chair*]
Change your bandage, Tomas. You're bleeding on the croissants.
[TOMAS *touches his head. Frowns. Goes back inside*]
Tell me about yourself. Tell me about your family. I just love hearing about families.

LIDUC Well ...

OLGA No. Please. It helps me. You said you wanted to help me.

LIDUC You said you didn't need help.

OLGA Well, I expected you to see that I was lying. Tell me. Please. Especially about your problems. Hearing about other people's problems somehow comforts me. [*a disturbing smile*] Please!
[LIDUC *stands*]

LIDUC My father was Chinese. My mother was a Jew. They were both incurably insane by the time I was ten. Some say they drove each other mad. Others say it was a bizarre game of one-upmanship. I was taken by the only relative I had. An uncle who was a convert to Catholicism. He was a fanatic. He died and I was put in the custody of the Church. That was twelve years ago. I just got out last month. I am a neurotic who is also like you say 'haunted.' And

I developed several habits along the way through my education. Among them, a desire for the bodies of lean young men, and an attraction to the joys of several drugs. The more dangerous the better. I am a potential source of deep embarrassment to the Church. Which is why I was sent here. This is where priests like myself and Father Ricci, who was an infamous sadist by the way, are sent in the hope that they will never be heard of again. So far a perfect record. Why is your mouth hanging open.

OLGA Would you like some tea.

LIDUC [*only now does he become mobile*] But the strangest thing. In the middle of all that and even now, my occasional relapse into total catatonia notwithstanding, I still have a relationship with God. I love him. And I trust him. And until I am done away with I will endeavour to bring him and his word to others. All I need now is a congregation. Do you think they'll come. If I wait long enough they will. They must.

OLGA Father. Would you like some tea.

LIDUC [*smiles*] Yes. I feel good. Thank you for the opportunity to speak. Yes I will have some tea.

[*He goes to get himself some*]

And what about you. Has hearing all this helped you. God is a reality, you know. He's better than even the best illusions.

OLGA Maybe. But he's not so accessible.

[ROCCO *comes out, in an undershirt. He is hung over*]

LIDUC Good morning.

ROCCO Liar. Don't you know that the sun is slowly dying. How can there be any *good* mornings? Where's your compassion. Ah, what a bunch of shit. Who wants to hear that shit. This isn't Italy. And I am no longer young enough to call out my reserves and hope for the best.

OLGA Is your work going badly. [*to* LIDUC] His work is his life.

ROCCO The freighter of my existence has struck a reef and all my chattels are getting wet.

[LIDUC *reaches into his pocket. Produces the money. Hands it to* ROCCO]

LIDUC From the lady called Rita.

ROCCO Excuse me. No. Don't. Who cares. [*starts back inside*]

OLGA [*to* LIDUC] He's trying to forget. He spends a lot of time trying to forget.

ROCCO [*turning around*] Shut up. Hear it?

OLGA What. [*pulls a small pistol from her skirt*]

LIDUC Why do you carry a gun.

OLGA Self-protection. We're surrounded by unhealthy people. You and I are the only ones around here who aren't paranoid.

ROCCO Shush. Hear it?

OLGA What?!

ROCCO Hear it now?

OLGA No.

ROCCO Hit the dirt!

[*They all duck. After a moment* ROCCO *stands. Looks through the open door into the house. The other two join him*]

OLGA What was it.

[ROCCO *scratches his head. Looks around. Tucks in his undershirt. Makes a meaningless gesture. Looks around. Smiles. Scratches his head*]

ROCCO Poison dart.

[*They all start slowly into the house, looking around cautiously.* OLGA *and* ROCCO *go inside.* LIDUC *changes his mind. Comes back down the steps. Looks around. Opens up his arms*]

LIDUC I have nothing to hide. In spite of everything I am still innocent. [*hears something. Whimpers. Puts his hands above his head*] [*Blackout*]
[*Drums, muffled and slow*]

SCENE SIX

Evening

The drums become gradually more distinct. Then they fade in and out throughout the scene

LIDUC *is still waiting with open arms. He moves only his eyes, which dash about in reaction to various noises from the bushes. Talking. Muttering. Footsteps. Branches breaking. Muffled screams. Complaints. Garbage cans banging. Babies crying. Birds screeching. And every once in a while a shot. A moan. And an explosion or two in the distance. And the sound of grass burning. Through all this* LIDUC *waits, moving only his eyes. Finally ...*

OLGA [*voice from inside the house*] No. Keep them out of my house.

ROCCO [*voice from inside the house*] What are you doing.

OLGA [*voice*] Keep away.

ROCCO [*voice*] Give it back.

OLGA [*voice*] Keep away.

ROCCO [*voice*] Don't do it.

OLGA [*voice*] Damn you! Damn you!

ROCCO [*voice*] No! Don't!

[*The sound of a bottle crashing*]

[*voice*] Oh my God. My work. My work.

OLGA [*voice*] Out of my house.

[*She comes through the door hysterically, covered with blood, her hands full of human organs, intestines and things.* LIDUC *turns away in disgust, starts to wander aimlessly around.* OLGA *throws them down on the ground. Picks them up. Throws them towards the audience. They don't go very far so she kicks them some more, closer to the audience, then closer.* ROCCO *comes out, in a rage, carrying a piece of intestine*]

ROCCO Stupid woman. Goddamn lunatic. You've ruined my work. No brains, woman. You've got mush for brains.

OLGA You brought them into my house. You put them on my dresser.

ROCCO Jesus. Simple Jesus. It wasn't me. It must have been Tomas.

OLGA I don't care. I saw them. I never wanted to see them. You're sick and evil and you let me see them. Damn you anyway. Damn you.

39

ROCCO Shut up. [*looks at his piece of intestine*] What did you do with
the rest.

OLGA Into the swamp. Threw it away. Threw it away.

ROCCO That was Old Peter. You threw away Old Peter. This is all that's
left.

OLGA Oh my God.

ROCCO I taught that man how to play chess. It took me two years.
Because he was a dumb native. Two wasted years reclaimed for my
experiments. And you've thrown him into the bushes to rot away
uselessly.

OLGA You're a butcher.

ROCCO I'm a scientist.

OLGA Scientists experiment with pigs.

ROCCO What a bunch of shit. Even a child could tell you that you
don't experiment with pigs to find out what's wrong with people.

OLGA You've lost your mind. It's for nothing. They'll look up your war
record and put you in prison forever. It's all for nothing.

ROCCO It's for my work. I will find the cure to end all cures. No matter
what it is. Or even that I do not know what it is. And even if I
never find it, I'm safe. Safe. Safe. In the bowels of the earth.
Because there's something about committing crimes against
humanity that puts you in touch with the purpose of the universe.

LIDUC That is the most intellectually obscene comment I have ever
heard.

OLGA [*hears something inside the house*] What's that.
[*She starts to go inside in a daze muttering 'Oh no, oh no*']

LIDUC God have mercy on the feeble, the diseased and the deluded.

ROCCO Woman! You will mean nothing to me in the end. I am a
scientist. And you are just a diversion. [*to the intestines*] I'm sorry,
Old Peter. This is the truth. Just between you and me. It's not glory
I'm after. It's redemption.
[LIDUC *utters a sentence in Chinese directed at the Doctor's condition*]
Nonsense. I am safe. I am sinking with confidence into the mire.
It's all out in the open and I'm safer than ever. I have finally
destroyed that fucking tower and now there are only three forces in
the world. God. Ignorance. And me.

[OLGA *screams inside the house. More a cry of anguish than a scream, actually*]

LIDUC Doctor, your soul is in serious trouble.

[OLGA *runs out of the house carrying a picture frame*]

OLGA We've been robbed. They've taken my Renoir. In retribution for your crimes. You've capsized me.

ROCCO My notebooks!

[*He runs into the house*]

OLGA My Renoir. My Renoir. My sanity.

LIDUC [*takes out his cocaine*] Have some of this.

OLGA No.

LIDUC Please. A touch of oblivion will settle you down.

OLGA No. I prefer to have a dream. Yes. I'm going to go inside. Lie down. And have a dream. A very vivid one. About the Victoria and Albert Museum. Yes. [*stands*] Masha will meet me at the station. [*starts inside*] Sloan Square. South Kensington. Gloucester Road. [*She disappears into the house*]

LIDUC [*sits. Sniffs some powder. Looks up*] I don't like the odds. [*sniffs some more*] But I will not give up.

[ROCCO *comes out*]

ROCCO My notebooks. My experiments. Gone. All gone. My safety is on the way. Now only to wait for the cataclysm.

[ROCCO *lies down on the operating table. The drums get a bit louder.* LIDUC *looks around. Looks at* ROCCO. *Chuckles. Goes and sits on the picnic table.* TOMAS *comes out of the bushes counting money, wearing a new suit, smoking a cigar. Sees the Doctor. Pulls a knife. Sneaks up towards him. His head is larger and more blood is showing on his bandage*]

LIDUC Be careful, Doctor. Behind you.

[ROCCO *sits up.* TOMAS *puts on a look of surprise*]

ROCCO What were you doing.

TOMAS Mistake.

ROCCO Go inside. Have a bath. Have two baths. Then crawl into bed with my wife. She's a bit frustrated. She needs sex. And I have other things on my mind. Inside. My wife. Sex. Understand?

TOMAS Yais. Sex. You come too.

ROCCO [*looks at him oddly*] No. [*lies down again*]

[TOMAS *starts inside. Stops. Goes to* LIDUC. *Sizes him up. Musses his hair*]

TOMAS You come too.

LIDUC Maybe later.

[TOMAS *laughs. Goes inside.* LIDUC *looks out at us*]

Clever. Clever. [*shaking a finger*] But I'm not going to be led into temptation. You naughty God you. [*laughs*]

[*We hear* RITA *approaching through the jungle, cursing to herself.* LIDUC *produces a bottle of pills from his coat pocket. Pops a couple. Laughs.* RITA *comes on, her bathrobe torn, black underwear beneath it, her face a bit soiled, muttering, walking oddly*]

RITA Those fuckers. Those mothers. Those lousy scumbags. Jesus. It's a double cross. Screwed on all sides. Where's Tomas.

ROCCO Busy. Come back later.

RITA He's done me in. He took their money and bought himself clothes. Fucking suits and ties and shoes. Clothes.

LIDUC What was he supposed to buy.

RITA Guns.

LIDUC What for.

RITA I don't know what for. For some stupid uprising, I guess. I don't know. And I don't care. I needed the money. The money.

LIDUC I'm sorry for you.

RITA What's that.

LIDUC I'm sorry for you.

RITA Oh, you are. Why.

LIDUC Because you're dumb. Because you've been exploited. Exploited by people who you were trying to exploit. And that's sad. Jesus doesn't mind losers but he has no patience for idiots.

RITA They raped me.

LIDUC Did you enjoy it.

RITA Hey, come on. Even Father Ricci never asked questions like that. You're weird.

LIDUC True.

[RITA *sits down on the steps. Pause*]

RITA I was caught off guard. Leaning against my tree. Sipping

Southern Comfort. Looking north towards the high grass.
Thinking everything was fine. Counting money in my head.
Figuring we had enough for a month's shooting. Thinking how
sorry Chad was every time he beat me up and how sorry I was for
calling the police that last time. And how sincere Chad looked
when he came into my hospital room with those cops. Leaning
against that tree with the flies in my ears. Getting really very deeply
into Susan Hayward in 'The Snows of Kilimanjaro.'
[*Drums start. Louder*]
And then they were on me with their funny talk and their wiped-
out eyes and their hands smeared with elephant fat. Sticking their
long dry dongs in me. And all the time asking where their money
was and telling me how they'd had to get that money by cashing in
empty soda bottles and stealing hub caps and costume jewellery
from all the white trash and that they were really pissed off that
they didn't have any guns to blow everyone's head off and set up a
new republic dedicated to socialistic democracy and put the white
European honky trash in little boxes with bars on them and feed
them gruel and hit their hands with long sticks.
[*Drums stop. Pause*]
But through all that I was fine. I was all right . Because I kept
telling myself it wasn't real. Nobody rapes me. Nobody ever raped
Susan Hayward or Rita Hayworth. And nobody rapes me. But,
Jesus, they said that if they didn't get their money or their guns
pretty damn soon they were gonna do it again. Only this time
torture me and take pictures of my mutilated body and send them
to all those cheap tabloids back home. That's when I passed out.
Because the idea of being on the front cover of one of those things
lying there like a matted rug just ran like vomit all through my
body and my mind. And I passed out.
[*A scream from the house.* TOMAS *runs out. Putting on his
undershorts*]
[*to* TOMAS] And it's your fault, you mother.
[*She steps towards* TOMAS. *He runs away. Before he disappears into the
bushes,* RITA *produces a pistol from her bathrobe and points it at*
TOMAS' *back. But does not shoot.* TOMAS *is gone.* RITA *drops the gun*]

I couldn't. He's still my only friend.

[*A gunshot from inside the house.* ROCCO *sits up*]

ROCCO She's shot herself.

[ROCCO *and* LIDUC *rush towards the door.* ROCCO *goes in.* LIDUC *stops. Returns for his Bible. Gets it. Runs in*]

RITA Sometimes I just feel like giving up.

[*Pause.* TOMAS *comes running on. Disappears into the bushes on the other side of the house. The* CORPORAL *comes running on. He is delirious and sweating profusely*]

CORPORAL Did you see him.

RITA A total blur.

CORPORAL A subversive. One of many. They're all over the place. Getting ready to attack. I've got an informant. He tells me they've got a new leader and a real sharpy he's supposed to be too. He's organized them and they're ready to move.

RITA You're sweating like a pig.

CORPORAL Fever. Malaria.

[*Drums start again.*]

[*producing a nylon stocking. Turning around feverishly*] Here we go. They followed me. It's all over.

[*He approaches* RITA *slowly*]

Listen I know you're in with them. Use your influence. It's me they want. They know I've been doing you-know-what with all their eleven-year-old daughters. Old Joseph's eleven-year-old daughter in particular. It was good. We both liked it. But she went funny. Stole my pistol and tried to shoot off my you-know-what. I liked that too. But then she started to cry and her eyes got all spongy and I knew she was in 'misery.' 'Evil whining misery.'

RITA You killed that little girl!

CORPORAL Shut up. It's a secret.

[*The* CORPORAL *puts the stocking around* RITA's *neck.* RITA *is gagging. The* CORPORAL *is squeezing.* LIDUC *comes out*]

LIDUC Olga has shot herself in the chest. Can we divert ourselves for a moment to pray for her.

[*The* CORPORAL *drops* RITA. *Turns on* LIDUC]

CORPORAL Shut up. You smell. I saw what you've got written on the

inside cover of your Bible. 'Prophecy is an escape from memory.'
Now what in the hell does that mean.

[*He raises the stocking and lunges at* LIDUC. LIDUC *ducks. Runs back inside.* RITA *has crawled to a chair. The* CORPORAL *is strangling himself*]

It means misery! Misery in the mind. Everyone's got it and everyone has to be put out of it. [*thinks. Drops the stocking*] But not me. I gotta live.

[*He grabs* RITA. *Lifts her in a bear hug*]

Help me.

RITA No.

CORPORAL I gotta live. Gotta overcome the disgrace of being drummed outta the Mounties. My father was a policeman.

RITA Cut the crap. And let me go.

CORPORAL My father was a bull. Deep murky brown eyes. Lips like pancakes. We called him Sarge.

RITA Let me go, you goddamn oaf.

[*Drums stop. The* CORPORAL *drops* RITA. *Looks around in a panic*]

CORPORAL What's going on here.

RITA It's a power struggle.

[*Pause*]

CORPORAL Yeah. That's it. Between who.

RITA You and me.

CORPORAL Yeah. Who's winning.

RITA I am.

[*He slaps her*]

CORPORAL Who's winning now.

RITA I am.

[*He slaps her*]

CORPORAL And who's winning now.

[*She knees him in the groin. He falls to his knees*]

RITA I am.

CORPORAL Don't look at me like that, eh. I know what you're thinking.

RITA I'm thinking how silly you look. Just like my man looked when I hit him with my cast in that hospital room.

[*The* CORPORAL *is crawling away from her*]

CORPORAL You're passing judgement on me. In times of crisis there are only two kinds of people. People who behave badly and people who pass judgement on the people who behave badly. And you're one of them. Just like my father. He's dead. But he never lets me forget.

[*The* CORPORAL *collapses. Face down.* LIDUC *comes out carrying his valise*]

LIDUC What's wrong with him.

RITA He's delirious.

[*Suddenly the* CORPORAL *gets to his knees. Draws his gun*]

CORPORAL I know what they want. I know what they all want. They want to be put outta their misery. And maybe they want a little sexual abuse too. Oh, and I'm just the man to give it to them. [*gets to his feet*] All right. All right.

[*The* CORPORAL *staggers off.* ROCCO *comes out of the house*]

ROCCO I've decided that I want to live. [*talking to the audience*] I'll do anything you want. Just let me get on with my work. My work is my penance. And my penance is everything. [*to* LIDUC] You. Priest. Go see if you can make them understand.

[*But* LIDUC *has taken the materials of a heroin user out of his valise. And is in the process of shooting up*]

LIDUC Okay. Sure. But first I have to get closer to God. I have the feeling we've been out of touch.

RITA Don't let them take any pictures of my mutilated body.

ROCCO Be quiet. I'm preparing myself to beg.

[OLGA *comes out of the house. Carrying her picture frame. Her chest is wrapped in bandages*]

OLGA Oh, hello Shirley.

RITA The name's Rita.

OLGA Your name is Shirley Morgan. But not to worry. Our secret. [*groans*] Enrico. I have a complaint to make about that animal you sent into my bed. His erection was monumental but his manner was disgusting. He took me in the rectum. Good taste died immediately. And I have decided to follow.

[*Pause*]

To die. On my way to Moscow. Finally leaving. Finally getting
there. Finally. Moscow. [*giggles*] Ah. What a bad joke it really is.
[*A scream from the jungle*]
Bravo.
[*She dies, leaning against a post on the porch*]

RITA Is she dead.

ROCCO I guess so.

LIDUC I can cope. No. I can't cope.

RITA Well, if it's gonna happen I wanna look my best. Or else everyone
will just look at my picture and say, 'She was a cheap porno queen
and she died looking like one.' And no one will ever believe that I
had what I had beneath all this shit. And the world won't be able to
remember me with love.
[*She takes a small compact and lipstick from her pocket. Begins to
apply the lipstick. The* CORPORAL *comes on. Minus one arm. Blood
dripping. A note attached to his sleeve. The note is plainly visible. A
child's handwriting. It reads, 'Entertain us'*]
Your arm.

CORPORAL Where is it.

RITA I don't know.

CORPORAL Then it's gone. They really took it off. Failed again. [*looks
up*] Sorry, Sarge.

ROCCO That note on his sleeve.

LIDUC [*chuckles. Looks up*] Amazing. I don't understand how you make
all this violence seem so gratuitous.

ROCCO What's it say. I'll do anything it says.

RITA [*reads*] 'Entertain us.'
[*Pause. They all look around. And from this moment there is a distinct
tendency for everyone to play outward*]

ROCCO [*pacing*] Entertain them? Entertain them.

RITA How.

ROCCO I'm thinking.

CORPORAL I'm bleeding to death! [*begins to cry*]

ROCCO Then do it quietly. I'm thinking.

RITA [*beginning to disrobe*] I won't do anything disgusting. I'll entertain
but I won't be cheap.

ROCCO You'll do what I tell you. Or I'll slit your throat.

RITA Hey. We're friends.

[*She crumples onto the steps*]

ROCCO I want to live.

LIDUC Excuse me. But what for.

ROCCO You give me a reason.

LIDUC To save humanity.

[*He whistles in self-approval*]

ROCCO Corporal. Shut up. You're whining.

[*The* CORPORAL *has been writhing on the ground*]

CORPORAL Whining? [*sits up*] Oh my God. I'm whining. Evil whining?

[*He wraps his one arm around* ROCCO'*s leg*]

Oh Doctor, you gotta put me outta my misery.

[ROCCO *shakes him loose*]

ROCCO No. You'll live. Till I'm safe. You'll bleed till I'm safe. All of you. We'll all entertain together. No one gets safe before me.

LIDUC [*points to* OLGA] Except her.

[ROCCO *grabs* RITA'*s lipstick. Goes to* OLGA]

ROCCO No. Not even her.

[*The* CORPORAL *is crawling towards us. Looking along the ground. Smiling insanely*]

CORPORAL Ants. Huge red ants. They've smelled my blood. And they've come to nibble on my stump.

[ROCCO *is using the lipstick to paint* OLGA'*s face: two tears and a huge obscene smile.* TOMAS *comes out of the jungle wearing priest's clothes, two crosses around his neck, carrying a spear and an enormous wad of money*]

LIDUC [*giddily*] Look at him. Where'd you get those clothes.

TOMAS God.

LIDUC Where'd you get those two crucifixes.

TOMAS God.

[LIDUC *has one moment of unbridled passion in this play. He stands. And projects*]

LIDUC Liar!

[TOMAS *attacks him. Pushes him down. Leans over. Massages his crotch. Whispers something terrible in his ear*] [*trembling*] It's true. Oh my God. It's true.

[TOMAS *laughs maniacally. Screams. Throws the money up and all over the ground*]

ROCCO I've got it! Hum. [*goes to* RITA] Everyone hum!

RITA [*singing*] 'We're having a heat wave ...'

ROCCO No. Something Russian.

[ROCCO *starts to hum 'Swan Lake.'* RITA *joins in.* ROCCO *goes to* LIDUC. *Drags him up. Gets* LIDUC *to join in. The* CORPORAL *is hearing humming noises*]

CORPORAL Locusts! Enormous pecking locusts!

[ROCCO *is now standing over the* CORPORAL. *Pulling his hair*]

ROCCO Hum!

[*Everyone is humming and singing 'Swan Lake,' staring hard at us and singing with increasing concern, getting louder and louder.* ROCCO *goes to* OLGA. *Drags her to a chair. Puts her on his knee. Sticks his hand up the back of her dress to her throat. And as 'Swan Lake' approaches a crescendo it is interrupted by a bizarre scream from* OLGA's *throat. Silence.* ROCCO *is manipulating* OLGA's *vocal chords, her head flopping lifelessly around until his is able to position her properly. He clears his throat. Moves* OLGA's *jaw. And the following speech comes from* OLGA, *in her own voice, but distorted and unbearably erratic.* ROCCO *silently mouths the words of* OLGA's *final speech:*]

OLGA 'The music is so gay, so confident. And one longs for life! Oh my God! Time will pass, and we shall go away forever, and we shall be forgotten, our faces will be forgotten, our voices and how many there were of us. But our sufferings will pass into joy for those who will live after us, happiness and peace will be established upon earth and they will remember kindly and bless those who have lived before. Oh dear sisters, our life is not ended yet. We shall live! The music is so gay, so joyful, and it seems as though a little more and we shall know what we are living for, why we are suffering ... Oh. If only we could know. If only we could know?!'

[*And* OLGA's *mouth is still moving as if there were more to say. But all we hear are groans and mutterings.* ROCCO *is smiling at the audience obsequiously. The others are staring in disbelief at* OLGA. TOMAS *looks*

at them. At us. Raises his arm and beckons. The drums explode.
Sudden violence and activity from the bushes, getting closer and louder.
Everyone on their feet now, edging towards the door of the house,
looking at the audience in confusion and growing anxiety—backing
up slowly]
[*Blackout*]
[*End*]

ZASTROZZI: THE MASTER OF DISCIPLINE

Zastrozzi was first produced at Toronto Free Theatre on 2 November, 1977 with the following cast:

ZASTROZZI Stephen Markle
BERNARDO George Buza
VEREZZI Geoffrey Bowes
VICTOR David Bolt
MATILDA Diane D'Aquila
JULIA Valerie Warburton

Director: William Lane
Designer: Doug Robinson
Lighting Designer: Gerry Brown
Sound Designer: Wes Wraggett
Fights arranged by: Patrick Crean

Persons

ZASTROZZI, *a master criminal, German*
BERNARDO, *his friend*
VEREZZI, *an Italian, an artist, a dreamer*
VICTOR, *his tutor*
MATILDA, *a gypsy, a raven-haired beauty*
JULIA, *an aristocrat, a fair-haired beauty*

Place

Europe, probably Italy.

Time

The 1890s.

Set

It should combine a simplified version of a Piranesi prison drawing with the ruins of an ancient city. There are interesting and varied chambers within and the walls are crumbling. The tops of several trees are visible and weeds are growing out of the stones.

Note

This play is not an adaptation of Shelley's *Zastrozzi*. The playwright read a brief description of this novella in a biography of Shelley and that provided the inspiration for *Zastrozzi: The Master of Discipline*, something quite different from Shelley's work.

PROLOGUE

Just before the storm
BERNARDO *is looking up at the sky*

BERNARDO It is not a passion. Passion will eventually reward the soul. It is not an obsession. Obsession will sustain you for a lifetime. It is not an idea. An idea is the product of an ordinary mind. It is not an emotion. It cannot be purged. It is not greed or lust or hate or fear. It is none of those things. It is worse. The sky is swelling. And all those with timid natures had better go hide. It will conspire with the sky, and the air will explode, and the world will break apart and get thrown around like dust. But it is not the end of the world. It is easily worse. It is revenge.
[*Blackout followed by a loud sustained volley of thunder. Deadly calm.* ZASTROZZI *lights an oil lamp and stands rigidly. His face is twisted with hatred*]

ZASTROZZI You are looking at Zastrozzi. But that means very little. What means much more is that Zastrozzi is looking at you. Don't make a sound. Breathe quietly. He is easily annoyed. And when he is annoyed he strikes. Look at his right arm. [*holding it up*] It wields the sword that has killed two hundred men. Watch the right arm constantly. Be very careful not to let it catch you unprepared. But while watching the right arm [*suddenly producing a dagger with his left hand*] do not forget the left arm. Because this man Zastrozzi has no weaknesses. No weakness at all. Remember that. Or he will have you. He will have you any way he wants you.
[*Lightning. A long pause.* ZASTROZZI'*s face and body relax. He looks around almost peacefully. He smiles*]
I am Zastrozzi. The master criminal of all Europe. This is not a boast. It is information. I am to be feared for countless reasons. The obvious ones of strength and skill with any weapon. The less obvious ones because of the quality of my mind. It is superb. It works in unique ways. And it is always working because I do not sleep. I do not sleep because if I do I have nightmares and when you have a mind like mine you have nightmares that could petrify

the devil. Sometimes because my mind is so powerful I even have
nightmares when I am awake and because my mind is so powerful
I am able to split my consciousness in two and observe myself
having my nightmare. This is not a trick. It is a phenomenon. I am
having one now. I have this one often. In it, I am what I am. The
force of darkness. The clear, sane voice of negative spirituality.
Making everyone answerable to the only constant truth I
understand. Mankind is weak. The world is ugly. The only way to
save them from each other is to destroy them both. In this
nightmare I am accomplishing this with great efficiency. I am
destroying cities. I am destroying countries. I am disturbing social
patterns and upsetting established cultures. I am causing people
such unspeakable misery that many of them are actually saving me
the trouble by doing away with themselves. And, even better, I am
actually making them understand that this is, in fact, the way
things should proceed. I am at the height of my power. I am lucid,
calm, organized and energetic. Then it happens. A group of people
come out of the darkness with sickly smiles on their faces. They
walk up to me and tell me they have discovered my weakness, a
flaw in my power, and that I am finished as a force to be reckoned
with. Then one of them reaches out and tickles me affectionately
under my chin. I am furious. I pick him up and crack his spine on
my knee then throw him to the ground. He dies immediately. And
after he dies he turns his head to me and says, 'Misery loves chaos.
And chaos loves company.' I look at him and even though I know
that the dead cannot speak, let alone make sense, I feel my brain
turn to burning ashes and all my control run out of my body like
mud and I scream at him like a maniac, [*whispering*] 'What does
that mean.'
[*Blackout*]

SCENE ONE

A vicious series of lightning bolts flash, illuminating the entire stage. A bed chamber. ZASTROZZI *is reeling about violently*

ZASTROZZI Where is the Italian Verezzi. Tell him I have come to send him to hell. Tell him that Zastrozzi is here. Tell him I am waiting. He can hide no more. He can run no farther. I am here. And I am staying. [*grabbing a flask of wine and drinking*] Ah, Jesus, this wine tastes like it was made by amateurs. I hate amateurs. Death to all of them. Remember that.
[BERNARDO *bursts into the chamber.* ZASTROZZI *throws a sabre at him like a spear.* BERNARDO *ducks. The two men look at each other*]
BERNARDO It's Bernardo.
ZASTROZZI Step closer. The light is tricky.
BERNARDO It *is* Bernardo, sir.
ZASTROZZI Ah, Jesus! [*turning and violently ripping all the coverings from the bed*] I thought I saw an Italian to be killed.
BERNARDO Not this one I hope. Please be more careful.
ZASTROZZI Don't worry, Bernardo. Of all the Italians worthy of killing I am interested in only one. [*sitting on the bed*] But my mind is becoming clearer by the minute and unless I get some satisfaction I may come to the inevitable conclusion that all Italians are worthy of killing for one reason or another.
BERNARDO Yes, I like your threats. They keep me alert.
ZASTROZZI Learn to smile when you are being ironic. It might save your life some day.
BERNARDO [*smiling*] The best advice is that of the best advised.
ZASTROZZI Remind me to order you to say that again when I'm not preoccupied.
BERNARDO It doesn't—
ZASTROZZI Have you found him.
BERNARDO He is here.
ZASTROZZI Where.
BERNARDO At least he was here. He has gone off into the countryside. But he is expected back.

ZASTROZZI How soon.

BERNARDO Eventually.

[ZASTROZZI *advances on* BERNARDO]

That is what I was told. And that is what I am reporting.

ZASTROZZI Told by whom.

BERNARDO The innkeeper where he stays.

ZASTROZZI Then you were at his rooms?

BERNARDO Yes.

ZASTROZZI How do they smell. What do they look like. Describe them to me. No, wait, first, are you sure it is the same man. Verezzi the poet.

BERNARDO Now Verezzi the painter.

ZASTROZZI Yes, yes. And before that Verezzi the dramatist. And before that Verezzi the dancer. His vocation makes no difference. Always changing. Always pleasantly artistic. But the man himself, Bernardo. A description.

BERNARDO The innkeeper described the same man.

ZASTROZZI Even so. Possibly a coincidence. But the important things.

BERNARDO Those as well.

ZASTROZZI A religious man?

BERNARDO Very.

ZASTROZZI Always praying?

BERNARDO Before and after every meal. Often during the meal. Occasionally throughout the meal.

ZASTROZZI And the ladies. Does he have a way with them.

BERNARDO Many ladies have visited him in his room. Most come back again.

ZASTROZZI What about the smile. The smile that I see clearly in my head even though I have never met the man who wears it. That smile is an unnatural thing, Bernardo. Empty.

BERNARDO 'He smiles an annoying much of the time.' I quote the innkeeper directly.

ZASTROZZI Then it is him. It is Verezzi the artiste. The Christian. The great lover. The optimist. I will have him soon. Are you happy for me, my friend.

BERNARDO I have watched you wanting him for a long time. I have grown fond of the force behind the search for revenge. I think I'll miss it.

ZASTROZZI At first I wanted him just for myself. For what he did to my mother. But what I have learned of this man, Verezzi, makes me want him for another reason. That smile, Bernardo, I will remove it from the earth. It is a dangerous thing. It raises a bigger issue than revenge. [*repeating this last sentence in German*]

BERNARDO Is this a new development.

ZASTROZZI Actually, it is still revenge. But in a larger sense. In fact it is revenge in its true and original meaning. And, therefore, some other word is probably necessary. It is 1893 and language, like everything else, has become pleasantly vague.

BERNARDO I'm not sure I understand.

ZASTROZZI Naturally. Because if you did then there would be two of us and there is only need for one. No. Call it revenge, Bernardo. Tell everyone else to call it revenge. If it will make you happy I'll even call it revenge.

[*Blackout*]

SCENE TWO

The countryside, a light rain is falling. VEREZZI *is sitting behind an easel, paintbrush in hand.* VICTOR *holds an umbrella over* VEREZZI's *head and examines the painting in silence for a while*

VICTOR Always tell the truth. Except when under pressure.

VEREZZI What does that mean.

VICTOR How can you paint a German landscape when you have never been to Germany.

VEREZZI My father was in Germany. He told me all about it.

VICTOR That's silly. You present a false image.

VEREZZI Perhaps. But my heart is in the right place.

VICTOR Unsuspecting people will look at your art and think they see the truth.

VEREZZI Perhaps my Germany is the real Germany. And if not, then perhaps it is what the real Germany should be.

VICTOR What is that supposed to mean.

VEREZZI I'm not quite sure. Yes, I am. Perhaps Germany is ugly. Or perhaps Germany is bland. What is the point of creating bland or ugly art.

VICTOR To illustrate the truth.

VEREZZI Art has nothing to do with truth.

VICTOR Then what is its purpose.

VEREZZI To enlighten.

VICTOR How can you enlighten if you don't serve the truth.

VEREZZI You enlighten by serving God.

VICTOR Then God is not serving the truth.

VEREZZI Is that a question or a statement.

VICTOR Both.

VEREZZI Then you are a heretic.

VICTOR And you are a liar.

VEREZZI A dreamer, Victor. A dreamer.

VICTOR The same thing.

VEREZZI Enough. I don't even remember asking your opinion.

VICTOR If I waited to be asked you would never receive my criticism and, therefore, no education.

VEREZZI You weren't hired as a tutor. You were hired as a servant.

VICTOR That was before either of us realized how monumentally ignorant you are.

VEREZZI Enough. What colours do you mix to make ochre.

VICTOR Ochre is unnecessary.

VEREZZI That hill should be shaded with ochre.

VICTOR On some other planet perhaps. On earth it's green.

VEREZZI Earth is boring.

VICTOR Why don't you ask God to move you.

VEREZZI Don't make fun of God.

VICTOR I was making fun of Verezzi.

VEREZZI The two are interchangeable.

VICTOR That sounds slightly narcissistic to me.

VEREZZI I am His messenger on earth.

VICTOR What.

VEREZZI [a revelation] I am His messenger on earth.

VICTOR This is a new development. Until recently you were His servant.

VEREZZI Through devotion and regular prayer, I have attained a new position.

VICTOR Then God encourages linear growth.

VEREZZI I beg your pardon.

VICTOR When will you be made Messiah.

VEREZZI Atheist. How do you sleep without fear.

VICTOR A secret. Besides, I am not an atheist. I just have a more pragmatic relationship with God than you do.

VEREZZI What is it.

VICTOR It is based on reality, Verezzi. You wouldn't comprehend it.

VEREZZI I should dismiss you. I think you mean to corrupt me.

VICTOR Can I ask you a question.

VEREZZI No.

VICTOR Not even a sincere one?

VEREZZI In all the time I've known you, you've never once been sincere on the subject of my religious experiences.

VICTOR Be patient. At least I don't laugh in your face anymore.

VEREZZI Ask your question.

VICTOR How do you reconcile being God's messenger on earth with the fact that you find earth boring.

VEREZZI That is my cross. I bear it.

VICTOR [*sadly*] Yes. Of course you do. You probably do.

VEREZZI Besides, I am an artist. Even if I was not a religious artist I would be dissatisfied. That is the nature of an artist.

VICTOR That is the opinion of a very silly man.

VEREZZI Enough. I have to finish.

VICTOR When are we going back to the village.

VEREZZI When I have completed my painting.

VICTOR And what will you do with the painting.

VEREZZI It contains His message. I'll give it to someone.

VICTOR Not sell it?

VEREZZI His message should not be sold. It's a gift. Besides I have no need of money.

VICTOR That's because your father was very rich.

VEREZZI Yes. So what.

VICTOR I was just wondering how a messenger of God would get by if he weren't independently wealthy.

VEREZZI You are a subversive.

VICTOR And you are a saint.

VEREZZI Oh. Thank you.

VICTOR No. It wasn't a compliment.

[*Blackout*]

SCENE THREE

A dining chamber, occasional thunder, lightning, and rain outside
MATILDA *and* ZASTROZZI *are some distance apart preparing to fight.*
They cut the air with their sabres. On the table are the remnants of a
meal. BERNARDO *sits in a chair, munching a chicken leg, his legs on*
the table. He describes VEREZZI'*s room*

BERNARDO The room smelled of lilacs, incense and mint tea. This
Verezzi is an orderly fellow for sure. Nothing about the room was
haphazard. Everything was neat and clean. In fact, the place
appeared to have been arranged by a geometrist, for all objects were
placed at perfectly right angles to each other. And between the two
halves of the room—one used for work and the other for
play—there was a perfect symmetry.
ZASTROZZI Then he has someone with him. A man like Verezzi is not
capable of symmetry.
[*Pause*]
Balance. A dangerous opponent in regulated combat. But get him
in an alley or a dark street and you have him disoriented.
Nevertheless, out of respect for his inclination, I'll cut him up into
thirty-two pieces of equal size. Are you ready, Matilda.
MATILDA First I want to make one thing clear. I do not suffer from
rapier envy. I just like to fight.
[MATILDA *and* ZASTROZZI *cross swords and begin to fight. As they*
progress it becomes clear that MATILDA *is very good even though*
ZASTROZZI *is not trying very hard*]
BERNARDO There were several of his paintings in the room. For the
most part he is a mediocre artist but occasionally he exhibits a
certain flair. It's naive but it's there. One painting in particular
caught my eye. An informal unrecognizable series of swirls and
circles in white, off-white and beige. He seems very fond of it
himself. He has given it a title.
ZASTROZZI What does he call it then.
BERNARDO God's Stomach.
MATILDA The man is a fool.

BERNARDO I would tend to agree.

ZASTROZZI Then how has he evaded us for three years.

BERNARDO I've been thinking about that.

ZASTROZZI Thinking?

BERNARDO Perhaps he doesn't know we've been chasing him.

ZASTROZZI Nonsense. He's a clever man.

BERNARDO But surely there are none more clever than the guileless.

ZASTROZZI Stop thinking, Bernardo. It causes you to have absurd poetic fantasies. I am clever. I am the most accomplished criminal in Europe. Matilda is clever. She is the most accomplished seductress in Europe. Do either of us seem guileless to you.

BERNARDO No. But you, sir, are motivated by a strange and powerful external force and Matilda has certain physical assets which allow her activities a certain ease.

MATILDA I also have a first-class mind, Bernardo, and it gives me self-confidence. But if I didn't and I heard that patronizing comment about my body I would take off your head.

BERNARDO If I ever have my head taken off I hope you'll be the one who does it. But not with your sword. I would like you to use your teeth.

MATILDA Are comments like that what you use to show sexual interest in someone.

BERNARDO Excuse me. [*standing and starting off*]

MATILDA Don't be shy, Bernardo. Are you being shy, Bernardo.

BERNARDO If you wish.

MATILDA Actually all I wish is that men in general could perform with the same intensity that they lust with.

BERNARDO I might surprise you.

MATILDA You might. But I think we both doubt that.

BERNARDO Excuse me. I think I'll go visit the inn again. [*starting off again*] Oh, I forgot. Here is one of his drawings. I took it from his room.

ZASTROZZI You stole it.

BERNARDO Yes.

ZASTROZZI Why.

BERNARDO Zastrozzi asks why someone steals something. Zastrozzi, who has stolen more than any man alive.

ZASTROZZI Put it back.

BERNARDO Why.

ZASTROZZI We are not thieves anymore.

BERNARDO Then what are we.

ZASTROZZI We are not thieves.

[BERNARDO *leaves*]

MATILDA I don't want to do this anymore. [*throwing down her sabre*] Let's make love.

ZASTROZZI I'm preoccupied.

MATILDA With what.

ZASTROZZI The image of Verezzi's painting.

MATILDA You didn't even look at it.

ZASTROZZI I saw it in my head. It is a colourful pastoral. An impression of a landscape. Impressionism. Distortion.

MATILDA Very interesting. Great material for preoccupation, I'm sure. But you were preoccupied the last time I came to you. And the time before that as well. We haven't made love in over a year.

ZASTROZZI Then go somewhere else. Making love is not an accurate description of what we do anyway.

MATILDA I realize that. I know what we do. We ravage each other. Nevertheless I miss it. Don't you?

ZASTROZZI No.

MATILDA Zastrozzi is hollow. I have come three hundred miles just to be reminded once again that Zastrozzi is hollow.

ZASTROZZI Drink. [*picking up a flask and drinking*]

MATILDA Don't you ever get physically aroused anymore.

ZASTROZZI No. All sexual desire left me the moment I realized I had a purpose in life.

MATILDA So now you have a purpose. I thought you just wanted to make people suffer.

ZASTROZZI Can't that be a purpose.

MATILDA I don't know. But I do know it can't stop you from desiring me. There's something you're not telling me.

ZASTROZZI Very well. I swore a vow of chastity.

MATILDA To whom.

ZASTROZZI The Emperor of Spain's mistress.

MATILDA Nonsense. When would you have met her.

ZASTROZZI When I robbed the Emperor's country estate. His mistress
    was there alone. One thing led to another and I raped her. Just as I
    was leaving she looked up and said, 'I can live with this if you vow
    never to be intimate with another woman.' I shrugged my
    shoulders, said 'all right,' and left.
    [MATILDA *laughs*]
    I knew you would understand.

MATILDA I'm the only woman alive who could. We belong together. It
    would be delicious while it lasted. There's no one alive we couldn't
    victimize in one way or another. And when we're finally caught we
    can go to hell together.

ZASTROZZI No, not hell. Some place less specific. Atheists don't go to
    hell. They don't know where it is. The Christians invented it and
    the only decent thing they've done is to keep its whereabouts a
    secret to outsiders.

MATILDA Then forget hell. Let's go to Africa instead.

ZASTROZZI Later. I have things to do.

MATILDA Ah, yes. This search for revenge on some God-obsessed
    Italian. You are letting it change your personality.

ZASTROZZI He murdered my mother.

MATILDA So find him. Then kill him. It's a simple matter. It should
    not be your purpose in life. Revenge is an interesting obsession but
    it isn't worthy of the powers of Zastrozzi.

ZASTROZZI I know. But Verezzi represents something which must be
    destroyed. He gives people gifts and tells them they are from God.
    Do you realize the damage that someone like that can do.

MATILDA Damage to what.
    [ZASTROZZI *makes a dismissive gesture*]
    I don't understand.

ZASTROZZI I don't need your understanding.

MATILDA Yes. I know that. I haven't been coming to you all these years
    because I think you need anything from me. It's that I need
    something from you.

ZASTROZZI Really. What.

MATILDA The whore sleeps with the devil so she can feel like a virgin?
ZASTROZZI Something like that. Yes. What a comfortable little
solution to guilt. Except that your devil is unpredictable.
[ZASTROZZI *hits* MATILDA *and knocks her down*]
Get out.
MATILDA Let me stay.
ZASTROZZI Get out. Or your devil might slit your throat just to show
the flaw in your argument.
MATILDA If I crawl across to you and beg, will you let me stay.
ZASTROZZI [*looks at her silently for a moment*] First, let's see how you
crawl.
[MATILDA *crawls slowly over to him, wraps her arms around his legs
and rests her head on his boot*]
MATILDA Let me stay. Do what you have to. Go send this Italian
Verezzi to hell and then let me stay forever.
ZASTROZZI Shush. [*thinking, breaking away from her and pacing slowly*]
Send this Verezzi to hell. [*chuckling*] Yes.
[ZASTROZZI *paces some more, stops and looks at* MATILDA]
I will. He is a Christian. He can go to hell. Or at least he thinks he
can. And the pain. Such excruciating pain. Much, much more than
if I were to merely kill him. He must be made to send himself in
his mind to hell. By killing himself. The most direct route to hell is
by suicide. Over a woman. The most desirable woman in the
world. She will entrap him then destroy him. And his destruction
will be exquisitely painful and it will appear to everyone to have
happened naturally as if it were meant to be.
[*Pause*]
You will do this for me, won't you, Matilda.
[MATILDA *looks at him. Stands. Straightens her clothes*]
MATILDA First, let's see how you crawl.
[*They stare at each other. Finally* ZASTROZZI *gets down and slowly
crawls over to her. He wraps his arms around her legs*]
ZASTROZZI Entrap him. Then destroy him.
[BERNARDO *walks in, sees them, smiles*]
BERNARDO He's back.
[*Blackout*]

Street scene. A light rain is falling. JULIA *is sitting on some steps,*
holding an umbrella above her head
VEREZZI *is standing centre stage, looking up, smiling, hitting himself*
on the head with both his hands and moving about delicately

VEREZZI I'm so happy. Life has once again given me the giggles. What
a surprise. In the ruins of an ancient city, on a foul, damp day in
spring, the soggy young artist, walking aimlessly about in search of
something to draw, meets the most beautiful and sensitive woman
alive.

JULIA You are kind. But you flatter me.

VEREZZI Not yet. But I will. I am growing silly with delight. [*reeling*
around a few times]

JULIA Good heavens. What's wrong with you. Why can't you just come
sit down and have a pleasant conversation.

VEREZZI You want me to be sober.

JULIA If you'd just stay still for a moment. We only met a minute ago.
All we said to each other was hello. And you started prancing about
and giggling.

VEREZZI Yes. A less perceptive person would think I was insane.

JULIA Well, you might be insane for all I know. Can't you even
introduce yourself.
[VEREZZI *sobers*]

VEREZZI Yes. Of course. [*walking over*] I am Verezzi.

JULIA My name is Julia.

VEREZZI [*spinning around*] Of course it is! Could it be anything else.
You are spectacular and your name is a song.

JULIA Sir. You will sit down. You will stop talking like a frenzied poetic
moron and will make rational conversation. It can be pleasant
conversation. It can even be romantic conversation. But it will be
rational or I am leaving.

VEREZZI [*sitting*] I am Verezzi.

JULIA Yes, you've said that.

VEREZZI And you are Julia.

JULIA And I have said that.

VEREZZI Will you marry me.

JULIA No.

VEREZZI I am depressed.

JULIA How old are you.

VEREZZI Twenty-five.

JULIA You have the emotions of a ten-year-old.

VEREZZI That is often the case with a visionary.

JULIA So you have visions.

VEREZZI [*a revelation*] I *am* a visionary.

JULIA So you ... have visions.

VEREZZI Yes. But don't tell anyone. I'm not ready to meet my followers yet.

JULIA Visions of what nature.

VEREZZI Religious.

JULIA Visions of God?

VEREZZI Of God. By God. For God. Through God.

[VEREZZI *smiles.* JULIA *just stares silently at him for a while*]

JULIA You are the first visionary I have met. At least the first one who has told me that he was one.

VEREZZI I hope you're not thinking I'm bragging.

JULIA No, that's not what I'm thinking.

VEREZZI Good. Because I worked hard to be what I am. At first I was just a person, then a religious person, then a servant of God, then a messenger of God.

JULIA And now a visionary.

VEREZZI Yes.

JULIA When did you have your first vision.

VEREZZI I haven't had one yet.

JULIA I don't understand.

VEREZZI Neither do I. I suppose I'll just have to be patient.

[*Pause*]

JULIA But you told me you had visions. Of God. By God. For God etcetera.

VEREZZI Yes. I was speaking hypothetically.

JULIA I'm sorry. But I don't think that makes any sense.

VEREZZI No. Then I was speaking metaphorically.

JULIA That neither.

VEREZZI Symbolically.

JULIA No.

VEREZZI Will you marry me.

JULIA No. [*standing*]

VEREZZI Where are you going.

JULIA Home.

VEREZZI May I call on you.

JULIA No. [*exiting*]

VEREZZI I love her. She is just the right kind of woman for me. She has no imagination and she takes her religion very seriously. God is creating a balance.

[VICTOR *enters*]

VICTOR Who was that woman.

VEREZZI Her name is Julia. She lives here. She is very bright. She is an aristocrat. She thinks I'm insane. I gave her that impression intentionally by making fun of religious states of mind. It was a test. She passed. I'm going to marry her.

VICTOR Shut up.

VEREZZI I won't shut up. You are my servant. You shut up.

VICTOR You're getting worse daily. You're almost insensate. There is danger here and you can't appreciate it.

VEREZZI There is no danger here. There is only love here.

VICTOR You are insane.

VEREZZI Who says so.

VICTOR I do.

VEREZZI You are my servant. You are not to say I am insane. I say you are insane. Yes, Victor, you are insane. So there.

VICTOR Shut up.

VEREZZI You shut up.

[VICTOR *grabs* VEREZZI *by the throat and shakes him*]

VICTOR Shut up, shut up, shut up.

[VEREZZI *raises a hand and* VICTOR *lets him go*]

Now are you ready to listen to me.

VEREZZI You hurt me.

VICTOR I'm sorry. You were in a daze.

VEREZZI I was?

VICTOR Yes. How do you feel now.

VEREZZI My throat hurts.

VICTOR But are you sensible.

VEREZZI Of course.

VICTOR I found out from the innkeeper that someone has been making enquiries about you. Do you know what that means.

VEREZZI Yes. My followers are beginning to gather.

VICTOR Shut up. You don't have any followers.

VEREZZI As of last count my followers numbered 454. I can describe each of them to you in detail.

VICTOR You've hallucinated every one of them. The man making enquiries about you was probably a friend of that man Zastrozzi.

VEREZZI Zastrozzi. Zastrozzi the German? The master criminal? The man who seeks revenge upon me?

VICTOR Yes.

VEREZZI He does not exist! He is a phantom of your mind. For three years you have been telling me I have been hunted by Zastrozzi and yet I have never seen him.

VICTOR Because I have kept us ahead of him. I have evaded him.

VEREZZI As only you could. Because he is a phantom of your mind.

VICTOR He was making enquiries about you.

VEREZZI That was one of my followers.

VICTOR Your followers do not exist. It was Zastrozzi.

VEREZZI Zastrozzi does not exist! I have 454 followers. Follower number one is short and bald. Follower number two is tall with a beard. Follower number three is ...

VICTOR Shut up. You are insane. And you grow worse every day. But I promised your father I would take care of you so I will.

VEREZZI You didn't know my father. I hired you. As a servant. You must be feverish in your brain. But I will save you. You are a challenge.

VICTOR Very well. But let's move on. You can save me at some other place.

VEREZZI I can't. The birds are here.

VICTOR I beg your pardon.

VEREZZI Look up. What do you see.

VICTOR A flock of birds.

VEREZZI Yes. They are the sign.

VICTOR What sign.

VEREZZI The one my followers will be able to see in order to know where I am.

VICTOR I don't believe this.

VEREZZI Try. Please.

VICTOR I will not.

VEREZZI Very well. But when my followers arrive you're going to feel very out of place. They all believe it.

[VICTOR *gestures in disgust and leaves.* VEREZZI *drifts off in his mind*]

Follower number 54 is of medium height but he limps. Follower number 101 is blind. Follower number 262 is … a Persian immigrant.

[BERNARDO *comes on dragging* MATILDA *by the hair. He is carrying a whip*]

BERNARDO Here's a nice quiet place for a beating. Strip to the waist.

MATILDA No, sir. Please forgive me. I won't do it again.

BERNARDO For sure you won't. Not after this.

[MATILDA *tries to run away. He intercepts and throws her down.* VEREZZI *raises his hand*]

VEREZZI Excuse me.

BERNARDO What do you want.

VEREZZI A little human kindness, sir.

BERNARDO Mind your own business.

[BERNARDO *raises the whip.* VEREZZI *approaches them*]

VEREZZI Leave her alone.

BERNARDO You have been warned. [*drawing his sabre*] Defend yourself.

VEREZZI Do I look like an angel of God, sir.

BERNARDO No.

VEREZZI Then you are in for a big surprise.

[VEREZZI *draws his sabre. Swishes it about. Trying to impress* BERNARDO *with his style.* BERNARDO *laughs. They fight.* BERNARDO *allows himself to be disarmed.* VEREZZI *has his sabre at* BERNARDO's

chest. Suddenly VEREZZI *drifts off in his mind*]
No. This is violence, isn't it. I shouldn't be doing this. This is
wrong. I am an artist. I am in touch with Him.
[BERNARDO *slips away.* MATILDA *goes to* VEREZZI *and seductively
runs her fingers through his hair*]
MATILDA Thank you.
[VEREZZI *looks up*]
VEREZZI You're welcome.
MATILDA No. Thank you very, very much.
[MATILDA *smiles.* VEREZZI *smiles*]
[*Blackout*]

SCENE FIVE

Evening
A secluded place. ZASTROZZI *is sitting inert*
JULIA *comes on with a picnic basket*

JULIA Excuse me, sir. But do you mind if I sit here.
[ZASTROZZI *slowly turns towards her and looks at her impassively for
a moment*]
ZASTROZZI It would be best if you did not.
JULIA But I always come here at this time on this particular day of the
week to have my picnic.
ZASTROZZI Without fail?
JULIA Yes.
ZASTROZZI Well, today you have been broken of a very silly habit.
Move on.
JULIA Why should I.
ZASTROZZI I want to be alone.
JULIA Then you move on.
ZASTROZZI I want to be alone. And I want to be alone exactly where I
am.
JULIA Well, today you are not going to get what you want. I am sitting
and I am eating.
[JULIA *eats and* ZASTROZZI *watches her for a moment*]
ZASTROZZI You are an only child from a very wealthy family.
JULIA Perhaps.
ZASTROZZI You don't have a worry in the world.
JULIA Perhaps not.
ZASTROZZI You don't have a thought in your head.
JULIA I have one or two.
ZASTROZZI And you are a virgin.
[*pause*]
Well, are you or are you not a virgin.
JULIA Why. Are you looking for one.
ZASTROZZI Go away.
JULIA In good time. Perhaps when I'm finished eating this piece of

cheese. Perhaps after I eat my apple. In good time.

[*Pause*]

ZASTROZZI Do you know who I am.

JULIA No. Who are you.

ZASTROZZI I am the man who is going to take away your virginity.

JULIA Many have tried. All have failed. It will never be taken away. It will be given. In good time.

ZASTROZZI Yes. Before you eat your apple to be exact.

JULIA I'll scream.

ZASTROZZI If you scream it will be the last sound you ever hear.

JULIA Then I'll go limp. You won't enjoy it.

ZASTROZZI It's not important that I enjoy it. It's important that you enjoy it.

JULIA Impossible.

ZASTROZZI Look at me.

JULIA No. I don't think I will.

ZASTROZZI Why not. Don't you find me attractive.

JULIA That's not the point. You've threatened to rape me.

ZASTROZZI Surely you knew I was joking.

JULIA You didn't sound like you were joking.

ZASTROZZI I was only trying to hide the embarrassing truth.

JULIA And what might that be.

ZASTROZZI That, like so many other men, I have admired you from a distance and could never gather the courage to approach you.

JULIA So you waited here knowing I was coming on this particular day.

ZASTROZZI Yes.

JULIA And you adopted an aggressive attitude to disguise your true and romantic feelings for me.

ZASTROZZI Yes.

JULIA Yes. I can believe that. Men have done sillier things for me. Do you still want me to look at you.

ZASTROZZI No. I'm too embarrassed.

JULIA I understand.

ZASTROZZI Just look ahead.

JULIA If you wish.

[*Pause*]

ZASTROZZI I hope you don't mind that I'm doing this.

JULIA What.

ZASTROZZI Running my hand through your hair.

[ZASTROZZI *does nothing. He will do nothing*]

JULIA Oh. I don't feel anything.

ZASTROZZI I am running my hand through your hair. Very softly.

JULIA Well, I guess it's all right.

ZASTROZZI You have a very soft neck.

JULIA Are you touching my neck. [*looking at him*]

ZASTROZZI Please just look ahead. [*looking at her*] Please.

JULIA All right. [*turning away*]

ZASTROZZI Very soft neck. Very soft shoulders too. And if I may just lower my hand a little.

JULIA Please, sir.

ZASTROZZI I'm sorry you spoke too late. Yes, your breast is also soft. But firm.

JULIA Please. No one has ever—

ZASTROZZI Both breasts so wonderfully firm. And my face so nice against your neck. If I could just reach down.

JULIA No, sir—

ZASTROZZI You should have said so earlier. Your stomach. My God. This is such a wonderful feeling, isn't it.

JULIA I'm not quite—

ZASTROZZI That's it. Lean back a little.

JULIA I shouldn't be doing this.

[JULIA *does nothing. She will do nothing*]

ZASTROZZI Back a little farther. Lie down.

JULIA All the way?

ZASTROZZI Yes.

JULIA But—

ZASTROZZI Lie down.

JULIA Like this?

ZASTROZZI Yes.

JULIA What are you doing now.

ZASTROZZI Kissing you on your mouth.

[*Pause*]

JULIA Yes. And now?
  [*Pause*]
ZASTROZZI Your breasts.
  [*Pause*]
JULIA Yes. And now?
  [*Pause*]
ZASTROZZI Relax.
  [*Pause*]
JULIA Yes.
  [*Blackout*]

The sky is rumbling again. ZASTROZZI *is drunk. He is at the doorway of his bed chamber. He drinks the last of the wine in his flask and throws it on the floor*

ZASTROZZI Where is my wine. I called for that wine an hour ago. I warn you it is in your best interest to keep me drunk. I am at my mellowest when drunk. Innkeeper!

A VOICE Coming, sir.

[ZASTROZZI *grunts. He goes and sits in a chair near the bed, picks up a book, reads, grunts, grunts louder, throws the book across the room*]

ZASTROZZI Liar! [*standing, pacing*] They're all liars. Why do I read books. What is this new age of optimism they're all talking about. It's a lie sponsored by the Church and the government to give the people false hope. The people. I care less about the people than I do about the Church or the government. Then what do you care about sin. I care that I should not ask myself questions like that. I care to be dumb and without care. I care that I should not ask myself questions like that ever again. [*sitting, pausing*] Sad. [*standing*] Wine! [*sitting*] Sad.

[VICTOR *comes in with the wine*]

Who are you.

VICTOR I own this inn.

ZASTROZZI No. I've met the owner.

VICTOR The former owner. I won it from him in a card game last night.

ZASTROZZI Congratulations. Put the wine down and get out.

[VICTOR *puts the wine down*]

VICTOR You are the Great Zastrozzi, aren't you.

ZASTROZZI I am a lodger in your inn.

VICTOR Are you ashamed of being Zastrozzi.

ZASTROZZI If you were to die in the near future would many people attend your funeral.

VICTOR No.

ZASTROZZI Then save yourself the embarrassment. Get out.

VICTOR I heard that Zastrozzi once passed through Paris like the plague. Leaving the aristocracy nearly bankrupt, their daughters all defiled and diseased, the police in chaos and the museums ransacked. And all because, it is said, he took a dislike to the popular French taste in art.

ZASTROZZI A slight exaggeration. He took a dislike to a certain aristocratic artist who happened to have a very willing daughter and one painting in one museum.

VICTOR And did Zastrozzi kill the artist, rape his daughter and destroy the painting.

ZASTROZZI The daughter was not touched. She had syphilis. Probably given to her by the father. The painting was not worth destroying. It was just removed from the illustrious company it had no right to be with. [*taking a drink*]

VICTOR But the artist was killed.

ZASTROZZI Yes. Certainly.

VICTOR Why.

ZASTROZZI To prove that even artists must answer to somebody.

VICTOR And what has Zastrozzi come to this obscure place to prove.

ZASTROZZI Zastrozzi is starting some new endeavour. He is going to murder only innkeepers for a year.

VICTOR I am not afraid of you.

ZASTROZZI Then you are stupid.

[*Pause*]

And you are not an innkeeper.

VICTOR They say that all Europe has no more cause to fear Zastrozzi. They say that for three years he has been single-minded in a search for revenge on one man and that all the rest of Europe has been untouched.

ZASTROZZI They think and say only what Zastrozzi wants them to think and say.

VICTOR They also say that any man can cross him, that any woman can use him. Because the master criminal, the Great Zastrozzi, is in a trance.

ZASTROZZI Ah. But then there are trances ...

[*He draws his sword and does four or five amazing things with it*]

... and there are trances.

[*He puts the sword to* VICTOR's *throat*]

Now, who are you.

[VICTOR *steps back. Afraid*]

VICTOR Your revenge upon Verezzi will be empty.

ZASTROZZI Who is he to you.

VICTOR I'm his tutor.

ZASTROZZI His what.

VICTOR Tutor. I teach him things.

ZASTROZZI Is that so. And what, for example, do you teach him.

VICTOR How to evade the man who wants to destroy him.

ZASTROZZI You are the one responsible for stretching my search to three years.

VICTOR Yes.

ZASTROZZI Interesting. You don't look capable of having done it. You look ordinary.

VICTOR I am.

ZASTROZZI No. In your case the look might actually be deceiving. But we'll soon find out. Where is your weapon.

VICTOR I don't have one.

ZASTROZZI Then why the innkeeper disguise. You must be here to intervene for your student.

VICTOR Intervention doesn't have to be violent.

ZASTROZZI I'm afraid it does. Haven't you been reading the latest books. The world is in desperate need of action. The most decisive action is always violent. [*repeating this last sentence in German*]

VICTOR Interesting. But all I'm saying is that I didn't think killing you would necessarily have to be the only way to stop you. I thought I could try common sense with you.

ZASTROZZI You were wrong. Try something else.

VICTOR Verezzi is insane.

ZASTROZZI I don't care.

VICTOR But revenge on an insane man can't mean anything.

ZASTROZZI Wrong. I don't share the belief that the insane have left this world. They're still here. They're just hiding.

VICTOR But he thinks he is a visionary.

ZASTROZZI Well, perhaps he is. I don't care about that either. That's between him and his God. This matter is between him and me. [*Pause*]

VICTOR I know why you seek revenge on Verezzi.

ZASTROZZI No one knows!

VICTOR I know of the crime that he and his father committed upon your mother.

ZASTROZZI Ah, yes. The crime. What version have you heard.

VICTOR The real one.

ZASTROZZI Is that so.

VICTOR I was a friend of his father. I was away studying. Hadn't seen him for years. Had never even met his son. A letter arrived. He said he was dying. And asked if I would protect his son who would probably be in danger.

ZASTROZZI And the letter described what they had done?

VICTOR Yes.

ZASTROZZI What did you think.

VICTOR It was horrible, of course.

ZASTROZZI Describe exactly what you mean by horrible.

VICTOR Bloody. Vicious. Unforgivable.

ZASTROZZI Wrong. Not even close. Horrible is when things proceed unnaturally. When people remain unanswerable for their actions.

VICTOR But the letter also told me why they had done it. This woman's son had killed my friend's daughter. Verezzi's sister.

ZASTROZZI No. It wasn't me.

VICTOR Then who was it.

ZASTROZZI Never mind. But even if I had killed her then the quarrel would be with me. Not my mother. That is usually the way with revenge, isn't it.

VICTOR You couldn't be found.

ZASTROZZI I was away. Studying. I was called back to examine my mother's corpse. And the father's letter actually did describe what they had done to her?

VICTOR Yes.

ZASTROZZI Imagine that. How could he bring himself to tell anyone. I thought he was a Christian.

VICTOR It was a confession, I think.

ZASTROZZI Are you a priest.

VICTOR I was at the time.

ZASTROZZI And you left the Church just to protect Verezzi?

VICTOR It doesn't matter why I left the Church.

ZASTROZZI Yes. That's correct. Only two things should matter to you. That Verezzi killed my mother in a horrible manner. And that I, her son, have a legitimate claim to vengeance.

VICTOR But he has no memory of the crime. He never has had. He must have blocked it out almost immediately.

ZASTROZZI I don't care. I seek revenge. Revenge is a simple matter. You shouldn't have turned it into such an issue by hiding him from me for all this time.

VICTOR But there's something else, isn't there.

ZASTROZZI I beg your pardon.

VICTOR I think there's another reason altogether why you want to destroy Verezzi.

ZASTROZZI What is your name.

VICTOR Victor.

ZASTROZZI No. You are not an ordinary man, Victor. But you would be wise to become one within the next few hours.

VICTOR When are you coming to take him.

ZASTROZZI I am here now. Are you going to run off again.

VICTOR No. He won't leave. He's waiting for his followers. Listen. I don't care much for violence. But to get to him you will have to go around me.

ZASTROZZI I have already done that. And I didn't even know you existed.

VICTOR How.

ZASTROZZI Never mind. Concern yourself with this. If what I plan doesn't work I will not be going around you or anyone or anything else. I will be coming directly at him. And if you are in the way you will be killed. Now go away. I'm tired. Tired of the chase. The explanation of the chase. Of everything. Of you specifically at this moment.

[ZASTROZZI *turns around.* VICTOR *pulls a knife from inside his shirt, raises it to* ZASTROZZI'*s back, and holds it there. Finally* VICTOR *lowers it]*

Go away.

[VICTOR *exits, passing* BERNARDO *coming in]*

BERNARDO   He had a knife about six inches away from your back.

ZASTROZZI   Why didn't you stop him. He could have killed me.

BERNARDO   I doubt it.

ZASTROZZI   Did you arrange for the introduction.

BERNARDO   Yes.

ZASTROZZI   I wonder now if it is a good enough plan.

BERNARDO   Probably not. [*starting off]*

ZASTROZZI   It doesn't matter. It's almost over. I sense it. One way or the other I have him. This way would be less violent but more satisfying. Where are you going.

BERNARDO   A young woman in the village smiled at me. She's very pretty. And obviously well-off. I think I'll seduce her and rob her blind.

ZASTROZZI   You know, Bernardo, that you don't have to do these things just to impress me.

BERNARDO   Thank you.

ZASTROZZI   You could try to become the nice young man you were before your one little mistake.

BERNARDO   And what was that.

ZASTROZZI   You murdered Verezzi's sister. Don't tell me you had forgotten.

BERNARDO   Yes, I had. I've murdered so many others since then.

ZASTROZZI   You really are a seedy little butcher, aren't you.

BERNARDO   Once you make your one little mistake, sir, you must continue or be destroyed. The insulation of evil is the only thing that makes you survive. I learned that from watching you.

ZASTROZZI   But sometimes your crimes are heartless enough to shock even me. Who is the dark personality here after all.

BERNARDO   You, sir. But I strive hard to be your shadow.

ZASTROZZI   Good. That man with the knife to my back. His name is Victor. He is Verezzi's tutor. He looks harmless, doesn't he.

BERNARDO   Yes.

ZASTROZZI He isn't. I give him to you. He'll probably present a
challenge.

BERNARDO Thank you. [*starting off*]

ZASTROZZI Oh, Bernardo.

BERNARDO Yes.

ZASTROZZI I don't expect you to understand why you are killing him.
But I do expect you to do it with some imagination!

[BERNARDO *leaves.* ZASTROZZI *takes a long drink*]

[*Blackout*]

[*Intermission*]

SCENE SEVEN

VEREZZI's *room.* VEREZZI *and* MATILDA *are making love. He is delirious. We know they are finished when he makes an absurdly loud and sustained groaning sound.* MATILDA *gets out of bed and looks at him in disbelief. She is clothed. He is naked*

VEREZZI I am in love.

MATILDA So soon?

VEREZZI I am enthralled. You were wonderful. What a new treat. Usually I am the one who is wonderful and the women are enthralled. Where did you get this strange power.

MATILDA It's something I was born with.

VEREZZI How do you know.

MATILDA What else could it be. It's not something you get from practice. I'm not a whore.

VEREZZI No. But you're not a saint either. I'd know if you were. Because ... [*a revelation*] *I'm* a saint.

MATILDA Of course you are.

VEREZZI Don't be intimidated. Saints are human.

MATILDA Why should I be intimidated. Saint or no saint. You are the one who loves me.

VEREZZI You mean you don't love me?

MATILDA No. Of course not.

VEREZZI I don't understand. Explain. But be kind about it.

MATILDA I love someone else.

VEREZZI Who.

MATILDA You saw him earlier.

VEREZZI That man who was going to beat you?

MATILDA Yes. Bernardo.

VEREZZI That's disgusting. How can you love someone who beats you.

MATILDA It's not *that* he beats me. It's *how* he beats me.

VEREZZI I don't understand. Explain. But be kind.

MATILDA He beats me like he could kill me. And I love him for that.

VEREZZI You should love me instead. I'm gentle. I'm an artist. I'm a saint. And I love you.

MATILDA Could you kill me. If you could kill me I might love you.

VEREZZI You're very strange. And you're very exciting. But I don't think you're very healthy. That's a challenge. I can help you. Stay with me.

MATILDA I can't! I love someone else.

VEREZZI Then why did you make love to me.

MATILDA A part of me is gentle. It wanted to thank you. But a larger part of me is something else. It wants to be beaten. [*starting off*]

VEREZZI Stay. I could beat you. A little.

MATILDA If you really loved me you could do better.

VEREZZI But I'm a saint. I love things. I can't hurt things. How could I face my followers. They're coming soon. Some of them are very vulnerable. Some of them are swans. Some of them are tiny little caterpillars who have been crawling for weeks to get here. I can't disappoint them. How can I preach love and human kindness to all my followers then go into the privacy of my bedroom and beat a woman unconscious.

MATILDA If you are a saint you can take certain liberties. People will understand.

VEREZZI But will the caterpillars. They are dumb. I love them. Honestly I do. But they are dumb. Crawl, crawl. That's all they do. Crawl. Life's dilemmas are multiplied for a saint. He has to deal with too many things at once. One of my followers is a Turk. I don't even speak his language. When he comes, how am I going to give him the message. I keep waiting for the gift of tongues but it never comes. God is handicapping me. And now you want me to beat you. I abhor violence. It makes me retch. But I love you. I'll die if you leave me.

[MATILDA *starts off,* VEREZZI *crawls out of the bed and over to her*]
Please don't go. I know. You can beat me instead.

MATILDA That just won't do.

VEREZZI But won't you even try.

[VICTOR *comes in*]

VICTOR What's this. Get up.

[VEREZZI *stands*]

[*to* MATILDA] Who are you.

VEREZZI She is the woman I love.

VICTOR And why were you grovelling on the floor.

VEREZZI Because she doesn't love me. What can I do, Victor. She's breaking my heart.

VICTOR It seems to me that I met the woman you love earlier. That virgin God sent for you.

[VICTOR *starts to pack*]

VEREZZI Yes. Julia. That's right. I love her. I'd forgotten. Oh, thank God. For a moment there I didn't know what I was going to do. It's all right, Matilda. You can go now.

MATILDA So you don't love me after all.

VEREZZI But I do. It's just that I also love Julia. And she's less of a challenge. She just thinks I'm insane. I can deal with that. But I don't know if I can ever deal with you, Matilda. You want me to want to kill you. That's unique. But it's not healthy. But I do love you. And if it weren't for Julia I would probably destroy myself over you. Or something to that effect.

MATILDA [*with clenched teeth*] Or something to that effect. [*starting off*]

VEREZZI Oh. Say hello to Bernardo for me. I think he likes me.

[MATILDA *looks at him oddly, shakes her head and leaves*]

VICTOR What was that all about.

VEREZZI One of the tests of sainthood, I imagine.

VICTOR Did you pass.

VEREZZI I don't know. Tell me, Victor, how do you suppose I can find out.

VICTOR Oh, shut up. Get packed. We're leaving.

VEREZZI Why.

VICTOR Zastrozzi is here.

VEREZZI Who.

VICTOR Zastrozzi. Zastrozzi!

VEREZZI Oh, yes. The phantom of your brain. You've dreamt him up again have you.

VICTOR I've seen him. I was at his rooms.

VEREZZI Oh, really. And what does he look like. Does he have fangs. Does he have horns. Does he have eyes dripping blood.

VICTOR No. He's a man. Just a man. Calm. Purposeful. And very experienced. Just a man. But a very dangerous one.

VEREZZI Well then, bring him along and I'll deal with him. A little human understanding should get him to leave you alone.

VICTOR You're no match for him.

VEREZZI Why not.

VICTOR Because he's perfectly sane. And you're a delirious lunatic.

VEREZZI And if I am, is it good and right for you to be telling me so. Would it not be more good and more right for you to be more understanding. That's an hypothesis—of a religious nature. I have decided that your degeneration has gone far enough. And I am commencing spiritual guidance with you immediately. [*sitting on the bed*] Now come sit at my feet.

VICTOR Get packed.

VEREZZI Lesson number one. When the Messiah speaks, listen.

VICTOR When did you become the Messiah.

VEREZZI Did I say Messiah. No.

VICTOR I heard you.

VEREZZI No. Not me. God. God said Messiah.

VICTOR I don't understand. Are you God or are you the Messiah.

VEREZZI I am Verezzi. I am whoever He wants me to be.

VICTOR You are exploring new dimensions of the human mind, Verezzi. But I don't think the world is ready for you yet. Get packed. We're leaving.

VEREZZI No.

VICTOR Please! I promised your father. It's the only promise in my life I've ever kept. It keeps me sane. Please get packed!

VEREZZI No. I have to go find Julia. I have to tell her that God is talking to me. I know she'll marry me now.

VICTOR Let me try to explain it to you in a way you will understand. [VICTOR *drops to his knees*]

VEREZZI Don't patronize me, Victor. I am not a moron. I am just a good and lovely man.

VICTOR Well, that could be a matter of opinion. But let us suppose you are in fact just a good man.

VEREZZI And lovely.

VICTOR Yes.

VEREZZI And very tidy as well.

VICTOR Yes. All those things. A good lovely tidy man. Who is gentle to all things living and dead, etcetera, and wishes only to carry about the positive uplifting spirit of God. Then doesn't it make sense that in order to do that you should become aware of the obstacles that lie naturally in your path. The forces of evil that wish to stop you. In effect, doesn't it make sense that a good man should also be a cunning man.

VEREZZI No.

[VEREZZI *leaves.* VICTOR *sits on the bed. Shakes his head*]

VICTOR I give up. Zastrozzi will get his revenge on the lunatic Verezzi. After three years he will finally destroy a vegetable. I don't know who to pity more. Zastrozzi, the poor vegetable, or whatever it was that created them both. Sad. [*shrugging*] No. I can't give up. I promised. I must save him. Even if I must hurt him a little.

[VICTOR *stands and searches the room for something heavy. He finds something, takes it, and runs out*]

[*Blackout*]

SCENE EIGHT

A lull in the storm. VICTOR *is walking through a dark alley*
Suddenly a torch is lit. It is held by BERNARDO. *He is standing with*
sword drawn in VICTOR's *way*

VICTOR Excuse me. Did a man pass by here recently. A young man.

BERNARDO Forget him. His time is almost here. You have business
with me.

VICTOR What do you want.

BERNARDO I am from Zastrozzi.

VICTOR And what does Zastrozzi want from me.

BERNARDO Your life.

VICTOR A bizarre request. Do you understand the reason for it.

BERNARDO No. I am a more simple man than Zastrozzi. I can only
understand simple reasons for killing a man. And very simple ways
of going about it.

VICTOR Interesting. What, for example, are the simple reasons for
killing a man.

BERNARDO To get his money.

VICTOR I have none.

BERNARDO If he has done some wrong to me.

VICTOR I don't even know you.

BERNARDO Or if he presents some kind of threat.

VICTOR Surely you can tell just by looking at me that I'm harmless.

BERNARDO Zastrozzi says you are not.

VICTOR Zastrozzi flatters me.

BERNARDO Zastrozzi sees things that others cannot.

VICTOR Perhaps that is because he is insane.

BERNARDO He is not the least bit insane.

VICTOR Are you absolutely sure of that.

BERNARDO Yes.

VICTOR Oh.

BERNARDO In fact, he is the sanest man I have ever met. He is also the
most perverse. The combination makes him very dangerous. You
do not upset a man like this. When he tells you to kill someone,

you do it. Even though you personally have nothing to gain from it. When he tells you to do it with imagination you try to do so. Even though you do not know why or even how to go about it.

VICTOR Poor fellow. You're in quite a fix.

BERNARDO While you on the other hand are not, is that it.

VICTOR I am probably going to die. That I can understand. You are going to spend the rest of your life fulfilling someone else's wishes that you do not understand. That, sir, is a state of mental chaos usually associated with purgatory. I pity you.

BERNARDO Shut up.

VICTOR I pity you like I would a diseased dog.

BERNARDO I said shut up.

VICTOR You are out of your element. Zastrozzi is the master of evil and you are just a thug.

BERNARDO I am more than that, I know.

VICTOR A thug. And a murderer. You cannot think of an imaginative way to kill me because you have no imagination. You stand there with a sword and threaten a man who is unarmed. That is the posture of a cheap murderer.

BERNARDO I could use my hands. Would you feel better about that.

VICTOR I am only thinking of you.

BERNARDO [throwing down the sword] It will take a little longer this way.

[He approaches VICTOR]

I'm going to have to strangle you.

VICTOR Well, it's not exactly inspired. But it's better than just cutting me down with a sword. Congratulations.

BERNARDO Thank you.

VICTOR But before you start, I have a confession to make.

[VICTOR quickly takes out the heavy object he has taken from the room in the previous scene and hits BERNARDO over the head. BERNARDO falls unconscious to the ground]

I lied about not being armed.

[VEREZZI comes on, in a daze]

VEREZZI Victor. I'm glad you're here. I can't find any of my followers. They must have gotten lost.

VICTOR [*pointing off*] No. There's one now.
   [VEREZZI *turns and* VICTOR *hits him over the head with his object.*
   VEREZZI *falls unconscious.* VICTOR *picks him up under the arms*]
   A place to hide. Some place quiet. I have to think about what is
   happening to me. That vacant prison I saw this morning. [*dragging*
   VEREZZI *away*] What's this. He's smiling. Even in pain he smiles.
   [*Blackout*]

ZASTROZZI's *room.* ZASTROZZI *is standing in the middle of the room, a blanket wrapped around him, shivering*

ZASTROZZI I am having a nightmare. It involves the final battle over control of the world between the forces of good and evil. It is the most terrifying nightmare I have ever had. Something so extremely unusual has happened that my mind in all its power cannot even begin to comprehend it. I am in charge of the forces of good. And I am winning. I think there is just the slightest possibility that there might be something wrong with my mind after all. The nightmare continues. I lead the forces of good with their toothy, God-obsessed smiles into the fortress of the commander of the forces of evil. We easily overcome the fortress and become gracious victors—not raping or murdering or even taking prisoners. We just smile and wish goodness and mercy to rain down on everyone. And I am smiling and wishing out loud for goodness and mercy as well except that inside I am deeply ill and feel like throwing up. And then we are taken to meet the commander of the forces of evil and he walks through a large wooden door and I see that he looks familiar. And he should. Because it is Zastrozzi. And even though I know that I am Zastrozzi I cannot help but feel extremely confused. And he reinforces this confusion when he opens his mouth and says, 'I am Zastrozzi.' At which point I feel myself smile even wider, so wide that I feel my skin tighten and I know that my face will become stuck forever like this in the widest, stupidest, most merciful and good smile ever worn by a human being. Then I die. But before I die I remember thinking—they are going to make me a saint. They are going to make me a Christian saint. The patron saint of smiles. The nightmare ends. I need a drink. I need to sit down. I need more than anything to stop having nightmares. They're getting worse every day. There might be something wrong with my mind. [*shivering*] The nightmare continues. Again. [*smiling*]
[MATILDA *comes on dragging a whip along the floor. She is furious*]

MATILDA Zastrozzi! [*swinging the whip around above her head, cracking it*] Zastrozzi! I'm going to whip you. I'm going to whip you for making a fool out of me. For sending me to entrap a man who is an idiot and feels nothing except idiotic things.
[*Pause*]
The nightmares. [*sighing and starting off; seeing him shaking*] No. [*turning back*] Zastrozzi, I have failed. Whip me.

ZASTROZZI I can't be bothered. [*turning to her, smiling stupidly*]

MATILDA Zastrozzi, you have a stupid empty smile on your face. Just like the one the idiot wears. You are standing there shivering under a blanket like a sick old man. You don't look like Zastrozzi. You look like an ass.

ZASTROZZI [*trying to concentrate*] And now.

MATILDA You are still shivering.

ZASTROZZI [*closing his eyes and concentrating*] And now.

MATILDA You are still smiling like an idiot.

ZASTROZZI [*closing his eyes and concentrating*] Now? [*approaching her slowly*] Now?!

MATILDA Now I feel like whipping you for threatening me.
[MATILDA *begins to whip him. He doesn't move*]
Don't ever make a fool of me again. Don't ever threaten me again. Who do you think I am. I am not one of those who quiver when they hear your name. I am your match, sir. I am every bit your match.
[MATILDA *throws the whip down*]

ZASTROZZI Are you.

MATILDA In every way.

ZASTROZZI In every way?

MATILDA Yes.

ZASTROZZI Ah, well. You must know. And if you know then I must agree. Correct?

MATILDA Yes. So you will let me stay? We'll be together?

ZASTROZZI I'm afraid that's impossible.

MATILDA Why.

ZASTROZZI We're too much alike. You've just said so. I am in love with someone else.

MATILDA Impossible.

ZASTROZZI Life is strange, isn't it. I met her just a short while ago. She is quite different from me. That is probably why I love her. She is pure and innocent and possesses a marvellous gentle sensuality that I have never experienced before. In fact, just thinking about her arouses me. I am thinking about her now and I am getting aroused now.

[ZASTROZZI *grabs* MATILDA]

MATILDA What are you doing.

ZASTROZZI I am going to make love to you. Haven't you wanted me to for a long time.

MATILDA Not while you are thinking about another woman.

ZASTROZZI I'm sorry. But that is the way it must be.

MATILDA I couldn't bear it.

ZASTROZZI But you are a match for me in all ways. And I could bear it. I could even enjoy it. In fact that is the way people like us should enjoy it. Try to enjoy it.

MATILDA I can't.

ZASTROZZI Try.

MATILDA No.

ZASTROZZI Are you crying.

MATILDA No.

ZASTROZZI You are crying, aren't you.

MATILDA No.

ZASTROZZI Are you sure.

MATILDA Yes.

ZASTROZZI Are you crying.

MATILDA Yes.

[ZASTROZZI *hits her and she is propelled across the room and falls*] What are you doing.

ZASTROZZI Making a point.

MATILDA You treat me this way because I am a woman.

ZASTROZZI Nonsense. Women, men, children, goats. I treat them all the same. I ask them to be answerable.

[BERNARDO *walks on, his head bandaged*]

[*to* MATILDA] Here. I'll show you what I mean.

[*He walks over to* BERNARDO]
I take it from your wound that you have failed.

BERNARDO Yes, I'm sorry.

ZASTROZZI That's not necessary. I don't want you to feel sorry. I don't want you to feel anything. Do you understand.

BERNARDO I think so.

ZASTROZZI Try to understand. Try to feel nothing. Are you feeling nothing now.

BERNARDO I'm not sure.

ZASTROZZI Try. Feel nothing. Are you feeling nothing.

BERNARDO Yes.

ZASTROZZI Good.

[ZASTROZZI *hits* BERNARDO's *face viciously with the back of his hand.* BERNARDO *staggers back, but doesn't fall*]
Fall down when I hit you, Bernardo.

BERNARDO Why.

ZASTROZZI Because it makes it appear that you are resisting when you don't. And you have nothing to gain from resisting.

[ZASTROZZI *hits* BERNARDO *again.* BERNARDO *staggers back but doesn't fall. He looks at* ZASTROZZI *and drops to his knees*]
Some advice for both of you. Get to know your limitations. Then remember that as you go through life there are only two things worth knowing. The first is too complex for you to understand. The second is that life is a series of totally arbitrary and often meaningless events and the only way to make sense of life is to forget that you know that. In other words, occupy yourselves. Matilda, go seduce Verezzi and if he is preoccupied remove his preoccupations. The plan to drive him to suicide is not the most inspired I have ever thought of but it will do to keep us occupied for a while. After you have done that, come looking for me and if I am in the mood we can play your silly whipping games. And as for you, Bernardo, go do something you at least understand. Commit some foul, meaningless crime. That village girl you mentioned earlier. Go abuse her and steal everything she values. And enjoy it as much as possible because eventually you will be made accountable. And now if you will excuse me, I am going to visit the

local prison. It hasn't been used in years. But I'm sure it is still full of wondrous sensations. I do some of my best thinking in prisons. Did you know that.

MATILDA Yes.

BERNARDO No.

ZASTROZZI It's true though. I've visited some of the best prisons in Europe. I find it invigorating. It helps to confirm my sanity. Only a sane person could function in those places as well as I do. Does that make sense.

BERNARDO Yes.

MATILDA No.

ZASTROZZI You see I must visit these prisons. It is the only way to make myself answerable. I have never been apprehended and I never will be. So I have to voluntarily submit to a prison in order to make myself experience judgement. When I have experienced enough, I escape. Do you understand.

BERNARDO Yes.

MATILDA Yes.

ZASTROZZI No, you don't.

[ZASTROZZI *smiles and leaves*]

BERNARDO He *is* crazy.

MATILDA Of course he is. He has always been crazy.

BERNARDO Not always.

MATILDA How would you know. You are crazy yourself. For that matter so am I. For wanting him the way I do. I should find a more simple man.

[BERNARDO *stands and goes to* MATILDA]

BERNARDO I am a more simple man.

MATILDA That's the problem. It is men like you who make me want men like him.

BERNARDO I could surprise you.

MATILDA You would have to.

BERNARDO I would like to make love to you.

MATILDA I know.

BERNARDO May I.

MATILDA I will be thinking of Zastrozzi.

BERNARDO I might surprise you.

MATILDA Well, you can try at least.

   [BERNARDO *grabs her and kisses her*]

   Harder.

   [*She grabs him savagely and kisses him*]

   [*Blackout*]

SCENE TEN

For the first time the focus is on the full set. Stripped of all furnishings, it should appear like an old dungeon. BERNARDO *comes on pulling* JULIA, *whom he has chained at the wrists. He takes her into one of the chambers*

JULIA What are you doing this for.

BERNARDO You smiled at me.

JULIA It was just an invitation for polite conversation.

BERNARDO What would that mean to me. What was I supposed to do after the conversation. Marry you? Settle into a wonderful, lawful, domestic life?

JULIA I really had no plans beyond conversation, sir.

BERNARDO You wouldn't. You spend too much time with civilized men. This will teach you never to smile at strangers.

JULIA Have I offended you.

BERNARDO No. I'm just accepting your invitation and using it in the only way I can.

JULIA What are you going to do with me.

BERNARDO Anything I please.

JULIA What is this place. I've never been here.

BERNARDO No, you wouldn't have. It's an old prison. It used to house the criminally deranged but now it's vacant. More or less. A friend of mine found it. He has a way of finding places like these. What do you think of it.

JULIA It's horrible.

BERNARDO Yes. It is, isn't it. It will do very nicely.

JULIA For what.

BERNARDO For whatever I please.

JULIA You're going to rape me, aren't you. You're going to rape me and murder me.

BERNARDO Not necessarily in that order, though.

JULIA You appeared to be such a nice young man.

[BERNARDO *grabs her hair*]

BERNARDO Nice? What would I do if I was nice. If a pretty woman smiled at me and we had a polite conversation could I marry her and be lawful and decent? No, I wouldn't do that now. My mind would explode. Yet I am a man. When a woman smiles, I must do something. So I do what I am doing.

JULIA You don't have to do this. Let me go. We'll start again from the beginning. We'll meet in the fresh air on a sunny day. Talk about healthy things. Develop a respectful attitude towards each other. Eventually fall in love on just the right terms.

BERNARDO Impossible. You're not the woman I could be in love with.

JULIA I could try.

BERNARDO Impossible. I can tell from your smile. There is a woman I love, though, who could love me on the right terms. But she loves someone else. His name is Zastrozzi. Have you heard of him.

JULIA I ... I think so.

BERNARDO He is the one they talk about in whispers in your circles. I am the one who follows him around like a dog. [*starting off*]

JULIA Where are you going.

BERNARDO Back to your house. To rob it of everything of any value at all. And to kill your parents.

JULIA Please don't.

BERNARDO Why not. And give me a reason I can understand.

JULIA They're dreadful people. You would only be putting them out of their misery.

BERNARDO Not bad. That's interesting. So there is something else behind that civilized smile. I'll be back.

JULIA If you leave me alone I'll scream until someone finds me.

BERNARDO [*walking to her*] You shouldn't have said that. That was a mistake.

[BERNARDO *hits* JULIA. *She falls, unconscious. He unlocks the chain*] She doesn't need these now. And I might have to use them. [*sadly*] I might want to use them. I might love to use them.

[*He leaves. In another corner of the set* VICTOR *comes on carrying the unconscious* VEREZZI *on his shoulders. He takes him into a chamber, puts him down and examines his head*]

VICTOR Perhaps I hit you too hard. You're barely breathing. Well, you were doomed anyway. At least this way you have a chance. [*looking around*] This place is horrible. But he'll be safe here I suppose. [*sitting*] Now what am I to do. The only way I can get him to run is to keep him unconscious and that's just not practical. I could leave him here and forget the whole matter. That's practical. Leave him here! Forget the whole matter! That's practical! But I did make that promise. And it's the only promise I've ever kept. I certainly didn't keep my promise to God. But I don't feel so bad about that, having met this Zastrozzi. If he is one of God's creatures then God must be used to disappointment. On the other hand, I just don't like the man. Everything he does, everything he represents unsettles me to the bone. Zastrozzi decides that an artist must be judged by someone so he kills him. Zastrozzi is to blame for his own mother's death in a crime of passion but hounds a poor lunatic because he cannot accept the blame himself. Zastrozzi steals, violates and murders on a regular basis, and remains perfectly sane. Verezzi commits one crime of passion then goes on a binge of mindless religious love and becomes moronic. Something is wrong. Something is unbalanced. I abhor violence. But I also abhor a lack of balance. It shows that the truth is missing somewhere. And it makes me feel very, very uneasy. Uneasy in a way I have not felt since I was... Yes, Verezzi, I will restore a truth to your lunatic mind and your lunatic world. [*taking* VEREZZI's *sword*] Zastrozzi.

[VICTOR *exits.* JULIA *groans, she slowly regains consciousness and gets up. She makes her way around the dungeon, sees* VEREZZI *and goes to him. She kneels down and takes his pulse*]

JULIA What's happening to me. I go for a series of walks in the street. Smile at two young men. One of them tells me he is a visionary. The other one abducts me and tells me he is going to rape and murder me, not necessarily in that order. Then he hits me like he would a man and knocks me unconscious. I wake up and find the young man who thinks he is a visionary lying on the ground bleeding to death from a head wound. What's happening to me.

[MATILDA *enters*]

MATILDA You must be the virgin. The one with the marvellous, gentle sensuality.

JULIA Who are you.

MATILDA My name is Matilda. I am your competition. I have a sensuality which is not the least bit gentle.

JULIA Really. What do you want.

MATILDA I want to kill all the virgins in the world.

JULIA Oh no. What's happening to me.

MATILDA Unfortunately for you, we are both in love with the same man.

JULIA [pointing to VEREZZI] Him? I don't love him. I don't even like him.

MATILDA Not him. Zastrozzi.

JULIA I've heard of him. He's the one who is whispered about in polite society.

MATILDA He is the evil genius of all Europe. A criminal. And I am a criminal too. We belong together. So we must fight and I must kill you.

JULIA Why can't I just leave.

MATILDA That won't do. Besides, I will enjoy killing you. It is women like you who make me look like a tart.

JULIA Nonsense. It's the way you dress.

MATILDA Stand up, you mindless virgin.

JULIA [standing] Madame, I am neither mindless nor a virgin. I am merely a victim of bizarre circumstance. A product of healthy civilization thrown into a jungle of the deranged.

MATILDA Yes, get angry. You are better when you are angry. If I were a man I would seduce you on the spot.

JULIA That's perverse!

[MATILDA takes a knife from under her skirts]

MATILDA Yes, get indignant. You are quite provocative when you are upset. Take off your clothes.

JULIA Why.

MATILDA We are going to make love.

JULIA Oh no, we are not.

MATILDA Yes, get confused. You are quite ridiculous when you are confused. And it is exactly the way someone like you should die. [She advances]

JULIA What are you doing.

MATILDA We are going to fight. And we are only going to stop fighting
when one of us is dead.

JULIA I would rather not. I would rather discuss some other possibility.
I'm only seventeen years old. People tell me I have so much to live
for.

MATILDA Oh. Name something worth living for and I might spare
your life.

JULIA But how could I. A woman like you could never appreciate what
I think is worth living for. No offence. But take your dress for
example. I would live to dress much better than that.

MATILDA You mindless, coy, disgusting virgin!

[MATILDA *attacks and they struggle. The knife falls and* JULIA
scrambles after it. MATILDA *leaps on her and somehow* MATILDA *is
stabbed. She falls over dead.* JULIA *feels her pulse*]

JULIA Dead. Oh my God. [*standing*] What is happening to me. First a
victim. Now a murderer! And I don't even know her. This is grossly
unfair. I'm young. I've had the proper education. My future was a
pleasant rosy colour. I could see it in my head. It was a rosy colour.
Very pretty. This is truly grossly unfair.

[BERNARDO *comes in. He sees* MATILDA*'s body and rushes to it*]

BERNARDO You killed her.

JULIA I had no choice. She attacked me.

BERNARDO She was the only woman I could have been in love with on
the right terms. You have blocked out my future.

JULIA I'm sorry. But she didn't love you anyway. She loved that
Zastrozzi.

BERNARDO You have closed off my life from my brain. It is exploding!

JULIA Well, if you'll pardon me expressing an opinion, I think she was
not entirely a rational person. Not at all the kind of person you
need. You are not a rational person either and you would be better
off with someone who could tame your tendency towards violence.
If you'll pardon my opinion, I mean.

[BERNARDO *approaches her*]

What are you going to do.

BERNARDO Stay still.

JULIA [*backing away*] No. This isn't fair. I shouldn't be involved in any of this. I didn't love him. I didn't hate her. I've only a strange and vague recollection of this Zastrozzi. And all I did was smile at you.

BERNARDO Stay very still.

JULIA Please.

[BERNARDO *strangles her.* ZASTROZZI *appears out of the darkness*]

ZASTROZZI Bernardo.

[BERNARDO *drops* JULIA, *who falls to the floor, lifeless. He turns to face* ZASTROZZI]

Another victim, Bernardo?

BERNARDO She murdered Matilda.

ZASTROZZI She was merely defending herself.

BERNARDO You saw?

ZASTROZZI I have been here for hours.

BERNARDO Why didn't you do something.

ZASTROZZI I was preoccupied.

BERNARDO Matilda is dead.

ZASTROZZI I didn't know you had such deep feelings for her.

BERNARDO It wouldn't have mattered to you. You only have one thought. Well, there he is. Verezzi the Italian. Take him. I am going to bury Matilda.

ZASTROZZI Verezzi will wait. You are not going anywhere. You have to face your judgement.

BERNARDO It will come.

ZASTROZZI It has.

BERNARDO From you?

ZASTROZZI Is there anyone better at it.

BERNARDO Judgement for what exactly.

ZASTROZZI For all your crimes. All the people you have murdered have spoken to me in my nightmares and asked that you be made answerable.

BERNARDO I am just a student to the master.

ZASTROZZI And only the master is qualified to judge. Draw your sword, Bernardo. Let us have the formality of a contest. But know now that you are dead.

BERNARDO Sir. Let me go.

ZASTROZZI No.

[ZASTROZZI *draws his sword.* BERNARDO *draws his. They fight. Viciously. Expertly.* BERNARDO *is good.* ZASTROZZI *is the master though, and eventually he pierces* BERNARDO*'s chest.* BERNARDO *drops to his knees*]

BERNARDO Sir.

ZASTROZZI You are dead.

[ZASTROZZI *knocks* BERNARDO *over with his foot.* BERNARDO *is dead.* ZASTROZZI *walks over to* VEREZZI *and stands silently looking down at him for a while, then sits down and cradles* VEREZZI*'s head*] Verezzi. Finally. Not dying at all. It's just a flesh wound. Your breathing becomes stronger. Soon you will wake up. I want you to be awake for this. It would have been more satisfying to have you destroy yourself. But you are too clever for that. Everyone thinks you are out of your mind. But I know you have just been hiding. Hiding from your crimes, Verezzi. Hiding from the crime of telling people you are giving them gifts from God. The crime of letting them think there is happiness in that stupid smile of yours. The crime of making language pleasantly vague and painting with distorted imagination. The crime of disturbing the natural condition in which the dark side prevails. Wake up, Verezzi. Zastrozzi is here to prove that you must be judged. You can hide no more.

A VOICE And what is Zastrozzi hiding from.

[ZASTROZZI *stands*]

ZASTROZZI What do you want.

[VICTOR *comes out of the darkness carrying* VEREZZI*'s sabre*]

VICTOR Sir. Tell me. What is this about. [*looking around*] All this death.

ZASTROZZI It is a continuing process of simplification. I am simplifying my life. These people came here to be judged.

VICTOR By you?

ZASTROZZI Is there anyone better at it.

VICTOR Apparently not. Well then, I too want to be judged by Zastrozzi, who judges for a profession.

ZASTROZZI Then step closer.

VICTOR Is there a fee.

ZASTROZZI Yes. But I take it from you quickly. You'll never even know it's gone.

VICTOR I have another idea. I think a man who enjoys his profession as much as you should be the one to pay the fee.

ZASTROZZI Perhaps. But I have never met anyone who would collect from me.

VICTOR You have now, sir.

ZASTROZZI I doubt it very much. You don't even hold your weapon properly.

VICTOR I have an unorthodox style. But it serves.

ZASTROZZI Let's see.

[*He draws his sword.* VICTOR *begins a short prayer in Latin which* ZASTROZZI *finishes for him.* VICTOR *looks at* ZASTROZZI. *Pause*]
[*in German*] Did you not know that I could see into your heart.

VICTOR [*in any Romance language*] Yes. But I can see into your heart as well.

ZASTROZZI [*in the same Romance language*] Then it will be an interesting battle.
[*Pause*]

VICTOR So.

ZASTROZZI So.

[*They approach each other, cross swords and begin to fight. The fight will continue and move across the entire stage at least once.* ZASTROZZI *tests* VICTOR. *He responds well but his moves are very unusual.* VICTOR *will gradually get better by observing* ZASTROZZI*'s moves*]
What are all these strange things you are doing designed for.

VICTOR To keep me alive.

ZASTROZZI Eventually I will find a way to penetrate your unorthodox style.

VICTOR That might be difficult. Since I am making it up as I go along.

ZASTROZZI You look silly.

VICTOR But I am alive.

ZASTROZZI Perhaps more alive than you have ever been. That is sometimes the way a person faces death.

VICTOR I intend to live.

ZASTROZZI Then you should have taken my advice and become an ordinary man.

VICTOR Sir. The point is that I am an ordinary man.

ZASTROZZI An ordinary man does not challenge Zastrozzi.

[ZASTROZZI *attacks him viciously.* VICTOR *defends himself well*]

VICTOR I am still alive. I am still waiting to be judged.

ZASTROZZI And growing arrogant as well.

VICTOR You talk about arrogance. The man who kills on a whim. Who kills an artist simply because he is mediocre. Who commits crimes against people because he believes he is the thing to which they must be answerable.

ZASTROZZI They must be answerable to something.

VICTOR There is always God, you know.

ZASTROZZI I am an atheist. If a man who is an atheist believes that people must be answerable, he has a duty to make them answerable to something.

VICTOR Answerable to your own demented personality.

ZASTROZZI I am what they are. They answer to themselves.

VICTOR All right, forget God. A man is responsible to humanity.

ZASTROZZI And I am part of humanity.

VICTOR The irresponsible part.

ZASTROZZI No. It is my responsibility to spread out like a disease and purge. And by destroying everything make everything safe.

VICTOR Explain exactly what you mean by safe.

ZASTROZZI Alive. Untouched by expectation. Free of history. Free of religion. Free of everything. And soon to be free of you.

[ZASTROZZI *attacks and* VICTOR *defends himself very well*]

VICTOR I am still alive.

ZASTROZZI But you are totally on the defensive.

VICTOR I don't have to kill you. I only have to survive. By merely surviving I neutralize you.

ZASTROZZI You cannot neutralize something you do not understand.

VICTOR We are approaching a new century, and with it a new world. There will be no place in it for your attitude, your behaviour.

ZASTROZZI This new world, what do you suppose it will be like.

VICTOR Better.

ZASTROZZI Describe what you mean by better.

VICTOR More humane. More civilized.

ZASTROZZI Wrong. Better is when the truth is understood.
Understanding the truth is understanding that the force of
darkness is constant.

VICTOR No, it is not. Your time is over.

ZASTROZZI Wrong again.

[ZASTROZZI *attacks him viciously.* VICTOR *defends himself and is
ebullient*]

VICTOR I am alive! Everything I said was true. You are neutralized. I
am the emissary of goodness in the battle between good and evil. I
have found God again.

[VICTOR *lunges forward wildly.* ZASTROZZI *plunges his sabre through*
VICTOR*'s heart*]

I am alive.

[VICTOR *falls down and dies*]

ZASTROZZI Ah, Victor. You understood what was in your heart. But
you did not know your limitations.

[ZASTROZZI *throws down his sabre.* VEREZZI *groans and slowly wakes
up. He sits, then stands, while* ZASTROZZI *watches him.* VEREZZI
*staggers around looking at the bodies and slowly regaining his
equilibrium*]

VEREZZI Look at all these dead people. What happened.

ZASTROZZI A series of unfortunate accidents.

VEREZZI Who are you.

ZASTROZZI Zastrozzi.

[VEREZZI *freezes*]

VEREZZI I thought you didn't exist.

ZASTROZZI Nonsense. You know me well.

VEREZZI Are you responsible for all these dead people.

ZASTROZZI No. You are.

VEREZZI That's quite impossible. I am a servant of God.

ZASTROZZI You are dead.

[ZASTROZZI *has drawn a knife*]

VEREZZI What are you going to do.

ZASTROZZI Cut open your stomach.

VEREZZI You can't. I'm immune. I am in touch with Him. Protected by Him. Loved by Him.

[VEREZZI *closes his eyes.* ZASTROZZI *approaches him*]

You can't hurt me. I'll just wait here. Nothing will happen.

ZASTROZZI Do you feel anything.

VEREZZI Yes.

ZASTROZZI Do you feel fear.

VEREZZI Yes.

ZASTROZZI Now who am I.

VEREZZI Zastrozzi.

ZASTROZZI And what is Zastrozzi.

VEREZZI The devil.

ZASTROZZI Nonsense. What is he.

VEREZZI A man.

ZASTROZZI What kind of man.

VEREZZI I don't know.

ZASTROZZI A sane man. What kind of man.

VEREZZI A sane man.

ZASTROZZI And what kind of man are you.

VEREZZI I don't know.

ZASTROZZI You feel fear when you are about to be murdered. And you are no longer smiling. You are a sane man too. From this moment on and forever. Do you understand. Perfectly sane and very, very afraid.

VEREZZI Yes.

ZASTROZZI Now get going.

VEREZZI Where.

ZASTROZZI You have to hide. I am giving you a day and I am coming after you. And do you know why I am coming after you.

VEREZZI No.

ZASTROZZI Because it will keep me preoccupied. Now leave. And hide well. I wish to be preoccupied for a long time.

[VEREZZI *slowly leaves.* ZASTROZZI *looks at all the corpses*]

[*smiling*] I like it here. Sad. No. I like it here.

[*He takes a cape off one of the corpses and wraps himself with it*]

I think I'll visit here again. It will help me stay sane.

[*Pause*]
Yes. I like it here.
[*Blackout*]
[*End*]

THEATRE OF THE FILM NOIR

Theatre of the Film Noir was first produced by the Factory Theatre for Onstage '81, Toronto's International Festival, in 1981 with following cast:

INSPECTOR CLAIR Steven Bush
BERNARD David Bolt
LILLIANE Susan Purdy
ERIC Jim Henshaw
HANK Peter Blais

Director: George F. Walker
Set Designer: Jim Plaxton
Costumes and Set Decor: Peter Blais
Music composed by: John Roby
Stage Manager: Renee Shouten

Persons

INSPECTOR CLAIR, *a police detective*
BERNARD, *a civilian clerk*
LILLIANE, *a former shop girl*
ERIC, *a German soldier*
HANK, *an American soldier*

Place

Paris.

Time

1944.

SCENE ONE

Under a street lamp. INSPECTOR CLAIR. *His hands deep in the pockets of his coat*

INSPECTOR The war is over. For us. But the evidence of war is everywhere. Some of the wounded are walking around. Pretending to function. Behaviour has no recognizable pattern. Morality is a question of circumstance. And guilt a matter of degree. For a police detective like myself this is not an easy time. I am used to a precise definition of my job. I am used to a pattern of behaviour, a clear consensus of morality and a belief in absolute guilt. For over five years I have been doing my job in a kind of fog. It's time I made it go away. It's time I stopped pretending to function. [*lights a cigarette*] On the night of the very day the liberation army marched into this city a young man was killed on a back street not too far from here. He was brutally murdered under the fog of recent circumstance. While thousands of people were celebrating freedom he fell down with a bullet in his stomach and bled to death. It's an interesting case. It could go any number of ways. It's supposed to be a case which cannot be solved. That's why they gave it to me. I specialize in difficult mysteries. I think I'm going to begin specializing in just making things clear. [*looks around*] Paris. The fall of 1944.
[*Blackout*]

SCENE TWO

Graveyard. BERNARD *is on his hands and knees searching for something on the ground. Muttering to himself*

BERNARD I've lost it. Jesus Christ, come help me. I've lost it.
[*He mumbles, groans, whines. Suddenly something on the ground catches his eye*]
What's that.
[*He whines, groans, whimpers. He crawls quickly along the ground. Stops. Picks up a small coin. Sighs, giggles*]
Where have you been. I was sick with worry. Now go back where you belong. [*puts the coin in his pocket*] And never try to escape again. Is my life cheap to you.
[*There is an open grave a few feet away from him. A wooden casket on the ground beside it. He walks over to it. Addresses the casket*]
I found it. I'll be all right now. [*sits on the casket, lights a cigarette*] I know you'd be laughing. And I know what you'd be saying. 'Bernard, you're a superstitious fool.' [*takes a drag on the cigarette*] Ah well, what of it. I found that coin the day the Nazis invaded. God whispered strangely in my ear. Here's a little two-headed coin for you, Bernard. A little token of my affection that will see you through the dark times ahead. It was one of those rare moments when God chose subtlety instead of outright terror. Nevertheless the point was well taken and I have kept this with me at all times. I know you'd be laughing, Jean. But I have been shot at with pistols, rifles, machine guns and cannons and I am still alive. True, I am a coward. But I am alive. [*crushes his cigarette, stands*] And you are dead. You should have let God whisper in your ear. You should have let him give you a coin. You should have learned to run and hide like me.
[*He opens the casket, takes out a bottle of wine, takes a long drink, puts the bottle back in the casket, closes the lid*]
[*Blackout*]

116

LILLIANE's apartment. LILLIANE *is sitting.* INSPECTOR CLAIR *is standing*

INSPECTOR You don't mind if I ask you a few questions?

LILLIANE No. But I've already told several other policemen everything I know.

INSPECTOR Of course. But this is such an unusual case ... I'm sorry I didn't notice, you have your coat on. Were you on your way out. I mean you did get the message that I was coming.

LILLIANE Actually I just got in.

INSPECTOR Really. I must have missed you.

LILLIANE What was that.

INSPECTOR On my way into your building I met an old friend. He kept me in conversation for almost an hour.

LILLIANE I came in the back way.

INSPECTOR Of course. You have a back entrance. That must have been very helpful over the past little while.

LILLIANE What do you mean.

INSPECTOR Well the war, the occupation made everyone so tense. So suspicious. It was difficult for an attractive young person ... to go about her business.

LILLIANE I've never paid any attention to other people's opinions of me.

INSPECTOR Good for you. And you have no political activity.

LILLIANE No. Unless you consider the business of survival a political activity.

INSPECTOR Under the circumstances, perhaps.

LILLIANE It would be easy to say I was in the resistance. So many people are saying that now, I know. But I was scared. Scared of starvation.

INSPECTOR Well no matter what we did or did not do for whatever reason, I suppose we must all begin again somehow.

LILLIANE If we can.

INSPECTOR Yes. Which unfortunately brings us back to your brother's death.

LILLIANE The Communists killed him.

INSPECTOR So you said in your statement. Because they suspected he was a spy, is that right.

LILLIANE Yes.

INSPECTOR But you didn't say why they suspected that.

LILLIANE Because I didn't know. Jean didn't tell me.

INSPECTOR He just told you that he was suspected.

LILLIANE He said they were giving him a rough time. He was afraid of them.

INSPECTOR That's all he told you. What I'm saying is, did he actually tell you they suspected him of spying on them.

LILLIANE That's what they fear most. That's what they always assume. I know how they are.

INSPECTOR You've had personal experience with them.

LILLIANE I have friends who were with Communists.

INSPECTOR You do?

LILLIANE Friends of friends. I gave the names already.

INSPECTOR Yes. None of them were helpful. By the time we reached them none of them were even Communists. Affiliations change so rapidly these days. One of these former Communists was also a known collaborator with the Nazis. He is now very friendly with the Americans. Ah, well. I suppose he too is just trying to survive.

LILLIANE I survived without affiliations.

INSPECTOR Good for you. On the night Jean was killed, he visited here. Correct?

LILLIANE We had dinner. We talked.

INSPECTOR Yes. Your apartment is so cozy. So safe. It was a nice relaxing evening?

LILLIANE He was tense. He was going to that rally.

INSPECTOR He expected trouble.

LILLIANE There was always trouble. The Communists attracted it like flies.

INSPECTOR But this time Jean wouldn't know which side his trouble would be coming from. Did he go to the meeting alone.

LILLIANE Someone picked him up.

INSPECTOR Who.

LILLIANE I don't know. There was a knock on the door. Jean answered it. Grabbed his coat and left. I didn't see who it was.

INSPECTOR None of this was in your statement.

LILLIANE None of these questions were asked.

INSPECTOR Of course. Well, even the police department is in the process of rebuilding.

LILLIANE But you are not new at this.

INSPECTOR Oh, no. No, I'm not new. I still make mistakes, though. Is that chocolate in your pocket.

LILLIANE Yes. Would you like a piece.

INSPECTOR Please.

[*She hands it to him. He breaks off a piece*]

American chocolate.

LILLIANE English.

INSPECTOR I thought only American soldiers had this.

LILLIANE English chocolate, Inspector. From a Free French soldier. They give it out freely. They give it to anyone. They give it to old women, young men, children. They just laugh and give it to you for no reason.

INSPECTOR Good for them. Well. The problem is we've talked to the Communists. They say they liked Jean. They say he had just been elected to a responsible position in the party. Their position does not make things easy.

LILLIANE They're lying.

INSPECTOR Perhaps. But they lie so well. In any event, it does not make things easy.

LILLIANE Did you expect they would be.

INSPECTOR No.

[*He hands her the rest of the chocolate*]

Can I visit you again. I might have more questions.

LILLIANE Any time.

[*She offers the chocolate to him. He smiles. Takes it*]

INSPECTOR Thank you. In the meantime good luck. What are your plans.

LILLIANE I'm not going anywhere.

INSPECTOR I meant for work.

LILLIANE I have a friend who knows an American soldier who makes films. I would like to be an actress.

INSPECTOR Be careful of that kind of American film.

LILLIANE I love American films.

INSPECTOR Yes, but ... Never mind. You would be very good in films, I'm sure. I hope you get the chance.

LILLIANE I will. I've made my mind up.

INSPECTOR I'll show myself out.

LILLIANE Be careful. The stairway is very dark.

INSPECTOR In that case, perhaps I should let myself out the back.

LILLIANE No.

[*Blackout*]

SCENE FOUR

Graveyard. BERNARD *is sitting on the coffin. Tossing his coin*

BERNARD Heads I stay. Tails I don't go. [*flips the coin, looks, frowns*]
Tails I stay. Heads I don't go. [*flips it*]
[LILLIANE *appears. Some distance away*]

LILLIANE Bernard.

BERNARD Over here.

LILLIANE Why can't you come here.

BERNARD I'm not moving. I'm standing guard.
[LILLIANE *hesitates then starts slowly toward him*]

LILLIANE You scared me on the telephone.

BERNARD I didn't say anything.

LILLIANE That's what scared me. So mysterious.

BERNARD I was drunk. I got carried away.
[LILLIANE *stops when she sees the casket*]

LILLIANE What's that.

BERNARD Coffin.

LILLIANE That's Jean's coffin, Bernard. What are you doing with it.

BERNARD I dug it up.

LILLIANE Why.

BERNARD Jean's still inside it. I checked. So that part of it's all right.
No mistake there.

LILLIANE I don't understand.

BERNARD Well, they sometimes forget to put the body inside. And
when that happens and they find it in the back room they just
throw it in the Seine.

LILLIANE That's ridiculous.

BERNARD The truth is the dead are very light. Four or five kilos at the
most.

LILLIANE You're still drunk, aren't you.

BERNARD Extremely. [*grins*]

LILLIANE I don't think it's funny.

BERNARD Neither do I.

LILLIANE Then why are you smiling.

BERNARD I'm drunk.

LILLIANE Why did you dig up my brother's body.

BERNARD His funeral was obscene.

LILLIANE I beg your pardon.

BERNARD When the priest was delivering the eulogy I got a hard-on.

LILLIANE You're degenerate.

BERNARD That's what I thought at first. Then I looked around.
Everyone had a hard-on. The priest. The pallbearers. The
choirboys. The concierge. And do you know who had the biggest
hard-on of all. Your mother. I didn't even know your mother had a
cock.

LILLIANE What in the hell are you talking about.

BERNARD The funeral was obscene and it made me hallucinate. I want
another chance to pay my respects properly. I want another funeral.

LILLIANE That's impossible.

BERNARD You're right. That's not why I dug him up. I did it because I
was lonely.

LILLIANE I know. Do you want to come home with me for a while.

BERNARD Don't look at me like that. That's not why either. The truth
is this. I want an autopsy.

LILLIANE You're not making any sense. You're just upset. I
understand—

BERNARD I want a fucking autopsy!

LILLIANE I'm going home. [starts off]

BERNARD No, don't go. Please listen. There's something wrong.

LILLIANE [stops] Go ahead.

BERNARD [looks around] The ghouls are out tonight. I can sense them.
I must be mad to be out with the ghouls. They might not know
that I'm a helpless coward. They might think I'm looking for
trouble. Listen ghouls, leave me alone, I'm harmless. Lilliane, is
that pity in your eyes.

LILLIANE Jean used to say you'd be lost without him.

BERNARD Jean had confidence. It was sometimes annoying. Do you
suppose that's why they killed him.

LILLIANE Who.

BERNARD Standing on top of that barricade. His clothes so tight against his body. His head above the smoke. His clothes so tight. His trousers especially. That's why I got a hard-on at the funeral. I could imagine the way he was filling out his trousers when he was killed. Jean had the best body in the Communist Party. There was a Free French radio operator who had an even better body. But Jean had the best of the Communists. As for his mind, well, it was all right. Your average nineteen-year-old. With idealism and a touch of stupidity mixed together. But we have to find out why they killed him in memory of his body.

LILLIANE You think the Party killed him, don't you.

BERNARD They wanted to make him a martyr. They knew he was too stupid to be of any other use to them.

LILLIANE He wasn't stupid.

BERNARD Did you love him.

LILLIANE Yes, of course.

BERNARD What did you love about him.

LILLIANE He was my brother.

BERNARD That's what you loved about him? That's just loving yourself.

LILLIANE I don't want to listen to your drunken philosophy.

BERNARD Then why did you come here. Does a sober man invite a person to a graveyard at midnight.

LILLIANE You made it sound important.

BERNARD Did you sleep with Jean.

LILLIANE No.

BERNARD He told me you did. I believed him.

LILLIANE He was lying.

BERNARD I still believe him. But what's that mean. I'm so stupid. Almost as stupid as Jean.

LILLIANE He wasn't stupid! He had a wonderful mind.

BERNARD It's disgusting and ridiculous that you could love his mind, that you could miss his mind and not miss his body. I loved his mouth, his thighs and his ass, and we both loved his cock.

LILLIANE If it's none of my business how you loved him it's none of yours how I loved him.

BERNARD My only contact with the outside was your brother. Now that he's gone it's just a matter of time before I slip back in to my hole. I've been hiding in basements for years learning how to speak English so I could ingratiate myself with the liberation army. I've seen the Americans and they scare me as much as the Nazis. I know they hate queers. I can tell by the way they chew their gum when I walk by. The truth is I thought ... [*he mumbles something*]

LILLIANE What was that.

BERNARD I thought that you and I could get married and live a life of convenience.

[*She smiles*]

Well give it some thought. I'd get a certain respectability from you. And you could take eternal satisfaction from being around the only other person Jean was intimate with.

LILLIANE You're joking.

BERNARD I don't think the Communists killed Jean. They didn't want him to be a martyr. Martyrs are no longer considered useful. I don't want an autopsy. That wouldn't be useful.

LILLIANE Then what do you want.

BERNARD For you to marry me. And someday love me.

LILLIANE And that's why you dug Jean's body up.

BERNARD Oh no. Well, I'm not behaving rationally. The truth is I wanted to kiss him. You see dead people don't turn cold. You see, when I kissed his lips they were warm. Even a bit wet.

LILLIANE Well, whatever. Even if you've gone insane I suppose you deserve an answer. I won't marry you of course. And now you should bury my brother. [*starts off*]

BERNARD But I have other things to say to you. The Communists didn't kill Jean. I don't want an autopsy. You won't marry me. I am a weak and cowardly man. There it is so clear and simple. But I still have other things to say to you.

LILLIANE [*circling him in the darkness*] Maybe we'll talk again sometime.

BERNARD But why did you come in the first place. Have you forgotten.

LILLIANE Because you said it was important.

BERNARD Yes. We've been through that. Because I was Jean's closest friend. And now you're leaving. Aren't I still Jean's closest friend.

LILLIANE Jean's dead, Bernard.

BERNARD And wasn't he dead when I talked to you on the phone.

LILLIANE Goodbye.

BERNARD Yes, he was. How silly. And yet you're leaving. Didn't you hear me. Just before I hung up. You weren't sure what I said, were you. And since I didn't bring it up you assumed I never really said it. But I did say it, Lilliane. I said—'Eric.'

[*She stops. He goes to the casket. Takes out the bottle*]

What are you doing out there in the darkness. If I were you I'd be scared half to death. All those ghouls out there and this drunken irrational fool over here. What a choice.

[*She is walking back toward him*]

Paris had just been liberated. Jean and I had stayed up the whole night celebrating. Making love and drinking. There was a certain potential for happiness that evening. Suddenly he turned to me and said, 'My sister has a lover. He's a German soldier. She's hiding him in her apartment.'

LILLIANE I understand that you're lonely and that you don't know what to do with yourself. I know you don't have any money. I have a little that I could give you. It's not much.

BERNARD No, it's not.

LILLIANE What do you intend to do. Report me?

BERNARD Well, I'm duty-bound of course. A patriotic Frenchman, a friend of the liberators, disgusted and shocked that a French lady of apparent taste and active conscience has taken in an enemy of all mankind. Taken him inside her night after night and hidden him from the forces of justice.

LILLIANE You're vermin. The biggest coward in Europe. Pissing in a private hole since the war began. Protecting your own skin and nothing more. Save your disgust for yourself. You have no right to judge me.

BERNARD Certainly true. However, it's the ideal that's important. Realistically I'm a self-serving mouse but ideally I am an enemy of fascism and a supporter of freedom. We are in a temporary state of peace. In times of peace, self-serving idealists surface and do well.

LILLIANE But you don't know him. Eric is not like the rest. He's a good man.

BERNARD And a terrific lover.

LILLIANE You're obsessive. Your mind is disturbed. Even before I met
you I wondered what Jean could see in you. After I met you I
wondered even more. If he had to sleep with a man he could have
done better without much effort.

BERNARD I wondered about you as well. Jean talked about you. 'She
lives an abstract life. Very introspective.' From the little he told me
I tried to imagine what you looked like. What your apartment
looked like. When I met you I wasn't surprised. But when I saw
your apartment it seemed all wrong. Too big. It seemed like you
were waiting for someone to share it with you. When Jean told me
about Eric I would imagine how well he fit in your apartment. I
saw him sitting in that big chair in the corner with his long legs
stretched out in front of him. I saw him in your bed beside you,
snuggling up against you. His legs wrapped around you. I
imagined in incredible detail with colours and sounds and odours.
I used to get very excited thinking about you and your apartment
and Eric. I don't know why. The notion of a man and woman
making love does not usually arouse me. I suppose it's because I
knew Jean had made love to you and that he wanted to make love
to Eric. Jean was such a ridiculous bastard. No discipline. No
control over all those ridiculous adolescent cravings. Fucking an
aging neurotic and his own sister and wanting to fuck his sister's
Nazi lover. Such a fine ridiculous boy.
[*He approaches her*]
We have to find out who killed him, Lilliane. Who put that
sickening hole in his head and made his body crumple like
garbage.

LILLIANE Stay away from me, Bernard—

[BERNARD *stops*]

BERNARD Was I scaring you.

LILLIANE No.

BERNARD Oh. [*turns around*] How kind of you to stay with me when
I'm drunk. Jean was right. You're very abstract and introspective.

LILLIANE Are you going to report me and Eric.

126

BERNARD I take that back. You're not at all abstract and introspective. You're brutal and realistic. Why are you talking about that. Why aren't you talking about your brother.

LILLIANE He's dead!

BERNARD But only for a week. His lips are almost wet. Even I know that to mourn properly you mourn longer than a week. Until the lips become dry. I read somewhere that that takes a month. Promise me you'll swear off everything for at least a month, Lilliane. Show us that you really loved him. Stop acting like a whore. Well, at least buy a black handkerchief for God's sake.

LILLIANE I owe you no explanations. Jean was a dear and lovely boy. I loved him in many ways. Eric and I met by accident and became fond of each other by accident.

BERNARD Yes. Tell me about Eric.

LILLIANE No. It's none of your business.

BERNARD Jean fought against the Germans.

LILLIANE But could have been killed by the Communists.

BERNARD But could have been killed by the Comm—! But fought against the Germans! There's a moral issue involved here.

LILLIANE Jean knew. He said nothing.

BERNARD Because he wanted to fuck Eric!

LILLIANE You're disgusting!

BERNARD Now he couldn't fuck—fuck Eric if Eric was locked up somewhere could he!

LILLIANE You're disgusting, Bernard!

BERNARD I am the moral conscience of the day.

LILLIANE Oh?

BERNARD Moral conscience! I am seeking justice. I will report you and your pretty German lover in his long tight trousers. I will go as a patriotic Frenchman and a friend of the liberators fluent in their language disguising my queerness as I walk past them chewing gum like they do and I will report your dangerous evil life with the German enemy of all mankind in incredible detail including colours, sounds and odours!

[LILLIANE *turns away*]

[*Blackout*]

SCENE FIVE

A bistro. HANK, *a young American soldier, is sitting on a stool. Playing an old guitar. Singing a blues song. He is drunk.* ERIC *sits at a table. His head is bowed. The collar of his overcoat up. His hands cupped around a drink on the table*

HANK [*sings*]
 Black and blue
 Black
 And blue
 Empty house
 Nothing to do
 Dead old friends
 And besides
 I'm black all over
 And blue inside

 Black and blue
 Blue inside
 Got no future
 That's all right
 Baby's gone
 Outta my life
 Mama's gone too
 Black all over
 Black and blue
 [ERIC *looks up sheepishly.* HANK *catches his eye.* ERIC *claps hands twice. Then a third time*]
HANK Thanks.
 [ERIC *looks down*]
 Hey.
 [ERIC *looks up*]
 Thanks.
 [ERIC *nods. Looks down*]
 Hey.

[ERIC *looks up*]

Thanks.

[ERIC *looks down.*]

Hey.

[ERIC *looks up*]

Hi ...

[HANK *falls off the stool.* ERIC *looks down*]

Ah, fuck. [*struggles to his feet*] Jesus. [*looks at* ERIC] You liked that song?

ERIC [*quietly*] Very nice.

HANK What.

ERIC [*whispering*] Very nice.

[HANK *moves toward* ERIC]

HANK Why are you whispering.

[ERIC *shrugs*]

You liked that song?

[ERIC *nods.* HANK *sits down at* ERIC's *table*]

You wanna whisper some more? It's all right. Don't let the uniform scare you. Why does this uniform scare so many people. It's American. It's supposed to make you happy. You like this uniform.

ERIC [*whispering*] Very nice.

HANK What.

ERIC Yes.

HANK Yeah? You want it? They're going to take it away soon anyway. You want it?

[ERIC *shakes his head*]

Court martial coming up. Conduct detrimental. Don't tell anyone.

[*He grabs* ERIC's *hand*]

Don't tell anyone.

[ERIC *shakes his head*]

In the meantime I'm hanging around. This is a lousy place to hang around. You wanna hang around some other place. Or maybe you like this place. Do you like this place.

ERIC Very nice.

HANK Very nice. [*laughs*] Jesus. No, it's not. Jesus!

[LILLIANE *comes in.* ERIC *sees her.* HANK *follows* ERIC's *eyes to*

LILLIANE. LILLIANE *goes to the table.* HANK *stands, knocking over his chair. Picks it up. Looks at* LILLIANE *and* ERIC *who are looking at each other*]

Excuse me.

[HANK *goes back to his stool.* LILLIANE *sits down at the table.* HANK *begins to play the guitar. Softly.* LILLIANE *looks at* HANK. *At* ERIC]

ERIC It's all right.

LILLIANE You should be more careful.

ERIC I was.

LILLIANE You can't go back to the apartment yet.

ERIC The policeman is still there?

LILLIANE Bernard knows about us.

ERIC Are you sure.

LILLIANE Jean told him.

ERIC Of course. We should have taken steps earlier.

LILLIANE Bernard is deranged, Eric. He's dug up Jean's body. I can't understand why. He called me. I went to the graveyard. It was so strange. Talking like his brain was exploding.

ERIC What does he want.

LILLIANE I don't know. He's deranged.

ERIC Give him what he wants. We can always take it away later.

LILLIANE I think he wants me.

[ERIC *touches her arm*]

ERIC Lilliane.

LILLIANE No.

ERIC Lilliane, it's a difficult life. You have hidden me. Broken the law. We could pay a high price. Be separated. Make a sacrifice. He could cause trouble. Where is he now.

LILLIANE I said I would meet him at my apartment.

ERIC Then you should go.

LILLIANE Eric.

ERIC You can always take it away later. When the time is right. When it's safe.

LILLIANE He scares me.

ERIC I scared you once.

[*Pause*]

You should go.
[*Pause*]
Go.
[*Long pause. She gets up. Starts off. As she is passing* HANK *he looks at her. Hands her a chocolate bar.* LILLIANE *smiles. She starts off.* ERIC *extends a hand.* LILLIANE *hands the chocolate to* ERIC. *She leaves.* HANK *looks at* ERIC. *Frowns.* ERIC *smiles*]
[*Blackout*]

SCENE SIX

LILLIANE's *apartment.* INSPECTOR CLAIR *sits in a chair. Legs outstretched. Reading a book.* BERNARD *comes in quickly. Looking around as he enters*

BERNARD Who are you. What are you doing here. I was to meet Lilliane here. She wanted to talk. This is her apartment isn't it. Yes, this is her apartment. I've seen it in my head. Who are you.

INSPECTOR A friend of Lilliane.

BERNARD You're no friend. You're a policeman. I can smell it.

INSPECTOR Why don't you sit down, Bernard.

BERNARD How do you know my name.

INSPECTOR Lilliane told me. Why don't you sit.

BERNARD No, I can't stay long. I left something unguarded. I have to get back. I only came here because I thought Lilliane wanted to talk. Do you know Lilliane. You're not romantically involved with her are you.

INSPECTOR Lilliane thought we should talk. I'm investigating the murder of her brother. You knew him.

BERNARD A long time ago.

INSPECTOR What does that mean.

BERNARD We'd grown apart. Recently we'd become like strangers. I know nothing about his death. Of course I have my suspicions. But don't we all.

INSPECTOR What do you suspect.

BERNARD I suspect that you are trying to implicate me. What did Lilliane tell you.

INSPECTOR She just suggested that you might have some information.

BERNARD Lilliane should be careful what she suggests. Have you established her innocence in this matter.

INSPECTOR Do you have something to tell me about Lilliane.

BERNARD Lilliane is a lovely girl. She can be very useful in times like these. She has a certain stability as you can tell from her apartment. Have you spent much time in her apartment.

INSPECTOR Where were you the night of Jean's death.

BERNARD In my room, of course. I never leave my room. Except in emergencies.

INSPECTOR Is this an emergency.

BERNARD Lilliane and I have to talk.

INSPECTOR What was it you were guarding.

BERNARD What did Lilliane tell you I was guarding.

INSPECTOR Why do you answer my questions with questions.

BERNARD What is that in your pocket.

INSPECTOR Chocolate. Lilliane gave it to me.

BERNARD German chocolate?

INSPECTOR American.

BERNARD American?

INSPECTOR No, I'm sorry, English. Would you like a piece.

BERNARD No.

INSPECTOR You were a clerk at the ministry of public works, weren't you.

BERNARD Can I see your identification.

INSPECTOR Certainly. [shows his card to BERNARD]

BERNARD You really are a policeman.

INSPECTOR You had doubts?

BERNARD I thought you were one of Lilliane's lovers.

INSPECTOR She has many lovers?

BERNARD How would I know. I just suspect. She has so much to offer. Her apartment. Chocolate. [begins to look around the apartment]

INSPECTOR You haven't worked at the ministry for the past two years.

BERNARD No. I had to quit.

INSPECTOR Why.

BERNARD I was too afraid.

INSPECTOR Of what.

BERNARD Getting there. It was difficult for me to get there. There were always people on the street who were hostile towards me.

INSPECTOR So what did you do instead.

BERNARD Stayed home.

INSPECTOR That's all?

BERNARD Well, it was difficult. Staying home was difficult. It was hard to make a living at home. And hard to make new friends.

INSPECTOR How did you eat.

BERNARD Friends brought me food.

INSPECTOR New friends?

BERNARD Old friends.

INSPECTOR Jean.

BERNARD Yes, he was one. People liked Jean. He had a way of getting things from people. I think it runs in the family.

INSPECTOR And other friends? People you knew from your days with the Communists.

BERNARD Are you investigating the Communists.

INSPECTOR I'm investigating a murder.

BERNARD It's just that it's hard to follow the pattern of your questions.

INSPECTOR I'm just stumbling around.

BERNARD I see. Well, I was never really a Communist. Oh, I read the books, but I didn't understand them when they talked. I was never officially one of them. I observed. Eventually they observed that I was just observing and asked me to leave ... [sits] It's too bad. I used to enjoy the meetings. When everyone had finished shouting, we'd have tea. I used to enjoy that. Also, the fact that no one seemed afraid of being discovered by the Germans. Some of them were resistance of course. Not all. But some. Some just liked to come to meetings. But no one seemed afraid. That was nice. Sometimes with tea we had biscuits. English biscuits. Michel, the custodian of arms, used to bring them from the countryside. He said the English dropped them by parachute. He went out looking for weapons but he said the English were only dropping biscuits. Good biscuits though. Good with tea ... But they weren't weapons, and Michel used this to arouse anti-English pro-Russian sentiment. The Communists were stupid. Not as stupid as the fascists because these things are relative. But stupid ... Even so, I enjoyed the meetings.

INSPECTOR What did you think of the Germans. Besides that they were stupid.

BERNARD Oh, I hated them of course.

INSPECTOR Of course.

[BERNARD *stands. Moves about aimlessly*]

BERNARD Are you investigating collaborators.

INSPECTOR I'm investigating a murder.

BERNARD You can believe me. I hated the Germans for my own reasons. Sexual reasons. They were particularly nasty to me.

INSPECTOR Jean had the same problem?

BERNARD I don't know.

INSPECTOR Your friends in the Party suggest he did.

BERNARD That should make you suspicious of them, shouldn't it.

INSPECTOR Why.

BERNARD Character assassination.

INSPECTOR Are suggestions of sexual preference a sign of character assassination.

BERNARD During certain times. Times like these.

INSPECTOR When you and Jean ceased to be lovers did you remain friends.

BERNARD He felt sorry for me. He brought me food. And cigarettes.

INSPECTOR German?

BERNARD Russian.

INSPECTOR Not German?

BERNARD Russian. Why.

INSPECTOR Lilliane's apartment is full of German cigarettes.

BERNARD You searched.

INSPECTOR Not too much. It wasn't difficult. They're not hidden.

BERNARD Lilliane has nothing to hide. She was just doing what so many others were doing.

INSPECTOR Yes?

BERNARD Getting by.

INSPECTOR Why did Jean feel sorry for you.

BERNARD Well, look at me. I'm pitiful.

INSPECTOR You seem fine.

BERNARD It's an act.

INSPECTOR What are you really like then.

BERNARD Afraid.

INSPECTOR But harmless?

BERNARD I think Jean's death was a political act. The Communists needed a martyr.

INSPECTOR That is possible of course. I'm looking into it. I came to the case late. A veil of contradicting evidence has been allowed to surround matters. It will take time. But I am looking to remove it.

BERNARD Can I go now.

INSPECTOR Yes.

BERNARD I have to go.

INSPECTOR Go ahead.

BERNARD I can go?

[*The* INSPECTOR *nods*]

Will I be seeing you again. Will your investigation involve me any further.

INSPECTOR We'll see.

BERNARD But I can go now?

INSPECTOR Yes.

BERNARD Thank you. [*starts off*]

INSPECTOR Oh, Bernard.

[BERNARD *stops. The* INSPECTOR *holds up a small package*]

Cigarettes. Here.

[*He throws the package to* BERNARD]

BERNARD Thank you.

[BERNARD *leaves.* INSPECTOR CLAIR *smiles weakly. Searches his pockets. Reaches under the cushion of the other chair. Takes out a pack of cigarettes. Takes one out. Lights it. Inhales. Frowns. Looks at the cigarette*]

INSPECTOR American.

[*Blackout*]

SCENE SEVEN

Graveyard. LILLIANE *waiting*
BERNARD *comes on*

BERNARD Get away from that coffin.

LILLIANE I'd thought you'd finally gone away.

BERNARD No chance.

LILLIANE Do you have your senses back.

BERNARD I met a policeman in your apartment.

LILLIANE I know.

BERNARD You arranged it?

LILLIANE No. I came home. Heard you talking, and went away.

BERNARD He liked me. He'd like to hear from me again. I might call him.

LILLIANE About what.

BERNARD You and Eric of course.

LILLIANE That would not be wise.

BERNARD I don't care.

[ERIC *has come slowly out of the darkness. A long wool coat on. The only sign of a uniform beneath it—his boots*]

ERIC Go home, Lilliane.

BERNARD My assassin. [*drops to his knees*]

LILLIANE How did you know where I was.

ERIC I followed you.

BERNARD A wily devil. I'm a goner.

LILLIANE Did you hear.

ERIC Yes. I was listening from the beginning.

BERNARD Trained by the Gestapo for sure. Are you going to torture me. I warn you now. I'll tell you everything I know and it won't make a bit of sense. Please excuse my glibness. In fact I am genuinely frightened.

ERIC I just want to talk. Will you excuse us, Lilliane.

LILLIANE I'm staying.

BERNARD Yes, let her stay. She'll make me feel more secure.

LILLIANE Odd that you should say that. I was just thinking of cutting your throat.

BERNARD Oh. Well, how was I to know. I'm not a mind reader.

LILLIANE There's no other way, Eric. He's demented.

BERNARD But harmless.

ERIC You threaten to report us.

BERNARD You want to cut my throat too.

ERIC I just want to talk.

BERNARD Then why do you want her to leave. You didn't want her to see the criminal in you. You wanted to send her away carefree and then cut me open in private. You have a technique for such things. Oh God, I'm so scared. I think I'm going to piss my pants. How pitiful.

[BERNARD *crawls into the grave. Pause.* LILLIANE *and* ERIC *exchange a look. They walk to the grave. And stand over* BERNARD]

ERIC Get off your knees.

BERNARD I'm too scared to move.

ERIC I'll help you up.

BERNARD Stay away from me. Why are you reaching inside your coat. You have a pistol.

[ERIC *produces a tiny box*]

ERIC Cigarette?

BERNARD I don't smoke.

LILLIANE He's lying.

BERNARD She's right. But it wasn't an important lie. Certainly no reason to punish me for it.

ERIC Certainly not. Do you mind if I smoke.

LILLIANE It was an example of his lying. He can't be trusted.

ERIC You're on edge. It would be better if you left.

LILLIANE I'm staying. I can't leave with this over my head.

ERIC I understand.

BERNARD You're very compassionate. I'm beginning to see what Jean saw in you.

ERIC Thank you. Will you have a cigarette now.

[LILLIANE *begins to pace*]

BERNARD Yes. Perhaps I will.

ERIC Will you get off your knees now.

BERNARD If you don't mind.

ERIC I would like it very much

[BERNARD *stands.* ERIC *gives him a cigarette. Lights it*]

BERNARD Turkish?

ERIC Dutch.

BERNARD Of course. I'm such a cretin.

ERIC Not at all. It's a stronger blend than the usual Dutch. It fools most people.

BERNARD You're very kind.

ERIC Thank you. Will you excuse me a moment.

BERNARD Certainly.

[ERIC *nods. Goes to* LILLIANE. *Whispers in her ear.* LILLIANE *shakes her head.* ERIC *grabs her. Whispers.* LILLIANE *nods. They kiss.* LILLIANE *goes to* BERNARD]

LILLIANE Will you excuse me for a few minutes, Bernard.

BERNARD Of course.

LILLIANE Just a few minutes.

[*She smiles. Leaves*]

ERIC She is just going for a walk.

BERNARD It's a nice evening for a walk. That is if the ghouls and their associates don't feel hostile towards you.

[ERIC *laughs*]

Does that make sense to you.

ERIC Very much.

BERNARD Really. Then would you mind explaining it to me. I'm afraid it's just one of the many things I'm prone to saying that make no sense to me.

[ERIC *walks slowly to* BERNARD. *Smiling*]

ERIC That is often the case with a complex mind like yours.

BERNARD Is it. Why are you reaching inside your coat again.

[ERIC *produces a package. Hands it to* BERNARD. *As* BERNARD *undoes the package,* ERIC *removes his overcoat to reveal a German officer's uniform. The package contains an officer's hat and* BERNARD *stares at it. He turns to* ERIC *and gasps. Puts the hat on* ERIC'*s head. Whimpers and turns away as if offering the back of his head as a target for the assassin.* ERIC *smiles*]

[*Blackout*]

LILLIANE's apartment. LILLIANE is sitting in a chair. HANK stands beside her, emptying his pockets of chocolate bars and dropping them into her lap. Two from one pocket. Two from another. Five from another. Six. Seven. About fifty chocolate bars. All gently dropped. When he is finished, pause. LILLIANE looks up

LILLIANE Thank you.

HANK You're welcome.

[She stands. The chocolate bars fall to the floor. HANK watches them. LILLIANE puts her arms around HANK's neck]

LILLIANE Thank you.

[She kisses his forehead]

Thank you.

[She kisses his cheek]

Thank you. Thank you. Thank you.

HANK You're ... welcome.

[LILLIANE turns]

Are you crying.

LILLIANE I'm sorry.

[HANK hands her a handkerchief]

Thank you. *[turns toward him]* Thank you. *[turns away]*

HANK Are you crying.

LILLIANE I'm so sad.

HANK Don't be sad.

LILLIANE I need ... what do I need.

HANK Cigarettes?

LILLIANE No. *[turns toward him]* Thank you.

HANK What do you need.

LILLIANE Help.

HANK I can help.

LILLIANE Can you.

HANK Can I ... May I.

LILLIANE It's politics. Everything is politics. I'm a victim of other people's beliefs. I'm a stranger in my own country. I don't understand these new influences. The radio plays American jazz. That's political. I'm just trying to survive. But the demands are frightening. One man in particular is frightening. He wants to destroy me for political reasons only. I try to explain that I am not responsible. But he won't listen.

HANK Someone should make him listen. Maybe I could make him listen. Maybe I could try. If that's all right with you. If that's what you want. Is that what you want.

LILLIANE Thank you.

[*She puts her arms around him*]

Thank you very much.

[*Tentatively he puts his arms around her. Tentatively he smiles*]

[*Blackout*]

SCENE NINE

Graveyard. BERNARD *is lying on the coffin.* ERIC *is standing over him, his tunic undone. Smiling*

BERNARD Why are you reaching inside your new pocket.

ERIC Would you care for a piece of chocolate.

BERNARD What kind of chocolate.

ERIC American.

BERNARD Does it have nuts in it.

ERIC No. I'm sorry.

BERNARD Don't apologize. I prefer chocolate without nuts.

ERIC Should I break off a piece for you.

BERNARD Yes. Not too big a piece though.

ERIC Is this about right.

BERNARD Yes.

ERIC Here.

BERNARD Thank you. [*eats the chocolate*] Good. Where did you get this American chocolate.

ERIC Lilliane got it for me.

BERNARD And where did Lilliane get it.

ERIC From the Americans.

BERNARD She must be very cunning.

ERIC She gets many things from the Americans for me.

BERNARD She must love you very much.

ERIC Yes.

BERNARD You're very lucky.

ERIC Yes, I am.

BERNARD Lilliane and I have had our disagreements. But basically I admire her. Especially for her introspection.

ERIC I too.

BERNARD Well, it's a rare thing in a beautiful woman.

ERIC And an even rarer thing in a beautiful man.

BERNARD You refer of course to Jean.

ERIC A beautiful young man.

BERNARD But stupid.

ERIC Yes.

BERNARD Yes.

[*Pause*]

ERIC More chocolate?

BERNARD No, thank you.

ERIC Here, take the rest.

[*He hands it to him*]

I insist.

BERNARD All right. I'll save it for later. [*puts it in the coffin*] If it's not too presumptuous of me to think there will be a later for me.

ERIC Not at all. I hope we both will lead a long healthy life.

BERNARD But I'm a stranger to you.

ERIC Jean spoke of you often.

BERNARD Really. What else does Lilliane get you from the Americans.

ERIC Many things. Even money.

BERNARD She must be very cunning indeed. So you had a conversation with Jean.

ERIC Yes. We got along very well.

BERNARD He liked you?

ERIC We got along very well.

BERNARD And he would not want me to report you. Is that what you are trying to say.

ERIC I believe he liked me. He didn't report me.

BERNARD Well, I was very fond of Jean as you know. I was his lover, as you know. I am respectful of his memory, as you know. These things are all very important and must be considered when I decide whether to turn you in or not. That is the rational way to proceed. Am I not a rational man. We have been having a rational discussion have we not. A very polite discussion. You have offered cigarettes and chocolates and I have accepted and made complimentary remarks about your lover, and always in a controlled fashion, never once—never once—referring to the spectacle of Jean's fine muscular body upon that barricade and the hideous sickening bullet hole which made him crumple like garbage onto the ground or the fact that he fought Germans like you, the enemy of all mankind, that he left me alone below the surface to fight his stupid fight, or the agony of the obscene nature of his funeral when everyone there had a grotesque erection, or that suddenly out of the corner of my eye I saw you for the first time leaning against the door of the church with a smile on your face. No, I have not even mentioned that, the most obscene and vivid thing of all because I am rational. I am calm. I am intuitive. I sensed that you wished me to be this way and I obliged.

[*Pause*]

But be careful. Because I am capable of regressing.

ERIC [*smiles*] Perhaps I was smiling. I sometimes smile when I'm embarrassed.

BERNARD Was Jean's funeral embarrassing you.

ERIC Yes.

BERNARD Why.

ERIC I am Lilliane's lover.

BERNARD Surely there must be more.

ERIC I had also been intimate with Jean.

BERNARD Oh, what a delicate way of putting it. No, I don't believe it. Yes, I do. What a stinking disappointment. I was sure I was the only one. But of course not. He was so undisciplined. No, it's stinking Nazi propaganda. You will not demoralize the degenerates, I warn you. Take it back or I'll suck out your intestines.

ERIC I'm sorry.

BERNARD Well what of it. Jean's dead. Look inside that coffin if you don't believe me. No. We must unite. We have a common goal now. We must find Jean's murderer and avenge the corruption of his body. But first we must strike a bargain. Are you agreeable.

ERIC What is the bargain.

BERNARD I agree not to turn you in.

ERIC I knew you would see it my way.

BERNARD And you agree to give me Lilliane.

ERIC But we are in love.

BERNARD She can be in love with me.

ERIC It's not so easy.

BERNARD Isn't it. Well, I wouldn't know. I've never been in love.

ERIC You loved Jean.

BERNARD That moron? I was fond of his skin. I want to be in love with Lilliane in a legitimate manner so that I can surface and have her bring me things from the Americans.

ERIC You frighten me when you talk like this, Bernard.

BERNARD Do I. How.

ERIC I worry that you really might be demented and that I won't be able to reason with you. That I will have to use other means.

[*He slaps* BERNARD]

BERNARD He reveals himself to me.

[ERIC *slaps him again.* BERNARD *drops to his knees*]

My assassin.

[ERIC *pushes him.* BERNARD *falls face down on the ground*]

Oh Jesus, I'm so scared.

[ERIC *puts his foot on* BERNARD'*s head*]

Jesus come here. I'm so fucking scared.

[ERIC *pulls a pistol from his coat. Kneels. Puts the pistol to* BERNARD'*s head*]

Don't. Please don't. I'm harmless.

ERIC You are forcing me to be brutal with you. I don't like this at all.

BERNARD I'm sorry.

ERIC I prefer polite conversation.

BERNARD I'm sorry.

ERIC I prefer peaceful negotiation.

BERNARD Very, very sorry.

ERIC I've seen enough violence. I've been forced to kill enough. I've done my share. I have vast experience with violence. My victims were of several nationalities.

BERNARD You poor man.

ERIC It caused me great turmoil. Basically I'm a tranquil individual. Just because I am German doesn't mean I am violent, rigid and heartless. That's a cliché!

BERNARD Yes, it is.

ERIC I hate clichés!

BERNARD So do I.

ERIC War is a cliché!

BERNARD Be careful with that gun.

ERIC Death is a cliché!

BERNARD Don't let your finger slip.

ERIC Peace is a cliché.

BERNARD I'm going to piss.

ERIC Peace is obscene! It's hypocritical. It puts war criminals on trial. It turns cowards into vengeance seekers. Where were the cowardly vengeance seekers when it mattered. Don't blame the criminals. Blame the victims. Without victims there wouldn't be criminals, would there. That makes sense, doesn't it. That *makes* sense, doesn't it. That makes *sense,* doesn't it. Das ist richtig, nicht vahr?!

BERNARD I suppose.

ERIC What.

BERNARD Yes. Of course.

ERIC What?!

BERNARD Yes, yes. Of course. Of course.

[*Pause*]

ERIC Yes. [*stands. Puts the gun away*] I owe you an apology. Please shake my hand.

[BERNARD *looks at him*]

Please.

[BERNARD *gets up slowly. Extends a hand. They shake*]

I frightened you.

BERNARD I almost wet myself.

ERIC I'm sorry. But now you see why we must keep our conversation rational. Certainly we are both capable of becoming quite disturbed and incoherent but in the long run that course will only prove disastrous. Do you agree.

BERNARD Yes.

ERIC Now where were we.

BERNARD I'm not quite sure.

ERIC What have you done with your chocolate.

BERNARD It's in my pocket.

[ERIC *looks at him oddly*]

No, it's in the coffin.

ERIC Why don't you have a bite.

BERNARD I'm not hungry.

ERIC Then would you like a cigarette.

BERNARD No.

[ERIC *grabs* BERNARD's *jaw*]

ERIC You're not being very agreeable. You should be more agreeable.

BERNARD Yes. You're right. Would you like one of my cigarettes.

ERIC Thank you very much.

[BERNARD *takes out package of cigarettes. Gives* ERIC *one. Takes one himself*]

I'll light them.

BERNARD No, I'll do it.

ERIC I insist.

BERNARD Very well.

[ERIC *lights the cigarettes. They both inhale*]

ERIC This is a very good cigarette. Turkish?

BERNARD American.

ERIC How stupid of me!

BERNARD Not at all. It's difficult to tell.

ERIC No. I should have known. I spent a year in America doing serious espionage work.

BERNARD You should tell me about it sometime.

ERIC It's a part of my life I would greatly like to forget.

BERNARD I understand.

ERIC Although I had an American lover there. I don't mind remembering him. He was eighteen years old.

BERNARD Does Lilliane know this.

ERIC Lilliane and I are in love.

BERNARD A respectable love.

ERIC But dangerous. We live constantly in fear. My nerves are very bad.

BERNARD Did your lover wear his trousers as tightly as you do.

ERIC Yes. Do you like the way my trousers fit.

BERNARD It suits you.

ERIC Thank you. But we should be careful where this conversation leads. We have both been living underground too long. We don't have all our faculties.

BERNARD Mine come and go.

ERIC I've noticed.

BERNARD Sometimes I'm perfectly sane.

ERIC In fact, you seem sane right now.

BERNARD And so do you.

ERIC And polite.

BERNARD And so are you.

ERIC But you could be just trying to manipulate me.

BERNARD And you could be doing the same.

ERIC And yet of course if that were the case it could lead to a
confrontation in which I would be superior. If it led to a violent
confrontation I could seize hold of your head and squeeze your
brains out into my hands.
[BERNARD *puts his hands in his pockets. Walks over to the coffin. Sits
on it. Bows his head*]
I've frightened you again. I'm sorry.

BERNARD I'm so sad. Jean is dead. I'm nothing without him. You could
crush my skull and you would be crushing the skull of a nothing.
[*Pause*]

ERIC Are you crying.
[BERNARD *nods.* ERIC *walks over, sits next to him*]
You really are a poor pitiful person.

BERNARD Yes, I am.

ERIC I get genuinely moved by a person like you. You have no hope.

BERNARD And yet if I could surface.

ERIC How could you.

BERNARD I could have Lilliane. She would be my respectability.

ERIC Poor man. Lilliane loves me.

BERNARD But you don't love her.

ERIC She gets me many things from the Americans. She lets me sit in
her big chair in the corner. She makes my life comfortable and
dangerous at the same time.

BERNARD You could get someone else.

ERIC Lilliane was the best choice. I selected her carefully. When I
occupied the city and knew eventually the liberators were coming
and that I couldn't go home to be caught in the web, I looked for
someone to hide me. I looked for a girl with special qualities. A girl

who led a special life.

BERNARD An abstract life.

ERIC An introspective life.

BERNARD But you *could* find someone else.

ERIC I cannot surface to search.

BERNARD Neither can I. I must have Lilliane.

ERIC I could eat your ears off. And let you bleed to death.

[BERNARD *has put his hand on* ERIC'*s leg and is running it slowly up and down*]

BERNARD I could have Lilliane and forget about Jean and seeking revenge for the corruption of his body.

ERIC I could stick my fist into your mouth and force it all the way into your stomach, destroying your insides.

[BERNARD *lays his head in* ERIC'*s lap*]

BERNARD You could lead a dangerous life with someone else. You wear your trousers so tight you could meet someone so else easily.

ERIC I think I should kill you now.

[ERIC *covers* BERNARD *with his overcoat*]

BERNARD You would be killing nothing.

[BERNARD *is doing something under the overcoat*]

ERIC I have killed many nothings.

BERNARD You should wait a minute.

ERIC [*suddenly smiling*] I should do it now?

BERNARD Wait for just a minute.

ERIC [*breathing heavily*] Now?

BERNARD Soon.

ERIC [*his eyes closed*] Now?

BERNARD Soon.

ERIC Why not now.

BERNARD [*muffled*] Soon.

[*A gunshot.* ERIC *slumps.* BERNARD *struggles out from beneath the overcoat.* ERIC *falls over.* BERNARD *walks cautiously to* ERIC'*s body. Bends down. Singing, off key*]

Deutschland, Deutschland, ha-ha, ha-ha-ha.

[*Pause*]

ERIC [*opens his eyes. Struggles up onto his elbows*] That is in very bad

taste. [*coughs*] It is also a cliché. [*coughs*] I hate clichés. [*coughs, dies*]
[**BERNARD** *grabs* **ERIC**'*s ankles and begins to drag him to the grave*]
[*Blackout*]

Graveyard. LILLIANE *is standing some distance from the coffin. Hands in pockets.* BERNARD*'s head is peering up from behind the coffin*

LILLIANE Where's Eric.

BERNARD Eric who.

LILLIANE [*looking around*] Eric?!

BERNARD Don't shout. Please don't shout. You know, out there, the G ... H ... O ... U ... L ... S.

LILLIANE Where is he.

BERNARD [*standing*] He tried to kill me. He was very aggressive. He proceeded aggressively. With confidence. Too much confidence. His confidence became arrogant. Did he know he'd lost the war. Didn't you tell him. Didn't you bring him newspapers in your apartment. Didn't he ever look out the window.

LILLIANE Where is he!

BERNARD Dead. Over here. Come and look.

[*She walks over slowly. Looks down*]

LILLIANE You did that?

BERNARD He tried to kill me. You look upset. Why.

[LILLIANE *just shakes her head*]

Why.

LILLIANE I loved him.

BERNARD Ah. That's sad. Because he didn't love you. He told me he just used you.

LILLIANE I used him as well. We had an understanding.

BERNARD But you loved him.

LILLIANE Yes!

BERNARD Well, he's dead now. You can love me instead. He killed Jean, you know. He confessed. Honest. He was a murderer. A mass murderer. You made an awful mistake loving him. But I'll forgive you. As the years flow by I'll forgive you. As long as you keep me safe in your apartment. As long as you bring me things from the Americans. Or the Russians. Or whoever. Come here.

LILLIANE No.

BERNARD I scare you, don't I.

LILLIANE Yes.

[HANK *is moving up behind* BERNARD. *Slowly. A nylon stocking stretched between his hands. He is wearing a plain overcoat*]

BERNARD No. I don't scare you. I wonder why. I know. [*pointing back over his shoulder without turning*] Because of him.

[HANK *stops.* BERNARD *turns to him slowly*]

Well, look at this then. [*to* LILLIANE] A new friend? Is there no end to them. Is there no end to what they'll do for you. [*to* HANK] You should have met her brother. He had many of the same qualities.

HANK You should be letting this lady alone.

BERNARD You speak my language. But you have an accent. Would you mind taking off your coat.

HANK You upset the lady.

BERNARD [*producing a gun*] Would you mind taking off your coat.

[HANK *takes off the coat. Lets it drop*]

I recognize that uniform. I've looked at it many times over the collar of my coat. Like this. [*demonstrates, lifting his collar, his eyes peering out*] That uniform has made me behave strangely in public. And earned me many anxious moments. I don't like it. I don't like uniforms in general. They shouldn't be allowed. They always show up uninvited and cause anxiety. For example, who invited your uniform here tonight. Don't move. Please. You moved. Just a bit, I know. But you moved. Don't.

HANK She said she needed my help.

BERNARD Did she tell you you might be putting your life in danger.

HANK I don't care.

BERNARD Do you love her.

HANK I don't care.

BERNARD Does she love you.

HANK I don't care.

BERNARD [*to* LILLIANE] He has a very limited vocabulary. These are complex issues we're dealing with. How is he going to manage with so few words.

LILLIANE Why don't you let him go.

BERNARD He tried to kill me. He's under your spell. He'll try to kill me again. [*to* HANK] Won't you.

HANK [*pounding his fists against his thighs*] I don't care!

BERNARD [*to* LILLIANE] You know, I think this man has problems of his own. It would have been kind of you not to involve him in ours. But of course you had to, just in case Eric failed. Or perhaps he was brought here to kill Eric if he didn't fail. You're often difficult to figure out, Lilliane.

HANK I don't care about nothin' anymore. You hear me?

BERNARD [*to* HANK] I think I understand you.

HANK I don't care!

BERNARD I don't care either.

HANK Jesus. Jesus. Jesus!

BERNARD [*laughs*] I don't care.

HANK Jesus I tell you. I don't care. Really. I don't.

BERNARD [*laughing*] Me neither. Me neither.

HANK Jesus!

[HANK *attacks* BERNARD. BERNARD *shoots him.* HANK *falls. Dead. Pause*]

BERNARD I did understand him. I did. I saw into his brain. It was broken into little pieces. And the pieces were talking to each other. Just like mine. Exactly like mine. [*looks at* LILLIANE. *Smiles*] In my darker moments, of course. You don't look well.

LILLIANE I'm going to pass out.

BERNARD Haven't eaten? Can I get you something. Chocolate? Biscuits? Some wine? A cigarette? Chocolate? Biscuits? Nylons? Winter boots? Coffee? Furniture? Electric heaters? Trips to the country? A week in the Mediterranean? What is it you want, Lilliane. What is it you haven't got yet.

LILLIANE I want you dead. Rotting in the ground. Off the world. Out of my mind.

BERNARD Be careful or I'll report you.

LILLIANE Be careful or I'll have you killed.

BERNARD You already tried that. Twice. Which reminds me. Did I tell you how Eric died. A nasty wound to the groin. He was aiming for my head. I nudged the barrel away with my nose and repointed. Like this. [*demonstrates with a finger*] Disgusting image, isn't it.

[BERNARD *is in a daze. He walks over to* HANK*'s corpse. And sings, off key*]

O-O say can you see, ha-ha, ha-ha-ha.

[*He stares at* HANK*'s corpse. Turns to* LILLIANE. *Speaks*]

Don't look like that. He killed your brother. And he was a fascist.

[LILLIANE *looks at the grave. At* HANK. *At the grave again*]

LILLIANE Eric was with me the night Jean was killed.

BERNARD [*pointing at* HANK] He was a fascist. No. [*pointing at the grave*] He was a fascist. Capable of dark magic. Perhaps he was in two places at once.

LILLIANE The Communists killed Jean.

BERNARD Perhaps Eric was capable of being in two places at once as two different people. [*points at* HANK *and the grave*] Perhaps he was where Jean was killed as a Communist.

[LILLIANE *starts off*]

Where are you going.

LILLIANE Home. I'm tired.

BERNARD Don't go. We have plans to make.

LILLIANE [*leaving*] I'm tired!

BERNARD If you go, I'll follow you. And when I'm through following you, I'll report you. I'll tell the story of Eric and his cigarettes.

LILLIANE I don't care.

BERNARD Stop!

[*She leaves*]

Good. It's good that you stopped. Now that you've stopped we can talk. Make plans. About our life together. Certainly there will be some expedience about it, but also great comfort. And safety. Don't move. You moved. That's better. [*reaches into his pocket. Produces a chocolate bar, bites off a piece*] Now where were we ...

[INSPECTOR CLAIR *comes on*]

INSPECTOR Bernard.

[*But* BERNARD *is just eating the chocolate. His eyes are glazed*]

Bernard.

[*Without thinking,* BERNARD *lifts his gun and points it in the general direction of the* INSPECTOR, *who anticipates this and has his own gun pointing at* BERNARD. *Pause.* BERNARD *is still in a daze. The*

INSPECTOR *slowly lowers his gun. Stares at* BERNARD. BERNARD *looks at the* INSPECTOR. *Confused. The* INSPECTOR *looks at* BERNARD *for a long time. Suddenly he lifts his gun and fires.* BERNARD *falls. Dead*]
[*Blackout*]

A bistro. LILLIANE *is sitting at a table, staring into her drink.*
INSPECTOR CLAIR *comes on. They look at each other. Pause*

INSPECTOR May I join you.
LILLIANE If you want.
INSPECTOR [*sitting*] Thank you.
LILLIANE Would you like a drink.
INSPECTOR No. Thank you. How have you been keeping.
LILLIANE I'm all right.
INSPECTOR You don't look well.
  [LILLIANE *shrugs. Pause*]
  Perhaps you're not getting enough sleep. Perhaps your neighbours
  are noisy and keep you up. If that's the case, I could pay them a
  visit.
LILLIANE No. Thank you. I'm all right.
INSPECTOR Food?
LILLIANE What.
INSPECTOR Do you get enough food.
LILLIANE Yes.
  [*Pause*]
INSPECTOR Just a general anxiety then. Like so many of us.
LILLIANE Yes. I think so.
  [*Pause*]
INSPECTOR I'm afraid I have some bad news for you ... That friend of
  your brother. Bernard ... He's dead.
  [*She looks at him*]
  He killed himself. Of course he was not a stable personality. I saw
  that immediately when I questioned him. He was obviously
  capable of extreme action. Was that your opinion of him.
LILLIANE I didn't know him very well.
INSPECTOR I would say you were fortunate in that.
  [*Pause*]
  Something else. This might be more painful I'm afraid. He is the
  one who killed your brother.

LILLIANE Are you sure.

INSPECTOR Pretty much. Yes.

LILLIANE Your investigation proved this?

INSPECTOR We found a note on his body. A confession. They don't usually lie under those circumstances ... Are you all right. I'm sorry, I—

LILLIANE No. It's just that I don't understand why. I mean—

INSPECTOR Jealousy. In the note, Bernard said he was jealous of Jean's involvement with some German soldier. You see these friendships, Jean and Bernard, the soldier. They were intimate. You probably didn't know.

LILLIANE Did the note say anything else.

INSPECTOR No. Not really.

LILLIANE Nothing about me.

INSPECTOR No. Does that surprise you.

LILLIANE It's just that you say Bernard was unstable. He could have tried to slander me. Perhaps he was jealous of me and Jean as well. I mean, he could have imagined all sorts of things.

INSPECTOR Perhaps he thought of it. Perhaps he had a moment of generosity and decided to leave you out of it. Such an unstable personality, you see. Unpredictable. Damaged by the war. Severely damaged.

LILLIANE Yes. I think he was.

INSPECTOR But now it's over. Tied up. Complete. You must think of the future. I'm sorry about your brother. But think of the future. Eat. Sleep properly ...

LILLIANE Would you like a drink. I'll get one for you if you want.

INSPECTOR No. Thank you ... Here, I have something for you. [*takes out a card*] This is the address of a new company that is going to make films. I have a friend. I talked to him about you. Go and see him.

LILLIANE I have no experience.

INSPECTOR This is a new company. No one has any experience. I think you would be good in films.

LILLIANE I'd like to be in films.

INSPECTOR Take the address.

[*She takes the card*]

LILLIANE I'd like to be in films. I really would. I saw one last week. American. No. English … Anyway, I would have liked to be in it. I sat there thinking that I would like to live in a film. Just be alive in a film and nowhere else. I'd like that. I think somehow that would be better.

INSPECTOR Perhaps it would.

LILLIANE You've talked to them about me?

INSPECTOR Yes.

LILLIANE What did you say. What are they expecting me to be like.

INSPECTOR Just be yourself.

LILLIANE Would you like a drink. Maybe we can talk. You can tell me how to behave.

INSPECTOR No. I have to be going. Just be yourself. You'll be all right. [*stands*]

LILLIANE And that will be enough for them, you think.

INSPECTOR I'm sure it will. Goodbye.

LILLIANE Will I see you again.

INSPECTOR No … you'll be all right.

[*He leaves.* LILLIANE *takes out a cigarette*]

[*Blackout*]

SCENE TWELVE

Under a streetlamp. INSPECTOR CLAIR. *Hands deep in his pockets*

INSPECTOR What you can't make clear, you should at least make
complete. Who is responsible for crime when for so long there has
been no law. Can there be guilt where there is no innocence. Before
the war I had a chief inspector who taught me many things ...
including never to ask myself questions like that ... that police
work was simply a matter of jurisdiction and enforcement. But that
was before the war. Before I met Bernard ... and found myself
standing in the darkness of that graveyard listening to his pathetic
broken brain with its little pieces talking to each other ... I have
decided that the murder I was investigating was just something
that happened because of the war. Truth is, I don't know if Bernard
killed Jean. Or if Lilliane killed him to protect her lover. Or if the
Communists killed him because he was stupid ... I have decided
that none of that matters ... because Bernard had to die. He was
just a part of what we have become. But it was the saddest most
unpredictable part. Where would he go. How would he live. How
could the rest of us survive and prosper with him out on the streets
making other people sad and unpredictable too ... My behaviour
in this matter is obviously open to criticism. [*shrugs*] But I think
behaviour depends on circumstance. And circumstance often
depends on luck ... Lilliane will go on to become one of this
country's most successful film actresses. My luck will be to always
see and hear Bernard in the film that runs inside my head ...
[*He drops his cigarette. Snuffs it out with his foot*]
[*Blackout*]
[*End*]

THE ART OF WAR

The Art of War was commissioned by Simon Fraser University (Vancouver) as the keynote address to the Conference on Art and Reality, August 1982. It was first produced professionally by the Factory Theatre at Toronto Workshop Productions in February 1983 with the following cast:

POWER David Bolt
JAMIE Jim Henshaw
HACKMAN David Fox
BROWN Dean Hawes
KARLA Diane D'Aquila
HEATHER Susan Purdy

Director: George F. Walker
Stage Manager: Peter Freund
Lighting and Set Designer: Jim Plaxton
Costume Designer: Miro Kinch
Music composed by: John Roby

Persons

TYRONE M. POWER
JAMIE MCLEAN
JOHN HACKMAN
BROWNIE BROWN, *Hackman's aide, late forties*
KARLA MENDEZ, *Hackman's guest*
HEATHER MASTERSON, *a local citizen*

Place

In and around a large summer estate in Nova Scotia.

Time

In the dead of summer.

Note

If an intermission is included, it should occur between Scenes Four and Five.

PROLOGUE

The murder of Paul Reinhardt
Choreographed to heartbeat-rushing music
Just before midnight at JOHN HACKMAN'*s summer estate. The house is*
a translucent glass bunker set into the side of a hill. The audience sees
a man looking in the front of the bunker, then disappearing around
the side. He is wearing an overcoat and a hat and he walks with a
cane. The room is dimly lit, but we can make out a huge map of the
world with flickering lights, some high-tech equipment and a few
filing cabinets. The man enters from the side. Begins looking around.
Takes out a camera and starts photographing everything. Looking
through the files. In the distance we hear the voices of two men.
Talking. Laughing. Getting closer. The man in the room hears them.
Panics. Tries to tidy the room. Gives up. Tries to escape, but can't find
an exit other than the one the voices seem to be near. Suddenly and
simultaneously the two men are in the room. They are wearing
evening clothes. The man in the overcoat throws himself with his arms
out against the downstage wall of the bunker. It doesn't break and he
remains splayed there. One of the men turns the lights in the room to
full. The man in the overcoat tries to run between them. He is stopped.
Thrown back. One of the men in evening clothes produces a long, thin
knife. Advances. The man in the overcoat tries to rush out past him.
He is stopped. Stabbed. Stabbed again. He falls. The men in evening
clothes look at each other. Then one turns away
[*Blackout*]

SCENE ONE

Midnight
The beach. Two figures approaching. HACKMAN *is carrying a*
flashlight. BROWN *is carrying a corpse wrapped in a blanket over his*
shoulder

HACKMAN Is he heavy, Brown.

BROWN No, sir. Light as a feather. A burden of love.

HACKMAN Anywhere around here should do. Put him down.

[BROWN *drops the corpse.* HACKMAN *starts to dig*]

BROWN I'll do that, sir. You'll get yourself covered in sand.

HACKMAN Thank you, Brown.

[*He hands* BROWN *the shovel.* BROWN *starts to dig*]

It's a lovely night, isn't it.

BROWN Yes, sir. Shame to waste it in the company of strangers.

HACKMAN Oh, he's no stranger, Brown. He's the enemy.

BROWN He was the enemy ... And not a very good one if I may say so, sir.

HACKMAN You killed him well, Brown. He didn't have a chance.

BROWN Thank you, sir.

HACKMAN Reminded me of the killing you used to do in the old days.

BROWN Afraid I'm a little out of practice. Had to stick it in twice.

HACKMAN Well, perhaps you rushed it a bit. Didn't take time to appreciate the act fully. Nevertheless, it was an exciting thing to watch. It had an artistic touch. You're a bit of an artist in your own way, did you know that Brown.

BROWN Never thought of it that way, sir.

HACKMAN You can you know, from now on, if you want.

BROWN I'm not much on art and artists, sir.

HACKMAN Well, it's all how you look at it. I suppose I'll be meeting a lot of artists in my new job. Most of them won't be very good I imagine. This dead man was an artist of sorts. A writer.

BROWN How deep do you want this, sir.

HACKMAN Oh, not too deep. I don't suppose anyone will be looking for him. Yes. It's a lovely night. Stop for a moment, Brown. Look at it. The night.

BROWN [*stops. Looks around vacantly. Then looks at the corpse. Smiles*]
Why you're right, sir. It is.

HACKMAN You see, Brown. You just have to take the time to appreciate
things. A lovely night. A lovely killing.

[BROWN *starts to dig*]

[*Blackout*]

SCENE TWO

Dawn
On a nearby cliff. POWER *and* JAMIE. POWER *is looking down*
through a pair of binoculars. JAMIE *is sitting on the grass, chin in his*
palms. There is a pile of camping gear nearby
POWER *is middle-aged. Balding. With a walrus mustache. Glasses.*
Wearing an overcoat. JAMIE *is in his early twenties. Sort of wiry. In*
jeans and a sweater

JAMIE What are you doing.

POWER Looking for signs of strange behaviour.

JAMIE Well, you can look at us, Power. I'd say our behaviour is pretty
strange. Sitting on top of a cliff a thousand miles from home at five
o'clock in the morning.

POWER The guy who lives down there is a maniac.

JAMIE You seem to be developing an obsession with him. Why.

POWER He's a maniac. Whatya mean, obsession. I'm not obsessed. He's
up to something, that's all. Something vile and dangerous I'll bet.
He needs to be watched.

JAMIE Then maybe we should tell the authorities.

POWER 'Authorities'?! You make it sound like an agency of the Lord or
something. This guy down there, this John C. Hackman, retired
general, is the authority. He's an adviser to a goddamn cabinet
minister in the goddamn government. And he's a maniac. When he
was adviser to the Minister of Defence he was suspected of cooking
up bizarre arms deals with lunatic Third World politicos and
military types.

JAMIE That's why he was fired?

POWER He wasn't fired. They just got him off the front pages. They
shuffled him over to the Ministry of Culture.

JAMIE I didn't know we had a Minister of Culture. What does he do.

POWER It's a secret. I'm not even sure the Minister of Culture knows.
It's not exactly a high-priority position. And just to prove it they
make Hackman his special adviser. The guy is a career soldier. His
idea of a cultural event is bombing an opera house.

JAMIE I think your bias is screwing up your judgement, as usual. I haven't noticed anything strange about him.

POWER You've only been working for him for a week. He's being cautious around you. Checking out your references. Did you take care of your references.

JAMIE No problem.

POWER Be more specific.

JAMIE When they check they'll find that I've been a gardener at some of the best homes in the area.

POWER How did you manage that.

JAMIE As one private detective to another, it took some doin' but it was done.

POWER Look. How many times do I have to tell you. We're not private detectives. I'm just a concerned citizen. And you're a punk who follows me around.

JAMIE Well, at least I'm a punk with a job. Good thing my cover on this one is to be gainfully employed because I'm starting to get the impression we don't have a client. We stand to make zippo on this case. Unless your friend Reinhardt is going to pay us.

POWER Reinhardt is dead. Hackman killed him.

JAMIE You know this for sure.

POWER I sense it for sure.

JAMIE All you know is he hasn't come home.

POWER He told me he was coming down here because he had a tip that Hackman was up to something. Reinhardt was the kind to dig in. He'd go right into the belly of the mess and all its danger. He wasn't subtle, but he was a good newspaperman.

JAMIE Oh, Jesus. You knew this guy Reinhardt when you were a reporter. You didn't tell me that. Is he your age.

POWER Just about. Why.

JAMIE For chrissake, Power. He's probably a disillusioned paranoid drunk just like you were when I met you.

POWER Shut up.

JAMIE You're all the same. That generation of yours. Scandals in every corner. Corruption on every level. I'm going home. If Reinhardt is dead, he died of alcohol poisoning.

POWER Reinhardt didn't drink. He was a whatyacallit.

JAMIE A junkie?

POWER Shut up. He was Born Again.

JAMIE Yeah. Well, I was only born once but it wasn't yesterday. And
I'm not putting my life in jeopardy under these increasingly
dubious circumstances. You led me to believe this was a simple job
of observation and that there was a lot of money to be made.

POWER Because that's the only way I can get you to do anything. By
talking about financial profit. You're a greedy money-grabbing
amoral smart-ass.

JAMIE And you're a cause in search of an issue. Life is precious, Power.
I don't want to waste it trying to reconstruct your social
conscience.

POWER The quality of life is precious. Life itself is meaningless.

JAMIE Quality is defined by quantity. Money buys you both.

POWER No. Money is just—

JAMIE I don't want to talk about this on this goddamn cliff at five
o'clock in the morning!

POWER Fine. We won't. We'll just do our jobs. You will report back to
work at Hackman's and keep your eyes and ears open and I'll
continue my investigation.

JAMIE Why.

POWER Why for me. Or why for you.

JAMIE Just why.

POWER Why for me is I think Hackman is up to something evil,
dangerous and destructive. Why for you is because you're the
smart-ass punk who has been following me around for a year and a
half and is now going to do something to pay me back for letting
you do it.

JAMIE Wrong. Why for me is I'm learning a trade. Because realize it or
not you're not the useless investigative reporter you used to be.
You've become a pretty fair private detective and I'm your partner.

POWER All right. Look at life in your own strange brittle romantic way.
You're a hard case. Just do your job. And when I show up at
Hackman's try to avoid recognizing me.

JAMIE How are you going to get in there.

POWER I think I've got a contact in the town who can help me. I'm meeting her for breakfast. I've got to get going.

JAMIE Why so early.

POWER Because it's five miles and I have to walk.

JAMIE Why didn't you rent a car.

POWER With what. I spent almost everything I had on my camping gear.

JAMIE We're pitiful. We're pathetic. We're poor. And why. Because you take these cases where there's no money involved.

POWER I'm poor because I'm a freelance writer with diminishing talent. You're poor because you don't work. You just follow me around. Reality, boy. Try it out. Goodbye. [*starts off. Stops*] Do me a favour. Throw my tent.

JAMIE Where.

POWER Right where it is.

JAMIE Oh, you mean put it up.

POWER That's what I said.

JAMIE The expression is 'pitch the tent,' Power. Not 'throw it.' Your grasp of contemporary idiom is scary.

POWER Goodbye.

[*He leaves.* JAMIE *starts to unpack the camping gear*]

JAMIE 'Reality, boy. Try it out.' The man's in middle age standing on top of a cliff talking about politicians and Third World lunatics and the quality of life and he worries about my sense of reality. He's gotta be kidding. What's this. [*from inside a duffle bag he produces a rifle with a telescopic sight on it*] He's gotta be kidding. Seriously.

[*Blackout*]

SCENE THREE

Midday
The patio and garden of HACKMAN'*s house.* HACKMAN, *in shirtsleeves,*
is sitting in a lawn chair reading a newspaper
KARLA MENDEZ *is pacing. She is a tall, dark, angular woman in her*
late thirties. Tastefully, simply dressed. Wearing dark glasses. She speaks
with a slight accent

KARLA The phone is not ringing.

HACKMAN Be patient.

KARLA He was to call at noon. It is now noon plus twenty.

HACKMAN He'll call.

KARLA I think something has happened. At the airport. It always
happens at the airport.

HACKMAN You worry too much. His papers are in order. I arranged
them myself.

KARLA You are not God.

HACKMAN I never said I was.

KARLA You speak sometimes like God. 'I did *that*. So this is what will
happen.' 'I made this arrangement so it is all right.' Only God can
make these assurances and you are not God. You are only a
politician. You work for the 'Minister of Culture.' [*laughs abruptly*]

HACKMAN How many more jokes are you going to make about that.

KARLA I think it is funny. I think it is ridiculous.

HACKMAN Ridiculous enough to be out of the limelight. But not too
ridiculous to keep the connections that allow me to make certain
arrangements.

KARLA We'll see. If he calls. We'll see.

HACKMAN Stop pacing.

KARLA I'm making you nervous?

HACKMAN It's annoying.

KARLA Do I care. Did I ask to be sent here.

HACKMAN I thought you did. I thought you wanted to be close to me.

KARLA I have not wanted to be close to you for over three years. Being
close to you is being close to disappointment.

HACKMAN Remember the month we spent together in Panama City?

KARLA No. See? I am over you. I even have no memory of you.

HACKMAN In Panama City you were not disappointed.

KARLA You misunderstand what I mean by disappointment. You misunderstand what I mean by everything. I should have taken my father's advice about you.

HACKMAN What did he say.

KARLA He said 'Keep it strictly business with that man. He is good for business. Bad for everything else.'

HACKMAN Your father is a great man and he will be a great leader for your people but about things that concern you he has no judgement. He's just a father.

KARLA Nevertheless. You soon proved him right. Several times in fact.

HACKMAN Fidelity. That's what this is about. Loyalty to you.

KARLA Or to anything. [*checks her watch*] Call the airport. Perhaps the flight is delayed.

HACKMAN If it's delayed, it's delayed. Be patient. He'll call.

[JAMIE *comes on, walking by, pushing a wheelbarrow full of rocks*]

You. Stop. Excuse me, what's your name again.

JAMIE Jamie. Jamie McLean.

HACKMAN Yes. Well, Jamie. Would you mind telling me what you're doing.

JAMIE Taking these rocks over to that flower bed.

HACKMAN Aren't those the same rocks you removed from that flower bed yesterday.

JAMIE No, sir. These are the rocks I took from around the shrubs out front and put around the rose bushes at the side. The rocks I took from that flower bed I put around the shrubs out front. You're probably wondering what rocks I'm going to put back around the rose bushes now that these are gone.

HACKMAN No, I'm wondering why, since you've been employed as my gardener for over a week, all you've done is move rocks around.

JAMIE It's my personal concept in gardening. Work from the outside in. Get the look of it before you deal with the substance.

KARLA Typically North American.

HACKMAN Some of the roses are dying.

JAMIE Don't worry about it, sir. They'll be all right as soon as I get the right rocks in place. Roses are sensitive. They know they're not yet properly showcased.

HACKMAN You're not a flake are you, Jamie. You talk like a flake.

JAMIE Trust me, sir.

HACKMAN You come highly recommended. But you talk like a flake and you seem to be obsessed with rocks.

JAMIE Trust me, sir. I'm an innovator.

HACKMAN See, that's what I mean. 'I'm an innovator.' What kind of thing is that for a gardener to say.

JAMIE Sorry. Would you prefer I kept my conversation more rustic.

KARLA Really, John. So much fuss over a bunch of flowers.

HACKMAN I'm very fond of my garden! It's a kind of passion.

[*The phone rings. It is on a small table next to* HACKMAN. *He answers it*]

[*on phone*] Yes … Good … Yes … Goodbye. [*hangs up. To* KARLA] He's here. You should leave. He's expecting you.

KARLA Where.

HACKMAN The airport.

KARLA The airport?

HACKMAN Yes. [*to* JAMIE] Excuse me.

JAMIE Yeah.

HACKMAN Why are you standing there.

JAMIE Awaiting further instructions, sir. Are there any.

HACKMAN Yes. Stop messing around with rocks. And take care of my garden. I love my garden! Understand?

JAMIE [*gulps*] You bet. Goodbye ma'am. Goodbye, sir.

[*He goes off, leaving the wheelbarrow*]

HACKMAN Yes. The airport.

KARLA Dangerous.

HACKMAN It's arranged. I'm having him watched. I don't want him leaving there. He'll be too hard to follow.

KARLA I don't like doing this kind of business in public places.

HACKMAN Just go. It's arranged.

KARLA You go.

HACKMAN He won't talk to me. It has to be you. That's why you were sent here. Now go.

[KARLA *stares at him for a moment. Then starts off*]

Oh, Karla.

KARLA What.

HACKMAN [*reaches under his lawn chair. Produces an attaché case*] It's money. He'll want money.

KARLA No he won't.

HACKMAN He's doing this for money, Karla.

KARLA I don't believe that. He's doing it out of loyalty to my father.

HACKMAN Well, if you're absolutely sure, don't take it.

[KARLA *mutters an obscenity. She grabs the attaché case. Leaves.*
HACKMAN *returns to his newspaper.* JAMIE *comes back on sheepishly.
Starts to push the wheelbarrow off quietly.* HACKMAN *peers over his
newspaper.* JAMIE *catches his eye*]

JAMIE I don't have any plans for these rocks, sir. It's just that I need the wheelbarrow for ... for ... dirt.

HACKMAN Dirt?

JAMIE Soil.

[HACKMAN *disappears behind the newspaper.* JAMIE *leaves. Shaking
his head.* BROWN *comes on. In a crisp business suit*]

BROWN Heather Masterson is here to see you.

HACKMAN Send her away.

BROWN She claims to have an appointment.

HACKMAN She's lying. I'm on vacation. This is my summer residence. I don't make appointments here.

BROWN You do when you are very drunk, sir. You were at a party together last Wednesday night. You probably made the appointment then.

HACKMAN Let her in.

[BROWN *goes off.* JAMIE *comes on carrying a small bush. Whistling.
Crosses in front of* HACKMAN. HACKMAN *watches him leave.* HEATHER
MASTERSON *and* POWER *come out of the house onto the patio. She is
in her late twenties. Preppie.* POWER *is in shirtsleeves. His coat thrown
over his shoulder. Hands in his pockets. Sweating*]

HEATHER Good morning, General.

HACKMAN Hello.

HEATHER I'm glad you remembered I was coming. I was afraid you wouldn't. [*to* POWER] The General came to my birthday party last week. He and my daddy are old friends. My daddy got him a little bit loaded and I decided to take the opportunity to bamboozle an official appointment. [*to* HACKMAN] Oh, I'm sorry. This is Mr. Power. He was just dying to meet you and I didn't think you'd mind. Do you mind.

HACKMAN I'm not sure.

[*He looks* POWER *over. Then extends a hand. They shake*]

Mr. Power.

POWER General. I've followed your career for many years.

HACKMAN Idle curiosity?

HEATHER Mr. Power is a writer.

HACKMAN Really. Of what.

HEATHER Oh, you can talk to him in a minute. I've got the official appointment, remember.

HACKMAN Very well. Would you like to sit down.

HEATHER No, thanks.

POWER I will if you don't mind. I had a long walk this morning. And I think I'm dying. [*sits in a lawn chair*]

HEATHER You're about twenty pounds overweight.

POWER It's the fresh air. They say it's like poison if you're not used to it.

HEATHER A man your age has to be careful. My daddy is careful.

POWER Your daddy is rich. He can afford to be careful. I'm poor. I have to take chances.

HEATHER I didn't get that. [*to* HACKMAN] Did you.

HACKMAN Heather. I thought you had something to ask me. I've got a busy day ahead of me.

HEATHER Right. Sorry. Well, as you know I am a member of the local Historical Board. It's great. It's local. It's historical.

[POWER *looks at her*]

And we have been trying unsuccessfully for two years to open our own museum. So when we found out that you had been made an adviser to the Minister of Culture we were sure you could—

HACKMAN Excuse me. [*picks up his phone, buzzes*] Brownie, get out here. [*hangs up*] This might save us both some time.

[BROWN *comes out*]

Do we have anything to do with the allocation of funds to museums.

BROWN No, sir. Minister of Education handles that.

HACKMAN Sorry, Heather.

HEATHER But surely the Minister of Culture—

HACKMAN Heather. It's a new position. Just created. We don't know exactly what it means yet ourselves. [*laughs*]

POWER When will you.

HACKMAN I beg your pardon.

POWER When can we expect an official statement of the Minister's responsibilities.

HACKMAN You asked that question like a journalist, Mr. Power.

POWER Is that good.

HEATHER Listen, General, I promised the Historical Board that you would help.

HACKMAN Heather. That conversation is over.

HEATHER Well that really pisses me off. You didn't even listen, and that really is a piss-off! I'm leaving! I mean it.

[*Pause, no response. She starts off*]

I'll wait for you in the car, Mr. Power.

[*She leaves.* BROWN *starts to follow her.* HACKMAN *signals him to stay.* BROWN *stands beside* HACKMAN. *Arms folded*]

HACKMAN The name Power sounds familiar ...

[BROWN *whispers in* HACKMAN'*s ear.* HACKMAN *smiles*]

There was a T.M. Power who used to write a syndicated political column. Is that you.

POWER Yes.

HACKMAN I hated every word you wrote.

POWER In my own way, so did I.

HACKMAN Hated with a passion. Hated all journalism. Hated the media in general. Of course that was when I was adviser to the Minister of Defence. Now that I'm working for the Minister of Culture I have a different attitude.

POWER You just don't give a damn. Politically speaking, I mean.

HACKMAN The Minister of Culture officially supports the power of the written word. And the spoken word.

POWER What about song lyrics.

HACKMAN [*smiles*] Oh, he has a Deputy Minister that handles music. I'm afraid the Minister is a bit of an ignoramus in that area.

POWER Please don't apologize for him. I mean think about it. There are only twelve notes. Musicians just move them around. What's all the fuss.

HACKMAN I get the feeling you sometimes speak to hear your own voice, Mr. Power.

POWER It's a habit I got into when I was covering the capital. Talking to politicians. There was nothing coming my way. I had to compensate.

HACKMAN Why did you want to meet me.

POWER I'm working freelance now. I'm fishing around for something to write about.

HACKMAN You think the creation of a Minister of Culture is a joke.

POWER Don't you?

HACKMAN What do you know about me.

POWER You're a soldier.

HACKMAN I was a soldier.

POWER Some old soldiers never die. They just start pan-American right-wing organizations.

HACKMAN That of course is an old and unfounded rumour.

POWER Then why were you moved off the defence portfolio.

HACKMAN I wanted a change. A chance for a middle-aged man to develop a new passion.

POWER Come off it, General. Men like you have room for only one passion in their lives. And yours is not art and culture.

HACKMAN What is it then.

POWER Oh God. Well, let's simplify it. Let's call it the communist menace.

HACKMAN [*groans*] And you don't believe in the communist menace.

POWER Actually I do. The communist menace. And the fascist menace. The menace of the Church. The menace of channelled information. The menace of ignorance. The menace of indifference. The menace of war. I'm sort of a menace specialist.

HACKMAN No. You're just a liberal.

POWER What's that supposed to mean.

HACKMAN You think the human race is going on a journey. To peace and enlightenment. And that it's a journey everyone has the ability and the right to make.

POWER And you don't.

HACKMAN Let's just say I don't insist upon it. And another thing. You probably have an unholy fear of something which I take more or less for granted.

POWER What.

HACKMAN The vast darkness.

[BROWN *looks at* POWER. *Smiles*]

POWER The vast darkness. The existential version?

HACKMAN No, let's simplify it. Let's call it war. The new war. The inevitable destruction of everything. Life-ending war. But even without war, it ends. Everything we build now will be ruins in, what, a thousand years, anyway.

[*He looks at* BROWN. BROWN *gestures a shrug with his hand*]

War is a way of taking temporary control, that's all. Try thinking about war that way and it won't scare you so much. Something wrong?

POWER [*rubbing his forehead*] I've suddenly developed one hell of a headache.

[HACKMAN *signals* BROWN]

BROWN Sir, it's getting late. You have several letters to dictate. And a telephone call to make. Miss Masterson is waiting in the car for this gentleman. And also ... also ... [*rubs his head*]

HACKMAN [*checks his watch*] I didn't realize it was getting so late.

POWER Time flies when you're talking about fun stuff.

[BROWN *is rubbing his head furiously*]

HACKMAN Are you all right, Brownie.

BROWN Sir. In a minute, sir.

POWER What's wrong with him.

BROWN [*advancing*] War wound!

HACKMAN Quite serious when it flares up.

POWER Sorry to hear that. [*rubs his own forehead. Stands*]

[HACKMAN *puts his arm around* POWER]

HACKMAN Look, Mr. Power, if you're going to be around for a few days perhaps we could talk again. Actually I'd like to insist upon it. If you're going to write anything about me, I'd like a chance to balance some of your preconceptions. Next time we'll talk about art not war. You'll see that there's more to me than most people think.

POWER Oh, I'm sure of that.

HACKMAN I really want to make the Ministry of Culture work. You could say I'm like anyone else who's new on the job and anxious to make a good impression. How can I reach you.

POWER Through Heather.

HACKMAN You're staying with the Mastersons?

POWER No. But I'll be contacting her.

HACKMAN Then where are you staying.

POWER Around. Here and there.

HACKMAN Why so secretive.

POWER Habit.

[*He frees himself from* HACKMAN. *Starts off. Stops*]

By the way. How did you get on with Paul Reinhardt.

HACKMAN I'm sorry. I don't know what you mean. Who is he.

POWER A journalist friend of mine. He was coming down here to interview you. Never showed up, eh?

HACKMAN Not as far as I know. Brownie?

BROWN No, sir.

POWER Odd. [*rubs his head*]

HACKMAN How bad is that headache.

POWER I'll live.

HACKMAN That's it. Think positively.

BROWN I'll show you out. [*rubs his forehead again*]

POWER No, thanks. I can find my own way. You better get some rest.

[BROWN *just looks at him.* POWER *leaves*]

HACKMAN Three things. Find out what he's been up to since he stopped writing that ridiculous column. Find out what his connection is to Heather Masterson. Find out what he and our late friend Paul Reinhardt had in common besides the fact that they were both bad writers.

[JAMIE *walks by carrying a bunch of flowers*]

What are you doing with those flowers.

JAMIE It's a surprise, sir.

[*He leaves*]

HACKMAN One more thing. Check that kid's references out again. He's murdering my garden. I love that garden!

[*Blackout*]

SCENE FOUR

Late evening
On the cliff. The tent is up. The area is lit by a gas lantern placed on a
campstool. POWER *is lying unconscious on his sleeping bag, half in and*
half out of the tent. An empty liquor bottle beside him. Sound of
someone approaching
JAMIE *comes on, cautiously*

JAMIE Power? Power, it's me. Don't shoot.
[*He sees* POWER]
Tyrone.
[*He goes to him*]
He's dead. [*bends down*] He's dead drunk. I knew it would come to
this. The man has no self-discipline. He is doomed to a life of self-
abuse.
[*He shakes* POWER]
Power. Power, wake up, you're disgusting.
[POWER *whimpers, twitches*]
Don't whimper. It's really pitiful when you whimper. Wake up.
[*He shakes him*]
POWER [*raises an arm. Speaks just above a whisper*] Leave me alone.
JAMIE Wake up!
POWER Leave me alone. Please! [*whimpers*]
JAMIE Stop whimpering!
[*He shakes him violently.* POWER *sits up suddenly*]
POWER What's going on?!
[JAMIE *stands. Moves away*]
What were you doing. Trying to pick my pocket? Looking for loose
change?
JAMIE You were having a bad dream. I thought I'd better wake you up.
POWER What time is it. I must have dozed off.
JAMIE Give me a break. You were drunk. You passed out. I thought
you were through with the booze. Don't you know how disgusting
you are when you drink.
POWER A temporary relapse.

JAMIE How many times do I have to tell you. You're an alcoholic. You have a serious drinking problem.

POWER [*getting up slowly*] No, you have a serious drinking problem. A man has a few sips and you get all sweaty and start sermonizing. You have an unnatural fear that anyone who touches liquor will turn out like your father.

JAMIE Leave my father out of this.

POWER Look, Jamie. All I'm saying is that I'm not a common drunk like he was. [*pouring himself a coffee from a thermos*]

JAMIE Oh, no. Not you. You drink for the pain in the universe and the soul of mankind. You're not a common drunk. You're a common pretentious drunk.

POWER It was Hackman. He drove me to it.

JAMIE Power. I was eavesdropping. I overheard your entire conversation. He sounded perfectly rational. You sounded perfectly obnoxious.

POWER He drove me to being obnoxious. His kind always does. A knee-jerk reaction. What do you mean he sounded rational. Didn't you hear him talking about the vast darkness.

JAMIE He was egging you on. It was a joke.

POWER It was no joke. It was his definition of reality. He was speaking from the heart of his moral code.

JAMIE I didn't understand a word of it.

POWER That's because you don't have a moral code of your own to cross-reference with. He was speaking from the heart of his moral code and the heart of my moral code picked up the signals and got very, very depressed.

JAMIE And made you go out and buy a bottle of scotch.

POWER No. I had it with me. I had a feeling I might need it before we were through.

JAMIE Yeah. Well, anticipation is the better part of cowardice.

POWER I'm not afraid of him. He just depresses me.

JAMIE Oh yeah? [*picks up the duffle bag and takes out the rifle*] Well, if you're not afraid of him what are you doing with this.

POWER He killed Reinhardt. I know he killed him. I had a feeling about it when I was there. A kind of mental picture. And he's up to something!

JAMIE Are you going to shoot him down, Power.

POWER Someone has to shoot him down.

JAMIE What.

POWER I was speaking metaphorically.

JAMIE Oh, so this is a metaphor. It's not a rifle. And you're not going to shoot him because you're not afraid of him even though you saw him kill your friend Reinhardt in one of your moments of psychic clarity because he's up to something which is vaguely concerned with some lunatic Third World politico and you want to find out what it is. Or maybe you don't want to find out what it is. You just want to create a mental metaphor for what it is. Then why do you have this *fucking rifle!*

POWER Because he's dangerous!

JAMIE And you're afraid of him!

POWER Yes!

JAMIE Thank you. I thank you. All of us who desperately believe in holding on to reality thank you.

[*Pause*]

Power?

POWER What.

JAMIE I'm afraid of him too.

POWER Why. What did he say.

JAMIE It's not what he says. It's how he says it. And it's who he hangs around with. That guy Brown.

POWER Killer eyes.

JAMIE Yeah. You noticed them, eh. He's an ex-commando. A sergeant-major.

POWER How'd you find that out.

JAMIE He told me.

POWER Exchanging pleasantries?

JAMIE I think it was a threat. There's a room in that house full of filing cabinets and high-tech machinery that I'm not even allowed to go near. It was his way of explaining why it's not guarded. Sort of a challenge. 'I'm an ex-commando and you're a skinny little kid. You want to try sneaking in that room late at night you better bring an army.' I got the message. So, Power, if you're going to suggest I do some after-hours snooping, don't.

POWER Off limits, eh. Private chambers, eh. What did I tell you. A nefarious sneaky dangerous vile disgusting plot!

JAMIE Calm down. Maybe it's just where he keeps his love letters.

POWER Love? Him? Mr. Vast Darkness. I can't imagine him having sex. Unless he's drilled a hole in an ICBM.

JAMIE There is a lady. She's staying there.

POWER What's her name.

JAMIE Karla.

POWER Her last name.

JAMIE Don't know.

POWER What's she look like.

JAMIE Terrific.

POWER Be a little more specific.

JAMIE Tall. Dark. Intense. Terrific.

POWER Did she have an accent.

JAMIE Sort of.

POWER What kind.

JAMIE Foreign.

POWER You've got a mind like a computer.

JAMIE I meant foreign in a general way. As a way of saying I couldn't pinpoint it.

POWER Mendez. Karla Mendez. It could be her. And you think they're lovers?

JAMIE Well, there was something going on between them. I could sense it. It was kind of exciting. He's different with her. Still dangerous but also kind of warm somehow.

POWER Shut up. You're making me sick.

JAMIE Sure. I know. I'm sensitive to those things in a way you're not. You're good at sensing paranoid things like death and misery. That's why you won't live long. That's why you're a disgusting drunk.

POWER And you're a romantic fool. Put any man and any woman together and you have a delirious feeling of self-projection. Have you asked her to walk on your face yet.

JAMIE You hate women, don't you.

POWER Look. Crawl out of my subconscious, will you. Why are you always saying things like that to me.

JAMIE Because you've never had a successful romance and I think that has a lot to do with your problems. Besides, you started it.

POWER I was just trying to bring you back to earth. You were falling in love with Karla Mendez or at least falling in love with the idea of falling in love which is more your style, and that could be very dangerous.

JAMIE Why.

POWER She's a terrorist. And a fascist. The daughter of a supreme fascist. A killer. Her father's in prison and she's wanted all over the world.

JAMIE Sure. And she's sitting down there casually as a guest of Hackman's.

POWER Why not. Who could see her.

JAMIE Me. I saw her.

POWER But you're just a gardener.

JAMIE Yeah. But even so—

POWER Shush. Someone's coming.

[*Someone is*]

Quick. The rifle. Pick it up.

JAMIE You pick it up.

POWER Pick it up and point it.

JAMIE It's your rifle. You pick it up.

POWER I hate guns. You know I hate guns. You're the one who loves guns. Now pick it up. Someone's out there.

JAMIE I don't love guns.

POWER Oh, you do so. You love them. Playing with them. Talking about them. Being a private eye. Being tough. Using force. Except now when we might be killed. Now pick up that goddamn rifle!

JAMIE All right!

[*He picks it up.* POWER *gets behind* JAMIE]

POWER Who's out there.

HEATHER [*appears from behind the tent*] It's just me.

POWER Oh, hello. What are you doing out here so late.

HEATHER Tyrone, would you mind asking your friend to lower the rifle.

POWER It's okay, Jamie ... Jamie.

[*But* JAMIE *is in love. He is smiling like a moron.* POWER *looks at* JAMIE. *Looks at* HEATHER. *At* JAMIE. *Shakes his head. Takes the rifle from* JAMIE]

JAMIE Is she a terrorist too.

POWER No.

JAMIE Good.

HEATHER What's going on here. [*to* JAMIE] You're the General's new gardener. [*to* POWER] What's he doing here.

JAMIE Moonlighting. I thought I'd earn a few extra bucks by offering to landscape this gentleman's campsite. Now if we put a few rocks over there—

POWER Shut up, Jamie. It's all right, Heather.

JAMIE Is she on our side.

POWER Yes.

JAMIE Good.

HEATHER I don't understand.

POWER He works for me.

JAMIE Actually I work *with* him. Can I get you a seat. Some coffee. How about something to eat.

POWER Good idea, Jamie. Cook us up a three-course meal. The stove's over there.

[JAMIE *goes over and starts to putter around with the stove*]
What is it, Heather.

HEATHER Hackman called. You're invited to dinner tomorrow night.

POWER Good.

HEATHER He also grilled me for a while about how I knew you.

POWER Do you think he suspects you.

HEATHER No. He thinks I'm an airhead. That's why he bought all that crap about the local museum so easily. He suspects you though. But that might be all right. He thinks you're just down here to do a journalistic hatchet job on him.

JAMIE [*approaching them*] That's the idea. Everything is right in place. I'm in place. Tyrone's in place. And now you're in place.

HEATHER Who is this guy, anyway.

JAMIE [takes her hand] Jamie McLean. I'm his partner.

HEATHER Partner in what.

POWER We're still working out the details.

HEATHER Why didn't you tell me about him.

JAMIE. Hey. That's his style. Close to the vest. You gotta respect it. It gets results. He didn't tell me about you either. What's your part in this.

POWER Heather is a friend of Paul Reinhardt's.

JAMIE Ahhh ... You were his girlfriend.

HEATHER What do you mean 'were'?! Oh my God. You've found out that he's dead, haven't you, Tyrone ... [staggers]

POWER Here, sit down.

[He helps her onto the campstool]

Good work, Jamie.

JAMIE I'm sorry. [goes behind the tent. Sits]

HEATHER I knew. He had to be dead. He left me that night to sneak into Hackman's house. And when he didn't come back I knew. What else would Hackman do. How did you find out.

POWER I didn't. But I'm sure he is, Heather.

HEATHER But to get Hackman we have to prove it.

POWER We will.

JAMIE We will?

HEATHER How.

JAMIE Yeah, how.

POWER Patience. We'll let Hackman make some moves first. I want the larger picture of what he's up to. Paul would have wanted it that way.

HEATHER Ah come on, Tyrone. Paul was no crusader like you. He just wanted Hackman's balls on the line because it would have been a good story. He was a good reporter but he had no mission. Just get Hackman. I feel so damn guilty. It was me who tipped Paul off that Hackman was up to something.

POWER Why didn't you tell me that before.

HEATHER Because I thought my father might be involved. It was something I heard them talking about.

POWER Go ahead.

HEATHER My father. Can you leave him out of this.

POWER Should I.

HEATHER Jesus. I don't know. I think Hackman was after his help. I don't think my father was directly involved. Hackman just wanted money from him.

POWER Your father shares a lot of Hackman's views.

HEATHER Well, they're from the same old world, Tyrone. But I think my father's ideas about how to sustain that world stop short of forming private armies and things like that.

JAMIE Private armies? I don't like the sound of that.

POWER That's why Mendez is in prison. He was forming a large illegal mercenary force. The rumour is that Hackman was a 'consultant.' Heather, what did Hackman want the money from your father for.

HEATHER I can't say for sure. I could speculate.

POWER Me too. Maybe to get someone out of prison in a foreign country? An operation like that could cost a lot of money.

HEATHER Simon Mendez.

POWER Simon Mendez. Yes.

HEATHER Right. That's what Paul thought too.

POWER Why.

HEATHER Because he found out Karla Mendez was staying with Hackman.

POWER For chrissake. Paul went into Hackman's place knowing that Karla Mendez was there. Was he insane.

HEATHER You're going there tomorrow night for dinner. Are you insane.

[POWER *has wandered over to the cliff's edge. Is staring down*]

JAMIE No, he's on a mission.

POWER Not me. Hackman's the only one with a mission. And to make it he's got to play a dicey double-edged game. He's got to stay close enough to government circles to be useful to his fascist friends and that means convincing sceptics like me that he really is nothing more now than the insignificant adviser to an insignificant Minister of Culture. But at the same time he's got to make his moves. This operation doesn't begin or end with setting Mendez free. They're going to make some big insurgent move somewhere. He's afraid of me. Afraid of what I'll write. So he wants to talk cultural policy and convince me. I'll let him. And then maybe he'll think I'll write something that will convince everyone else. And then he'll make his moves with confidence. And then I'll get him. And I'll get Mendez. And I'll get everything they both stand for.

JAMIE But it's good to know you don't have a mission.

POWER There's something going on down there on the beach in front of Hackman's place. Hand me the rifle.

JAMIE No way. You've worked yourself into a frenzy, Power. You can't just shoot him.

POWER The telescopic sight is infrared.

JAMIE So what.

POWER It sees in the dark. It was the only way I could get one. I had to buy the whole rifle. Hand it over.

[JAMIE *hands him the rifle.* POWER *looks through it*]

JAMIE Well? ... Well?

POWER It doesn't work. Nothing I buy ever works. Have you noticed that. That new typewriter I bought last month doesn't work.

JAMIE That 'new' typewriter is twelve years old.

POWER But I bought it. And it doesn't work. I bet it worked before I bought it. Life does things like that to people like me. Why is that. Why doesn't life do things like that to people like Hackman. Think about it. I want you to think about that. I'm going down there for a closer look.

[*He leaves*]

HEATHER You shouldn't let him go by himself.

JAMIE He likes to be alone when he's like this. He likes to ask himself questions like 'Why does life do these things to me' and he likes to give himself answers like 'Because life is stupid, Power. Life doesn't know that you're the only person alive with his own moral code. The only person who can save the whole world from destruction and spiritual emptiness.'

HEATHER It's from all those years in the newspaper business. It can do things to them. It made Paul reckless.

JAMIE [*checking the telescopic sight*] It does work. You just have to adjust it. He's so lousy with mechanical things. I think he's in the wrong century. I'm sorry about Paul.

HEATHER Thanks.

JAMIE Had you been together a long time.

HEATHER We hadn't 'been together' at all.

JAMIE But Power said—

HEATHER No, he didn't. He said I was his friend. And that's all I was. Just a good friend.

JAMIE Oh ... How did you meet Power.

HEATHER Through Paul. He taught a journalism course I took. Power used to lecture us sometimes.

JAMIE Was he tedious.

HEATHER Well, let's just say he took his subject seriously. In fact it seemed to depress him. [takes a flask of whisky from her purse]

JAMIE Yeah, that's Power. If he knows about it, he's depressed about it. [notices the flask] Are you a journalist.

HEATHER Yes. [takes a drink] My father owns the local newspaper. I work for it.

JAMIE You work for your father. But you don't agree with his politics.

HEATHER He tolerates me. Maybe because he thinks I'm stupid. Like the General does. I don't mind. I'm biding my time. Someday the paper will be mine. And its politics will be mine too.

JAMIE And your politics are like Power's, I guess.

HEATHER Yeah. Sort of. What are yours.

JAMIE Ah, I don't know. All I know about politics is that it's depressing. It seems to suck the spontaneity right out of most people. And it makes others, like Power, well ... deranged.

HEATHER How did you meet him. Power.

JAMIE I was a janitor. I used to clean offices part-time while I was going to school. I cleaned his office. Have you ever seen his office. It was a mess. Just like him. Drunk all the time. Writing this dumb novel he's been trying to finish for about a hundred years. I changed his life. I cleaned his office and infected him with my contagious spirit. Do you sense my contagious spirit.

HEATHER It's overwhelming me.

JAMIE I like you. We'll be close, I can tell.

HEATHER That sounds like a threat.

JAMIE You'll learn to love it. Just like Power did. He's alive. Sure he doesn't make sense most of the time. But he's got spirit.

HEATHER And now he's got a mission.

JAMIE I think he thinks it's a war. That's why he dragged us down here a thousand miles. All the way on the train his eyes were funny and he was talking about the new world fascism and the military mind. And when we got here he got worse. Like he was smelling Hackman even before he met him. Like he was sniffing in the air for the enemy. It's so ironic on top of all that, Hackman being this cultural adviser thing. Power hates art. He thinks it's 'the leisurely reflection of a dying society.' Those are his words, not mine. It just twists and turns, this thing between him and Hackman. And it's growing. I'm beginning to feel it myself. It would be funny if Hackman really did care about culture. You know, the fascist who cares about culture. And Power wants to destroy him. But isn't culture a fine thing. Isn't that what we're told. So it keeps twisting and turning this thing. It's got me thinking about it and I don't usually think about these things. I'm too smart. It kills you. But this is war. This is Power's war. And dammit, now I'm thinking about it too.

HEATHER So am I.

[POWER *returns. Sombre looking*]

JAMIE Did you see anything down there.

POWER Death. I saw death down there. [*takes a flask of whisky from a pocket. Drinks*]
[*Blackout*]
[*Intermission*]

SCENE FIVE

Later

The patio. Lit by several Japanese lanterns. BROWN *is looking around through a pair of binoculars*

KARLA *comes out*

KARLA Where is he.

BROWN On the beach.

[KARLA *mutters*]

How did your meeting at the airport go.

KARLA He agreed to help us.

BROWN You mean he agreed to let us pay him to help us. I notice you no longer have the briefcase.

KARLA I would like a drink please.

[*There is a small, portable bar in a corner of the patio.* BROWN *leaves the binoculars on a chair, goes to the bar*]

BROWN What would you like.

KARLA I don't care.

[BROWN *makes a drink.* KARLA *picks up the binoculars. Looks through them*]

What's he doing down there.

BROWN Digging.

KARLA Why.

BROWN You'll have to ask him.

KARLA I'm asking you!

BROWN [*hands her the drink*] I'm sorry you're upset, miss. The fact that your father's old friend took money from you must be hard for you to swallow. You don't understand the mercenary mind, miss.

KARLA Your mind, Brown?

BROWN I'm no mercenary, miss. I have a loyalty.

KARLA To what.

BROWN The General.

KARLA It's strange how he attracts certain kinds of personalities to him.

BROWN The General will set the world right, miss. The General and men like him.

KARLA No. Men like my father will set the world right. Men like the General are their tools.

BROWN Beg your pardon, miss, but your father's rotting in a South American prison. I don't remember the General ever getting himself in a position anything like that.

KARLA He has a way of looking out for himself.

BROWN No, miss. He's just not easily beguiled.

[KARLA *mutters.* HACKMAN *comes on from the beach. Carrying a shovel*]

HACKMAN Good evening, Karla. You look upset. Didn't it go well.

KARLA Well enough.

HACKMAN Good. Brown, could you pour me one of those. A double.

BROWN Sir.

[*He goes to the bar*]

KARLA He said he'd have my father out within a week.

HACKMAN Then why don't you look happy.

KARLA I don't trust him.

HACKMAN Because he took the money? Just because he's practical doesn't mean he can't be trusted. Relax. He'll get your father out because he knows if he doesn't I'll kill him. That's how the world works, Karla. By contract. I thought you knew that. I thought that's what you believed in.

KARLA I believe in my father.

HACKMAN And your father believes in force. The force of contracts.

[BROWN *hands* HACKMAN *his drink*]

Thank you.

BROWN Did you retrieve it, sir?

HACKMAN Yes.

KARLA Retrieve what.

HACKMAN [*reaches into his pocket. Produces a small notebook*] This. A journalist's notebook. You know, Brown, it would have been far less unpleasant to have searched him before we buried him.

BROWN An unforgivable lapse, sir. I can only say that I must be out of practice.

KARLA You killed someone.

HACKMAN He was a trespasser. This is my property. I own it. I have a deed. A contract. People in this world must learn that certain things are inviolate. Besides, dear, he was spying on us.

KARLA So you are suspected.

HACKMAN It appears so.

KARLA Are there others.

HACKMAN There is one other. A friend of the dead journalist. That's why I retrieved the notebook. To see what he had written down and possibly passed on to his friend. Mr. Power. Brownie, do me a favour. Take a quick read through this and brief me later.

BROWN [takes the notebook] I won't take long, sir.

HACKMAN Take your time. Let's not let them panic us. Let's not change our style, Brownie. They are the foolish ones, remember.

[BROWN nods. Leaves]

You know, Karla, I might have to leave here. Run away. That would be sad. I like it here. I like my garden. I like the ocean. I could have even grown to like my new job. I do like artistic things, Karla. Did you know that about me.

KARLA No.

HACKMAN Art is the leisurely reflection of an elite society. Who said that.

KARLA I don't know.

HACKMAN Perhaps I just made it up then. I'm getting poetic in my old age. Karla, if I have to leave, we'll go together. We'll join up with your father and work for his future success. Would you like that.

KARLA If it was a useful merger. You can be useful. I suppose.

HACKMAN It could be like the old days. Panama City. Madrid. Places in between. You are a woman I could love.

[He touches her hair]

KARLA You said that once before.

HACKMAN You see? I never repeat myself unless I mean it. I must love you. And somehow you must love me.

[He touches her neck]

KARLA Don't ... [shrugs] Of what exactly are you suspected.

HACKMAN Of helping you. And your father. Of helping to free a charismatic right-wing lunatic who wants to change half the world. Change it into a place where contracts are honoured. And duty is done. And loyalty is kept. Change it into our kind of world.

[*He touches her cheek*]

KARLA I have no loyalty to you.

HACKMAN But I've helped your father. Put myself in danger. And I may have to run. You could comfort a man on the run.

KARLA Comfort, maybe. But that is not love.

HACKMAN Let me be the judge of that.

[*He grabs her*]

KARLA No.

HACKMAN Let me.

[*He puts his arms around her. Kisses her. She laughs*]

KARLA How do you plan to use me.

HACKMAN How do you wish to be used.

[*They kiss*]

[*Blackout*]

SCENE SIX

The beam of a flashlight. The sound of someone moving around, some metal clanging. Suddenly the flashlight is dropped. Darkness. A groan. A louder groan. A thud
Pause. Lights
A small room in HACKMAN's *house full of filing cabinets.* BROWN *is standing with his foot on* JAMIE's *throat.* JAMIE *is lying on the floor in front of him.* HACKMAN *stands to the rear, hands in his pockets*

BROWN Don't move, laddie. If you move you die. Are you armed. Don't lie, laddie. If you lie you die.
[JAMIE *shakes his head*]
HACKMAN Let him up.
BROWN [*removes his foot*] Up you get.
[JAMIE *gets up slowly*]
HACKMAN Make him comfortable.
[BROWN *picks* JAMIE *up and puts him on a filing cabinet. The filing cabinet is about four feet high.* HACKMAN *approaches* JAMIE. JAMIE *is rubbing his throat*]
Let's make it simple, shall we. We know you're not a gardener. We know you're an associate of Mr. Power's. We know you've been spying on us. All we don't know is why. And you're going to tell us that right now.
JAMIE He paid me! I'm a paid lackey. I do anything for anyone who pays me. Would you like to pay me to spy on Power. No problem. I'll do it. Trust me.
BROWN Shut up, laddie. [*rubs his forehead*]
HACKMAN You're telling me you don't share his political beliefs.
JAMIE He's a washed-out liberal. Liberals, conservatives, communists, fascists. Who cares. Not me. I'm a working-class pragmatist. I believe in the politics of staying alive.
HACKMAN Under the circumstances I would say that makes you quite idealistic.
[*He nods at* BROWN. BROWN *pulls a stiletto from his sleeve. Places it at* JAMIE's *throat*]

BROWN The man is telling you that you're not saying the things he wants to hear.

JAMIE [to HACKMAN] I'm just trying to say I'm not interested in your political involvement.

HACKMAN My only political involvement is as cultural adviser.

JAMIE Right. And I can help you there too. They say this country has no real working-class art. And I think that's because it's always presented by a bunch of middle-class academics who patronize the shit out of the working class with a lot of romantic bullshit. Now, if you pay me enough, I could set up a study, hold regional meetings, write a report on my findings and—

BROWN Please do shut up, laddie. [now rubbing his forehead furiously]

HACKMAN Steady, Brown.

BROWN I'll be all right, sir. [turns his back, goes to a corner]

JAMIE Why is he always doing that. Rubbing his forehead like that.

BROWN [advancing] War wound!

[HACKMAN gets between them. Gestures. BROWN returns to his corner]

HACKMAN Steel plate.

JAMIE Steel plate?!

HACKMAN Please. You'll embarrass him.

JAMIE I'm sorry.

HACKMAN Let's continue without him, all right.

JAMIE Sure.

HACKMAN Are you uncomfortable. Not too ill at ease.

JAMIE No, actually I'm starting to feel okay.

HACKMAN Yes. Well, that's a mistake.

[HACKMAN suddenly and viciously grabs JAMIE's collar and throws him off the filing cabinet across the floor and into another filing cabinet. JAMIE slowly collapses to the floor]

How are you feeling now.

JAMIE How do you want me to feel.

HACKMAN Scared.

JAMIE Okay.

HACKMAN Three questions. What were you looking for in my files. What did Power learn from Reinhardt. Has Power passed on anything he's learned to anyone else.

[JAMIE *just looks at him*]

Answers.

[*He kicks* JAMIE *in the side*]

JAMIE [*groans*] Okay. Stop. I've got something to say. [*groans*] But I gotta get up. [*getting up slowly*] I gotta be on my feet. [*up*] Okay, I'm up.

[*He straightens, looks at* HACKMAN. *Inhales. Exhales*]

Go fuck yourself.

[HACKMAN *hits him and* JAMIE *falls to the floor. Unconscious.* HACKMAN *is standing over* JAMIE]

BROWN [*joins him*] I'm sorry you had to do that yourself, sir.

HACKMAN It's all right, Brown. You were there in spirit.

BROWN But a man like you shouldn't have to do things like that, sir. Those are things that a man like me should do. I've been letting you down quite a bit lately I'm afraid. It's the head. Always acts up at these times. I think it's the excitement. The promise of violence, if that doesn't sound too barbaric, sir.

HACKMAN Not at all, Brown. You're a soldier. You have instincts. And this is war.

BROWN Is it, sir.

HACKMAN Oh yes, I think so.

BROWN Have we lost it. Is that why we have to get out of the country.

HACKMAN No, that's something else. Something larger. A chance to prepare for the real war to come. This is something a bit unreal. This is a little war we have to fight before we go. A matter of conflicting points of view. This is a war between me and Mr. Power.

BROWN I hated him on sight, sir. I hated his flabby belly. I hated all the books he'd read and the schools he'd gone to. Just like that. Without even knowing him.

HACKMAN You know him. He's the enemy. The humanist. The egalitarian. The constant appeaser. He wants to turn the world into Jello. [*points to* JAMIE] And that's the enemy's spy. When he wakes up, do it again. And keep doing it until he talks. He has nothing to tell us but we should make him talk. It's a matter of principle. It's a battle of wills. His against ours.

BROWN Not exactly an even battle, sir.

HACKMAN I know. Sad, isn't it. It's a pathetic little war. But it's the only one we've got!

[*He leaves.* BROWN *looks at* JAMIE. *Rubs his forehead. Advances*]

[*Blackout*]

SCENE SEVEN

The patio. POWER *and* HEATHER. *Drinks before dinner. They are dressed casually.* POWER *is pouring himself a glass of wine*

HEATHER Why are they keeping us waiting.

POWER So we'll get nervous.

HEATHER It's working. I'm starting to sweat. I don't know if I can go through with this.

POWER Be strong. Have a drink.

HEATHER No, thanks. I'd rather stay alert. I think it would be good if you stayed alert too.

POWER I'm just having enough to give me a fighting edge.

HEATHER We should have called the police.

POWER Nah. They'd ruin everything. Besides, vengeance is mine saith the Lord, and since the Lord isn't here tonight I'm standing in for him. Vengeance, therefore, is mine.

[BROWN *comes on. In a suit*]

BROWN Are you comfortable.

POWER Absolutely.

[HEATHER *smiles. Nods*]

BROWN [*to* HEATHER] Would you like another cocktail.

POWER No. I've just been helping myself to the wine.

BROWN So I see. How unique to drink the wine before the dinner.

POWER I was beginning to get afraid there wasn't going to be a dinner.

BROWN Of course. Patience is the virtue of a confident man.

POWER I don't know. I'm a confident man. And I'm just rarin' to go.

[BROWN *starts off*]

HEATHER [*looks at* POWER] Oh, Brown.

BROWN [*stopping*] Yes.

HEATHER Is your gardener around. I thought I might ask him about the mixture in my compost heap.

BROWN No. I'm sorry. He had a little accident. We had to send him away.

HEATHER [*stands*] What kind of—

[POWER *grabs her arm*]

BROWN Something wrong, miss?

POWER No. She's fine.

[BROWN *nods. Leaves*]

HEATHER They've killed Jamie.

[POWER *stares into his glass*]

Tyrone. They've killed him.

[POWER *doesn't respond. Just stares down*]

Tyrone. Do something.

POWER I will. [*looks up*] I will.

[*Suddenly the patio is filled with music. A heart-pounding, lush, symphonic march. Very loud.* HEATHER *and* POWER *have to shout over the music*]

HEATHER What the hell is that.

POWER Psychological warfare! [*grimaces*] Unbelievable! This guy is unbelievable!

[HACKMAN *and* KARLA *enter. Arm-in-arm. Pose at the door and begin a slow regal walk to the table and around it once and then stop.* HACKMAN *is wearing a perfectly tailored tuxedo. Military ribbons on his chest.* KARLA *is wearing a black evening gown. And a red sash with a small insignia on it.* POWER *and* HEATHER *are just staring at them.* HACKMAN *makes a subtle gesture and the music stops. And simultaneously* BROWN *is there with a camera to take a picture of* KARLA *and* HACKMAN. BROWN *leaves. Pause*]

HEATHER Quite an entrance.

HACKMAN Thank you. We were aiming for something stylish.

POWER Unbelievable.

HACKMAN Too much, do you think.

POWER Oh, no. It was just right. I had an orgasm. [*to* HEATHER] How about you.

HEATHER No. Sorry.

POWER I think she probably likes more foreplay. But for me, the earth moved. It really did.

HACKMAN If you're finished, I'll make the introductions.

POWER Of course, how moronically rude of me to keep the charming lady waiting. [*stands*] And she's wearing her favourite battle dress, too.

HACKMAN Mr. Power. Heather Masterson. Allow me to present Karla Mendez.

[POWER *kisses her hand*]

POWER Daughter of Simon Mendez. Widely known banker and ultra-conservative patron of the political movement affectionately known as 'lunatics for a better world.'

KARLA [*sits*] Are you drunk, Mr. Power.

POWER A bit, perhaps.

KARLA Then it would be wise if you watched your tongue.

HACKMAN [*sits*] It's all right, Karla. Mr. Power has what he considers to be an original conversational style. Even though to others it may seem more like the rantings of a desperately under-equipped intellect. In any event I think we should not respond to him too hastily nor take him too seriously.

POWER There are parts of that speech I actually agree with. You gotta guess which ones though.

[KARLA *and* HACKMAN *laugh.* POWER *and* HEATHER *frown and slump in their chairs*]

HACKMAN How are you this evening, Heather.

HEATHER What is the purpose of this dinner party, General.

HACKMAN To eat. To make conversation.

POWER To strike a deal.

HACKMAN Yes. Perhaps later to even strike a deal.

HEATHER I think it stinks. If we've got things to say let's say them.

HACKMAN This is my house, Heather. We'll do this my way. You've changed, Heather. You're not the little girl I used to know.

HEATHER I never was. I've hated your kind all my life.

HACKMAN Well, you've been very good at keeping it a secret. Was this so that you could spy on me.

HEATHER Yes.

HACKMAN For whom.

HEATHER Friends.

HACKMAN Like Mr. Power here. No. Not Mr. Power himself, of course. People like him though. Of his ilk, so to speak.

HEATHER If that means people who believe in things like a free press and elections and ... and ...

POWER Peace.

HEATHER Peace. Well, yeah then. Yeah.

HACKMAN You're still a child, Heather. Naive and self-righteous.

HEATHER And you're a murdering son of a bitch. And I'm not going a bit farther with this crap. [*stands*] I'm going for the police.

KARLA I think you should sit down, little girl.

HEATHER Don't little girl me. I know your story. You throw bombs at people to get what you want. And you've already got three million dollars in a Swiss bank. You're just a common greedy criminal.

[KARLA *is muttering furiously*]

HACKMAN Mr. Power, explain to her why she should sit down.

POWER The General has a pistol under his jacket.

HEATHER So what.

HACKMAN The full sentence should have been 'The General has a pistol under his jacket which he will use.'

POWER Sit down, Heather. Our time is coming.

HACKMAN It's here now, Mr. Power. I'm afraid Heather has ruined the mood for dinner. I was prepared to dazzle you with my suggestions for a cultural policy. But of course that sham will be unnecessary.

POWER You got any other shams you want to try out.

HACKMAN I have your friend, Mr. Power. I have him and it's up to you to get him back.

POWER He's alive?

HACKMAN More or less.

POWER If you've hurt him I'll—

HACKMAN Oh please, Mr. Power, you'll what. Lash me with your tongue? Write a nasty article about me? Put my name on a petition and send it to all your friends?

POWER That's not a bad idea. Ban the Fascist.

HACKMAN An unfortunate choice of words, in the modern context, I mean. I'm someone who just wants to rid the world of chaos, get the economy moving again, and restore order.

POWER General, I've been waiting all my life to say this to someone like you. [*stands*] Any asshole can get the trains running on time! Any asshole can do that, but it takes something more to get the people on the trains for any reason other than the fact that they're

scared shitless of the asshole who got them running on time. And
another thing. It's too bad you didn't get a chance to infect me with
your contrived ideas on culture because I was ready for that too.

HACKMAN Strangely enough my ideas on culture are quite sincere.

POWER Oh, I bet they are. All concerned with harmony and beauty
and the glorious heart within. That piece of schlock that
accompanied your musical ride into dinner was probably a good
example.

HACKMAN You would have preferred an earthy folk song, no doubt.

[POWER *is fuming.* HEATHER *is gesturing him on.* KARLA *and*
HACKMAN *are shaking their heads. Muttering*]

POWER That's it. That's the point! I wouldn't have preferred. I don't
dictate. If you'll pardon the pun. Culture is like everything else. Just
is. It evolves out of just being. Like everything else. Like society. A
changing society. An evolving society! Oh God Almighty I want
you dead and rotting in the ground! And if I could I'd reach back
into history and remove every trace of every person you have
anything in common with and right all the wrong they've done in
the name of all that is brutal and elitist and just plain goddamn
vicious and greedy!

[*In one quick move* KARLA *pulls a small pistol from under her dress,
stands, points the gun at* POWER *and shoots.* HEATHER *yells. Pause*]
Am I shot? [*checking his body*] Am I shot? [*to* HEATHER] See any
blood? I don't feel anything. Maybe I'm in shock. Maybe I'm
dying.

HACKMAN Brutal, elitist, vicious, greedy, but decisive, Mr. Power.
Quite decisive.

POWER Well, am I dying or not. Isn't anyone going to tell me.

KARLA I aimed wide.

POWER Thanks. [*sits*]

KARLA Next time I won't. John, I think the little girl was right. Must
we go on with this. This man is intolerable.

HACKMAN But just a little bit amusing, no?

KARLA No. Intolerable and tiring. Very tiring. And we have a long
journey ahead of us tomorrow.

HEATHER Going away for good, General.

HACKMAN I'm afraid so. I'm afraid your friend Mr. Reinhardt has probably made it impossible for me to stay.

HEATHER You killed him. You killed him but he got you. For sure he got the word out that Miss Murder here was your guest and people will put that together with whatever you're planning to do to help her father.

HACKMAN Well, I can't be sure, but I can't take any chances either. We do have a meeting with destiny, you know.

POWER What about us.

HACKMAN You have a meeting with your own destiny, Mr. Power.

POWER Ah, yes. The vast darkness. Chaos and death.

HACKMAN I hope to make it a clean death, Mr. Power. No chaos. Just a bullet. I was hoping to play with you some more but you're too boring. Besides, you have nothing I want and all you want from me is to listen to you rant. It really is a pathetic little war, Mr. Power. No thunder. No lightning.

POWER [*has his hands under the table. Is leaning forward*] I have a little lightning under the table, General. It's a .38-calibre special. And it's pointed straight at you.

KARLA He's lying.

POWER Try going. Find out.

HACKMAN It doesn't matter. Brown probably heard that shot. He'll be coming in soon, Mr. Power. And no mere .38 is going to stop him.

POWER He'll just walk into it, right. He'll march into his death for you.

HACKMAN Try him. Find out. In the meantime, perhaps it's a standoff.

HEATHER What do we do.

POWER I'm thinking.

[*Long pause*]

KARLA John. He's bluffing.

HACKMAN We'll see soon enough.

HEATHER Tyrone.

POWER I'm thinking.

[*Long pause. The sound of footsteps. Someone approaching. They all look. Pause.* JAMIE *stumbles in. His face bloodied. Limping*]
Jamie.

JAMIE Power. He beat the shit out of me. Old Killer Eyes. He's a mean bastard ... Power, help me ... Power ... [*falls*]

[HACKMAN *makes a move to get up, but* POWER *stands.* POWER *does have a gun. He grabs* KARLA *and puts the gun to her head, while almost simultaneously* HACKMAN *is doing the same thing to* HEATHER. JAMIE *is struggling to get to his feet*]

HACKMAN This looks like a standoff for sure.

POWER Can you get up, Jamie.

JAMIE Yeah. [*struggling up*] He hurt me. He came back to hurt me some more but ... his head started to bother him pretty bad and I knocked him down and pushed a filing cabinet on top of him.

POWER Don't worry, Heather. We'll get you out.

HACKMAN Not by going to the police, Mr. Power. That would mean she dies. I promise you that.

POWER Get up, Jamie. We're leaving.

JAMIE [*on his feet. Staggering*] Yeah ... sure ... great idea. Old Killer Eyes is lying under a filing cabinet. He looks real stupid. But he's not dead ... kind of wish he was. God he hurt me.

POWER Get going. I'm right behind you.

[JAMIE *starts off.* POWER *is backing up. Holding* KARLA]
Is this better, General. Is this a better quality war. I mean now we've both got prisoners. Exciting, eh.

HEATHER For chrissake, Power. I don't much feel like sacrificing myself so you can get your rocks off.

HACKMAN Yes. Why make the ladies suffer. How about a prisoner exchange.

POWER That's not how it's done, General. Even I know that. You don't exchange prisoners in the enemy's camp. You find a neutral territory.

HACKMAN Where.

POWER You'll hear from me.

JAMIE Where am I.

POWER Just keep going.

JAMIE Where.

POWER Left foot. Right foot. Leave the rest to me.

JAMIE [*in a daze*] Left foot. Right foot. Left ...

[JAMIE, POWER *and* KARLA *are gone.* HACKMAN *lowers his gun. Lets go of* HEATHER]

HEATHER He'll go to the police.

HACKMAN I don't think so. That would spoil his fun.

HEATHER What is this. Are you two playing some kind of game or something.

HACKMAN He is, I think. But not me. And that's the basic difference between us which Mr. Power will soon find out about.

[BROWN *comes on. Soiled. Walking slowly*]

BROWN How did it go.

HACKMAN More or less as planned. Your part as well, I gather.

BROWN I think I gave a brilliant performance, if I may say so, sir.

HACKMAN Did he hurt you.

BROWN The fool threw an empty filing cabinet on me. Wouldn't hurt a fly. The kid thinks he's real tough.

HACKMAN They both do, Brown. They both do. [*laughs. Picks up a glass of wine. Drinks. Laughs again*] I love this!

[*Blackout*]

SCENE EIGHT

Dawn

In different areas, eventually all merging into one. The campsite on the cliff. KARLA *is sitting on a campstool. Her hands tied behind her back.* POWER *is kneeling next to* JAMIE, *washing the blood from his face*

POWER Does it hurt.

JAMIE Yeah.

POWER I was right about Hackman, wasn't I. He's nuts.

JAMIE Yeah. You were right.

POWER [*shrugs*] Yeah. Well, good for me. I guess. What possessed you to sneak in there in the first place.

JAMIE You. Your disease. Whatever you've got I had for a while.

POWER But you don't have it anymore.

JAMIE Killer Eyes knocked some sense into me. Power, I think we should call the authorities.

POWER No. This is my job.

JAMIE Really. Who gave it to you.

POWER Look. I'm sorry this happened to you but—

JAMIE No you're not. You're not even here. What is it exactly you want from Hackman. I've got to know, Power. I feel like I've been run over by a truck and I hate thinking there's no reason for it.

POWER I want him dead.

JAMIE Really? No metaphors? You don't mean in a larger spiritual way. You know how you usually talk? You mean really dead?

POWER Yeah.

JAMIE Why. Because he killed your friend Paul Reinhardt?

POWER Sure. That's a good reason. There are others of course.

JAMIE Of course. [*shakes his head*] Are *you* going to kill him, Power.

POWER If I get the chance.

JAMIE You can't. It's not in you.

POWER Oh, I think it is. I've got a feeling.

JAMIE You've been drinking again.

POWER Yeah. To make the feeling go away. But it won't.

[*He picks up the rifle. Wanders over to the cliff's edge*]

JAMIE Is it a scary feeling.

POWER Yeah.

KARLA I wouldn't worry. I doubt if you'll get the chance to do anything about it.

JAMIE I'm not in love with her anymore. [*to* KARLA] I used to love you from a distance. When I got closer I noticed you had serious flaws in your personality.

KARLA That is preferable, is it not, to having no personality at all.

JAMIE You can't insult me. You and your buddies are just about finished. My friend here is a formidable opponent. Aren't you, Power.

[POWER *is looking through the sight, pointing the rifle down towards* HACKMAN's *house*]

Aren't you, Power.

POWER [*looks at him*] I don't know.

[*Lights out on this area. Lights up on the patio.* BROWN *is sitting there. In commando gear. Loading a rifle. Looking off towards the cliff*]

BROWN Come on, laddies. Come on down. Be tough. Be big tough boys. [*rubs his forehead furiously*] Oh, man. I'm getting that old barbaric feeling. We're waiting, laddies. Won't you please come down. [*rubs his forehead, then raises the rifle to check the sight*]

[*Lights out on this area. Lights up on the beach.* HACKMAN *is sitting on a rock.* HEATHER *is digging a hole with a shovel*]

HEATHER What am I digging.

HACKMAN A grave.

HEATHER Whose.

HACKMAN Well, it's not mine.

HEATHER It's pretty sick to make a person dig her own grave.

HACKMAN How pessimistic, Heather. No, you're just not the same little girl I used to know. Journalism has dulled your imagination. Your friend Power is probably watching you dig. Do you suppose he's come to the same conclusion.

HEATHER [*stops digging*] You're baiting him.

HACKMAN [*waves his gun*] Keep digging, Heather.

HEATHER You're a sadistic murdering bastard.

HACKMAN Would you like to hear the speech on culture I prepared for

Mr. Power.

HEATHER Not really.

HACKMAN Well, you're going to hear it anyway. I worked too hard on it for it to go to waste .... Art. Art is the leisurely reflection of a discriminating society. Classical art is the historical reminder of earlier discrimination. The best art is the art of superficial spectacle which demonstrates the beauty of art for art's sake.

[*Lights start to fade*]

Give five discriminating artists enough money to create five superficial spectacles and you will have a definition of a nation's culture. Culture? Culture is ... oh ... Culture is ...

[*Lights out on this area. Lights up on the campsite*]

POWER [*looking through the sight, the gun pointed down at the beach*] I've got to get down there.

[*He hands the rifle to* JAMIE]

Here, take this. Watch her.

JAMIE You don't look well.

POWER I can't win. I just realized that.

JAMIE Then don't go.

POWER I have to get Heather away from him. But dammit. I can't win. Even if I get him. He's the only one who can win. Violence is his way, not mine. Life is always doing things like this to me. Have you ever noticed that. Think about it. [*leaving*]

JAMIE Be careful.

POWER I don't understand. Why me. I must be doing something wrong. I wonder what it is.

[POWER *is gone*]

KARLA He has no chance at all. [*laughs*]

JAMIE A momentary loss of faith. A little moral crisis. He has them all the time. [*looks at the rifle*] I hate guns.

[KARLA *laughs.* JAMIE *looks at her.* KARLA *laughs louder. Lights out on this area. Lights up on the patio.* BROWN *has the rifle to his shoulder and is pointing it towards the cliff*]

BROWN [*sings*]

There once was a man called Power

Who set himself up in a tower

But when someone shot him
They all soon forgot him
And dead, Power decayed and turned sour.
[*He laughs, then sings*]
Getting to know you
Getting to know all about you
Getting to like you
Getting to hope you like me.
[*laughs*] Come on down, laddie. That's it. Here he comes. Are you
ready, Sergeant. Yes, sir. How do you feel, Sergeant. [*rubs his
forehead*] Ooh. There's a pain I can live with, sir. A real burden of
love.
[*The lights start to fade. He sings*]
That old black magic's got me
In its spell
That old black magic that we
Love so well.
[*Lights out on this area. Lights up on the beach*]

HACKMAN Opera. Opera is an example of what I mean. Many people
think opera is a wasteful and irrelevant art form. But I believe its
strength lies in its wastefulness. Its arrogant belief in its own—

HEATHER Shut up! Will you please shut up. Shoot me. Strangle me.
But please don't make me listen to any more of this garbage.

HACKMAN [*waves his gun*] Just keep digging.
[*Four rifle shots*]

HEATHER What was that.

HACKMAN The first two shots froze Mr. Power in his tracks with fear.
The third shot blew off his foot. He of course fell down. The
fourth shot hit him in the shoulder. He is dying. Very slowly. With
plenty of time to think. I have a picture of it in my head. Very
finely etched. Very tasteful, in its own way. A very creative ending.
Not only does he get to watch his own death, but from where he's
lying he can see yours too.

HEATHER You're insane.

HACKMAN Please. Say something more original. Something
creative. Because it will certainly be the last thing you'll ever

say. [*lifts his gun*]

HEATHER Mr. Power has his gun pointed at your back.

HACKMAN Well, that's creative. But it's not very original.

POWER [*walking out of the darkness. Holding his gun with both hands*] I think she was going for the documentary approach.

[HACKMAN *smiles*]

Get his gun.

[HEATHER *grabs* HACKMAN's *gun*]

Turn around.

HACKMAN What are you going to do now.

POWER I'm thinking.

HEATHER Do you know what this is, General. This is justice. You murdered Paul Reinhardt and now you're going to pay. Hooray for us, Power. I'll go call the police.

[*She runs off*]

HACKMAN Now's your chance. All you have to do is pull the trigger.

POWER Maybe there's another choice. I could hold you for the police.

HACKMAN No. If you don't shoot I'm leaving. I'll be gone, out of the country before the police arrive.

POWER Where can you go. There are international police agencies. And extradition treaties.

HACKMAN Where I'm going I can't be touched. I'm going to burrow just beneath the surface of a foreign society. You'll know I'm around though. Occasionally you'll read something in a newspaper. A story about a return to order somewhere. The setting of things right. And you'll know I've been working ... Well, Mr. Power. Can you kill me.

POWER I'm thinking.

[*Lights out on this area. Lights up on patio.* BROWN *is sprawled unconscious in a chair.* JAMIE *is standing over him. Looking in a daze at his rifle*]

HEATHER [*runs on*] What happened.

JAMIE He was aiming for Power. He was going to shoot him. I saw it all through this telescopic sight. I had to stop him.

HEATHER You killed him?

JAMIE I tried. I missed. Three times I missed. The fourth time I hit that lantern and it fell on his head. He's unconscious. I hate violence. I really do. This is not private-eye work. Private eyes don't use rifles. They take divorce cases. And make money. There's no money in this. There's only misery in this. Where's Power.

HEATHER On the beach. With Hackman.

JAMIE Are you all right. I've been worried about you. I know we just met but I felt we made a psychic connection. I'm sensitive that way, you know.

[HEATHER *touches his cheek*]

HEATHER I'm all right. What about you. You seem to be in a daze.

JAMIE I am. I just tried to kill someone. I've never done that before. I think it changed my life. [*sits*]

HEATHER You better get down to the beach. Power might need your help.

JAMIE Helping Power makes me miserable. I just tried to kill someone to help Power. It's a habit I've got to break.

HEATHER This is no time to go soft. This isn't defeat. This is victory. Justice. These guys killed Paul Reinhardt.

JAMIE Politics.

HEATHER No. Murder.

JAMIE No. War. Yes. I'm seeing it all now. I'm seeing how it works. I'm learning. This is a battle between two men. One of them, Power, wants the world to work properly with justice and equality and all those things. The other one, Hackman, just wants the world to work. Period. I figured all that out a while ago but I couldn't figure out my part in it all. But I learned. Experience taught me. I'm a pacifist. Will you marry me.

HEATHER What.

JAMIE I know you like me. I want to get married. Have children. Buy a small farm someplace. Will you marry me.

HEATHER No.

JAMIE Is that your final answer.

HEATHER This isn't the time. Power might be in danger. And there's something I'm supposed to be doing. I'm supposed to be calling the police. [*starts off*] Hey ... Hey. I liked you better when you had spirit.

[*She leaves*]

JAMIE Pacifists have spirit. I know. I can sense it growing inside me. A great spirit.

BROWN [*groans. The groan turns into the first note of 'As Time Goes By'*] You must remember this
A kiss is still a kiss
A sigh is just a sigh
The fundamental things apply
As time goes by.

JAMIE [*in a daze, joining in*] And when two lovers woo ... [*continues*] [BROWN *sits up suddenly. Sees* JAMIE. *Advances.* JAMIE *raises two sets of fingers in the peace sign.* BROWN *sees this. Recoils. Rubbing his head furiously, he wanders off. And together he and* JAMIE *continue to sing. Fade out. Lights up on the beach.* POWER *is pointing the gun at* HACKMAN. *Thinking. Rubbing his head. Mumbling to himself. Gesturing.* HACKMAN *is looking at him curiously.* KARLA *appears. Walking quietly, slowly up behind* POWER]

HACKMAN No, don't bother him. He's thinking.

KARLA About what.

[POWER *turns. Caught between them. The gun moving from one to the other*]

HACKMAN The sanctity of life, probably. The moral implications of taking action. The pros. The cons. The pros. The cons. Ad infinitum, right, Mr. Power.

POWER How did you escape.

KARLA I got mad. It's easy if you get mad.

HACKMAN She's right. Perhaps you should try getting mad, Mr. Power.

POWER I am.

[HACKMAN *and* KARLA *advance slowly*]

HACKMAN No. You're indignant. You're outraged. You just don't understand, do you. Anger is a weapon. Allowing you to be brutal. Brutality is another weapon. Allowing you to take action. In this way, you build your arsenal. Until you have the ultimate weapon. Immorality. Which allows you to take any action in any way at any time. Immorality is a great weapon. And you don't have it.

POWER I don't need it. I've got a gun. See?

HACKMAN So what.

POWER I just thought it was a good time to remind you.

HACKMAN The point is, you can't use it.

POWER Just because I can't use it, doesn't mean I won't use it.

KARLA What is he talking about.

HACKMAN The gun is philosophically confusing to Mr. Power. Perhaps you could do him a favour and take it away from him.

[KARLA *moves towards* POWER]

POWER Stay put.

KARLA That's impossible. To take the gun I have to be closer.

POWER Stop right there.

KARLA One more step. [*takes a step. Stops*]

POWER Be careful.

KARLA All right.

[*She pulls a fancy move. Kicks the gun out of* POWER'*s hand. Picks it up*]

POWER Shit. I knew she was going to do that. I hate myself.

HACKMAN No chance, Power. You had no chance. She hates you. She'd risk everything to beat you. You have to risk taking action! Let's go, Karla. It's over. [*starts off*]

KARLA Almost.

[*She shoots* POWER. POWER *drops to his knees. Holding his shoulder*]

HACKMAN Did you do that for me.

KARLA [*walking past him*] No.

[*She leaves. Muttering*]

HACKMAN Power ... Power?

POWER What.

HACKMAN Don't die. Try to live. It would be more interesting if you lived and we met again. There's so much I could teach you.

[POWER *is trying to get to his feet*] No. Please. No need to stand on my account. Besides, I want to remember you just as you are.

[*He smiles. Pats* POWER *on the head. Leaves, humming an aria.*

POWER *struggles to his feet. Turns in a circle. Falls on his rump*]

POWER This is very, very depressing.

[JAMIE *runs on*]

JAMIE Power? Power.

POWER Over here.

JAMIE [*rushes over*] What happened.

POWER You tied Karla's hands, didn't you.

JAMIE Yeah.

POWER You did a lousy job.

JAMIE Oh my God. You're shot.

POWER She shot me. She got loose because you didn't tie her up properly and she came down here and shot me. Why can't you do anything properly. Why can't we do anything properly. It's so goddamn depressing.

JAMIE Does it hurt.

POWER Yes.

JAMIE It looks bad.

POWER I could have killed him. But I didn't. I just thought about it. You're right about me. I think too much. Thinking doesn't help.

JAMIE Power. It looks really bad. Your wound is serious.

POWER I'll be all right. You better get after them. Karla and Hackman. They're getting away.

JAMIE I can't leave you. You're wounded. You may be dying.

POWER No. I'm not. Get going. You can at least try to follow them.

[JAMIE *is cradling* POWER's *head. Rocking back and forth*]

JAMIE I can't. You're dying.

POWER I'm not dying.

JAMIE Yes, you are.

POWER No, I'm not. Get going. Let go of me.

JAMIE Oh my God, Power. You're dying.

POWER Dammit. Dammit. Dammit. I am not dying. Let me go. Get after them.

JAMIE I'm sorry, Power. I'm so sorry. Don't die. Don't die.

POWER I'm not. I'm not.

[*Lights start to fade*]

JAMIE It's so bad. It's so awful. Don't die.

POWER I can't stand it. They're getting away. We're letting them get away. We're failing again. I can't stand it. It's killing me.

JAMIE You're dying.

POWER No, it's killing me.

JAMIE You're dying.

POWER It's so depressing.

JAMIE Please don't die.

POWER For God's sake, I'm not dying. I'm just depressed. It's just so damn depressing ... Jamie?

JAMIE What.

POWER We have to do better in the future. Promise me next time you tie someone up you'll do it properly.

JAMIE I promise.

POWER And I promise next time I go to war I'll win ... or at least try to break even. I'm tired of losing. It's so ... depressing.

[JAMIE *is rocking back and forth.* POWER *is shaking his head.*
HEATHER *runs on. Goes to them. Kneels. Suddenly they all look up.
And on the cliff* KARLA, BROWN *and* HACKMAN *are looking down.
Waving*]

[*Blackout*]

[*End*]

CRIMINALS IN LOVE

Criminals in Love was first produced at Toronto's Factory Theatre on November 7, 1984 with the following cast:

JUNIOR Ted Dykstra
GAIL Gina Wilkinson
WILLIAM Peter Blais
HENRY Dean Hawes
SANDY Lesleh Donaldson
WINEVA Barbara Gordon

Director: George F. Walker
Set Designer: Reginald Bronskill
Lighting Designer: Sholem Dolgoy
Music composed by: John Roby

Persons

JUNIOR DAWSON, *nineteen, Gail's boyfriend*
GAIL QUINN, *eighteen, Junior's girlfriend*
WILLIAM, *forty-five to sixty-five, a bum with a slight Eastern European accent*
HENRY 'SENIOR' DAWSON, *early forties, a cheap crook*
SANDY MILES, *nineteen, lean, alert*
WINEVA DAWSON, *late thirties, former earth mother, going to seed*

Place

Various locations in the working-class east end of a big city. The set should be simple, suggestive, allowing spaces for inventive lighting.

Time

Almost summer.

'When you believe in things you don't understand, you suffer.'

— *Stevie Wonder*

SCENE ONE

Dusk
A schoolyard. A small grassy slope. GAIL *and* JUNIOR *are entwined. She is on her back with her hands behind her head. He has one leg over her thighs and his head under her sweater. He is making many varied and muffled sounds of pleasure. Her mild enjoyment turns gradually to restlessness and eventually impatience*
Behind them, some distance away, a bum is curled up against a wall

GAIL Junior? ... Junior.

JUNIOR [*something muffled*]

GAIL God, Junior, it's time to move on ... try some other part of my body. Sex does not begin and end at my chest. Do you realize how much time you spend under my sweater.

JUNIOR [*something muffled*]

GAIL I'm beginning to think there's something wrong with you.

JUNIOR [*pulls his head out*] I love them. I ... I can't think of anything else to say.

GAIL But what can I do to you when your head is under there. I'm tired of running my fingers through your hair.

JUNIOR That's all I need. My hair is sensitive. It's exciting, really.

GAIL Let's stop. Let's talk.

JUNIOR Five more minutes.
   [*He goes under the sweater again*]

GAIL No, now.

JUNIOR [*something muffled*]

GAIL Junior. Get out of there!
   [*She grabs a fistful of hair. Twists. He yells. Sits up suddenly. Pause. She grabs her jacket from the grass beside her. Puts it on. Zips it up*]

JUNIOR Will you marry me.

GAIL You just had a vision didn't you. The two of us married and always together. Twenty-five or thirty years with your head under my sweater.

JUNIOR I dream about you. You're my salvation.

GAIL I hate it when you say shit like that. I don't think you even know what it means.

JUNIOR You save me.

GAIL From what.

JUNIOR My true destiny.

GAIL Which is.

JUNIOR Fuck all.

GAIL Pathetic. I hate it when you talk like this.

JUNIOR Fuck all is what I came from. Fuck all is where I'm going without you.

GAIL Just knock it off, okay.

JUNIOR Why do you like me.

GAIL What.

JUNIOR I just want to know why you like me.

GAIL I love you, honey.

JUNIOR Because I love you probably.

GAIL Probably, yeah. You give me your full attention. The first time we kissed even. You threw your arms around me. Closed your eyes and just held on. It wasn't the world's greatest kiss, but I said to myself here's a guy who can concentrate on what he's doing ...

JUNIOR Will you marry me.

GAIL When I get a job. ·

JUNIOR I've got a job.

GAIL I know you've got a job. I didn't forget. The answer to your question was when I get a job.

JUNIOR Why.

GAIL You know why. Why.

JUNIOR So you won't have to be afraid I'll fuck up.

GAIL No. Jesus. Pathetic. Not that you won't fuck up. Just so I'll know there's something I can do to control things. Keep things moving. Whatever happens.

JUNIOR Well, whatever happens just has to be me fucking up. I've been thinking about it and there just isn't anything else that can go wrong.

GAIL There are things in this world beyond your control. Your plant could close. You could be laid off. You should have voted to unionize that place, you know.

JUNIOR You should go to university, Gail. You're smart enough to be anything.

GAIL Thanks. [stands] I need your advice really badly.

JUNIOR Why are you getting pissed off.

GAIL Don't tell me what I should do.

JUNIOR It wasn't an order or anything.

GAIL Look. Let's not get into the habit of talking about what we should do. What we could do. It's a dumb way to live so let's just kill that way of thinking right away. Let's just talk about what we want to do. I want to get a reasonably good job. Period.

JUNIOR I want to get married.

GAIL Great. Now we've got a plan. Something to aim for.

[*He stands too. Puts his arms around her*]

JUNIOR You look great. When you stood up like that your body looked amazing. When you talked ... you talked like a lawyer. You're perfect.

GAIL So are you.

[*They kiss*]

JUNIOR I need some advice.

GAIL [*suspiciously*] Yeah?

JUNIOR I'm supposed to visit my dad tomorrow.

GAIL Yeah.

JUNIOR In jail. He's in jail.

GAIL Yeah, I know that, Junior.

JUNIOR Well, should I.

GAIL Don't you want to.

JUNIOR He's ridiculous you know. He's the most ridiculous man in the whole world. He's a crook. That's bad enough. But he's a ridiculous crook. He can't even steal hub caps.

GAIL Where's this leading.

JUNIOR He's my legacy.

GAIL What.

JUNIOR I mean he's my destiny. I mean he's my family. I mean ... he scares me. He's so ridiculous he's terrifying.

GAIL Why don't you just take him a present. Something he can use in prison. A mission of mercy.

JUNIOR He gets sentenced tomorrow. After my visit. That's why they brought him into the city jail ... So?

GAIL What.

JUNIOR Well, I could estimate, I guess. Five years anyway. I mean I'd have to buy him something that would last.

GAIL I know you want to talk about this, really talk about it ... but it's hard, eh. We do this all the time, Junior. Talk about your dad. You use me to figure out what he means to you. Maybe you should just figure it out for yourself once and for all.

JUNIOR Without you?

GAIL Tonight. Before the visit.

JUNIOR But without you.

GAIL I'll go home.

JUNIOR What'll I do.

GAIL You can stay here. It's quiet here. You can think here.

JUNIOR Sure. I guess. Are you leaving now.

[*She kisses him*]

GAIL It's okay, honey. It's not a big deal. You've made him a big deal in your life. Think of some way to make him just what he is.

JUNIOR That sounds good.

[*She starts off*]

GAIL Call me later.

JUNIOR Be careful. Walk quickly. Walk on the side where the street lights are. Don't talk to anyone.

[*She is gone*]

Walk real fast. No, run instead. You can run beautifully. Go ahead. I'm watching! No one is following you. Run!

[*He sits.* GAIL *comes back on. Firm look in her eyes*]

GAIL Look. Just relax. I can make it home just fine. I was brought up in this neighbourhood. I got along fine in it before I met you. I'm leaving now. I'm not going to run. I'm going to walk. And I'll be all right! So relax!

[*She leaves. Pause.* JUNIOR *leans back on his elbows.* WILLIAM, *the bum against the wall, sits up suddenly*]

WILLIAM What ... What's all the ... Please don't kill me. Please. I don't eat garbage. Don't make me eat it. There's dead flies ... Please. What ... Where.

[*He looks around.* JUNIOR *is staring at him. Long pause*]

JUNIOR Bad dream?

WILLIAM Another garbage-eating dream. It's recurring. Terrifying in its detail ... Where's your girlfriend.

JUNIOR Gone.

WILLIAM Argument?

JUNIOR Nah. You all right?

WILLIAM I'll have to check. [*checks his body*] Okay, so far. Just let me examine the essentials. [*puts his hand in his pants*] Dry as a bone, as the saying goes. I recognize you. You're one of the local kids. I've been seeing you around since you were this high. Ten, twelve years. You've certainly changed with time.

JUNIOR You haven't. You're even wearing the same coat.

WILLIAM Passing ships in the night. That's what we are in a way. Urban freighters. I'm not carrying though. Absolutely without contents.

JUNIOR What.

WILLIAM I'm saying we've known of each other's existence all these years and we've never talked.

JUNIOR My mom wouldn't let me talk to bums.

WILLIAM She's had a change of heart, dear woman.

JUNIOR She's dead.

WILLIAM Ah. So what's the impediment. Can I join you.

JUNIOR Sure.

WILLIAM Or you could join me. Your preference, entirely.

JUNIOR It's more comfortable on the grass.

WILLIAM If you say so. [*stands with difficulty*] Actually I've found that grass is fine during the day but concrete is better for evening restings. No dew, you see. Doesn't get wet. I hate getting wet. It's the worst thing about my way of life. Involuntary bladder activity. Absolutely the worst thing there is.

[*He sits next to* JUNIOR. *Puts out his hand*]

WILLIAM William.

JUNIOR Junior.

[*They shake*]

WILLIAM William ... William.

JUNIOR Yeah, I got it the first time.

WILLIAM No. It's just that there used to be a last name that went along with it and I'm trying to remember what it is.

JUNIOR Seriously?

WILLIAM Please, no pity. I think it began with a K. William K ... K ... Well, I won't push it. Don't want to hemorrhage. [*groans, falls over*] Jesus. That was a pain. Probably the spleen.

JUNIOR Listen, the liquor store's still open. I could go get you a bottle.

[JUNIOR *is picking* WILLIAM *up*]

WILLIAM Oh God, you think I'm an alcoholic. How quick they are to judge, Lord. We the meek of the earth. Absolutely without defence.

JUNIOR I'm sorry. I thought …

WILLIAM Oh. I drink. I drink much. Often. Almost non-stop. But I know, and here I use a relative term, when I've had enough. Therefore, honestly, and without smiling, I can say I am not an alcoholic. A bum, yes. There's a tricky distinction here. But enough of me. Why aren't you out with your peers. Pushing buttons in the electric amusement places. Fucking the dog. And the puppies too if the worst of us have our way.

JUNIOR I've got some thinking to do.

WILLIAM About your girlfriend?

JUNIOR She's part of it.

WILLIAM A fine girl. Very sturdy. I've observed her over the years as well.

JUNIOR Yeah?

WILLIAM From a discreet distance. No hands. Honestly. No touching ever. Of course I can't be responsible for my private thoughts and they are truly disgusting.

JUNIOR You're kind of weird.

WILLIAM But I function as a gentleman. When I function. What's the problem. The obstacle … The overall … the absolute thing you're wrestling with.

JUNIOR Nothing easy to describe. Just how to get by. Hang on.

WILLIAM Hanging on is the true problem of the age. I wrestle with it daily myself. So often I think of just giving up and letting myself plummet into the depths of degradation. Into the absolute pit. I'm so tired of this bourgeois existence.

JUNIOR Mister, I kinda know what that word means, and it ain't you.

WILLIAM Once again I call upon the rules of relativity. From my perspective, I see a great distance yet to fall. I feel positively middle-class in comparison.

JUNIOR You're a bum.

WILLIAM Truth is, I'm just pretending. Yes, I have a bank account! I can withdraw money at any time. Check into a hotel. Order up a steak. Have an all-night bath with bubbles. Drink cognac. Live splendidly.

JUNIOR Why don't you!

WILLIAM Why should I!

JUNIOR Why shouldn't you. Or why don't you.

WILLIAM You have a truly devastating aptitude for logical debate. I think I'll answer the first question. I don't do these things because I am not destined to live like that.

JUNIOR What.

WILLIAM I was about to tell you about the 'call of the pit.' Its great echoing voice. 'Come down, William,' it says. 'We know you want to.'

JUNIOR You said destined. You know about destiny?

WILLIAM I am the inventor of the modern connotation.

JUNIOR I've got a thing about destiny.

WILLIAM Then we should talk more.

JUNIOR No. It's a bad thing. I should go.

[JUNIOR *stands.* WILLIAM *pulls him down*]

WILLIAM Sit down. Destiny as a concept of the mind and soul is what you're afraid of. I'm talking pure economics, politics, social patterns. I'll have to tell you my entire story for you to understand.

JUNIOR That'd be great. Sometime soon.

WILLIAM What's wrong with now.

JUNIOR I thought I'd go for a walk. I think better walking.

WILLIAM I talk well sitting or walking. I'll come along. You don't have to listen. But seriously do you mind. I would love some company.

[*They look at each other. Pause*]

JUNIOR Sure. Okay.

[*He helps him up*]

WILLIAM Where to.

JUNIOR We'll just walk.

[*They start off*]

WILLIAM It's always hard to leave a place you're fond of. Goodbye, wall. Goodbye, concrete. Goodbye, grass. Now where were we. Ah, yes. My life. My absolute history ...

[*They are leaving*]

[*Blackout*]

SCENE TWO

Visiting room in the city jail. A table. Two chairs. JUNIOR *in one. His father* HENRY *in the other*

HENRY So didya hear what happened to Joe Meecher. Someone knifed him in the laundry room. He's in the infirmary. They can't get his blood to clot. [*shivers*] He's gonna die.
[*Pause*]
You don't seem concerned.

JUNIOR I'm not. Joe Meecher's a turd.

HENRY He's your godfather.

JUNIOR Like hell.

HENRY Didn't your mother ever tell you. Joe held you at your christening. He's your goddamn godfather.

JUNIOR I'll pray for him, all right?

HENRY You don't pray. Don't give me that. Just show a little concern.
[*Pause*]

JUNIOR I was talking to your lawyer.

HENRY Stay away from my lawyer. If you talk to my lawyer that's technically a consultation. He could add a hundred bucks to my bill.

JUNIOR You're on legal aid, you don't pay.

HENRY You dumb fuck. Sure I pay. When I get out they garnishee my wages.

JUNIOR If you get a job.

HENRY That goes without saying.

JUNIOR If you get out.

HENRY That goes without ... Whatya mean if I get out.

JUNIOR Your lawyer says that technically you're a chronic offender.

HENRY My lawyer has no regard for me as a human being! I could tell by the way he picked his teeth during my trial. I wanted to put my fist in his mouth and yank all those teeth right out of there.

JUNIOR It has nothing to do with him. It's up to the judge.

HENRY Now I'm worried. You've got me worried. I hope you're happy. They could put me away for twenty years.

JUNIOR I just thought you should be prepared.

HENRY You're all heart.

JUNIOR Listen. Maybe the judge will feel sorry for you. I mean what's the farthest you ever got from the scene of a crime. Fifty yards?

HENRY You still seeing that girl. Grace.

JUNIOR Gail.

HENRY She's good looking isn't she. Healthy. Right? I'm just making small talk.

JUNIOR Yeah. Listen, I brought you something.

[JUNIOR *puts a small packet on the table*]

HENRY What's that.

JUNIOR A pen.

HENRY A pen?! Is it a Parker T-Ball Jotter. Ooh, I always wanted one of them.

JUNIOR I don't think they make them anymore. This is a Scriptomatic. It glides across the paper. And it's got a clock in it. I thought you could use it.

HENRY You were wrong. [*picks up the box*] But thanks anyway.

JUNIOR It's guaranteed. You can get refills. It's a good pen.

HENRY Cost a lot?

[JUNIOR *shrugs*]

How's the job.

JUNIOR Good.

HENRY Shipper, right?

JUNIOR Assistant.

HENRY Little things? Big things?

JUNIOR A graphics company. Little things. We use couriers mostly. Lots of stuff to the airport. Deadlines. That kind of thing.

HENRY Don't let the pressure get to you.

JUNIOR I won't.

HENRY The pressure got to me. It was just the pressure. Before the pressure I didn't do crime.

JUNIOR The pressure got to you early in life, eh?

HENRY What's that mean.

JUNIOR You botched your first break-in when you were seventeen. Who knows how many there were before then.

HENRY That was the first. I got caught first time out. [*laughs*]

JUNIOR Yeah. That's what I figured. Dammit, Dad, couldn't you have just got the message.

HENRY What message.

JUNIOR That you weren't very good at it.

HENRY I was young. I had my whole life stretching out in front of me. You have to expect some early failures. That's my advice to you. Expect some early failures.

JUNIOR It's great advice.

HENRY Look. We haven't got much time. I want to tell you about your Uncle Ritchie.

JUNIOR Did he get knifed.

HENRY No. He's out. He's made connections. The thing is, he'll be contacting you.

JUNIOR Why.

HENRY He needs a little help on some of his projects.

JUNIOR No way.

HENRY He needs to use the house to store some things on an on-and-off-and-on-again basis.

JUNIOR No fucking way.

HENRY He'll be calling you.

[*Pause*]

JUNIOR Listen. I've been thinking about us. You and me. I think we should end our relationship.

HENRY What are you talking about, you dumb fuck. We're father and son. That's not a relationship. It's destiny.

JUNIOR What.

HENRY You know ... destiny.

[JUNIOR *stands*]

JUNIOR You don't even know what that word means!

HENRY Calm down. Sit down. Sit down!

JUNIOR I gotta go. I'm late for work.

HENRY You help your Uncle Ritchie. He's my brother. You owe me.

JUNIOR For what.

HENRY Okay. You don't owe me. But there'll be money in it for you. You need all you can get. Your future isn't secure. You're not equipped. You should have stayed in school. No one quits school at sixteen anymore.

JUNIOR I'm nineteen now. I'm doing all right.

HENRY Your future sucks. I'm sorry. But the odds say that you'll be doing crime in a few years.

JUNIOR Never.

HENRY I've been thinking about it. It's in the blood.

JUNIOR What are you doing. Are you insane. Saying things like that to me.

HENRY There comes a time to be honest. This is it I guess. If you didn't want to face your true destiny you should have stayed in school.

[JUNIOR *stands*]

JUNIOR There's that word again. You haven't got a lousy clue what that word means and you keep throwing it in my face. Listen. Let's remember something. I quit school because one day while I was sitting in English class, you decided to rob the bank across the street. You failed miserably like usual and me and my friends and my teacher got to watch you from the classroom window being handcuffed and thrown into the paddy wagon. Embarrassment. Embarrassment made me quit school. No fucking destiny!

HENRY I don't want to talk about the goddamn past. Sit down!

[JUNIOR *sits*]

Now listen, this is the truth. I owe your Uncle Ritchie this favour. If I welch he'll have me knifed. He's got friends inside. You gotta talk to him when he calls.

JUNIOR I can't.

HENRY I just told you the truth, you dumb fuck. We're talking about my life here.

JUNIOR I can't.

HENRY You'll do it.

JUNIOR No.

HENRY I'm telling you to do it. Don't say no.

JUNIOR No.

[*Suddenly* HENRY *grabs* JUNIOR's *hair. Pulls his head hard on to the table.* JUNIOR *groans.* HENRY *lifts* JUNIOR's *head*]

HENRY Don't say no.

JUNIOR No.

[HENRY *pulls* JUNIOR's *head down on the table.* JUNIOR *groans.* HENRY *lifts* JUNIOR's *head*]

HENRY Don't say no.

JUNIOR No.

[HENRY *pulls* JUNIOR's *head down and up three times fast.* JUNIOR *falls off his chair. Holding his forehead.* HENRY *stands. Looks at*

JUNIOR. *Shakes his head*]

HENRY Guard! [*looks at* JUNIOR. *Snaps his fingers*] Hey, get up. Stand up. Quick get up. Sit in the chair. You want to get me in trouble. Get up.
[JUNIOR *struggles into his chair*]
Good boy ... Guard!
[*Blackout*]

SCENE THREE

A booth in a corner of one of those burger places. GAIL *and* SANDY. SANDY *is drinking a Coke. Eating fries. Smoking. Wearing a burger-worker uniform.* GAIL *is writing*

GAIL What happened then.

SANDY They flipped a coin. The tall one lost. The short one and me caught an elevator and went to his room.

GAIL Were you scared.

SANDY On the outside, no. But on the inside, yes.

GAIL No one gets scared on the outside, Sandy. The outside is hair, skin, nails ... You mean you didn't let it show.

SANDY Is that what you're writing.

GAIL Yeah.

SANDY Then I guess that's what I meant.

GAIL So you're inside his room.

SANDY First we're outside his room. At the door. He thinks the maid is in there. We wait. We whisper. He listens at the door. Stupid little jokes.

GAIL Is this going anywhere important. Was the maid inside.

SANDY No.

GAIL Okay. You're in the room. The door's locked. Get to it.

SANDY We did it.

GAIL Go back just a bit.

SANDY He said let's have a drink. I said no. He said let's talk. I said no. He said let's have a shower. I said no. I said let's get undressed. We got undressed. Then ... we did it. He did it.

GAIL How.

SANDY Badly.

GAIL But how.

SANDY What do you mean. Was he on top.

GAIL Not exactly. I'm looking for a feeling. Describe the feeling.

SANDY Nothing.

GAIL Not the sex. The feeling in the room.

SANDY Nothing. I don't know what you're getting at. I did it for the money.

GAIL Was it sad. I want to know if you felt sad.

SANDY You said we wouldn't talk like that. You know it's not sad. It's money. I don't know. Jesus, this was my first time.

GAIL This is a lousy idea. No newspaper's going to buy this.

SANDY Diary of a Teenage Hooker. I think they'll all buy it. Some of them will want pictures.

GAIL Let's stop. Don't do it anymore.

SANDY I'll do it for the money, if I need it. I've made up my mind.

GAIL It'll make you sad.

SANDY Don't say that!

[JUNIOR *and* WILLIAM *come on.* WILLIAM *has* JUNIOR *by the arm.* JUNIOR'*s head is bandaged.* GAIL *jumps up on the table to grab* JUNIOR'*s face*]

GAIL What happened to you. Look at you. Look at him.

JUNIOR Let me sit down.

[JUNIOR *slides in next to* GAIL. WILLIAM *stands at his side*]

SANDY Gail, get off the table. They're all looking at us.

[GAIL *sits*]

GAIL What happened.

JUNIOR I'm a little dizzy. But I'm all right.

GAIL Your dad did this, didn't he.

JUNIOR I didn't handle him very well.

SANDY Your head is swelling up like a melon.

WILLIAM Okay. Everyone should relax. This is not a serious injury. Totally superficial, without doubt. I have the doctor's word on this.

GAIL Who's he.

JUNIOR William.

GAIL [*whispering*] He looks like a bum.

SANDY [*whispering*] He smells really bad.

JUNIOR You get used to it.

WILLIAM It takes time. But I can assure you it's worth the effort. I have much to offer.

JUNIOR He took me to the hospital. He was waiting for me outside the jail and he took me straight to the hospital. He's had an incredible life. Well, not for the last ten years. For the last ten years he hasn't done a thing. But before that, wow.

WILLIAM Excuse me. I'm being overcome by nostalgia.

[*He slides down on to the floor*]

SANDY Hey. Get up. This is a public place. You wanna get me fired?

WILLIAM A pain. Somewhere near the heart. I rule out indigestion absolutely. Because I haven't eaten in a week.

[JUNIOR *grabs* SANDY's *box of fries*]

JUNIOR Here. Eat these.

SANDY Those are mine, Junior.

JUNIOR I'll buy you more. If he doesn't eat he won't have the strength to get up. [*to* WILLIAM] Take it.

[WILLIAM *takes the box*]

WILLIAM French fries. One of my all-time absolute favourite foods. Good even cold. I've had many a vicious battle in the garbage with the neighbourhood cats over these beauties.

[*He takes one. Sucks on it*]

SANDY He's making me sick. I'm going back on duty. [*stands*] I'll try to keep the manager in the kitchen till you get him out of here. They're fanatics about cleanliness in this place.

WILLIAM You have wonderful legs.

SANDY Who asked you to say anything about my legs.

WILLIAM Perhaps if you could imagine the way I looked before I looked like this, before the mighty fall, you could treat it like a compliment.

SANDY But who the hell asked you!

[*She leaves*]

JUNIOR She seems edgy.

GAIL She turned her first trick.

JUNIOR You can't be her friend anymore, Gail.

GAIL I'll forget you said that.

JUNIOR But if she's going to be a hooker, I don't think you'll …

GAIL Listen. She tried it out to see if she could do it. So she'd know in an emergency.

JUNIOR What kind of emergency.

GAIL Financial.

WILLIAM That makes sense. Always be prepared.

GAIL Look! Either he gets up and sits down like a human being or he leaves!

JUNIOR Can you make it into the seat, William.

WILLIAM I'm willing to try. I have deep respect for this young woman's tone of voice. [*gets to his knees*] Just a little help if it's no bother.

[JUNIOR *helps him into the booth.* WILLIAM *slides off the chair onto*]

the floor. JUNIOR *picks him up. Puts the fries in front of him.*
WILLIAM *sucks on some more fries*]

JUNIOR William. Would you like a coffee.

WILLIAM No.

GAIL What's wrong, Junior, what are you trying to avoid telling me.

JUNIOR Nothing.

GAIL Why aren't you looking at me.

WILLIAM It's a sad story.

GAIL What is.

WILLIAM I weep. Look, a tear on my cheek. I have been reached
personally and sincerely by this tragedy.

GAIL What tragedy.

WILLIAM He'll tell you. In his time.

GAIL Junior, what the hell is it.

JUNIOR Nothing really. Just dumb bad luck. My head hurts.
[JUNIOR *lays his head on* GAIL's *shoulder*]

WILLIAM A little comfort. There, there. Shush. Sleep. Dream.

GAIL Please be quiet. [*to* JUNIOR] Tell me, honey.

JUNIOR Tell her, William.

GAIL How can he tell me. What's he got to do with it.

JUNIOR He's good with words. Really. He'll tell it good. You'll probably
enjoy the telling even if the story itself depresses you.
[*Pause*]

WILLIAM I have your permission?

GAIL Go ahead, William.

WILLIAM First a summary. It has been a bad day for your loved one,
my friend here. His father refused to end their relationship. Then
beat him up. Later in the afternoon he got fired from his job.

GAIL Oh Jesus.

WILLIAM But that's not the worst. This is the worst. He has been
coerced into an involvement in criminal activity.

GAIL Oh no. Oh Jesus.
[*She is petting* JUNIOR's *head*]

WILLIAM That was the summary. Let me rinse my mouth and give you
the poetic details.
[*He picks up what's left of* SANDY's *Coke*]

GAIL Jesus. Shit.

JUNIOR [*to* WILLIAM] Excuse me.

238

[JUNIOR *lays his head in* GAIL'*s lap.* WILLIAM *wipes away a tear. Touches* JUNIOR'*s arm affectionately, then* GAIL'*s.* GAIL *looks up towards the ceiling*]

WILLIAM I speak now from the heart of experience. I use words like destiny and fate and despair. I talk of the great abyss which beckons us all. I speak of the great underclass of our society, the doomed, the forgotten, the outcasts. I describe the fine line which separates the lands of function and dysfunction. I put it in terms which cover the spectrum. The political. The philosophical. The poetic. Occasionally I use the vernacular. I talk of the great fuck-up. Of getting shafted, getting screwed up the ass. Without even a kiss. I describe the human condition. I tell you Junior's story. Your story. And if I may be so bold, our story ... Because aren't we all in this together. Aren't we all friends here. Can't you feel the bond. Isn't this the absolute truth.

[*And* WILLIAM *continues ... gesticulating, wiping away tears*]
[*Fadeout*]

The living room of JUNIOR's *sad little house. A sofa and a lamp.*
WINEVA DAWSON *is standing in the middle of the room. A cigarette in*
her mouth. Holding a cardboard box. Looking around. She mutters
something, puts the box down behind the couch. Looks around again.
Leaves
JUNIOR *comes on from another direction with a glass of water and a*
bottle of aspirin. Takes a few. Washes them down. Takes the cushions
from the sofa and opens it up into a bed. Blankets and sheets already
in place. Strips to his underwear. Lies down under the covers
GAIL *comes on*

GAIL Take the aspirin.

JUNIOR I did.

GAIL Feel better?

JUNIOR Not yet. Did you call your mom.

GAIL Yeah.

JUNIOR Is it okay for you to stay over.

GAIL Come on, you know I don't ask her permission for things like
that. I'm eighteen. I just let her know I'm all right.

JUNIOR Did you send her my love.

GAIL Sure.

JUNIOR You didn't, did you.

GAIL It would make her nervous if I sent her your love, Junior. I'm not
sure she'd know how to take it.

JUNIOR I like your mother.

GAIL She likes you.

JUNIOR That's not really true, is it.

GAIL She thinks you're ... interesting. She thinks we're an interesting
match. She's not totally against it. Not totally.

JUNIOR Well, maybe if you'd start sending her my love like I ask you,
for chrissake!

GAIL Don't worry about my mother. How she feels about you isn't an
issue. How'd you lose your job.

JUNIOR William explained it. Weren't you listening.

GAIL I must have phased out after he got to the part about your Uncle
Ritchie.

JUNIOR Yeah. Terrifying wasn't it. He made it sound terrifying. William seemed to know all about my Uncle Ritchie. Maybe he's met him.

GAIL Where is William.

JUNIOR Sleeping on the pantry floor. I told him he could sleep inside but he said he couldn't re-enter civilization too quickly. He had to do it in stages.

GAIL Why's he doing it at all. Really, why's he doing it around you.

JUNIOR We've got a bond. He thinks I need a teacher.

GAIL A what? Never mind. We'll talk about William later. Tell me about your job.

JUNIOR Let's not talk about it. It's pathetic.

GAIL I want to know.

JUNIOR They received an anonymous call.

GAIL They?

JUNIOR Whoever owns the company. Well, maybe not the owners. Someone. I don't know. I don't know much.

GAIL Do you know what the call was about.

JUNIOR That car I stole when I was a kid? I've been trying to think if there's anything else.

GAIL You mean they didn't tell you.

JUNIOR The plant manager said he was under orders to let me go. Couldn't say why. Said he'd give me a hint though. Anonymous call.
[*Pause*]
So?

GAIL I'm thinking ... This wouldn't have happened if that place was unionized.

JUNIOR What should I do. Do you have a plan.

GAIL Give me a while, I'm thinking.

JUNIOR Well while you're at it, what do we do about my Uncle Ritchie.

GAIL Would he really have your dad killed.

JUNIOR For sure. He's a real scuzz. The true criminal pig my dad could never be.

GAIL If he's so good at it, why does he need you. Why does he need this place.

JUNIOR Well listen, he's no fucking mastermind. I mean, he's good at it in comparison to my dad. He doesn't get caught every single time or anything.

GAIL Well, we can't go along with it.

JUNIOR We can't?

GAIL You know we can't. You know that.

JUNIOR Sure. Because it's my true destiny and we have to avoid it at any cost.

GAIL Listen! Don't let this get to you. Keep it small. It's still small. Nothing's happened yet.

[*She is rubbing his head*]

JUNIOR Yeah. And anyway he'd just be using my house if worse came to worst.

GAIL It can't happen! Not because it's your true destiny. We can't do it, that's all. We can't start.

JUNIOR I could let him kill my dad.

[*Pause*]

GAIL Could you.

JUNIOR I wish.

[WILLIAM *comes on*]

WILLIAM Hello. Apologies for the interruption.

JUNIOR Is it too cold out there.

WILLIAM No. Absolutely fine. I was just wondering ... well, it's been almost twenty-four hours.

GAIL He needs a drink.

WILLIAM Nothing fancy. Some wine? Domestic will do.

JUNIOR Sorry. Don't have any.

WILLIAM Perhaps I aim too high. Almost anything works. Aftershave. Hair tonic. Vanilla extract ... Just a sip. For the shaking.

GAIL Are you suffering withdrawal.

WILLIAM This is a possibility. I just had a lengthy argument with a large mongoose. It was speaking Japanese. [*starts to cry*] I tried. I tried so hard to understand. But it's such a difficult language.

GAIL [*to* JUNIOR] D.T.'s. [*jumps up*] Come with me, William.

[*She grabs his hand*]

WILLIAM With you I will go anywhere. You are the child I never had.

GAIL Yeah. You remind me a little of my father too.

JUNIOR Where are you taking him.

GAIL The bathroom.

WILLIAM Yes. Good. Aftershave was honestly my first choice.

GAIL [*to* JUNIOR] A shower. Cold water.

[*They leave.* JUNIOR *takes a couple more aspirin.* WINEVA *comes on. Stands there. Holding another box*]

WINEVA Are they gone. Those voices. Are they gone.

JUNIOR Who are you.

WINEVA Are you Junior.

JUNIOR Yeah.

WINEVA I'm Wineva.

[JUNIOR *gets up*]

JUNIOR Do I know you.

WINEVA I'm Wineva. I'm your Aunt Wineva. Your Uncle Ritchie's wife.

JUNIOR He's married? Since when.

WINEVA Two years. Well, common law. It's the same thing. We're family. Aren't you going to give me a kiss.

JUNIOR Maybe later.

WINEVA Give me a kiss. Come on over here and give me a kiss. I'm your aunt.

[JUNIOR *goes over. Kisses her cheek*]

Was that so bad. Try to be a little friendlier from now on. We're family. Here.

[*She hands him the box*]

Put this behind the couch with the other one.

[JUNIOR *looks behind the couch. Looks at* WINEVA]

JUNIOR Where'd that come from.

WINEVA They're heavy aren't they.

JUNIOR What.

WINEVA That box. It's heavy.

JUNIOR Yeah.

WINEVA So why don't you put it down.

JUNIOR Sure.

[*He does*]

WINEVA So ... Give me another kiss ... I'm trying to establish contact here.

[*He kisses her on the cheek*]

That wasn't so bad. We're family. It's good for a family to have warm feelings for each other. I'm getting warm feelings for you. How are your feelings for me.

JUNIOR What's in the boxes.

WINEVA Why do you ask.

JUNIOR I shouldn't ask?

WINEVA I didn't ask. Why should you.

JUNIOR So you don't know what's in them.

WINEVA Why should I.

JUNIOR How many more in your car.

WINEVA It's a van.

JUNIOR So there's a lot?

WINEVA There's more. What's a lot.

JUNIOR How many more!

WINEVA A lot more!

[*Pause*]

JUNIOR And you're bringing them all in here?

WINEVA So are you. We're doing it together. Like a family. It's a family business.

JUNIOR Yeah. What kind of business is it that the family's ... in.

WINEVA Maybe you should get dressed before you go out to the van.

JUNIOR Sure.

[*He starts to get dressed*]

So what kind of business is it. You didn't say.

WINEVA A family business. You work out, or what? In a gym, or what? You're in fair shape. Your body is in fairly good shape. I'm not getting excited or anything but it's decent to look at.

JUNIOR Yeah. Great. Thanks. You go ahead. I'll catch up. You shouldn't leave the van unguarded. Those boxes are valuable.

WINEVA Is that what you think.

JUNIOR You don't?

WINEVA Did I say that.

JUNIOR Are they valuable.

WINEVA It depends what's in them, doesn't it.

JUNIOR You go ahead. I'll catch up.

WINEVA Sure. Give me a kiss.

[*He walks over. Kisses her cheek*]

That's real nice. You see, a warm feeling is developing. That's the important thing, right.

JUNIOR Sure.

WINEVA No matter what's in the boxes, no matter what the

consequences, it's the warm feeling that'll see us through, keep us together, keep us loyal. Protect us from the shit. Once more for good measure.

[*She grabs his cheek. Hard. Kisses his lips hard. Taps his face. And leaves*]

JUNIOR Holy fuck! [*turns in a few circles*] Shit.

[*He runs off after* GAIL. WINEVA *comes on with another box. Looks around. Frowns. Puts down the box. Goes out.* GAIL, JUNIOR *and* WILLIAM *appear bending down in a tight grouping in a far corner of the room.* WILLIAM *is wearing an old bathrobe*]

GAIL Where is she.

JUNIOR Outside I guess. Look. A box. That makes three.

GAIL We have to stop her.

JUNIOR You can do it. I know you can.

WILLIAM And as a last resort, there is always me, of course.

JUNIOR No offence, William. Gail has a way with people like this.

GAIL She's coming back.

JUNIOR Do you have a plan.

GAIL No.

WILLIAM It might be a good idea to begin by standing up. That way for sure we don't look so foolish.

JUNIOR Yeah.

[*They straighten.* WINEVA *comes in. Another box. Another cigarette*]

WILLIAM You. Madame. Put that box down.

JUNIOR No.

WILLIAM No? No. I mean do not put that box down. We do not want that box.

[WINEVA *puts the box down*]

WINEVA All of you. Over here. Come on.

[*They move closer to her*]

Over here.

[*They move closer*]

You must be Grace.

GAIL [*to* JUNIOR] Who's Grace.

JUNIOR [*to* WINEVA] Her name's Gail.

WINEVA I've been told all about you. By the family. Give me a kiss ... Come on. I'm Junior's aunt. It's the custom. Give me a kiss.

[GAIL *goes and gives her a kiss on the cheek*]

There. That was innocent enough. This must be your father.

GAIL My ... uncle.

WINEVA Good enough ... Give me a kiss, oldtimer.

WILLIAM First the matter of the boxes.

WINEVA First the kiss. We have to be on terms before we go any
further. Put it here.

[*She points to her cheek.* WILLIAM *kisses her cheek*]

Oh. Whew. Jesus. What's that smell on your breath. You been
drinking Old Spice? [*laughs*]

WILLIAM Yes. As a matter of fact I have.

WINEVA Now all of you. Remember the bond. The warm feeling. You,
Grace, especially. It will be a pleasure to be your aunt. You I like.
You've got a very nice body. Ah, come on, relax. You can always
stop me if I go too far.

WILLIAM You have been sent by the notorious Ritchie, I assume.

WINEVA Junior knows why I'm here. All we need from you is the
loyalty of a loved one.

WILLIAM But I—

WINEVA Butt out. [*to* JUNIOR] Come on now, we've go a lot more out
there.

[*She goes*]

JUNIOR What should I do.

GAIL Go ahead.

JUNIOR Have you got a plan yet.

GAIL No.

JUNIOR I'll play along. Buy you some more time.

[JUNIOR *goes out*]

GAIL Why does he think I can stop this. He thinks I can do anything.
He has this picture of me in his head about twenty times the size of
life. [*sits on the bed*]

WILLIAM Don't give up.

GAIL These things have their own momentum, you know.

WILLIAM I think we should ask for a meeting with the uncle himself.

GAIL Wouldn't help. I met him once. He's a real swine. He drools. You
should see it. And it's not from drink. He's sober when he drools.
He just stands there, gets some really evil thought in his head, and
the saliva pours. Man, just thinking about him is making me sick.

[WINEVA *and* JUNIOR *come on. Put down their boxes.* WINEVA *starts off*]

WILLIAM After you leave we will dispose of these boxes. They will be taken away. Lost in the vastness of the dark city.
[*She stops*]
This is a definite truth. I am not bluffing.
[*She turns*]

WINEVA Maybe you didn't kiss me hard enough. Maybe there wasn't enough feeling in it. Come here. Now!
[WILLIAM *walks over.* WINEVA *grabs him by the collar*]
This is big business. Ritchie has plans. This is just the beginning. There's more to come. We'll all do very well if we don't let each other down. If the bond holds. But if the bond breaks, people will get seriously hurt. Junior's father will be the first. It might not stop there. You could get hurt too.
[WILLIAM *begins to cry*]
What's wrong. Did I scare you.

WILLIAM No. It's pain ... Pain deep inside. All my organs are rotting away, you see. This feels like the liver.

WINEVA This will make you feel better.
[*She kisses him. Hard. With tongue. Starts off*]
Come on, Junior.
[*They both leave.* WILLIAM *sits down next to* GAIL]

WILLIAM She is a truly terrifying kisser.

GAIL I can feel a dark shadow hanging over our heads. Descending slowly. Junior and I are doomed. It's young love gone wrong. Dead man's curve. Teenage wasteland. In a couple of years we could have made it to the suburbs ... no, the suburbs are fucked up too. The country's the only answer. If we'd just had more time, the country ... an unlisted phone. Two good jobs.

WILLIAM In times similar to these over the years, always, I have found it helpful to put things in historical perspective. We are dealing here with an absolute definite class. The criminal element.

GAIL You guessed that much, eh.

WILLIAM The point is, threats don't work. Neither will reason, nor compassion, obviously. No normal social dialogue. The logic is not there. The mind bent from years of repression.

GAIL You think the problem with these people is that they're repressed.

WILLIAM The class is repressed. When the class is repressed, it produces a certain percentage of moronic immoral slimy offspring.

GAIL Is this taking us anyplace useful.

WILLIAM It's a process. It takes time. We begin in the abstract.
Eventually we move on. Settling finally in the area of logic. A
problem exists. A solution also. It is necessary to the laws of the
universe.

GAIL And meanwhile the shadow hangs.

[WINEVA *comes on with a box.* JUNIOR *follows with two*]

WINEVA Finished.

WILLIAM So soon?

WINEVA How's your liver.

WILLIAM Better. Thank you.

WINEVA Great. [*to* JUNIOR] When I leave you have to put these boxes
in the basement. Those are the instructions. Any problem with
that.

[*They all shake their heads*]

No looking in the boxes. We'll know if you've looked. So no
looking. Any problem with that.

[*They all shake their heads*]

Good. No hard feelings. I'm just doing a job. Doing my part. I'm
married to the main man. [*to* GAIL] It's just a marriage of
convenience. But it's still family. There's no sex but there's a bond.
By the way, do you all understand what I really mean by 'family.'

[*They all nod*]

This is just the beginning. There's more to come.

JUNIOR More boxes?

WINEVA Just more. When you're needed you'll be contacted. Any
problems with that.

[JUNIOR *shakes his head*]

The oldtimer and the girl too. They're family now. They're
informed. They're in. Right in the centre. Understand?

[*They all nod*]

Good. Great. Now kisses goodbye. Hard ones. With feeling. Come
on.

[WILLIAM *goes to her. Kisses her cheek.* GAIL *goes to her. Kisses her
cheek.* WINEVA *runs her hand through* GAIL*'s hair*]

Nice. Very nice. [*to* JUNIOR] Your turn.

[JUNIOR *just stares at her*]

Come on.

[*Pause*]

Your kiss. It's mine. And I want it. Now!

[JUNIOR *kisses her cheek*]

Thanks.

[*She leaves. Long pause. They all wander around the room in a daze*]

JUNIOR When I was little I always wanted an aunt.

[*He sits between* GAIL *and* WILLIAM *on the edge of the bed*]

I'm sorry.

[*He kisses her*]

I'm sorry you're involved in this.

GAIL It's not your fault.

JUNIOR I'm sorry anyway.

[*He kisses her once, twice*]

GAIL Wait. Why is it you always get affectionate at times like these. The worse things get, the more you kiss.

JUNIOR Kissing you makes me forget. That's all I can say about it really. If I couldn't live my life under your sweater, I'd like to live it attached to your mouth.

GAIL [*to* WILLIAM] Sad guy, eh. I think he probably means it too. [*to* JUNIOR] Don't you.

JUNIOR Sure.

GAIL Sure.

[*They hug. A long sustained kiss*]

WILLIAM This love is a precious commodity. The two of you. I love this love you have. It should be nourished and protected. I will rise to the occasion. I will surround your love with an iron will! [*groans*] Ooh. Go away pain. Recede. Liver, spleen, bladder. Head. Heal. Ooh. Please. Jesus. Oh. [*sliding off the bed*] Oh God. Not the pancreas. The kidneys.

[*He is on the floor, writhing.* JUNIOR *and* GAIL *stop kissing. Look at him*]

Don't worry. I'll protect you. This is a promise. Ohhhh! Arrgh! Geeezz!

[*Blackout*]

SCENE FIVE

Late night
Lights up on a section of street. SANDY *is pacing. Dressed in high heels,*
tight jeans and sweater. Smoking. Looking around. After a moment
she walks off. Lights out on this area
Lights up on an alley off the street. JUNIOR, GAIL *and* WILLIAM *are*
each sitting against a garbage can. WILLIAM *is wearing a baseball*
jacket, sneakers. Ill-fitting but reasonably clean

WILLIAM This I stress. I absolutely stress the following point. To
understand the possibility of progress you must first identify the
force which keeps you static. Is it external. Does it lie within. To
find the answer you require self-awareness. Self-awareness is the
thing. Junior, seriously, this is important stuff.

JUNIOR William, excuse me for a minute. You know, Gail, I'd feel a lot
better if you were home.

GAIL I'd feel better if you were home too. Too bad for both of us.
[WILLIAM *is staring at his hand*]

WILLIAM I look at my hand. I picture it lying on the sidewalk, on the
end of my arm. Limp. I picture someone stepping on it. Crushing
my bones. Truly. I ask myself, could this have been avoided. Did
this person step on my hand intentionally. On the other hand,
what was my hand doing there in the first place.

GAIL You'd passed out.

WILLIAM I was speaking in the abstract, but yes, in fact, I had passed
out.

JUNIOR What time is it.

GAIL Ten past midnight.

JUNIOR They're late. We could leave. If they ask we could say … you
were late.

GAIL So they'll call us again tomorrow night. The night after. We've
got to get involved a bit before we can take a stand. Get some
information.

WILLIAM There is of course a moral in the story of the crushed hand.

JUNIOR Look, William, people will step on your hand every chance
they get.

GAIL Yeah, William, I mean listen, maybe you bring all this pain on yourself, did you ever consider that.

WILLIAM Exactly my point. Good for you both. So we go on. We move slowly through the abstract darkness. Point by point we nail things down. But first I must take a piss.

[*He wanders into the darkness*]

JUNIOR I could have bought a gun. And when they showed up just shot them dead.

GAIL Now you're thinking.

JUNIOR Ah, this is a sad situation we've got here. They've got us on a leash. They're going to lead us around for the rest of our lives. We'll be slaves. Low-life criminal slaves. Until we're caught. God I can't stand the idea of you in jail. I've been thinking about it for hours. It's driving me crazy. Please go home.

GAIL No.

JUNIOR Please.

GAIL Shush. What's that noise.

JUNIOR Is it a pissing sound.

GAIL Voices ... Listen.

[*There are voices in the distance. Down the alley. Getting closer. Voices. Arguing voices. One man. One woman. Getting closer. Suddenly* WINEVA *appears out of the darkness*]

WINEVA Good. You're here.

GAIL Are you alone.

WINEVA You have a problem with that?

GAIL I heard two voices. A man and a woman.

WINEVA Wrong. Just me.

[GAIL *and* JUNIOR *look at each other*]

Where's the oldtimer. I told you. I wanted all three of you. What have we got here, a crack in the wall?

JUNIOR What.

WINEVA The bond. Is it breaking.

[WILLIAM *is wandering back*]

WILLIAM You know something, this alley looks familiar. This building. I know this building. [*sees* WINEVA] Oh, hello.

WINEVA Come here. Quickly.

[WILLIAM *rushes to her. Kisses her cheek. She breaks away*]

There's no time for that shit. Now listen, this runs like clockwork. Everyone does their part. The girl keeps a watch. On the street. Go.

JUNIOR She stays with me.

WINEVA Did someone die and leave you in charge. Do you know
something I don't.

JUNIOR Look, lady—

WINEVA The clock is running. Remember your father.

GAIL I'll be all right.

[GAIL *starts off.* JUNIOR *grabs her*]

JUNIOR If anything happens. Run. Get away. Promise.

GAIL Yeah.

JUNIOR No, promise. Jesus, promise. I'll go crazy.

GAIL I promise. [*starts off*]

JUNIOR Anything at all, and you run. No. Take a cab. It's late.

[GAIL *is gone*]

WINEVA Finished?

JUNIOR You've got no right involving her in this. You and Uncle
Ritchie are shit. Insane shit too.

WINEVA Finished now?

WILLIAM You want us to do something. Please, why don't you tell us
what it is.

WINEVA Well, I'm trying, aren't I. Now it's simple. That's the door of
the loading dock. We break it open.

JUNIOR How.

WINEVA The usual way.

JUNIOR Yeah, what's that.

WINEVA They told me you were a dumb fuck. They didn't tell me you
were the dumbest fuck. Look, haven't I tried to be nice to you.
Didn't I go out of my way to establish contact. Why the
aggravation.

JUNIOR I just wanted to make sure you know what you're doing.

WINEVA Watch me. Now the door is my job. Don't worry about it.
When I break it, you head in. A few feet inside along the left wall
is a pile of about fifty boxes.

JUNIOR [*to* WILLIAM] More boxes.

WILLIAM Fifty boxes. That's a lot of boxes.

WINEVA It goes like this. The kid hands them to the oldtimer, the
oldtimer lines them up. In the meantime I'm getting the van which
is parked at the end of the alley. I bring it back. We load. It's
simple.

JUNIOR What happens then.

WINEVA Jesus. We leave.

JUNIOR What happens to the boxes.

WINEVA Guess.

JUNIOR You bring them to my house. That's my house, you know. It's not Ritchie's. It's not my dad's. My mom left me that house. I have a responsibility to that house. It was never intended for work like this. My mother wasn't like that. Jesus.

WILLIAM Perhaps we could find another place to store them.

[WINEVA *approaches* WILLIAM *making kissing noises*]

WINEVA I've got instructions. The instructions say the house.

WILLIAM [*to* JUNIOR] It's gotta be the house.

JUNIOR Like a fucking slave. Jesus, William when are we going to do something about this. What's the historical lesson here. I mean, come on!

WINEVA What's wrong with him.

WILLIAM A touch of nervous energy. He'll be fine.

WINEVA Here's hoping ... Okay, on the count of three.

JUNIOR Jesus.

WINEVA One. Two. Three!

[WINEVA *yells.* JUNIOR *and* WILLIAM *yell, fall on the ground.* WINEVA *picks up one of the garbage cans. Puts it over her head and attacks the loading door. Blackout on this area. Lights up in the street.* GAIL *is waiting. Nervously. Someone is coming. She turns her back.* SANDY *comes on*]

SANDY Hey, I know you.

[GAIL *turns*]

GAIL What are you doing here.

SANDY Well, I sure hope it's not the same thing you're doing here.

GAIL Look how you're dressed. You look stupid.

[SANDY *looks at herself*]

SANDY Hey, it's the going fashion. It's not my idea. What am I supposed to do, break new ground.

GAIL You promised you wouldn't work the street.

SANDY You followed me, didn't you.

GAIL No ... Yes ... No. Never mind. What are you doing, Sandy. You said if things came to the worst, if there was no money, no job, no husband, no future, you'd turn a trick or two in the hotels. That was the plan, the hotels.

SANDY Suppose I got bounced from the hotels. I had to know if I could do it on the street. The plan wasn't complete. I'm completing it.

GAIL It's dangerous.

SANDY It's worth it. It's for my peace of mind. Relax. I know what I'm doing. What are you doing.

GAIL Nothing. I'm still looking for work. I had an interview yesterday with a bank.

SANDY I was sort of talking about now, right. You followed me, didn't you.

GAIL No. I'm ... I'm standing lookout.

SANDY For what.

GAIL I don't know ... the cops, I guess. Listen, this is a secret. Junior's breaking into a building down the alley.

SANDY Why don't you just admit you followed me. You've got a right. You're my best friend.

GAIL He's not alone. He's with William.

SANDY That bum?

GAIL And his aunt.

SANDY The bum's got an aunt?

GAIL Junior's aunt. She's the brains, I think. I don't know. Maybe she's the brawn. I don't know. I'm scared shitless.

SANDY So. This is the truth, right.

GAIL Yeah.

SANDY Really.

GAIL Yeah.

[*Pause*]

SANDY I'm going to tell your mother.

GAIL Get real. Come on.

SANDY No, I'm serious. She told me to. Any sign that Junior was corrupting you and I'm supposed to report to her directly. I swore an oath.

GAIL It's not Junior's fault. He's being blackmailed.

SANDY I don't give a flying fuck about Junior. I'm telling your mother!

GAIL Go ahead. I'll tell yours.

SANDY Okay okay, forget the mother-telling thing. Listen. This is crime, Gail. What you're doing is serious crime. We should stop them.

GAIL It's not so easy. There are complications.

SANDY Nothing's more complicated than this. This is the first step to disaster. We should stop them. Figure the rest out later.

GAIL Maybe.

SANDY For sure.

GAIL Yeah, maybe.

SANDY Let's do it.

GAIL Yeah? ... Okay. Yeah.

[*Two gunshots. They take two or three steps and are frozen by the wailing sound of a burglar alarm*]

SANDY Too late.

GAIL What should we do.

SANDY Run.

GAIL No. Junior's back there.

SANDY Junior would want you to run.

GAIL No. Take a cab. He wanted me to take a cab.

SANDY A real criminal genius for sure. Let's go. Come on. Come on!

GAIL No, no I can't.

[SANDY *grabs* GAIL's *arm. And pulls*]

SANDY Come on!

GAIL Junior!

[*A spotlight catches* GAIL *on the street, while another catches* JUNIOR *grimacing in pain in the doorway of the loading platform*]

[*Blackout*]

The visitors' room at the city jail. HENRY DAWSON *and* WILLIAM.
Staring at each other across the table. Long pause

HENRY Do I know you ... There's something familiar about you.

WILLIAM I am a psychiatrist.

HENRY Oh. Well, that's good. I'm glad you're here. Because they want
to put me away for keeps. But I can be saved. I want to turn myself
around. Society never gave me nothing but dirt. But I don't want
to hold a grudge no more. I want you to reach right inside my
head, reach right inside and turn it around. I'm willing. I'm ready.
I'm able.

WILLIAM Bullshit.

HENRY No. Honest.

WILLIAM Bullshit.

HENRY Ah, come on. Really. Honest. Give me a break. Don't be cruel.
Try me out.

WILLIAM You are a big stupid shit-spewing asshole. One of the world's
truly pathetic empty spaces. An enormous nothingness on legs. A
total waste of time. Vomit. If I had a gun I'd shoot you.

HENRY I want another doctor.

WILLIAM Shut up. I warn you. If you make me angry I'll kill you with
my bare hands.

HENRY You are a lousy psychiatrist. I've seen a few of them. And you
are the worst.

WILLIAM It's a lie, stupid. I told it so they would let me see you. Now
shut up and listen. Your son was nearly killed two nights ago.

HENRY How do you know my son.

WILLIAM Shut up. To be coerced into crime is one thing, to be coerced
by incompetent fools is another. I could live a criminal life. I've
seen the abyss. I've felt the pull. Even philosophically, I could come
to terms with certain actions. Perhaps against large corrupt
institutions. This is hypothetical. I don't expect you to understand
what I'm saying.

HENRY Thanks.

WILLIAM But to attempt to steal food from the Salvation Army
headquarters is beneath contempt. Unjustifiable.

HENRY So Ritchie finally knocked over the Sally Ann. He's been planning that job for two years.

WILLIAM Then he is, and this I find almost impossible to believe, more stupid than you are.

HENRY [*smiles*] Really. You think so.

WILLIAM Oh, yes. Because in those two years he wasn't even able to discover that the warehouse is guarded by two armed security men.

HENRY So Ritchie screwed up bad.

WILLIAM And your son was wounded.

HENRY That's rough. I'm sorry. Tell him I'm sorry if you see him, will you. So Ritchie screwed up. So. So who's the dumb fuck, eh. Tell me who the first-place dumb fuck is in this family.

WILLIAM It's a crowded field. Look for a photo finish.

HENRY What. Yeah. So you know my kid. Hey. Wait a minute. Now I know what's familiar about you. It's your clothes. They're mine. You're wearing my clothes. Where'd you get my clothes.

WILLIAM In your closet.

HENRY Hey, wait a minute. You were in my closet? You know my kid and you're in my closet. What is this. Are you taking over my life. This is weird. That's my life. Get your own.

WILLIAM You have no life. You have no son. Now shut up because you are starting to make me angry. I want you to get word to your brother. From now on we do things our way.

HENRY Our way.

WILLIAM My way! And Junior's. Truth is if I had just my way I'd let them cut you open. But for some reason your son can't let this happen. Maybe because unfortunately he cares for you. Maybe because he really believes he's supposed to turn bad. That it's predestined or some such nonsense.

HENRY It's true. It's in the family. The bad turn. It takes place in the head. You can't fight it. You have to give in.

WILLIAM Tell your brother we want to meet with him personally. To discuss a ... new approach. A meeting is essential. These are further instructions.

[*He hands* HENRY *an envelope*]

I've written them down because we don't expect you to be able to remember them.

HENRY Thanks.

WILLIAM Do this quickly. If not I will trick Junior somehow and make sure that we adopt an attitude that prompts your brother to hurt you.

HENRY Suppose I don't believe you.

WILLIAM Personally I hope you don't believe me. I honestly do. Coming in contact with your type is revitalizing me. I'm gaining strength by the minute. A hatred of the purest kind is making me powerful. This is true. It's amazing. I could kill you on the spot and feel terrific.

HENRY Mister. I don't know where you come from. But you're hard. What'd I ever do to you. Look at me. My life's a disaster. You should be nicer.

WILLIAM I have great sympathy for the truly sad cases of our world. The victims. I have felt so badly that I fell amongst them. This is the truth. This is not melodrama. Their misery made me useless. I fell. But for you, I feel nothing. You use your own boy. Ruin his life. And he's a good one potentially. Have you seen him with his girl. This is love. You wouldn't know it anyway. I have to leave now. I feel my temper rising. [*groans*] Also a slight twinge in the lower intestine. [*stands*] Just one more thing. Please lean over a bit. Yes. A bit more.

[HENRY *obeys.* WILLIAM *leans on the table*]

I have a question. I want you to tell me the truth. I'll know if you lie and I'll take steps to have you hurt. Understand?

[WILLIAM *is pointing a finger at* HENRY]

HENRY Yes.

[WILLIAM *notices that* HENRY *seems mesmerized by the finger*]

WILLIAM The anonymous call to Junior's employer. This was made by his Uncle Ritchie, to somehow make Junior vulnerable?

HENRY Yes.

WILLIAM But how did Ritchie find out who Junior's employer was.

HENRY I don't know.

WILLIAM That's a lie, isn't it.

HENRY Yes.

WILLIAM You gave him the name of the employer.

HENRY I had to.

[*Pause*]

WILLIAM You had to. Yes. I know. It was ... predestined.

[WILLIAM *grabs* HENRY'*s hair. Pulls his head down hard on the table. Starts off*]
Hurts. Doesn't it.
[*Blackout*]

SCENE SEVEN

JUNIOR's *living room.* GAIL, JUNIOR *and* SANDY. GAIL *is just finishing changing a bandage on* JUNIOR's *leg.* SANDY *is watching and grimacing*

JUNIOR Finished?
[GAIL *nods*]
Let me walk. I feel like walking.
[*He gets up.* GAIL *just lowers her head. Sits there*]
It could be worse. My head doesn't hurt much anymore. I wish my mother was still here. We could have a little talk. I could get really scared and she'd understand. She's the only person I could let myself get totally scared in front of. I get close with you, Gail. But with her I could lie down on the floor and pretend I was Jello. I knew this was coming when I was nine. Nine years old. I saw a picture of some guy getting hanged in a book my dad gave me. And I knew right away I'd hang too someday.
GAIL Please. Stop. You're not going to hang.
JUNIOR I feel already hung. They just have to take my body down. Bag it. Send it off for burning. I'm scared.
[GAIL *throws herself onto the floor. Her arms around* JUNIOR's *legs*]
I should have stayed small. Tried to get smaller. Really, really small. This big. So no one would notice. I know I was never really big but I wasn't small enough. Someone noticed I was around. Why are you holding onto my legs.
GAIL Just holding.
JUNIOR Yeah. But it looks pathetic. You're not pathetic.
GAIL Neither are you.
JUNIOR I'm not? She thinks I'm pathetic. [*to* SANDY] Don't you.
SANDY You don't look so good at the moment, but I wouldn't say you were pathetic. She likes you. You must have something. I've been asking her for months what it is, but she won't tell me.
JUNIOR I want to thank you for buying the first-aid stuff. I want to thank you for helping Gail get away ... Thanks.
SANDY Yeah ... Hey, maybe that's it. [*to* GAIL] Is it because he's polite.
JUNIOR Gail. Please get up.
GAIL I know what my problem is. I'm too emotional. I'm an emotional

mess. I'm not thinking clearly. It's the downside of love. I've got to stand back a bit. I know I can solve this mess. I just know it.

JUNIOR I know you can too. [*sits on the couch*]

GAIL Nah. You're being nice. I've let you down. I've got to stand back.

JUNIOR Get up. Please.

GAIL I mean fuck them. [*stands*] Those insane bastards. We've just got to get those rotten insane bastards out of our life.

JUNIOR Did you call your mom.

GAIL She's fine. I sent her your love.

JUNIOR Yeah? How'd you do it.

GAIL Just slipped it in. Junior sends his love.

JUNIOR How'd she take it.

GAIL All right. Nice. She said that was nice.

[*She sits beside* JUNIOR. *They hug*]

JUNIOR Too late though. Junior sends his love. Oh, by the way, I won't be home for awhile. I'm going to prison. Junior? Oh yes, don't worry he's going too. Separate prisons though. Christ, that's right. Gail. Separate prisons. I'll go nuts.

SANDY No one's going to prison. There's a plan.

GAIL What is it.

SANDY I have to let the bum tell you. It's his plan.

JUNIOR His name's William. Don't call him the bum, please. He's my only friend. He's from Europe you know. He used to be something big. He's been around. He's been in four revolutions. He grows on you.

GAIL That's kind of true.

[WILLIAM *comes on*]

WILLIAM [*raises his arms*] Look at me. I'm different.

[*He is. He is wearing a new suit, shirt, shoes. Carrying a new briefcase. Hair is neat. They are all staring at him*]

It's an impressive sight, isn't it. I wish I could be you. Looking at me.

[*Long pause*]

Someone must say something to break the ice.

GAIL There's a purpose to this? This is taking us somewhere constructive? I mean I've got a guy here with a bullet wound. The future looks grim.

JUNIOR How'd you get all this stuff.

WILLIAM With money. From my bank account.

[JUNIOR, GAIL *and* SANDY *look at each other. Shake their heads*]

GAIL Sandy says you've got a plan. What is it.

WILLIAM This.

GAIL A new suit?

WILLIAM Exactly. The suit is the answer. It is the cruise missile of social conflict. It exerts power. We need power. We must go on the offensive. To the disgusting underclass of society the suit is like garlic to Dracula. It makes them grab their genitals. It's an inbred reflex action based on years of grovelling. Even though you know in your heart that grovelling won't stop you from taking it in the groin. Because the suit ... shows ... no ... mercy.

GAIL This is a thin plan, William. This seems pretty fragile.

WILLIAM I'm going to demand we escalate. Demand a higher quality crime. A world beyond their grasp. It will scare them shitless. They'll back off.

GAIL Desperate.

WILLIAM Exactly. But sometimes desperate works.

[WINEVA *comes on. Carrying two boxes*]

WINEVA All right. You're here. That's good. Who's this.

GAIL Just a friend. She can go. Go ahead, Sandy.

SANDY I'm staying.

WINEVA If she stays now, she stays forever. She's in or she's out.

GAIL Get out, Sandy.

SANDY Suppose the hooking fails. Suppose I lose my job. I'll be broke. I should know if I can do crime. I should know, just in case.

WINEVA That makes sense.

WILLIAM Yes. She's just looking for security. Other people invest in bonds.

WINEVA Nice suit, oldtimer. [*to* SANDY] I'm going to do something to you now. It's just a thing we do. Don't get excited.

[*She hands the boxes to* WILLIAM. *She kisses* SANDY *on the cheek*]

WILLIAM Where do these boxes come from.

WINEVA My van. The only two you managed to get out before the kid here screwed up.

JUNIOR Come on. There were two guards. Twenty feet away. I almost got killed.

WINEVA You screwed up. That was a big job and you blew it. You are the one to blame. We're blaming you. Get it?

WILLIAM Stealing cartons of food is to you a big job?

WINEVA There's a problem with that? You think food isn't important? Food is food, you dumb ass. It's the one thing we all need. It moves fast. It keep its value.

GAIL It's a cheap crime.

WINEVA It's the best kind of crime. We've got a right to food. It's like bread. Everyone has a right to bread. In court you can say you were hungry. Who's to say we aren't hungry. Who's to say it wasn't a crime of necessity.

JUNIOR Me.

GAIL And me.

WINEVA Be careful now. Watch the bond. Keep it tight.

WILLIAM I asked for a meeting with Ritchie.

WINEVA Yeah? Is that why you bought the suit.

WILLIAM We want him here. I've got plans. I'm a powerful man. Look at me clearly. I'm making demands here. Things are going to be different. Get Ritchie.

WINEVA He's busy.

JUNIOR With what.

WINEVA Mugging pensioners. Stealing change from children. Stamping on cripples. All the usual stuff.

WILLIAM He's the boss. We want to talk to him and only him.

WINEVA He's the boss?

[*She starts to laugh. It's a moderately high-pitched laugh. She throws her head back. It gets deeper. She doubles up. And the voice plummets into a deep roaring sound. The rest of them back away a bit. She straightens suddenly*]

He's the boss when I need it that way. To push out front. To make introductions sometimes. Sometimes I let him plan something. The Salvation Army job was his. It had his stamp on it for sure. Pure fucking stupidity. He drools. He walks into walls. He reads five words an hour. I use him mostly when I want someone mauled. You annoy me anymore and you'll meet him all right. I'll have him come over here and set your clothes on fire. He likes shit like that. Maybe he'll just molest you all. You keep annoying me and you'll find out! Now oldtimer, you said you've got plans.

WILLIAM You wouldn't like them. I'm dealing here with a very large crime.

WINEVA That's good. I'm up for that. That job the other night was just a test of your loyalty. I like suits. If suits is what you all want, we'll buy them. We'll do suit jobs. That's no problem. Let's talk. Oh, I forgot. We made the papers.

[*She takes a rolled-up section of a newspaper from her pocket. Hands it to* GAIL]

It's circled. Read it to them ... Come on.

GAIL 'Police speculate that the break-in at the Salvation Army headquarters is the work of a new gang of thieves based in the east end of the city. In conjunction, the mayor and several aldermen are demanding a crackdown on street crime, prostitution—'

WINEVA Etcetera, etcetera. We've made an impression. They're squirming. Their bond isn't strong like ours. It can be cracked. We're going to make history.

WILLIAM Criminals make no history. They just make news.

WINEVA You dumb ass. You don't get it, do you ... Here it is. I'm going to give it to you fast. Right now. This isn't crime. It's politics. It's you know ... destiny. I'm no criminal. I'm a fucking revolutionary!

[*They all mutter and look at each other. Pause*]

You have a problem with that?

[*Blackout*]

SCENE EIGHT

A long path of light. GAIL *and* SANDY *are walking through it. Both wearing trenchcoats*

SANDY There's no future in revolution.

GAIL Depends on the revolution.

SANDY Well, there's no money in it for sure.

GAIL Sometimes there's enough.

SANDY Hey, are you for this.

GAIL No. I was talking about revolutions. What I've read about them. This is something different. Suicide probably. We'll all die young.

SANDY I could leave. I don't know why I'm going with you.

GAIL You should leave.

SANDY On the other hand it's an experience. I might learn something I can use later in life.

GAIL Besides, she said if you didn't show up she'd track you down and slit your throat.

SANDY There's that too. She's mentally ill, right. I mean she's not quite human.

[*They are leaving*]

GAIL At least now we've got a purpose. Before it looked like we were being dragged along by a bunch of sub-moronic creeps without a clue. Now at least I know what it is we're supposed to do. We're supposed to destroy the world.

[*The path of light dims. Lights up in an alley.* JUNIOR *and* WILLIAM *are each sitting against a garbage can*]

WILLIAM These alleys all look the same to me.

JUNIOR The garbage cans are newer.

WILLIAM My insides feel like one enormous throbbing ulcer. I'm bleeding to death internally. I'm almost certain of this.

JUNIOR If we get out of this alive, I think you should see a doctor. Maybe a few doctors.

WILLIAM Terrifying. Where would they begin. Once they got a look at my insides they'd have to give me the bad news. I've always been able to live with the possibility that these pains might be imaginary. But once the doctors tell you you're sick then for sure you're sick. Doctors can kill you with words ... You know something, for a few brief hours this afternoon I felt entirely well.

JUNIOR You looked good too.

WILLIAM The theory of the suit is an old one. People used to be extremely afraid of them ... I've been out of touch.

JUNIOR We're sinking, aren't we. I mean this is it. What you call the deep pit. I can feel it for sure. We're inside, about halfway down.

WILLIAM I'll be honest with you. Yes.

JUNIOR And no way to get back up?

WILLIAM Some people would tell you just to think positively. These are people, of course, who have been able to spend all their summers outdoors. Probably their grandmothers had a lot of money. Others would tell you to pick yourself up by the bootstraps. These are people who have forgotten anything they might have known about life. Still others would call for a critical examination of many different factors. A searching for alternatives. I used to be one of those. But I've taken this trip before. At a certain point you just hold your breath till you reach the destination. The bottom, so to speak.

JUNIOR With a thud.

WILLIAM Pretend you're a feather. Think about it. Try to float down. Gently. At this point, this is my only advice.

JUNIOR Thanks.

WILLIAM But I have been known to make miraculous comebacks. We'll see. Maybe I'm just in a mood.

[SANDY *and* GAIL *come on*]

JUNIOR You came.

GAIL That's right. You thought I wouldn't?

JUNIOR I prayed you'd meet someone on the way, and fall in love.

GAIL Just stop it, okay. You're not responsible for me in any way.

JUNIOR You think you're responsible for me. Why can't I feel the same way.

GAIL Because when you feel that way it just turns you to mush ... Where is she. Is she late again.

JUNIOR & WILLIAM Yes!

JUNIOR Let's leave. Let's just go somewhere.

GAIL Where.

JUNIOR Someplace warm. Where we can be naked. Lie down. Sleep.

GAIL With what. You've got money?

JUNIOR It doesn't matter. I can't go. They'll kill my dad.

WILLIAM This is a true equation of the world. These four lives are made equal to the life of your father, that pile of vomit. I'm starting to get angry again.

SANDY What's that noise.

[*Two voices coming. One deep. One high*]

GAIL It's Wineva.

SANDY And someone else. Listen.

[*The two voices have stopped their progress and are having a loud argument*]

GAIL No, just Wineva. She has two voices.

SANDY Yeah, well one of them is speaking Spanish.

WILLIAM With this woman, I'm afraid we are dealing in extreme schizophrenia.

GAIL Like a split personality.

WILLIAM No ... Pretend my fist [*holds it up*] is the place we all know as reality. Things happen here. Shopping. Eating. Going to work. We all spend most of our time here. But the schizophrenic just visits this place occasionally. [*uses a finger from his other hand to demonstrate*] Usually this person spends most of the time out here. In the special place. The place of personal definition. The other reality. It has great detail, this other place. It takes a great imagination to invent it from scratch. An imagination that can be truly terrifying.

[SANDY *has been nodding knowingly.* WINEVA *tumbles out of the darkness. Carrying a knapsack. Wearing a red beret*]

WINEVA Whew! That was a rough one. He thought he had me. Tried to use his voice on me. But I won't wash his floors. I won't stay home and wash his fucking floors while he goes out and changes the world.

WILLIAM He? You mean Ritchie?

WINEVA No. This is some other guy. This is the guy who follows me around making demands. Wants me to be docile. Stay at home. Be his good little woman. He's kinda handsome. But he's very demanding. And he's starting to piss me off ... So you're all here. Good. When I call the army it comes. Wait a minute. Where are the hats.

[*They all produce black berets*]

Come on. Put them on.

[*They obey*]

Good. When it's all over we'll gather round for kisses. Why are you staring at me like that ... You think you detect a weakness. Forget it. Don't ever make the mistake of thinking you know more about my disease than I do. Now gather round for the plan.

[*They do*]

This is the back of a building owned by one of the largest banks in the country. They do business out of this building with some of the world's biggest creeps. Missile builders. Drug lords. Any life-sucking asshole with a few billion to hide ... Tonight we're sending them a message.

[*She takes off her knapsack*]

JUNIOR What's in there.

WINEVA You like mechanical things? Who here likes mechanical things. Who appreciates a job well done.

[*She takes out a gizmo*]

WILLIAM That is a bomb.

WINEVA 'That is a bomb.' I expect more from you, oldtimer. Maybe some appreciation of the difficulty involved here. Or maybe you think it's easy.

WILLIAM You're going to detonate it.

WINEVA You have a problem with that?

WILLIAM Why do you need us. The bang will speak for itself.

WINEVA Any asshole can detonate a bomb.

WILLIAM My point exactly.

WINEVA Be careful ... What I'm saying is I have plans beyond the bomb. These plans involve you.

JUNIOR You know, I thought we were going to steal something.

GAIL Me too.

WINEVA Really. What about you.

SANDY Oh, I just came along. I thought I might learn something useful. Pick up a skill.

WINEVA You're quite the little self-starter aren't you. [*to* GAIL] What the hell is it you thought we were going to steal.

GAIL Documents.

JUNIOR Yeah. Documents. You know, something important.

GAIL Something vital.

WINEVA All right. Sure. Okay. We'll steal something. I'll incorporate theft into the plan.

JUNIOR Okay. But no bomb. People could get hurt.

WINEVA People are supposed to get hurt, you dumb fuck. Try to picture the scenario where the world gets destroyed without anyone getting hurt ... Look, all right, I know the problem here. You don't really care if anyone gets hurt, not really. You just can't live with the responsibility. Revolutionaries have always had this problem. But I've solved it. I've solved the problem of responsibility. You wanna know how? None of your fucking business. Now here's the plan.

JUNIOR No way.

GAIL He's right.

JUNIOR No way at all. No.

WINEVA Watch it. Be careful. You've been warned.

WILLIAM No bomb.

WINEVA But the bomb's just for openers. Then we're going to kidnap the chairman. He's in there now, working late. It's all planned.

GAIL No bomb.

WINEVA I'm willing to throw in a theft. We can steal anything you want.

JUNIOR No goddamn bomb. And that's it.

WINEVA Really?

GAIL We're all together on this.

WILLIAM We stand firm. This is a certainty. There will be no explosion. No bomb.

WINEVA You're sure about that.

  [*She is holding it*]

WILLIAM We are determined. We stand here together. United.

WINEVA Well, if you stand here longer than twenty seconds you'll be dead. I just set it. It's going off.

WILLIAM This is a bluff.

WINEVA The hell with you. No one tells me I can't use my bomb. No one! I should have kissed you much much harder. I should have kissed you to death.

WILLIAM [*to the others*] I truly believe this is a bluff. She is unstable. But not necessarily suicidal.

WINEVA Suicidal, my ass. We'll all be martyrs. Ten seconds. Eight seconds.

[*They swarm her. Wrestle.* WILLIAM *gets the bomb from her. Holds it up proudly*]

WILLIAM Got it!

JUNIOR Jesus Christ! William!

WILLIAM Oh.

[WILLIAM *throws the bomb.* JUNIOR *grabs* GAIL. *They all run*]
[*Blackout. Sound of an explosion*]

SCENE NINE

JUNIOR's *living room.* WINEVA *is sitting on the floor in a corner. Wrapped in a blanket. Chewing an edge of it.* WILLIAM *is pacing. With a slight limp.* GAIL *is bandaging* JUNIOR's *arm. They are on the pullout bed*

GAIL You know Junior ... you didn't have to fall on top of me to protect me.

JUNIOR Yeah. I did.

GAIL I mean we could have just kept running.

JUNIOR Stuff was flying all around. Better it hit me than you.

GAIL Why. Never mind ... This hurts I guess.

JUNIOR But the leg is better. And the head doesn't bother me at all anymore. You know I've been thinking. Maybe this will only stop when I've got a wound on every part of my body. Maybe that's the destiny.

WILLIAM I absolutely forbid the use of that word from now on. Add to that fate. Also legacy ... Please forget those words. You will do this for me and I will not talk about the abyss ... This way we can begin to recover ... Even now I am thinking of ways to do this.
[WINEVA *makes a loud prolonged hissing noise*]

GAIL How long has she been sitting there. It seems like hours.

JUNIOR She's the scariest person I ever met in my life. I mean no one else is even close.

GAIL And the noises she makes. What are the noises all about. What was that honking noise she made an hour ago about. Do we have to spend the rest of our young tragic lives listening to her honk and whinny and whistle.

WILLIAM [*points to* WINEVA] I want to kill her! Get me some wire! I want to put it around her neck! She's doing no good with her bomb! She's just ruining lives here. [*to* JUNIOR] Do you have any wire? No, seriously. She's badly damaged. We'll put her out of her misery.

WINEVA I heard that. [*getting up slowly*] Harsh. It was harsh.
[*She goes and sits on the bed next to* GAIL *and* JUNIOR]
I didn't mean to make a bad impression. I was just trying to provide leadership. I love you people. You're the people I do my

work for. You're the working class. The peasant class. Everything I've ever done I've done for you.

[*She puts her head on* GAIL's *shoulder*]

I've got some books for you to read. If you don't know how to read I'll teach you. Teach you how to rise up. Get free. Smash the barriers that keep you hopeless. But first I need some sleep. [*lies down*] It's so hard. Being the last person in the world who really gives a shit is just ... so hard.

[*She closes her eyes.* SANDY *comes in. Carrying a newspaper and a bag of groceries*]

SANDY We're famous. No, that's wrong. [*to* WILLIAM] What's the word when you're famous but it's not good.

WILLIAM Infamous.

SANDY That's it. I knew I was close. That's what we are. It's kind of scary.

[*She hands* GAIL *the paper*]

The front page. At the bottom.

[GAIL *is reading to herself*]

WILLIAM This could be important. I'm thinking here of public opinion, when we come to trial. What does it say.

GAIL We're terrorists ... Or we're desperate criminals. Or we're trying to start a race war ... They can't seem to make up their minds. It was all a prank. Organized crime. No, no. Yes. Here ... They settled on one. We're definitely terrorists. But with a strong local criminal element.

JUNIOR Barbados.

GAIL What.

JUNIOR Barbados. I've seen the ads. It looks great. We could just walk slow. Everyone walks slow. Everything is done slow. Maybe I could get a job fishing. Slow fishing. One hour to bait the hook. One hour to let out the line. Six hours sitting. Waiting. Keeping your eyes closed. Can you picture it.

GAIL Yeah. [*her eyes are closed*] Yeah. I'm picturing it now.

[*He puts his arms around her. They kiss. Lie down*]

WILLIAM I like it when they do that.

SANDY Yeah. Why are you looking at me like that. You're not getting any ideas are you.

WILLIAM I'm too old for you probably.

SANDY Yes. You are.

WILLIAM It's been so long.

SANDY I don't care.

WILLIAM I'm sorry. Occasionally I regress. Circumstances force me into a dark corner. Turn me into a beast. I look at your legs. And my old self has the vilest thoughts.

SANDY Thoughts are one thing. I can live with thoughts. Just don't get any ideas for action.

WILLIAM But you don't mind if I visualize in my mind. That's okay?

SANDY Sure. I guess.

[*He is looking at her. She squirms a bit*]

All right. That's enough. I mean it! I'm going to make something for us to eat.

[*She leaves*]

WILLIAM That's all right. You don't have to be here. I've got the picture. It's in my mind. We're on a beach. You are the same. I am younger. [*closes his eyes*] All right. Yes! It's better there, so we'll go there. We'll leave! Children. Sit up. Please.

[*JUNIOR and GAIL sit up*]

There's no other choice. It's the only way I can protect you. I thought we had to stay and fight this through. I thought you had a stake in this world here. That running away would solve nothing for you. But running away is absolutely the best thing to do when the world tries to make you insane. Sure. Barbados. Wherever. Somewhere warm. We'll go.

JUNIOR How.

WILLIAM I have money. In a bank. I told you but you didn't believe me.

GAIL We still don't believe you.

WILLIAM You'd feel a lot better if you did. Part of your problem is an absence of positive options. This makes you think in circles. I mean you have to believe in something. You might as well believe in me.

JUNIOR How'd you get this money.

WILLIAM The usual way. I acquired it in my previous life. I put it away anticipating my fall. I heard the voice from the pit and I opened a daily interest savings account. For emergencies. This qualifies.

GAIL Can we. Really.

WILLIAM We must.

GAIL How.

WILLIAM We just go.

GAIL But things ... My mom. Things.

WILLIAM We'll solve all problems eventually. But first we become safe. We put distance between us and the negative force.

JUNIOR My dad. If we leave ... Remember what they said they'd do to him.

WILLIAM Your father doesn't deserve any consideration.

JUNIOR But ... it's for me. How I'd feel.

[*He lowers his head. Long pause.* GAIL *looks at* WILLIAM. WILLIAM *gestures* GAIL *towards* JUNIOR]

GAIL Junior ... I'm going to ask you for something. You have to look at me. This is the last time I'll ever do this. I promise ... Do this for me. Let's go.

[*Pause*]

JUNIOR All right ... I'd have gone any time you asked.

GAIL I know.

[*Pause*]

WILLIAM Wonderful. This is wonderful. This is a way to protect you. I have a purpose. The pain recedes.

[*He hugs them.* SANDY *comes on*]

SANDY What's going on.

JUNIOR We're leaving.

GAIL We're escaping.

WILLIAM We're going somewhere better.

SANDY Where.

WILLIAM South. Do you want to come.

SANDY I don't know. What's south. Are there opportunities there. How's the economy.

[*Suddenly the room is flooded by two or three strong shafts of light. A voice booms through an electric megaphone*]

VOICE Attention in there. This is the police. All occupants outside. Hands behind their heads. Repeat. This is the police. Come out. We have armed men all around you.

JUNIOR Get down.

[*They all get down on the floor*]

WILLIAM This is more than bad luck, you know. There is something else at work here. I absolutely refuse to believe this had to happen.

VOICE We're going to give you five minutes! I repeat. Five minutes!

[WINEVA *sits up suddenly*]

WINEVA What. Who's giving me five minutes. What's going on here.

GAIL The police. The police are outside.

WINEVA Yeah? Great. [*jumps out of bed*] You. Kid. Where'd you put that first bunch of boxes.

JUNIOR In the basement.

WINEVA And you didn't look inside?

JUNIOR No.

WINEVA Boy, are you in for a surprise.

[*She runs off*]

WILLIAM If I could just put my finger on why this is happening.

[*A knock.* HENRY DAWSON *comes in*]

HENRY Don't shoot, eh. It's me. Your dad.

JUNIOR What are you doing here.

HENRY They sent me in to talk some sense into you. To bring you out peacefully.

WILLIAM Now it makes sense!

[WILLIAM *screams. And attacks* HENRY. *Grabs him by the collar. Shakes him. Throws him on the bed. Sits on top of him*]

I'm going to ask you a question, moron. If you lie I'll bite your jugular vein in two. Understand?

HENRY Yes!

WILLIAM How did the police know we were here.

HENRY They had an informer.

WILLIAM This next question will be more difficult for you. But I urge you to answer properly. Who was the informer.

HENRY It was ...

WILLIAM You. Say it, moron. Say 'It was me.'

HENRY It was ... me ... I had no choice. A chronic offender. This gets me ten years off my sentence. I read about those two jobs you pulled in the paper. I put two and two together.

WILLIAM And for the first time in your whole life you got the right fucking answer!

HENRY I was due for a break ...

[WILLIAM *grabs* HENRY's *neck. Starts to squeeze*]

WILLIAM This isn't working. I want to kill him. Junior get me some wire. No wire? A shoelace will do. Anything.

JUNIOR It doesn't matter, William.

WILLIAM It matters more than anything in the history of the entire world. It matters more than God. Take my word for it.

JUNIOR William. I'd feel better if you didn't.

[*Pause*]

William.

[WILLIAM *looks at* JUNIOR. *Gets up. Sits on the bed.* HENRY *sits up. Rubs his neck*]

HENRY Thanks, son.

[*Pause*]

Hello, Grace. Long time no see, eh.

[WINEVA *rushes on. Carrying a box. Ripping it open*]

WINEVA All right. It's coming down, the total shit is coming down right here. They've been begging for this. And I'm the person who's going to give it to them. Everyone catch.

[*She is tossing grenades to them from the box. They are juggling them. Yelling*]

Total armageddon. Apocalypse Now, my ass. Apocalypse *now*. Right now. Get me the Wagner. I know what to do with that Wagner crap. I'll blow their assholes through their brains. No time for kisses. But I love you all. Where's the goddamn pin on this thing. Ah, here's the little bugger.

[WILLIAM *tackles her.* JUNIOR *grabs her grenade.* WINEVA *is squirming. Yelling*]

Get off me! This is my war! I'm warning you, man. You're interrupting history. Get off. Get the fuck off.

WILLIAM You better help me. She's strong.

[JUNIOR *helps him pin her down.* SANDY *and* GAIL *jump on her too*]

WINEVA That's nothing. Four to one. That's not enough. Jesus! Just let me throw one. Just one. Please. Goddammit you scuzzy know-nothing dumb fuckhead asshole pig-screwing losers!

[SANDY *hauls off and knocks her out with her fist. Pause*]

WILLIAM Thank you.

SANDY Yeah ... You know something ... These grenades are real.

[SANDY *walks off. Staring at grenades.* WILLIAM *and* JUNIOR, *out of breath, plop down next to* GAIL. HENRY *walks over to* WINEVA. *Looks down*]

HENRY That's your Uncle Ritchie's girlfriend, eh. So. So, she's supposed to have all these brains. If you hear him tell it she's something special ... So what ... It still happens doesn't it. It still goes like this.
[*They are all looking at him*]
This is the way it goes, Junior. This is the way it goes. You better come out ... [*starts off*] See ya later!
[*He leaves. Pause*]
GAIL You opened up that wound again.
JUNIOR It's all right.
GAIL Let me look at it.
JUNIOR I just remembered something he said to me once when I was a kid. My dad. We were out in the park. I don't know why. And there were some kids playing baseball. We sat there quietly watching them for a while and then he looked at me and said, 'What's the purpose of this game?' I thought he meant something important by it at first. That it was one of those meaning-of-life questions. Then you know what? I realized the dumb jerk just didn't understand the rules. I mean baseball. Where'd he spend his life. In a cave? I gotta believe he blackmailed my mother into marrying him. I gotta believe it was something like that or I'd go crazy.
[*Light shafts flash. The voice comes on*]
VOICE Come out. We want you to come out now.
GAIL I guess we better go.
WILLIAM I will of course be arranging for a first-class lawyer. Things will not be too bad. Unfortunately this is just speculation.
GAIL It's ... just so frustrating.
[*She puts her head on* JUNIOR's *shoulder*]
Where's Sandy.
SANDY Right here.
[SANDY *walks on*]
GAIL Where were you.
SANDY Down the hall. Looking out the window. You should see the crowd out there. Fifty cops. Two hundred people. Five TV cameras. It's kind of scary.
GAIL Are you going out.
SANDY Nah. I'm going upstairs. I need a hot bath.

GAIL They'll just come in and get you.

SANDY I can handle that. I need a bath. [*starts off, stops*] Ah, what's the use. I might as well go out there and get it over with. [*starts of in the opposite direction*] I'm just a bit confused here. If there was only something I could gain from this. Just about anything would do.

WILLIAM Are you looking for anything in particular.

SANDY Profit. Profit is the best thing. I understand that the best.

WILLIAM Well, perhaps you could sell your story to the press. Diary of a Teenage Terrorist or something to that effect.

SANDY Really?

WILLIAM You'd have to jazz it up.

SANDY I could do that.

WILLIAM Tell a few colourful lies. Talk about your past. Truly exploit yourself and everyone you know.

SANDY I could do that. If you guys don't mind.

GAIL Okay with me.

JUNIOR Sure. Go ahead.

SANDY Yeah. I will. See you later.

[*She leaves.* WILLIAM *gets up*]

WILLIAM I'll go out too. Tell them you'll be along. Take your time. I'll tell them a long story to keep their minds occupied. I'll use poetry. They'll be dazzled. You could have an hour or two alone, if I reach top form.

JUNIOR What about her.

WILLIAM I'm taking her with me.

[*He goes over to* WINEVA]

This is a person of terrifying logic here. I would very much like to attend her trial. Just to hear her defend herself. And scare the jury out of their minds ... Listen ... I'm sincerely sorry. I thought for sure I could save you.

JUNIOR You were wrong.

GAIL Yeah, it's bigger than you, William. Whatever it is ... is enormous.

WILLIAM Other people would want to talk in terms of social patterns. Real things, like economic reform. Re-education. They'd dismiss the theory of the hanging shadow with a sneer. These are people who are members of another class. The skiing class. The long-outdoor-summer class. Historically, philosophically, they make me sick. The hanging shadow of course exists. I say fuck it, but it exists. Take your time coming out, please.

[*He picks up* WINEVA. *Puts her over his shoulder*]

I love you both.

[*He starts off.* WINEVA *raises her head*]

WINEVA Hey. Where are we going.

WILLIAM We're going out there to give them a piece of your mind.

WINEVA Great.

[*They leave.* JUNIOR *and* GAIL *are sitting on the edge of the bed.* JUNIOR *puts his arms around* GAIL]

JUNIOR What happens now.

GAIL We go to jail.

JUNIOR No, seriously.

GAIL What do you mean. You still think I can solve this mess, don't you. You've got a picture of me in your head a million times bigger than everyone else. Standing there, with some magical tool, fixing the world like it's a car or something.

JUNIOR Well, if anyone could do that it'd be you.

GAIL We're going to jail. Young lovers doomed, taking the plunge. This is that cliff, Junior. That one I read about in a dozen books ... In the books it was a bit romantic.

JUNIOR You'll think of something.

GAIL Please. Stop saying that. You're going to drive me nuts.

JUNIOR Sure. What do you want me to say instead.

[*He kisses her forehead*]

GAIL Just be ... realistic.

[JUNIOR *puts his arms around* GAIL]

JUNIOR Sure. Okay ... Okay, we're going to jail. But it won't be too bad. There's no serious time inside involved here. You might even walk away. There's ... what's that called.

GAIL Extenuating circumstances.

JUNIOR Yeah. That's right. There's that. Don't worry.

GAIL I'm not. Not about that. Not really. Any separation would be kind of lousy.

JUNIOR Really.

GAIL But it's not that ... Tell me this isn't the start of something bad. Just the beginning of a bad life, you know.

JUNIOR It's not ... Now you tell me.

GAIL It's not.

JUNIOR You're sure?

[*Pause.* GAIL *shrugs*]

GAIL No. And that's what really scares me.

[*Pause*]

JUNIOR You know what scares me? I could get mad. I could get really mad ... I could ... kill someone.

GAIL Anyone could feel like that sometimes.

JUNIOR Could you.

GAIL Yeah, I think so.

JUNIOR Could you kill someone.

GAIL I think so.

JUNIOR Who.

GAIL Anyone. It would depend.

JUNIOR Depend on who made you mad ...

GAIL Yeah.

JUNIOR Could be anyone ... Scary.

GAIL Yeah ... I don't want to go out there.

[*He kisses her head*]

JUNIOR Then let's see if they've got the stomach to come in and get us.

GAIL Yeah. Let's. In the meantime ...

[*She starts to pull his shirt off over his head*]

JUNIOR Now?

GAIL Now.

JUNIOR What about them. Outside.

GAIL The hell with them. I mean it. The hell with them.

[*She kisses him. They wrap themselves around each other. Settle back.* GAIL *leans back. Smiles. Holds out the bottom of her sweater.* JUNIOR *smiles. Slowly puts his head inside*]

[*Blackout*]

[*End*]

BETTER LIVING

Better Living was first produced by Toronto's CentreStage Company at the St. Lawrence Centre on May 15, 1986 with the following cast:

JACK Peter Blais
JUNIOR Doug Greenall
GAIL Catherine Disher
NORA Marion Gilsenan
MARY ANN Nancy Palk
ELIZABETH Dixie Seatle
TOM Michael Hogan

Director: Bill Glassco
Set Designer: Douglas A. McLean
Lighting Designer: Lynne Hyde
Costume Designer: John Pennoyer

Persons

NORA, *late forties*
JACK, *early fifties*
GAIL, *seventeen*
MARY ANN, *twenty-seven*
ELIZABETH, *thirty*
TOM, *early fifties*
JUNIOR, *late teens*

Note

There is an intermission between Scenes Five and Six.

SCENE ONE

The kitchen of an old run-down house in the east end. Upstage centre a screen door leading to an overgrown backyard. Stage left the fridge and stove and a doorway into a hall. There is a radio on the fridge. Along the stage right wall are a door leading to the basement, a row of tin cabinets and the sink. Off-centre, an old kitchen table and chairs. In one corner a wicker rocker. Beside the rocker a pile of yellowing newspapers. The linoleum floor is warped and slopes badly. The walls are partly painted, partly papered
As the lights come up the kettle is whistling on the stove. The radio is blaring with rock and roll. And there is a priest knocking on the screen door
The priest hollers hello a few times then comes in. Looks around. Frowns. Hollers hello a couple of times. Gives up. Turns off the radio. Goes to the stove. Turns it off. Takes the kettle and starts to make himself a cup of tea. As he is doing this a young man in his underwear walks in from the hall. Sees the priest. Turns. Runs off. The priest takes his tea to the table. Sits. A young woman in her underwear leans in from the hall

GAIL Oh, hi. I thought it was you. Just checking.
[*The priest smiles. Nods. The young woman turns her head to yell down the hall*]
It's okay, Junior. It's just my uncle. [*entering kitchen*] Uncle Jack, you gave my boyfriend a real scare. He thought they'd come to get him.
JACK He's a fugitive from the Church?
GAIL Nah. But you know what I mean.
JACK I never know what you mean, Gail. His name is Junior?
[GAIL *makes herself some tea*]
GAIL Yeah. He rides a motorcycle.
JACK Is that why his name is Junior.
GAIL Yeah. I guess. Maybe. Listen, you're not going to tell me it's a sin or something are you.
JACK I had a motorcycle once.
GAIL Not motorcycles. Sex. Sex outside the Church.
JACK You've been having sex outside the church? Well as far as I know

285

nobody's seen you.

GAIL Outside the Church's domain. The domain of marriage.

JACK The domain of marriage is in trouble. You can screw your brains out and it's not going to make a bit of difference. As for the sin of it. Who cares.

GAIL Are you saying you don't care how I lead my life, Uncle Jack.

JACK You got it.

GAIL You used to.

JACK No. I just said I did. Where's your mother.

GAIL I don't know. In the basement probably. She's building an addition to the house.

JACK You mean turning the basement into a rec-room? Panelling? That sort of thing?

GAIL No. Tunnelling. Digging. That sort of thing. The addition is going to be underground. Under the backyard. She's got this plan. A big square room under the backyard. Don't you think that's weird.

JACK A bit.

GAIL Junior thinks it's weird. He says it won't work. You need beams. Big beams for support. Where's she going to get beams.

JACK She'll probably give up when she reaches the outer wall. It's concrete.

GAIL It's gone. She rented a jackhammer. The wall went last week. She's four feet out from the house now. You wouldn't believe the mess down there. Mud. Sludge. It's like a mine shaft. I think she's gone crazy. You should talk to her. She's your sister. She'll listen to what you say.

JACK What should I say.

GAIL Say we don't need an extra room. Say Mary Ann and the baby can have my room. And I'll sleep in the attic.

JACK Oh. Mary Ann is coming home. I see.

GAIL No surprise there, right. Not for me anyway. I knew that marriage wouldn't last. You know why? Because Mary Ann's just like Mom and Mom kills marriage. She killed her own, right.

JACK Not exactly.

GAIL Well where's my father. Gone. Dead? Insane? Some new life somewhere? He's not here though is he.

JACK People have been telling you for years that wasn't your mother's fault.

GAIL Lies. Ask me how I know.

JACK I don't want to.

GAIL No. No one ever wants to ask me how I know.

JACK Then why the hell don't you just tell me.

GAIL Because I'm not sure how I know. It's blurry. When I figure it out, I will. Don't worry. I'm not bluffing. Do you want more tea.
[GAIL's *clothes, a sweater and jeans, are on the kitchen chair. She starts getting dressed*]

JACK No.

GAIL You don't look so good.

JACK How's school.

GAIL I'm gonna quit. Are you going to try and talk me out of it.

JACK No. Quit. Become a hairdresser. Who cares.

GAIL Stylist. Hair stylist.

JACK A worthwhile existence, no matter what it's called.

GAIL I'm not smart enough for anything better.

JACK Oh. You're plenty smart enough for lots of things better and you know it.

GAIL I knew you'd try and talk me out of it. I love you.
[*She kisses his head*]
Okay. I'll stick it out for one more year. But that's it.

JACK Like I said. Who cares.

GAIL I love you. And do you know why.

JACK Why.

GAIL Because you love me. It's that simple.
[JUNIOR *appears. Dressed. Jacket over his shoulder*]

JUNIOR Let's go. It's time.

JACK Time for what.

GAIL Time to go. Junior, this is my Uncle Jack.

JUNIOR Pleasure to meet you, Your Honour.

GAIL Junior's a Protestant. 'Your Honour' is just for judges, Junior.

JACK Force of habit, eh.

JUNIOR I guess. Well, it's time.

JACK Actually it's past time. Look at the clock. You're late.

JUNIOR For what.

GAIL He's kidding.

JUNIOR Yeah? [*to* JACK] Kidding. That's great. Good for you. I mean that.

JACK I'm sure you do.

GAIL Get going. I'll catch up.

[JUNIOR *leaves*]

Try not to judge Junior too harshly. It's his father who's the real criminal. A record this long. I'm trying to reform Junior. I've told him he has singing talent. He doesn't. But it'll keep him busy for a while. See you soon. Talk to my mother.

JACK I will.

[*She leaves.* NORA *sticks her head out from the basement door. She is wearing a floppy black rubber rain hat*]

NORA Are they gone.

JACK Yes.

[*She enters the room. She is also wearing a black rubber raincoat and rubber boots and is covered in mud. She is carrying a shovel*]

NORA Criminals. She brings criminals into my house. He's a burglar. He steals from pensioners. He has a record this long.

JACK How do you know.

NORA I have friends in the police department. He better watch his step or I'll have him put away for intent.

JACK Intent to do what.

NORA I think he's casing the place for a break-in. I've hidden the valuables. But his kind knows exactly where to look. Besides, he's got someone on the inside.

JACK Don't worry. Your daughter won't betray you.

NORA Gail's been acting crazy. I think she's over-stimulated. Too much copulation. You know generally I don't mind. I even encourage it up to a point. All my daughters have been encouraged to copulate to a degree that is good for their general health. But Gail's had too much. She's at this guy's mercy for copulation. He's probably just too damn good at it. A machine. A sex machine. And a break-and-enter artist. I was hoping she'd do better. Have you noticed how much Gail looks like her father.

JACK It's true.

NORA I'm not superstitious, Jack. But I think it's a possible case of possession. It's possible her father is possessing her. Do you think you could investigate.

JACK Exorcism is frowned upon, you know.

NORA Generally speaking, a wise position. Religious hysterics abound.

Why, in this neighbourhood alone I could name twenty of them.
But in Gail's case it could be the genuine thing. Be discreet, dear.
But the next time you see her, give her a whiff. You remember
Tom's smell. Give her a whiff and see if the odour is familiar.

JACK I'll try.

NORA Tea?

JACK I have some.

NORA I'll join you. I don't like the stuff much but it gives us all
something to do with our hands. [*making herself a cup*] So you're
probably wondering why I'm covered in mud.

JACK Gail told me.

NORA She thinks I'm crazy. I know she has reasons for thinking that.
But they're stupid reasons. She doesn't understand my initiative.
Where would my family be now without my initiative. We need
more room. I can't go up. It's expensive. I can't build on the left.
Attached. I can't build on the right. Attached. I could have built on
the back but then we wouldn't have a yard. The kids, the little ones
will need a yard.

JACK Digging a room under the ground is dangerous, Nora.

NORA Beams, right? I know all about beams. Gail's criminal friend
thinks he knows more about beams than me. I've got friends who
are architects. They made drawings. They drew up plans. Eighteen
feet by eighteen feet. Six and a half feet high. A perfect room and
just four beams. Any fool can arrange for four beams. I'll put them
in myself. I'm developing strength by the day. Sure there are
dangers. I had a cave-in last week. But the little ones will need a
backyard. So underground is the only choice.

JACK By 'little ones' I assume you mean Mary Ann's baby.

NORA It won't stop there. My daughters are coming home. It's the
economy I guess. It's turned bad. I don't understand it myself. But
just because they're home why shouldn't they have babies. I'll
encourage it. Mary Ann will have more. Elizabeth will have some
as soon as she's established in her profession.

JACK Elizabeth has been practising law for five years, Nora. That's
reasonably established I would think.

NORA Elizabeth does not want to practise law as a profession, Jack.
Law is just an inroad to her true destination.

JACK Which is what.

289

NORA Elizabeth will enter politics and eventually be in charge of foreign affairs, so she can send huge amounts of foreign aid to Third World countries to feed their poor. Our Elizabeth has a heart the size of a mountain. She's like you.

JACK She's like you.

NORA She's like us.

JACK Nora. I have something to tell you.

NORA You're ill.

JACK No.

NORA Please, be honest. If you're ill, tell me. I know you've lost your faith but you shouldn't let it kill you.

JACK Nora, I haven't lost my faith. I've just lost my enthusiasm. And that won't kill me, it will just make me pathetic. Now sit down. This is going to be shock.

NORA [*sitting*] I can't be shocked. I won't let myself be shocked. Wait. Don't tell me. Maybe I can't be shocked. But I can be upset. Destabilized.

JACK I received a phone call this morning. From Tom.

NORA Tom who.

JACK Your husband.

NORA He's dead, thank God. I saw him die. In my dreams. Hundreds of dreams. Hundreds of deaths. Cruel, slow, painful.

JACK He's living here. In a hotel. Has been for three months.

NORA You say he called. But do you believe what you're saying. I mean do you know what you're saying. This could be more than I can bear to hear. So you could just stop talking now and it would be all right by me.

JACK He called. He wants to come home.

NORA [*stands*] Excuse me. I have work to do. For my daughters. And their daughters.

[NORA *goes downstairs.* JACK *sighs. Stands, wanders around. Then goes over to the basement door*]

JACK Nora! He said if you don't let him come home he'll go to the police. He'll go to the police with proof that we tried to kill him.

NORA [*from basement*] That's silly. A prank. Falseness. Stupidity. The stupidest thing I've ever heard.

JACK Nora! Listen. There could be proof. I just want you to think back a little. Remember just long enough to recognize the danger. We did try to kill him.

[*Pause. He leans against the wall.* NORA *appears at the top of the basement stairs*]

Can you remember.

NORA I can if you want me to, dear.

JACK We tried our best to kill him.

NORA If you say so, dear. It's hard to believe though.

JACK Yes, it is.

NORA I mean it's just not like us to fail at something like that. Especially when we're trying our best. Perhaps we weren't trying our best at all.

[NORA *goes back downstairs.* JACK *stares at the ceiling*]

[*Blackout*]

SCENE TWO

MARY ANN, *thin, nervous-looking, is in the middle of the kitchen, turning in a slow circle*

MARY ANN It's worse. Is it my imagination. No, it's definitely worse. How could she let it get worse.
[ELIZABETH *comes in from the hall. Carrying two pieces of luggage. Wearing a tweed suit. Looking annoyed*]
ELIZABETH It costs money to make it better.
MARY ANN Couldn't you give it to her.
ELIZABETH She wouldn't take it. I'm supposed to be saving for my campaign fund.
MARY ANN I can't stay here.
ELIZABETH So leave.
MARY ANN I already left. I left where I was living to come here. I can't go back.
ELIZABETH So get used to it. Fast. Before Mom comes home. You'll make her feel guilty. She does what she can.
MARY ANN No, she does what she *can't*. What she can, she doesn't.
ELIZABETH You're starting to talk like her.
MARY ANN Please don't say that.
ELIZABETH Listen. What's it matter. The roof doesn't leak. The furnace works.
MARY ANN It smells.
ELIZABETH I don't smell anything.
MARY ANN You're used to it.
ELIZABETH How. I don't live here.
MARY ANN Lucky you. Why can't I stay at your apartment.
ELIZABETH Because I don't want you there, Mary Ann.
MARY ANN You really like living alone?
ELIZABETH That's not what I said. I said I don't want *you* there.
MARY ANN Why not.
ELIZABETH Because I'd have to take care of you. Cook for you. Wash for you. Tell you cute little jokes. Make you forget your troubles.
MARY ANN Not true. I thought you loved me. You always said you loved me. Maybe you were lying. Were you lying. You can put my luggage down, you know. You don't have to stand there holding it

292

like a martyr. I know you think I'm weak.

ELIZABETH You are weak.

MARY ANN Please don't be cruel. You never used to be cruel. Being a
lawyer has made you cruel.

ELIZABETH Are you going to cry.

MARY ANN No.

ELIZABETH Go ahead. I know you want to.

MARY ANN I don't cry anymore. I'm much stronger. Marriage has made
me tough. Look at me. Take a fresh look at me and tell me if I'm
not tough.

ELIZABETH Go ahead. Cry if you want.

MARY ANN I never cry! I sometimes get very scared.

[*She bursts into tears.* ELIZABETH *sighs. Drops luggage.* ELIZABETH
goes to her. Puts her arms around her. Music is coming. GAIL *dances in
from the hallway. Carrying* JUNIOR's *portable Sony. Something terrific
playing. Starts towards the door.* ELIZABETH *gestures her over.* GAIL
*sighs. Goes to them. Puts her head in the huddle for a second. Breaks
away. Leaves.* JACK *comes up from the basement*]

JACK Ah. Happy reunions. The heart bursts. The stomach churns.
Words fail.

ELIZABETH Hi, Jack.

MARY ANN Uncle.

[MARY ANN *runs to him. Throws her arms around him*]

I'm home. My marriage failed. You knew it would.

JACK I did?

ELIZABETH You didn't?

JACK We can discuss this in more detail with even less clarity a little
later. Elizabeth, can I talk to you outside for a moment.

ELIZABETH Sure.

[*They go into the backyard.* NORA *is standing at the basement door*]

NORA Don't feel left out. They were always close. They both have
mountainous hearts. He just wants to confide in her. He's lost his
faith. He'll fall a great distance if he doesn't get it back. Great
people do. He's a great man. He played hockey when he was
young. And he had an interesting sexual life. He sacrificed a lot to
become a priest.

MARY ANN Hi, Mom.

NORA I'm covered in mud or I'd give you a kiss. You know that don't you. I kissed you a lot when you were younger. I have nothing against kissing. I encourage it. Remember?

MARY ANN Yes.

NORA Where's the baby.

MARY ANN I left her with Larry.

NORA Who's he.

MARY ANN My husband.

NORA Does he like babies.

MARY ANN He likes his own. What's wrong, Mom. You seem funny.

NORA I was hoping you'd bring me a baby.

MARY ANN She's coming. I needed some time on my own.

NORA Why.

MARY ANN To … you know. Adjust.

NORA To what.

MARY ANN It's hard to say.

NORA Well, in the meantime take my advice. Get your baby back. Your husband could become fond of it. Stranger things have happened. I can't afford the legal costs if we have to go to court to get her back. And don't expect Elizabeth to work for nothing. She's saving for her political campaign. Take my advice. Call Barry.

MARY ANN Larry.

NORA Call him. The phone is in the living room.

[ELIZABETH *comes in*]

Tell her to call Barry!

ELIZABETH Call Barry!

MARY ANN Larry!

ELIZABETH Do it!

[MARY ANN *groans. Leaves*]

NORA She still does what you tell her. I like that. The oldest still has influence. The family structure is intact. She looks awful, don't you think. Like a frightened person pretending not to be. Like a bird. Isn't she. A bird.

ELIZABETH Yeah yeah, she's a bird.

NORA I hate birds. I'm sure Mary Ann knows that. Maybe she's pretending to be a bird to get back at me for something awful I did to her when she was young. Did I do anything awful to her when she was young.

ELIZABETH No! Please be quiet for a minute.

NORA Are you thinking. You have your thinking look on. It used to scare me when you were young. I thought you were having severe stomach cramps.

ELIZABETH Uncle Jack told me. About Father wanting to come back.

NORA Your Uncle Jack is not well. Don't listen to him until he gets better. He drinks, you know. Not a lot. But enough to get him fantasizing.

ELIZABETH Listen to me. I'm going to say something important.

NORA You're frightening when you talk like that. When you say 'listen to me.' It's the tone of voice. I know it's necessary for your career but it scares the ones who love you. You sound like Franco. Like Mussolini. Like my grandfather.

ELIZABETH Listen. He's not coming back here. If that son of a bitch sets one foot in this house I'll kill him.

[MARY ANN *is standing in the doorway*]

MARY ANN So will I.

NORA Good. We could all kill him. That would be nice. If your father was alive he'd need killing, we all know that. But he's dead. He died in Swift Current, Saskatchewan. Five years ago. Run over by a runaway tractor. Crushed both his legs. He lay in the hospital for five days. In agony. Out of his mind with pain. And then he died. They buried him in Swift Current.

MARY ANN You never told us that. I never knew that. Did you, Elizabeth.

ELIZABETH She just made it up.

NORA You know I can't make things up, Elizabeth. I have no talent for that kind of thing at all. I've got a copy of the death certificate.

ELIZABETH Get it.

NORA It's in the vault. The bank vault. You know in the little box. I'll have to find the key.

ELIZABETH What about his pension. He was on the police force for fifteen years. You must have some money coming to you.

NORA I'll make enquiries.

ELIZABETH How are you going to keep this up, Mom, when that son of a bitch shows up at the door.

NORA He won't. Your Uncle Jack is telling stories. Outrageous. I should be angry. But he's in such turmoil. Mental fatigue. Ask his bishop. He called me. Told me. Of course this is privileged information of the Church so we have to keep it to ourselves. Now, you two make something to eat and I'll just finish up downstairs. Have to put the tools away. Always clean the tools. Put them away. Start fresh the next day.

[NORA *goes downstairs*]

MARY ANN She's worse. Isn't she. She's living in a fourth tense. She's taken past, present, future, and combined them somehow. Look, she's still got Dad's old car in the backyard.

ELIZABETH She says she'll sell it when she gets the right price.

MARY ANN It's been there for eleven years. She's worse. Listen to how she talks. Private. Obsessive. She's got private obsessive plans for that car.

ELIZABETH Don't talk like that about her. You're making it sound like she's nuts.

MARY ANN And you think she's just eccentric.

ELIZABETH Well, isn't she. Hasn't she always been. And she's not worse. She's just a bit more intense.

MARY ANN Well, why. Menopause?

ELIZABETH Give me a break. Menopause doesn't make women dig holes under the ground. Only intense, single-minded women ... dig holes under the ground.

MARY ANN That's what she's doing down there? That's what all the mud is from?

ELIZABETH You didn't ask?

MARY ANN I was afraid to.

ELIZABETH You're always afraid to. You always were.

MARY ANN With good reason. If I ask she gives me a private answer I don't understand. And I get scared.

ELIZABETH Because you're a bird.

MARY ANN What.

ELIZABETH A bird! You're a fucking bird! Listen, what are you trying to pull with this bird stuff anyway. You know Mom hates them. What did she ever do to you?!

MARY ANN What are you talking about?!

ELIZABETH Wake up. Take responsibility for your own problems. You're twenty-seven years old. Act it.

MARY ANN All right ... I'll try.

ELIZABETH So do you want to know why she's digging under the ground.

MARY ANN No. I'm sorry.

ELIZABETH I give up. Cook us something for supper. I've got to go get something. [*starts off*]

MARY ANN What.

ELIZABETH [*turning back*] Oh, are you sure you really want to ask that question.

MARY ANN No. I mean yes.

ELIZABETH A gun. Yes, that's what I said—a gun. Don't scream! You didn't believe all that stuff about Uncle Jack. He's all right. Father dear Father is coming home and I'm going to blow his head off. Sorry you asked?

MARY ANN No. I meant what I said before. I'll kill him too.

ELIZABETH We both can't kill him. I'll do it.

MARY ANN [*smiles*] Because you love me?

ELIZABETH Cook supper. And call Larry.

MARY ANN Barry! [*smiles*] Yeah, Larry.

ELIZABETH And get your kid back. Mom wants the kid here.

MARY ANN Okay. In time. After I've thought about it for a while.

ELIZABETH By the way when are you going to give that kid a name. We can't go on calling her 'the baby' forever.

MARY ANN What's the hurry.

ELIZABETH She's eight months old.

MARY ANN I'm worried about making a mistake. I could give her the wrong name and she'd be stuck with it all her life. I have to be careful.

ELIZABETH Goodbye. [*starts off again*]

MARY ANN Elizabeth.

ELIZABETH [*stopping*] What?!

MARY ANN You were just kidding about the gun, weren't you. Kidding about killing him. I was. You were too, weren't you.

ELIZABETH Oh, sure. What did he ever do to deserve to be killed. [*She leaves*]

MARY ANN [*smiles. Frowns*] It's worse. It's definitely worse. [*Blackout*]

SCENE THREE

Later

It's dark outside. MARY ANN, GAIL *and* JUNIOR *are sitting around the table.* MARY ANN *is reading a cookbook.* JUNIOR *has a leg on* GAIL's *lap.* GAIL *is drawing on one of his sneakers.* NORA *is busy putting a black tablecloth and candles on the table. And talking*

NORA It must have been a big maple. Maybe they cut it down because it was spoiling the view. Maybe it was diseased. Who knows. It would just be history except they left the roots. I came across them yesterday. Eight feet wide. Each root a whole foot around. They gotta go. They'll be right in the middle of the new room. Don't worry. There are ways. Dynamite maybe.
[*They all look at each other*]
Don't worry. I'll buy a book that tells me how to do it right. You know it's great, there are books out now that tell you how to do everything. In theory there's nothing you can't do if you can find the book. In theory I could build an airplane. But I'm too practical. I might write a book like that someday though. Maybe a book that tells other people how to find the right books for what they want to do. It's wonderful. Think about it. I'll get rid of that big maple's roots and learn a little about dynamite at the same time. [*lights the candles*] Okay. Finished. Gail. Get the lights.

GAIL I'm busy ... Mary Ann. Mary Ann?

MARY ANN [*not looking up*] What.

GAIL Turn off the lights.

MARY ANN Why.

NORA Everyone knows you can't call the dead into the light. It's harsh. Light is harsh. The dead don't like it. They exist in a soft subtle place.
[NORA *turns off the lights*]

MARY ANN Oh my God, it's a seance!
[MARY ANN *stands. Goes to the stove*]

NORA Not yet. It's not officially a seance till we clasp hands.

JUNIOR [*standing*] Hey. I've got stuff to do.
[*He starts off.* NORA *blocks his path to the door*]

NORA Tell him to stay put. We need a man.

GAIL Why.

NORA Because we're calling the spirit of a man. A man who only respects other men. I'm sorry we need your friend.

JUNIOR It won't work. I don't believe in this stuff. I exist on a realistic plane. I'll shatter the mood.

NORA Gail. I need him. Tell him it's a way of repaying me for all the food he's eaten.

JUNIOR Why doesn't she ever talk to me directly.

GAIL She's got a point. You owe her.

JUNIOR Sure. She's got a point. If you want to stretch a point. But didn't I give her advice about the beams.

NORA Non-professional advice. Tell him to do this or there will be no more uninhibited behaviour allowed in my house.

GAIL She means we can't do it here anymore.

JUNIOR She knows about that?

GAIL Jesus, Junior. Is she deaf. Is she blind.

JUNIOR I thought she was ... you know ... 'naive.'

[GAIL *grabs* JUNIOR. *Sits him down. Then* NORA *leads* MARY ANN *to table. They both sit*]

GAIL Jesus. Look, you have to do this. There's no escape. We do it all the time. Mom's psychic. We call the dead once a month. All her dead relatives. Aunt Violet comes sometimes. She's a hoot. Who are we calling tonight, Mom.

NORA Your father.

GAIL What.

MARY ANN [*standing*] Count me out. I've got spaghetti sauce on the stove. It needs watching.

[MARY ANN *goes back to the stove*]

GAIL Who says he's dead.

NORA I do.

GAIL Since when.

NORA Today.

GAIL He died today?

NORA No, I'm *saying* he died today. He died five years ago.

GAIL [*to* MARY ANN] Is this the truth or what.

MARY ANN I have to stir the sauce!

GAIL Mary Ann. Come on. She's telling me my father's dead. Is it true. Did you know.

MARY ANN No more questions. No answers. Leave me alone. I'm cooking.

GAIL I don't believe this. You're unbelievable, Mother. Don't you think we've got any feelings.

NORA I can see this is a sore point with certain people. A dead father usually is. I'm just trying to help.
[GAIL *turns the lights back on*]

GAIL How. This isn't helping. This is insane. You're supposed to be comforting in situations like this. You know, put your arms around me. Break it to me gently. Oh no, not you. You call a seance.
[JUNIOR *blows out a candle*]

NORA You fail to understand what I'm doing.

GAIL You fail to explain what you're doing.

NORA I forget to explain, Gail. I have a lot on my mind. Mary Ann, you tell her.

MARY ANN I'm not saying anything. I'm cooking. Then I'm going to sleep. I'm sorry I came.

GAIL Then leave.

MARY ANN I can't.

GAIL Then talk, you gormless twit.

NORA Be kind. She's nervous.

GAIL Jesus. Assholes. Assholes. Someone tell me what's going on or I'll go berserk. I'll break things. I'll yell. I'll scream.
[*She picks up a frying pan from the counter. Bangs it down hard*]
I'll kill!
[NORA *stands. Advances on* GAIL]

NORA Look. Her father's eyes. Her father's temper. Her father's dirty language. Gail, do you feel something inside you. Some alien presence. Some masculine force.

GAIL [*backing up*] What's she saying now.

MARY ANN Okay. One answer. Then leave me alone.

GAIL What's she saying!

MARY ANN She thinks you're being possessed by Father's ghost.

JUNIOR I gotta leave. Really.

GAIL [*in a deep violent voice*] Shut up! Sit down! Or you die!
[NORA *suddenly grabs* GAIL's *head with both hands*]

NORA Tom. You evil man. Leave this child. In the name of the Father and the Son and the Holy Spirit I command you to leave this poor innocent child. You evil murdering bastard!

[GAIL *screams. Faints*]

JUNIOR Holy fuck.

NORA It's done. He's gone from her. The seance isn't necessary. [*to* MARY ANN] Do you believe me now. Your father is dead.

[TOM *suddenly appears at the screen door. His face dimly illuminated by the outside light*]

TOM Bullshit.

[*He is a solidly built man. Tough. Worn. Wearing a plaid shirt. Work pants and boots. An old beaten fedora. They all look at him.* NORA *doubles over. Cups her mouth.* TOM *opens the door. Comes in*]

NORA Oh my God. A burglar! Hide your faces!

[NORA *covers her face.* MARY ANN *covers her face.* JUNIOR *covers his face.* TOM *is looking around*]

TOM Nothing changes. Things just fall apart. Be careful, the worst is yet to come.

[*Suddenly* ELIZABETH *appears from the hall. Wearing an evening dress. Holding a gun. She fires it five times in his direction*]

[*Blackout*]

SCENE FOUR

One hour later
TOM *and* JUNIOR *at the table. A bottle of whiskey. Two glasses*

TOM She knows I've got a bad heart. She was trying to scare me to death. Elizabeth is a wily coyote. But I can't be scared. I've been scared to the limit.

JUNIOR I was scared.

TOM The secret is in expecting the unexpected and expecting it to be bad. No use expecting anything good. It never comes. That's not the secret. The secret is in understanding the worst. It's patterns. When it's sneaking around. When it's just teasing. And when it's actually coming.

JUNIOR Sort of like defensive driving.

TOM Who are you, anyway.

JUNIOR Junior Dawson. I'm Gail's boyfriend. I guess.

TOM Gail's the youngest.

JUNIOR I know.

TOM She was only seven years old the last time I saw her. Which one of those women was Gail.

JUNIOR The one lying unconscious on the floor.

TOM Did she have a fit.

JUNIOR I don't know. Maybe.

TOM She had fits when she was a baby. Her mother was in labour for thirty-six hours. Gail was born with brain damage. She took medication. It cost a fortune but I paid it gladly. The fits went away. When did they come back.

JUNIOR I don't know.

TOM You should. If you're serious about her, get to know her liabilities and her strengths. What are her strengths.

JUNIOR I'm not sure. She's funny.

TOM Gets that from her mother's side. Wacko. The whole family.

JUNIOR No. I meant she's got a good sense of humour.

TOM She does? That's odd. What's she find funny.

JUNIOR Everything.

TOM That's really odd. What's so funny about everything. I'd be suspicious. When she was young she'd laugh before she got her fits,

302

you know. Maybe that's what brought them on. She'd laugh until she lost her breath and then her eyes would roll back in her head. We'll put a stop to it before it gets outta hand. Don't do anything that encourages her to laugh. You might start by dressing differently.

JUNIOR She says she likes the way I dress.

TOM Maybe it's just good for a laugh. Take precautions. Buy some real clothes. Do you have a job.

JUNIOR I'm a musician.

TOM What do you play.

JUNIOR I sing.

TOM Sing something.

JUNIOR Maybe later.

TOM Definitely later. Where do you live.

JUNIOR At home. With my dad.

TOM What's he do.

JUNIOR I don't wanna talk about it.

TOM What's wrong, you ashamed.

JUNIOR No. Well, yeah. I am.

TOM Never be ashamed of your father. Unless of course he's a crook. Is he a crook.

JUNIOR Yeah. He is.

TOM That's rough. But let's not dwell on it.

JUNIOR You were a cop, weren't you.

TOM That's right. Fifteen years on the force. Seven in uniform. Eight as a detective. Hold-up. Fraud. Missing persons. I did a bit of everything.

JUNIOR You do homicide?

TOM Sure. Who do you want killed. [laughs] Just kidding. A little policemen's humour. Do you pay board at home.

JUNIOR Sure.

TOM How'd you like to live here for nothing.

JUNIOR I don't think that would go down too good.

TOM No innovation ever does. Not here anyway. Patterns are dangerous. It's like politics. Why the country is in such bad shape. But that's another story. I want you to live here.

JUNIOR Why.

TOM I need a bodyguard. I need protection.

JUNIOR From who?

TOM Guess.

JUNIOR [*looks around*] Them? Your family?

TOM You said it. Not me. Just taking precautions. So it's a deal? You stay here until I say you don't.

JUNIOR Sure.

[ELIZABETH *comes on. Carrying an old duffle bag*]

ELIZABETH [*to* JUNIOR] You. Out.

JUNIOR But I'm supposed to be—

ELIZABETH Out. Shitface. Before I pull you out by the hair.

JUNIOR [*stands*] Okay. I'm leaving but it's not because I'm afraid. It's because I'm sensitive. I sense that you're—

[ELIZABETH *stamps her foot.* JUNIOR *leaves*]

TOM I knew he couldn't stand up to you. Gail needs someone better. I'll shop around.

ELIZABETH You look different.

TOM I am different. It's been a lot of years.

ELIZABETH Tell me about it. Do you recognize this.

TOM No.

ELIZABETH It's your duffle bag. The one you kept your old uniform in.

TOM Yeah, I know it's my duffle bag. I was just testing you. I sometimes test people. It does them a lot of good.

ELIZABETH It makes me violent.

TOM I'll keep that in mind.

ELIZABETH You won't have to. This uniform is the last item in your personal mythology around here. I'm sure it's what you came back for. Now you can leave.

TOM Sit down, Elizabeth. Let's talk.

ELIZABETH Let's not.

TOM I have a legal right to be here.

ELIZABETH That's not true. Do you know what I do for a living. I'm a lawyer.

TOM No kidding. How'd you manage that.

ELIZABETH Hard work. A fierce sense of competition.

TOM I meant the money.

ELIZABETH Prostitution.

TOM Student loans, or something?

ELIZABETH Prostitution.

TOM Come on, honeybunny. Tell me the truth.

ELIZABETH Don't call me that.

TOM I always called you honeybunny.

ELIZABETH You called Mary Ann honeybunny. You called me baby
doll. You called Gail pumpkin, puddin', peaches, puddles and
precious. It was sickening then. It's disgusting now.

TOM That was another test. I know I called you baby doll. And it
wasn't sickening. It was sincere, and you loved it.

ELIZABETH What are you doing here.

TOM It's time. It's time for me to be here. I'm needed.

ELIZABETH Yeah? You got a message, eh. Someone here sent you a
message that they needed you.

TOM I've seen everything. I've been everywhere. I have experience in
the real world. The Third World. I've seen the people. They're in
bad shape. They can't take it much longer. They'll be coming here
soon looking for relief. They want what we've got. Secret armies of
confiscation are being formed in the Libyan desert, in Bangladesh,
the jungles of El Salvador, the Philippines. I'm here to protect the
family.

ELIZABETH [smiles] You're nuts.

TOM Read the newspapers. Carefully. This idyllic existence won't last
much longer. This country's a greedy pig at the world's trough.
Takes up too much space. Eats too much. Those starving people
are getting restless. You'll need me. I know how to talk to them. I'll
lie. I'll tell them we're as poor as they are. I'll teach you how to hide
the food. Disguise your wealth.

ELIZABETH Look around. What wealth.

TOM This place is a palace compared to what they're used to ... How
much do you give your mother.

ELIZABETH Nothing.

TOM Nothing?

ELIZABETH Yeah, nothing. She won't take it.

TOM How does she get by.

ELIZABETH She works.

TOM Where.

ELIZABETH Here. She stuffs envelopes. And that's the last question I'm
answering. You're something, I'll give you that. You deserted this
family almost ten years ago. You left us in emotional and financial

ruin. But you seem to be operating without any knowledge of that fact. We resent you. We hate you. If you stay here we'll destroy you.

TOM   Who is 'we,' darling.

ELIZABETH   Look. You can't stay. My mother's been in the basement since you got here and she won't come up till you go. She's scared. You're a ghost. A bad smell from the past. There's a new world in this house. A new society ten years old. New laws. Self-reliance. You don't belong.

TOM   Ten years is nothing in the overall scheme of things. Wounds of the past heal. The danger is in the future. As for your mother. She's strange. She always spent a lot of time in the basement.

ELIZABETH   I know what you did here before you left. You're lucky they didn't have you locked up.

TOM   They're lucky I didn't have them locked up. You're a victim of vicious propaganda. But I forgive you. In time you'll come to love me again. The truth will be known when it's time to know the truth.

ELIZABETH   You're nuts. We're going in circles. I'm calling the police.

TOM   That would be a mistake. Talk to your mother first.

[GAIL *comes in. A blanket wrapped around her*]

GAIL   Yeah. Talk to Mom, I dare you.

ELIZABETH   Get back to bed.

GAIL   Who are you talking to, your filing clerk.

ELIZABETH   I mean it, Gail.

GAIL   'I mean it, Gail.' Give me a break. I'm seventeen years old for chrissake. And you don't intimidate me anymore.

ELIZABETH   Great. I don't want to intimidate you. I just want you to get the hell out of here!

[*She grabs* GAIL's *hair and drags her into the hall*]

GAIL   Ouch. Stop it. I mean it.

ELIZABETH   Upstairs. Out of sight. And stay there until I say you can come down.

[ELIZABETH *comes back into the kitchen*]

[*to* TOM] Now it's your turn.

[*Suddenly* GAIL *pounces from the hall. With the blanket. Throws the blanket over* ELIZABETH's *head. Turns her around. Forces her through the basement door amidst a lot of cursing and shouting. Closes the door. Locks it. Turns slowly to look at* TOM]

GAIL You're my dad, eh.

TOM Yeah. That's who I am, precious.

GAIL Precious. That's me, eh. I've missed you, you know. I don't even have a picture of you. They threw them all out. They were really pissed off at you.

TOM A little misunderstanding.

GAIL I know all about it.

TOM You do?

GAIL Well, I put two and two together. I drew conclusions based on certain things and I decided I was on your side.

TOM I'm glad, precious.

GAIL Look, you don't have to overdo the 'precious' thing. I mean it takes some getting used to. So are you hungry. We've got spaghetti sauce. It's good by itself. Just in a bowl. Mary Ann was cooking supper. She always leaves something out. This time she left out the spaghetti.

TOM [*laughs*] How is Mary Ann.

GAIL A wreck. A nervous wreck. And since she saw you, a totally hysterical nervous wreck. She's in bed. Really, you turned this place into a hospital ward. So do you want some sauce.

TOM With some bread.

GAIL Sure. [*sets about getting him something to eat*] So here we are. I had a dream about this. It was a bit different really. We kissed and hugged. It's okay though. Maybe that's awkward. Maybe it's not. Maybe it is. Who knows. Who knows.

TOM I can kiss you. I can do that.

GAIL Sure. I can do that too. Sure.

[*She goes to him. He stands. Kisses her cheek. She hugs him. Then she breaks away quickly*]

So listen. I'm quitting school. I've decided to become a hair stylist.

TOM Good for you.

GAIL Yeah. So that's all right, eh. It's not stupid?

TOM I don't know.

GAIL I'm not smart enough to be anything else.

TOM That's too bad.

GAIL You see, actually I'm smart enough to be anything I want. I'm smarter than Elizabeth and she's a lawyer. When you get to know me you'll see that. I just want to be a hair stylist because I've given up. I don't care. That's depressing, eh.

TOM Is it.

GAIL Sure it is. Someone as smart as me becoming a hairdresser is depressing as hell. The thing is I'm deprived. Emotionally deprived. Deprived of love. Mom's weird. She's been weird since you left. Not loving. Caring, if you know the difference, but not loving.

TOM Your mother was always weird. It's in her blood. Her whole family's paranoid schizo. I'm surprised she's not in the mental hospital by now.

GAIL That's kind of cruel. I don't want you talking about my mom like that.

TOM It's okay. I was just testing you.

GAIL Yeah? Oh. Anyway, you're missing the point. We're talking about me. I need love. Attention. So if you're going to stay you've got to do your job right. You've got to be a real father. Generous. Affectionate. You know … nice. And then maybe I'll stick it out in school one more year. No promises. We'll see how you do.
[*She bangs on the basement door*]
They're trying to escape. Don't worry. I'll protect you. I mean I'll do my best. They're awesome when they're aroused. Especially Elizabeth.
[*The door crashes open.* ELIZABETH *is carrying a baseball bat.* NORA *is carrying a shovel.* TOM *lowers his head over the bowl. Pulls down his hat. Eats.* GAIL *grabs the whiskey bottle from the table*]
Stay where you are. I won't let you hurt him.

NORA [*to* ELIZABETH] I told you. She has an unnatural affinity for criminals. She'll do anything to keep one alive. She's a criminal conservationist.

ELIZABETH What has he been telling you, Gail.

GAIL Plenty. Getting nervous?

ELIZABETH He can't be trusted. He lies.

GAIL [*to* TOM] She's nervous. The truth makes her nervous. She does all that legal aid work for down-and-outers. The truth about them is really frightening. Too much for her trendy liberal conscience to bear.

ELIZABETH Stick to the matter at hand, kid.

GAIL This isn't a courtroom. There's no procedure here. This is stuff from the heart, heartless wonder. The unleashing of my subconscious after years of mental inhibition.

ELIZABETH Oh, fuck off.

GAIL You fuck off. This guy's my dad. He's going to liberate me. You're liberated, why can't I get liberated.

ELIZABETH From what.

GAIL From her!

ELIZABETH Shut up. Do you want to break her heart.

GAIL She broke mine. She ignores me. She lives in her own world. Maybe it's in the basement. Maybe it's on another planet. I've got a space cadet for a mother. Jesus, Elizabeth, I gotta live here. I need a buffer. Dad stays.

ELIZABETH Sure. If he's alive when I'm finished with him, he can stay.

NORA Why is she calling the burglar 'Dad.'

ELIZABETH What.

GAIL Don't start, Mom.

NORA Who is this man. Do you know him.

GAIL She's starting. The antennae are out. Airwaves from space. Alien images flowing through her brain. [*cups her hands*] Earth to Mom. Earth to Mom. Beam in, Mom. We've got news from home. This is your husband!

NORA No. I'm sorry. I realize dead fathers are sore points with certain people but I don't think I should be expected to accept marriage to total strangers. I know this is a psychological dilemma for you, Gail. I've got professional friends who can help you.

ELIZABETH Are you saying this isn't Dad, Mom?

GAIL That's right, encourage her.

ELIZABETH He looks like Dad.

NORA Well, if it makes you happy, Elizabeth, this man can be your father. I didn't know you felt so strongly about it.

GAIL I'm gonna start smashing things!

NORA However, your real father is dead and now inhabits the body of your sister here. [*to* GAIL] Tom, I thought I told you to leave that child, in the name of the Father and—

GAIL That's it. This piece of shit goes first.
[*She picks up the rocker*]

NORA Oh, not the kitchen rocker. That belonged to my mother. He hates my mother. [*to* GAIL] Tom, put that down. I'll give you fifty bucks if you put it down.

GAIL   Don't call me Tom. [*to* ELIZABETH] Tell her to stop calling me Tom. Tell her that's Tom. Tell her she can't keep pulling this shit. Tell her we're on to her.

ELIZABETH   Mom. This is awful hard on us, you know. I mean it's taking an emotional toll. We better talk.

NORA   I'll talk to any of you anytime you want. I always have, haven't I. But first tell him to put that rocker down. Give him fifty bucks. Fifty bucks was his usual price to cease destruction.

ELIZABETH   Put it down, Tom.

GAIL   You called me Tom.

ELIZABETH   I'll give you fifty bucks.

GAIL   I get it. Humour her. Well, fuck you. I want a hundred!

NORA   It won't work. Only one thing works.

[*She rushes to* GAIL. *Sticks her own head inside the rocker with* GAIL. *And starts yelling into* GAIL'*s mouth*]

Out. Out you vicious bastard. Putrid love-killing madman. Leave this child alone. In the name of all the good things in life. Out out out out!

[GAIL *screams. Faints.* NORA *has hold of the rocker.* ELIZABETH *leans her head against the refrigerator.* JACK *bursts through the screen door*]

JACK   Who screamed.

ELIZABETH   Gail.

NORA   Not exactly.

JACK   [*kneeling over* GAIL] What's wrong with her.

NORA   It's all right. I think it worked this time. I exorcised him, Jack. I smelled him as he left her body. I had to do it. Don't be angry. I know it's not sanctioned.

[*But* JACK *is looking at* TOM. *He stands. Goes over to him. Lifts his hat. Looks at his face*]

By the way, Jack. Do you happen to know who this man is.

[ELIZABETH *takes a step towards* JACK. JACK *looks at* NORA *for a moment, then briefly at the others, then at* NORA *again for a long time*]

JACK   No.

[ELIZABETH *turns. Wraps her arms around the refrigerator and groans loudly as she tries to lift it*]

[*Blackout*]

MARY ANN *and* JACK. JACK *is sitting in the rocker. Smoking a cigarette. Drinking whiskey.* MARY ANN *is preparing to bake an apple pie from scratch. Including crust, excluding apples*

MARY ANN I'm worried. About my future. I'm worried that my past didn't prepare me for any future. I'm worried about a basic failure to understand how the world operates. I'm worried that I won't bring my baby up right. That I can't teach her how the world operates. I'm worried about the world. Even though I don't understand it entirely I'm worried that something is deeply wrong with it. With life in general. I'm worried that there's a general lack of faith and security in the world and in life. It's too much. Maybe it's all too much. I don't understand it but maybe that's because it's too much, too complicated. Yeah. Money. Love. Responsibility. Family. Work. Crime. Food. God. Children. Insanity. Friends. Sickness. Death. Shopping. Traffic. Teeth. Pollution. War. Poverty. Oil. Infidelity. Ignorance. Fear. Shoes. Hats. Nuclear power. Cats. Winter. Sex. Elevators. I worry about all those things and more. All the time. It's awful, really.

JACK Have you ever considered suicide.
[*She looks at him*]
Don't look at me like that. Officially I'm totally against it, but in your case it might be a legitimate option.

MARY ANN I had this dream once. I was outside somewhere with a whole bunch of people. It was a fantastic day. Everyone was happy. Birds were singing. There was an incredible rainbow on the horizon. All of a sudden the air was filled with beautiful music. And God appeared in the sky. Smiled down at everyone. Everyone smiled back. Then God beat me to death with a hammer.
[*Pause*]

JACK That's the saddest thing I ever heard.

MARY ANN [*goes to* JACK] No, wait. I think I understand that dream. You see I've always believed I'm prone to bad luck. And bad luck is just a bop on the head from God.
[*She puts the pie in the oven*]

JACK You forgot to put the apples in that pie.

MARY ANN You think I'm neurotic, don't you! Fussy and neurotic.

JACK I've always thought of you as one of life's chosen. Chosen to be worried, that is. Your saving grace is that you don't just worry for yourself.

MARY ANN Saint Mary Ann the Fretful. She didn't nurse the sick. She didn't feed the starving. She sat in a corner and trembled. But she trembled for us all. Don't you have any set pieces of advice you give to people like me.

JACK Sure. My best line.

MARY ANN & JACK Don't worry. It'll be all right.

MARY ANN It doesn't help.

JACK You're telling me.

[TOM *comes up from the basement*]

TOM Hi. Is there a tape measure around.

MARY ANN Are you asking me. I don't know. Look, if you're going to be staying here awhile you have to learn not to ask me questions.

TOM Sure. Okay.

JACK There's one in the bottom drawer, on the left.

TOM Thanks. [*opens drawer*] Yeah. Here it is. Thanks. Now we can get precise. Precision is poetry, that's my motto.

JACK It's a great motto.

TOM I've got others.

JACK I can hardly wait to hear them.

TOM Great. See ya.

[TOM *goes into the basement*]

MARY ANN Why is he still here.

JACK When your mother found out he was neither a burglar nor her husband she couldn't think of anything else to hold against him. So she … invited him to stay.

MARY ANN Why.

JACK I've got a motto of my own that might answer that for you. Here it is. Ready? 'Life. Is. Dumb.'

MARY ANN Are you drunk.

JACK I'm trying to get comfortable. I'm sitting here on my poor dead mother's rocking chair, bless her soul, having a whiskey and trying to get comfortable. Comfortable with the truth as we know it. Here's the truth I wish you to know. Tom. Our Tom. Your mother's Tom. Not the Tom downstairs. But the Tom of legends is really dead. This Tom. The new Tom, whose name really is Tom, was a brief acquaintance of the dead Tom. They met in Denver, Colorado, apparently a famous meeting place for Toms, about six years ago. They'd both been travelling around the underside of the world and apparently they jumped off the train at the same time. The dead Tom was in the process of dying, and over drinks one night told the new Tom about the family he had diseased and deserted and left for dead. Well, the old Tom was remorseful. But the new Tom was appalled. 'Precision is poetry,' he thought—here I speculate—'and someday, only Tom knows when, I'm going to make my way to those folks and right the wrong of this other Tom. Why, I even look like him. I bet I could just march right in there and with all this Tom-time gone by no one would know that Tom of the road was not Tom of the abode.' In other words—

MARY ANN Is all of this a lie.

JACK There's more.

MARY ANN I don't want to hear it.

JACK For your personal safety you have to.

MARY ANN Oh, please don't say things like that to me.

JACK Dead Tom was a troubled man. You know that. He committed revolting crimes. You know that too. But what you don't know is that your mother and I were forced to take action against him. This Tom, I'm afraid, might have certain knowledge which ...

[NORA *and* TOM *come up from the basement*]

TOM Yeah. It's a project I could sink my teeth into. It has ambition. It's flexible.

NORA [*to* JACK] He thinks it's ambitious and flexible. He saw the ambition of it right away. We had to discuss it for awhile before he saw the flexibility.

TOM All it needs now is precision.

NORA Precision is poetry.

TOM I'm gonna go measure the car. By measuring the car I determine the weight. We're selling it for scrap.

[*He goes out*]

NORA Ambition, flexibility and precision are things I have aspired to all my life. He knew that about me as soon as he saw it.

JACK I assume you're talking about that hole down there.

NORA No Jack, it's not a hole. It's a room. And it could be more. It could be anything. It could be a new way to live. An underground world. A place to keep vegetables. A safe place to hide. A bomb shelter.

MARY ANN A bomb shelter?

NORA If we get concrete. If we get lead. If we're nice to this man he'll get these things for us. He has connections.

JACK Nora, he can't stay.

NORA In theory, you're right. It would be a disruption of the family unit. Who is he anyway. We don't even know him. But he has a certain kind of knowledge of the world and maybe we should take advantage. He's got information we don't have.

JACK He's got nothing you need. He knows nothing you can't find out yourself. Remember there are all those books you can buy.

NORA In theory, you're right. I'm an independent person with strengths and initiative, and I certainly don't need a strange man to help me get by. I think I've proven that point. But what's the purpose of our life here on earth. Who knows. To live better? That's one purpose maybe, and he can provide knowledge that might be difficult for me to obtain. I'd have to travel the world to obtain his knowledge and I just don't have the time. I think we should let him stay if he can do things to help us live better.

JACK How is building a bomb shelter going to help you live better.

NORA Well, Jack, surely you'd agree that it's better to live without radiation poisoning. It's better to live with your own supply of food and water. It's better not to be scavenging in the wasteland through thousands of maggot-infested corpses.

MARY ANN Oh my God.

JACK He's turned you into a doomsday hysteric.

NORA He has certain knowledge. He has connections. He's seen the trends. He's read the newspapers. Carefully.

JACK We've all seen the trends, but some of us—no, most of us—prefer to remain optimistic.

NORA But he's got proof.

JACK Proof of what.

NORA The coming of bad times.

MARY ANN Gee Mom, are these the good times.

NORA Well, of course these things are all relative. But the bad times coming are very bad times and he's got proof.

JACK What.

NORA A letter. A highly official letter. A government letter. Written to someone in the government from someone else in the government. Someone who has access to information about the future. You see the future isn't really the thing we think it is. To people like us the future is an open space filling up with things we can't see until we get there. But for certain other people high up in the government the future is something you make. And these people have decided to make it bad.

JACK Why.

NORA They've got their reasons. High-up reasons. Overpopulation. The impurity of the social system, and big deficits, very big deficits. Also it's possible they're just mean. It's all in the letter.

JACK You've seen the letter.

NORA Yes, but I can't tell you its exact contents. It's a secret.

JACK And how did our new Tom get it.

NORA Also a secret. And please don't call him Tom.

JACK That's his name.

NORA Yes. But that doesn't mean we have to use it. It creates painful echoes. [to MARY ANN] Doesn't it, dear.

MARY ANN No comment.

NORA Of course, dear. You just continue what you're doing. Don't trouble yourself with any of this. I'll take care of it. I've decided I'll do anything to protect my family and create a higher standard of living.

[TOM comes in]

TOM Three hundred and fifty dollars. That's how much that car is worth for scrap.

JACK Precisely?

TOM Just about. The point is, it's worth nothing at the moment. It's just taking up space. By this time tomorrow we'll have the space back and three hundred and fifty dollars to boot.

NORA You see? Progress.

TOM Exactly.

JACK Precisely.

TOM This man's a sceptic. Too many years living in the shadow of God. It sucks the free will right out of a man. I've seen priests all over the world. They're in pain. Priests in the Third World are the worst off. Some of them want to help. Some of them even die to help. But it doesn't. Priests who die for a cause don't help anyone. And do you know why.

JACK Yes. Because they're perceived as being outside society in the first place and all their actions—even the sacrificial ones—are perceived as actions, once-removed, of personally motivated non-political symbols.

[*Pause*]

TOM More or less. Yeah. That's it. More or less.

JACK It's more or less the Marxist point of view on the subject.

TOM I'm not a Marxist. He's been dead too long. Too much has happened since he died. Priests have gotten smarter for one thing.

JACK Thanks. Nora, could you and Mary Ann leave me alone with Tom for a moment.

MARY ANN I'll go. I'd love to go. Where should I go.

NORA Where would you like to go.

MARY ANN To my room.

TOM Not much can be accomplished in your room. Why do you want to go there.

MARY ANN [*to* NORA] Tell him to stop asking me questions.

NORA [*to* TOM] Just until she gets used to you.

TOM Sorry. I forgot.

NORA By the way, Tom. Do you mind if we don't call you Tom. Do you mind if we call you Tim.

TOM Sure. Tim's okay with me. [*to* JACK] How about you.

JACK Sure. Call me Tim too. Who cares.

NORA Jack.

TOM Nora. Why don't you take Mary Ann somewhere and explain how we're going to expand the stuffing business.

MARY ANN I don't like the sound of that very much.

NORA My envelope-stuffing business. We've got plans to make it into a going concern. It could provide a solid base income. Come with me and I'll explain.

MARY ANN But I don't want to hear about it.

[NORA *goes to* MARY ANN]

NORA It's all right. I'll be gentle. I'll just give you an outline. No details, promise.

[*They're leaving*]

Details worry you more than anything, don't they, dear.

MARY ANN Yes.

NORA I thought so.

MARY ANN Details can be really scary.

NORA I know. I know.

[*They are gone*]

TOM Weird family.

JACK You think so.

TOM Sure do. Full of neurotic tendencies. Undirected energy.

JACK I suppose you think it's because they've been living without a man.

TOM Nah. I'm not simple-minded. I've seen the world. I've seen both sexes in the world. One does as well as the other. These people here are just not organized, that's all.

JACK These people here were traumatized ten years ago by a vicious madman. Lesser people would have crumbled. These people here just became ... disorganized.

[*While they talk,* TOM *checks out the kitchen's problems. A mark on the window. A leaky tap. One of the burners on the stove. The refrigerator door. The warped floor, etc. Then he opens the back door. Reaches out. Pulls in a large shallow box. Opens it. Takes out the contents—two or three sets of security bars. Begins to install them on the windows*]

TOM Sure. Listen. I never said they didn't have strength. They just don't have a system.

JACK You seem to be missing my point.

TOM You seem to be having a hard time making your point.

JACK You gotta go.

TOM You're worried about their safety.

JACK They're my family.

TOM I thought your family was supposed to be all of mankind.

JACK Knock it off. This is my family. My sister. My sister's kids.

TOM I'm not your problem. Your problem is that you once tried to kill a man. You don't think I'm dangerous ... You think you're dangerous. Try to get over it.

JACK You must be just about the most perceptive son of a bitch in the whole world. What's a perceptive son of a bitch like you need from these people anyway. Power? Sanctuary?

TOM No. Just a place to try out my plan ... I used to be messed up. I know that. It was my work. I saw a lot of anxious people. A lot of scum too. Messed me up after awhile. Not that I'm blaming the work. I'm not even blaming the scum.

JACK You gotta go! I want you to slip back into whatever crazy part of the world you came out of.

TOM Listen. Stop fretting. We're on the same side. I'm just trying to develop productive outlets for these people.

JACK Who asked you?!

TOM I saw the problems. I've got the solutions.

JACK Bomb shelters? Envelope stuffing? Selling scrap?!

TOM Look, we're going to create something here based on theories I've developed in my travels right here on earth. This isn't interstellar thinking, you know. What I'm talking about isn't a fantasy enterprise. It's a kind of socialism based on the reality of the place. In this place it's a kind of consumer socialism. The theory is if you can't stop buying things you should at least buy the right things for the most people. It's like a government. Like a society. A society within a society with its own government. Bomb shelters. Stuffing envelopes. These are make-work projects. In bad times you make work for two basic reasons. To get something done. And to keep people busy so they don't think. You gotta trust me. History is going to play a dirty trick on this country. The sins of imbalance are all coming home to roost and these people have to be prepared. Now if you'll excuse me I've got a schedule to follow in the basement. Five feet a day. [*starts off, stops at doorway*] By the way, all this worrying about what happened to this family ten years ago is garbage. What's going to happen in the future will make that seem like Christmas morning if we're not ready.

[*He goes into the basement.* JACK *seems dazed*]

JACK My God.

[*He sits.* MARY ANN *comes in looking through an encyclopedia*]

MARY ANN What's wrong with you.

JACK I'm worried.

[MARY ANN *sits*]

What's wrong with you.

MARY ANN She lied. She told me all the details. And they were really frightening ... Tell me, have you ever heard of something called consumer socialism.

[JACK *smiles. Shakes his head in disbelief. They sit in silence. Sound of a motorcycle in the backyard.* GAIL *comes into the kitchen from the hall. Carrying a knapsack.* JUNIOR *comes in from the backyard. Carrying a knapsack. They look at each other*]

JUNIOR What are you doing.

GAIL Moving out. What are you doing.

JUNIOR Moving in.

GAIL Who says.

JUNIOR Your dad.

GAIL He's not my dad. He's a fake. Another disappointment. That's all there is around here. Disappointment and strange behaviour. I can't take it anymore.

JUNIOR The real world's tougher. In the real world you're supposed to stand out. I got a feeling that in here I could just blend in. [*to* JACK] I think even though I've got natural talent I might be better off not using it. I'm gonna give it a try. [*to* GAIL] What about us.

GAIL What about us.

JUNIOR Well, I thought you'd be part of the deal if I moved in.

GAIL Who said.

JUNIOR Your dad.

[GAIL *hits him*]

I mean your fake dad.

GAIL Too much. Some total stranger walks in here and starts selling us into slavery. The only other place something like that could happen is the Twilight Zone. I gotta get out of here.

[*She goes to* JACK, *kisses his forehead*]

Goodbye.

JACK Goodbye.

GAIL Aren't you going to try and stop me.

JACK No.

[GAIL *shrugs. Goes to* MARY ANN. *Kisses her. Starts off*]

MARY ANN [*standing*] Okay. Listen. I think I should tell you it can be dangerous out there and you—

GAIL Shush. If you don't answer questions, you can't give advice. Fair? [MARY ANN *nods.* GAIL *walks to door. Shaking her head at* JUNIOR *as she walks by him. Reaches door*]

MARY ANN I just wanted to say be careful.

GAIL Don't worry.

MARY ANN Ha!

[GAIL *leaves.* JUNIOR *drops his knapsack*]

JUNIOR I'm starving. What's to eat.

[MARY ANN *and* JACK *look at each other. They both stand. Both leave.* JACK *out the back.* MARY ANN *down the hall. And* NORA *comes in and goes directly into the basement*]

Hey, it's working. People are ignoring me already. I'm blending right in. [*smiles*] All right!

[*He sits in a chair. Tries to blend in. Get smaller. Be insignificant. Begins to eat the sliced apples* MARY ANN *has forgotten to put in the pie*]

[*Blackout*]

[*Intermission*]

SCENE SIX

Night. A few days later
By candlelight, MARY ANN *is sitting at the table. Stuffing envelopes.*
Trying to do it quickly. Huge piles of envelopes and folded
advertisements. Some she stuffs properly. Others she crumples and forces
in. Then pounds flat
The light gets turned on. ELIZABETH *is standing there with her hand*
on the switch. Carrying a briefcase. Papers pouring out of it. A
trenchcoat folded over her shoulder. She looks like she has had a rough
day. Not tired—sort of unhinged

MARY ANN Turn that off. It's not allowed.

ELIZABETH What are you talking about.

MARY ANN The rules. We've got rules. This particular rule, the one
we're breaking now, is designed to save money on the power bill.
Please turn off the lights.

ELIZABETH No.

MARY ANN But we've got rules. And they're not yours! They're new!
There's a list posted on the fridge.

ELIZABETH How long has this been going on.

MARY ANN I don't know. Time flies when you're part of a social
revolution. Time flies for you too, I guess. You haven't been around
in ages.

ELIZABETH I've been busy. I've got a job to do, remember. If I don't
show up people go to jail. Get placed in mental hospitals or fined
ridiculous amounts of money.

MARY ANN I've got a job too. My job is part of the greater whole. I
stuff envelopes with advertisements for drugstores. But that's only
the first part of my job. The second part is to devise a more
efficient way of doing the first part. This requires thinking. For
most people thinking is a bad thing. But I'm the exception.
Thinking prevents me from worrying. Worrying is anti-productive.
If I worry too much I'll be sent away for reorientation. Sent where,
you might ask. Well I don't. Because I don't want to know. So I
stuff. I stuff well. And I think of ways to stuff better.

ELIZABETH Shut up.

MARY ANN With pleasure. Soon I'll stop talking altogether. Then I plan to stop moving. My ultimate goal is to become invisible. That way I'll be able to get my work done without taking up valuable space. Also I'll feel a hell of a lot safer.

ELIZABETH Mary Ann, it's wonderful that you're developing a sense of irony. It's less wonderful that you're becoming incomprehensible at the same time.

MARY ANN You're an alien. You just don't understand the vocabulary of consumer socialism. If you want to learn about it, ask Tim.

ELIZABETH Who's Tim.

MARY ANN Tim's what we call Tom.

ELIZABETH Why.

MARY ANN To avoid the painful echoes.

ELIZABETH I mean why do you call him anything. Why is he still here.

MARY ANN Why was Gandhi in South Africa.

ELIZABETH I'll bite.

MARY ANN To learn. To teach. And to prepare. For what you might ask. Well I don't. Because frankly I don't want to know. I just want to become invisible. Shush. They're coming.

[NORA *comes out of the basement in her rain gear and boots, followed by* TOM *in similar gear and also a miner's lamp around his hat, followed by* JUNIOR *wearing just trousers, rubber boots, and his motorcycle helmet. His upper body is bare and covered in mud. They all pick up lunch pails from the counter, wave at* MARY ANN *and go into the backyard in a line*]

That was the night shift. It's their dinner break. They like to eat outside so they won't disturb my work.

ELIZABETH It's like a scene from 'How Green Was My Valley.'

MARY ANN 'The Good Earth.'

ELIZABETH What.

MARY ANN It's more like 'The Good Earth.' Politically speaking. You see no one is being exploited. It's a shared experience. In 'How Green Was My Valley' the happy workers were exploited by the mine owners but didn't seem to notice. These happy workers work for themselves. For me. For all of us. You too if you want to join.

ELIZABETH I'm beginning to feel like Gail feels.

MARY ANN How is Gail.

ELIZABETH What do you mean.

MARY ANN She left. We assumed she went to live with you.

ELIZABETH No.

MARY ANN I'll have to call a meeting of the family unit. This could
cause great anxiety for the maternal leader.

[ELIZABETH *rushes to* MARY ANN. *Shakes her*]

ELIZABETH Knock it off, Mary Ann.

MARY ANN I can't knock it off. If I knock it off I'll go nuts. I've got to
go with the flow. People like me have to. People like you can resist.

[*She hugs* ELIZABETH]

Oh Elizabeth, please resist. You're our only hope.

[TOM *comes in.* MARY ANN *quickly goes back to work*]

TOM How are we doing tonight.

ELIZABETH We're upset. We're very upset. We seem to have wandered
into the wrong house. We seem to have wandered into some
perverse Pavlovian experiment. We think it sucks. We think it
should stop. We think if it doesn't stop we'll mangle your face!

TOM You don't trust progress?

ELIZABETH I don't trust you.

[*He goes to the fridge. Takes out a bottle of orange juice*]

TOM Things are improving around here. Life is improving. Life is
organized. Things are working again. The back burner on the stove
is working. The light in the refrigerator is working. The broken
faucet is working. The broken stairs are repaired. All of them.
Front. Back. Basement. The shower doesn't leak. The toilet flushes
the first time. The windows have been caulked. The doors all have
locks. There are five hundred cans of stewed tomatoes in the root
cellar—

MARY ANN Tomatoes retain their vitamin content the longest.

TOM And work on the basement sanctuary is right on schedule. Is
there anything that shouldn't be trusted in any of that. Speak.

ELIZABETH Why do you call the basement a sanctuary.

TOM Why do you call the sanctuary a basement. It's all in your point
of view, if you get my drift. Take some advice. Change your point
of view. Fast!

ELIZABETH I want to talk to my mother.

TOM Good. She's missed you. I have to get back to work.

[*He goes into the basement.* ELIZABETH *goes to the door*]

ELIZABETH Mom, could you come in here please. Not you, Junior. You
just stay put. [*to* MARY ANN] What's Junior doing here anyway.

MARY ANN In theory, he's your brother.

ELIZABETH Jesus Christ.

MARY ANN He's not too bad. He just works, eats and sleeps. He says he's had a realization that he's actually a very normal person. And now he just wants to blend in.

ELIZABETH This is no place for a normal person to blend in.

[NORA *comes in. Reading a book. And an atlas*]

NORA Good evening, dear. You've gained weight.

ELIZABETH No, I haven't! ... [*calms herself*] No Mother, I haven't.

NORA You look much heavier in comparison to your sister.

MARY ANN I think I've lost weight, Mom.

NORA That's all right, dear. It's for a good cause. What you don't eat gets eaten by someone else more needy. Isn't that right, Elizabeth.

ELIZABETH No Mother, it's not.

NORA Well, of course that's just a theory. And it's not my theory so I'm not sure about it. The ebb and flow of political theory is so complex. But of course you know that, Elizabeth, because you're familiar with politics. You'll have to be patient with me though because I'm just learning.

ELIZABETH That's great, Mom. Tell me what you've learned so far.

MARY ANN This is not the time to humour her, Elizabeth. This is the time to be direct.

ELIZABETH Be quiet. Go ahead Mom.

NORA I'm learning how the world operates. Do you know it's scary. It's complex and scary. So far I've learned that it's far too complex to really learn anything, but I'll keep trying.

ELIZABETH Maybe it is complex and scary. But you don't change that by hiding away.

NORA We're not hiding.

ELIZABETH What about the barbed wire.

[JUNIOR *comes in and goes directly downstairs. They watch him leave*] The barbed wire?

NORA Yes dear, what about it.

ELIZABETH It's strung all around the backyard. And there are bars on the windows. Bars on the doors.

NORA We're just protecting ourselves from looters.

MARY ANN Tim says we have to protect those stewed tomatoes, no matter what the cost. I expressed the opinion that any looters would more likely be after the television and the piano. Tim immediately went out and sold the television and the piano.

ELIZABETH Our piano.

MARY ANN Yes, but he bought five hundred more cans of stewed tomatoes. They arrive tomorrow. I can hardly wait. It promises to be the event of the week. [*looks at her watch*] Excuse me it's time for some fresh air. If I don't get fresh air I lose efficiency. If I lose efficiency I get sent away for reorientation.

[MARY ANN *goes out back*]

NORA Have you noticed that your sister has developed a strange way of speaking.

ELIZABETH She says it keeps her sane.

NORA But it's odd. Don't you think it's odd. She sometimes uses a dozen sentences to say the simplest thing. I think it's because she's unhappy. She's trying to express her unhappiness but it's too complicated for her to deal with so she expresses herself about anything that comes into her head. Remember when she used to use short sentences. Sometimes just single words. She was happier then. She was worried, of course, but I was used to that.

ELIZABETH What do you think is the source of this unhappiness. Do you think maybe she's having trouble fitting into your new ... lifestyle.

NORA No, it's sex. She believes I'm having sex with you know who. [*points downstairs*] And it's upsetting her. Who knows, maybe she even finds the idea disgusting. What do you think of the idea.

ELIZABETH Is it just an idea, Mom.

NORA It's an idea that would make the situation ... complete.

ELIZABETH But it hasn't happened yet?

NORA I've been approached. It's been hinted at. I've never had anything against sex, if you remember. And I'm still a vital person. I'd just like a second opinion.

ELIZABETH Look, I'd rather not talk about sex.

NORA Is it embarrassing for you, dear.

ELIZABETH No. It's just that I don't know much about this guy.

NORA That's all right. It's me he wants to have sex with.

ELIZABETH I know that. But aren't we jumping too far along. I mean this is all happening so fast. I mean what is it that's happening here. Is this a new life or something for you. Is this your second

chance or what. What's going on here. I don't understand. I mean really I don't understand a thing. Barbed wire. Organized work projects. A thousand cans of tomatoes. Some strange man digging a bomb shelter in the basement. You, talking about sex. Listen, I'm overloading here. I've had a hard day. I lost two cases. [*pulls an envelope from her briefcase*] You know what this is? A letter from the senior partner. You know what she says? She says I'm messing up. And she's right, the jerk. My mind isn't on my work. My mind is on my family and my family is—well, my family is—really fucked up! Maybe I'm wrong. If I'm wrong I'll just go away, divorce myself from the whole thing, let you get on with it, whatever it is, and I'll just step back, try to get some objectivity. But it's hard, you know. I need an aspirin. Have you got an aspirin. Never mind. I'll just lie down. [*lies down on the floor. Screams. Gets up*] Can I go upstairs and lie down. I think I'm overloading. [*leaving*] It's just too much. [*whispering*] Too much. Too much …
[*She's gone*]

NORA Sex. I never should have brought it up. The idea of their parents having sex can drive children almost clinically insane. It makes them talk funny and use lots and lots of sentences. It's like most other things when you come right down to it. I'll have to follow my own instincts.
[*She takes off her rain gear. Checks her hair by looking in the toaster. Straightens herself. Goes to the basement door*]
Tim. Oh, Tim. Can you stop that for a moment. Can you come up here.
[TOM *comes up*]
Let's talk. Let's have a nice talk.
[*Pause*]

TOM So talk.
[*She mumbles something. Smiles. Starts towards him. Mumbles something. Puts her arms around him. Mumbles something. Kisses him. He puts his arms around her*]
[*Blackout*]

SCENE SEVEN

The next day
MARY ANN *and* ELIZABETH *are stuffing envelopes*

MARY ANN I don't understand. Don't you have to be at work.

ELIZABETH I'm taking some time off.

MARY ANN Don't worry about me. I can manage all this. I've got a system.

ELIZABETH Be quiet. It has nothing to do with you.

MARY ANN If it's Mother—

ELIZABETH Mother seems just fine. Leave me alone.

MARY ANN But it's important for me to understand why you're doing this.

ELIZABETH This is therapeutic work. A part of me likes this better than practising law. A part of me really hates practising law, did you know that.

MARY ANN Of course I know that. But did you have to take this particular time to become reflective. I was counting on you to resolve this mess.

ELIZABETH It's rough out there. Rough on my mind. Political involvement often causes moral confusion. I mean, unless you're mentally rigid. You know, most of my friends have found a single direct path through a minefield of socio-political issues. Describe the politically correct position on the following issues. Welfare. Daycare. Capital punishment. Nuclear disarmament. No, that's easy. How about unilateral nuclear disarmament. Foreign aid. Who gets it. Only the governments we trust? And abortion. Let's talk about abortion in depth. Philosophically, morally, politically, legally, and even religiously …

MARY ANN Please, Elizabeth. I'm going to throw up.

ELIZABETH Relax. Take deep breaths. The danger as I see it is throwing the baby out with the bath water.

MARY ANN I know you think I've deserted my baby! Why don't you just come right out and say it?!

ELIZABETH Hey! Get your guilt under control until we have time to get you professional help. I was speaking about the situation here. Certain things are worth retaining. The income from this job is worth retaining. The knowledge of how to fix things is worth retaining. Mother's happiness is worth retaining. Her ideal of a better lifestyle is worth retaining. Only one thing doesn't have to be retained, if we're careful.

MARY ANN What.

ELIZABETH Tom.

MARY ANN [*whispers*] You mean Tim.

ELIZABETH [*whispers*] I prefer to call him Tom.

MARY ANN How do we get rid of him.

[ELIZABETH *stands. Kisses* MARY ANN]

ELIZABETH There are ways. A long-range strategy to undermine his influence. A series of compromising situations we could place him in. An attitude of resistance to everything that comes out of his mouth. Or we could just kill him.

MARY ANN We'd have to kill him without upsetting Mother.

ELIZABETH We'd have to be inventive.

MARY ANN Or sneaky.

ELIZABETH Or really, really brave.

MARY ANN Is it worth it.

ELIZABETH He has a history that could be filled with anything. When he shows his true nature we could all be in real trouble. He could be an axe murderer or something. He can't be allowed to march in here and set himself up as some kind of chairman of the committee. People who do that are dangerous by nature. Sometimes deranged by nature.

MARY ANN I had a dream about Dad last night. About what he did.

ELIZABETH We don't talk about what he did.

MARY ANN Maybe we should. Maybe it would help. Maybe it would have helped me with Larry.

ELIZABETH Dad had nothing to do with that. A lot of marriages fail. We're not screwed up about men if that's what you're trying to say. I like men. Some of them. I just don't like the ones who show up here. We have to be mature about these things. And we have to maintain our mental health. Like Mom did when Dad left.

MARY ANN Like Mom did, more or less, is what you mean.

ELIZABETH She did just fine for chrissake. She just didn't learn how to fix the goddamn stairs!

[JUNIOR *comes in from the backyard. Carrying a carton*]

JUNIOR The tomatoes are here.

[*He goes downstairs*]

MARY ANN I didn't know he was out there. Do you think he heard anything. Do you think he'll tell.

ELIZABETH Not with my fist in his mouth he won't. Listen, Junior's no threat. I know when men are threatening. I have a certain amount of experience, remember.

MARY ANN I don't want to talk about that part of your life.

[*Pause.* ELIZABETH *is looking at* MARY ANN. *Hard*]

ELIZABETH What part of my life is that, Mary Ann.

MARY ANN The part I don't want to talk about.

ELIZABETH I'm not sure I know what you're referring to here, Mary Ann. You're going to have to help me out. Describe it. Use a word that describes it. Come on. Just one word. Use it! Say it!

MARY ANN I can say it. Don't make a big deal about me saying it.

[JUNIOR *comes up. Goes outside*]

Prostitute! You were a prostitute. So there. I can say it. I just don't want to talk about it.

ELIZABETH What else is new, Mary Ann?!

MARY ANN That's right. I never wanted to talk about it. And I still don't.

ELIZABETH Good for you.

[*Pause*]

MARY ANN Except to say this ... You were amazing. Money was needed. So you went out and got some. Money for us. For our survival. Money for you to be what Mom wanted you to be. It was very, very brave of you. Of course I was disgusted and depressed by the whole thing. But that's just me. That's what I do. I get disgusted and depressed. But you did something that took real courage. And I'll respect you and love you forever for that. And that's all I want to say. Let's never talk about it again.

[ELIZABETH *takes* MARY ANN's *hand in her own.* MARY ANN *lifts* ELIZABETH's *hand to her mouth and kisses it gently.* JUNIOR *comes back in with another carton*]

JUNIOR The tomatoes are here. Except, guess what. They're not tomatoes. They're canned fruit. It's a surprise from Tim. Peaches, pears, apricots, melons, oranges. It's a gift from Tim because we're doing so good.

[*He goes downstairs*]

ELIZABETH The Santa Claus syndrome.

[TOM *comes in from the hall. Wearing a bathrobe. Carrying three different newspapers*]

TOM Good morning, girls.

[MARY ANN *lowers her head. Continues working.* TOM *plugs in the kettle*]

ELIZABETH Where did you get those newspapers.

TOM At the corner store.

ELIZABETH Dressed like that?

TOM I'll go anywhere, anytime, to get newspapers.

[JUNIOR *comes up*]

JUNIOR The peaches and pears are here. I'm putting them away.

TOM Thatta boy.

[TOM *sits in the rocker. Opens a paper*]

JUNIOR I just wanted to say thanks. It was a nice thing for you to do. I like canned fruit. I like canned fruit a lot.

[JUNIOR *goes outside*]

ELIZABETH All work and no play seems to be making Junior a bit simple-minded.

TOM The happiness found in small things is the only happiness of troubled times. What are you doing here. Don't you work anymore.

ELIZABETH I'm working now. If you mean my law practice, I'm giving it up. Why work in the world when the world won't be around much longer. A truly sane optimist knows when to cut the shit. Maybe all my life I've been looking for the exact moment to cut the shit. Maybe this is it. It's possible that this work will suit me fine.

[TOM *stands, walks over to them*]

TOM I sense a threat here. A possibility of some connivance. A deep cynicism.

ELIZABETH You're paranoid. I know a good psychiatrist. You should go see him. He lives in Australia.

[ELIZABETH *smiles.* MARY ANN *lowers her head. Covers her mouth to stop a laugh*]

TOM I've seen the spoilers of the world. I know what they look like. I know how they talk. How their talking leads to plotting, the plotting to confrontation.

ELIZABETH Great. But I just want to stuff envelopes.

TOM And I just want to let you know that I'm alert.

ELIZABETH Kettle's boiling.

TOM Coffee?

[*Pause*]

Mary Ann.

MARY ANN [*startled*] What?!

TOM Coffee?

MARY ANN Yes. Please!

ELIZABETH Me too, please.

[TOM *fills the cups with instant coffee.* NORA *comes in from the hall. In a bathrobe. She looks gloomy*]

MARY ANN Good morning, Mom.

NORA Good morning, Gail, Jack. [*snaps her fingers*] Mary Ann.

ELIZABETH Good morning, Mom.

NORA Good morning, Elizabeth.

TOM Good morning, Nora.

NORA [*lowers her head*] Thank you.

TOM Well, now that Mother's here, Mother can make the coffee. I'll go get dressed.

NORA Thank you.

[TOM *starts off. Stops*]

TOM Mary Ann.

MARY ANN What?! What's wrong. I'm stuffing the best I can.

TOM No, no, Mary Ann.

MARY ANN No, no, Mary Ann what?!

TOM I was just going to say now that your sister's here working on the envelopes maybe you can be doing something else.

MARY ANN What?!

TOM We'll think of something, won't we Nora.

NORA Yes. Thank you.

[TOM *leaves*]

ELIZABETH You look awful, Mom.

NORA You don't want coffee, do you.

[*She unplugs the kettle*]

ELIZABETH & MARY ANN No thanks.

[*They look at each other.* MARY ANN *looks away first*]

NORA Coffee isn't even good for keeping your hands busy. You drink it in gulps. Eventually it kills you. Like everything else. [*looks around*] This place is a mess. How did it get to be such a mess. That wallpaper used to be so pretty.

ELIZABETH What's wrong.

NORA I'm a little worried.

ELIZABETH About Gail?

NORA I worry about Gail all the time. I guess I've become used to worrying about Gail.

ELIZABETH You know something. I worry about Gail all the time too. [*to* MARY ANN] What about you.

MARY ANN Yeah, she's on my list.

NORA It's not Gail.

ELIZABETH Well Mom, if it's not Gail, what is it.

NORA You don't want to talk about it.

ELIZABETH [*goes to her*] Sure we do.

NORA It's sex.

[ELIZABETH *turns away*]

I had a sexual experience last night. It began with a bath.

ELIZABETH Wait. You're not going to give us all the details are you.

NORA If I don't give you the details I can't explain what happened. The whole thing is about details.

MARY ANN I'm scared of details, Mom.

NORA You're using short sentences again, dear. That's good. I'm glad your unhappiness is gone. [*sighs*] Life's like that. Some people are happy. They just lose their sadness. Others find a new sadness.

ELIZABETH Okay. Go ahead. Details.

NORA We had a bath together. He soaped me. I soaped him.

ELIZABETH No. Jesus Christ, I can't listen to this.

MARY ANN Maybe you could just skip all that, Mom. And get to the thing that made you sad.

NORA But if I don't lead up to it properly I don't see how you'll understand.

ELIZABETH Listen, we're both experienced. The details tend to be the same.

MARY ANN Give or take a few.

NORA Well, intimacy is a wonderful thing. Loving, kissing, hugging. Orgasms are wonderful things too. I'd forgotten. It's been so long.

Orgasms are incredibly interesting sensations. That's not the problem.

MARY ANN Lucky you.

ELIZABETH Be quiet.

NORA As for oral sex, well, I can take it or leave it.

ELIZABETH Oh please Mom, just get to the problem!

NORA Power. And dominance. And violence. I think if you take the hugging and kissing and the orgasm away that's what last night was really about.

ELIZABETH Did he hurt you.

NORA He wanted to. Once or twice I saw it in his eyes. I remembered that look. Like your father. Not all men have that look you know. That's why it's so easy to pick it out. Tim is much more like your father than he lets on. Sexually speaking. But sex connects to other things. I've got friends who know all about it. Sociologists. I think I made a mistake becoming intimate with Tim. I felt it was expected. I wonder now if it's too late to stop. You see, I don't like looking into his eyes in bed and thinking he could kill me.

[JUNIOR *comes in with three cartons*]

JUNIOR I can carry three of them. I'm getting stronger. I'm gaining strength.

[*He goes downstairs*]

NORA That boy's happy. That boy's rehabilitated. He's become normal. Tim knows how to get things working and how to rehabilitate criminals. In general terms he's brought a lot of improvement to our life here. [*stands*] I just wish he didn't want to kill me.

[*She goes out, down the hall*]

MARY ANN That's really frightening. You were right about Tim. He's really frightening. You have to do something about him! You have to.

[ELIZABETH *explodes*]

ELIZABETH Tim this! Tim that! Why are we always talking about Tim. Why do I have to deal with Tim. Who is Tim. Who the hell is Tim that I have to deal with him. Really. Think about it. It's an obsession. It's bullshit. He'll just go if that makes Mom happy. He'll just stay if that makes Mom happy. He'll turn into a pile of steaming dog shit if that makes Mom happy! But that'll be the end of it. We'll go on with our lives. Who the hell is Tim to stop us

from going on with our lives?!
[*She storms outside*]
MARY ANN [*smiles*] Now she's mad. Now he's in trouble. Go get him!
[*Blackout*]

ELIZABETH *looks angry. She is standing at the table. Stuffing envelopes furiously.* TOM *is measuring the floor*

ELIZABETH I've developed a new system for doing this. I've increased productivity one hundred percent. I've created a flow pattern. Watch me, it's amazing. Watch me.

TOM I'm busy.

ELIZABETH Watch me.

TOM I'm busy!

ELIZABETH You're not busy. I'm busy. I've taken a rough idea, a basic idea and made it work. Made it flow. Doubled its capacity. And do you know why. Because I'm smart. I'm really, really smart. Watch me!

TOM I'm busy.

ELIZABETH You're just fucking around.

TOM I'm fixing the floor. The floor is warped. Haven't you noticed. The floor is a hazard.

ELIZABETH You're not fixing the floor. You're measuring the floor.

TOM How can I fix the floor if I don't measure the floor. You gotta measure so that when you come to fixing you come prepared.

ELIZABETH I think you're primitive. You've got ideas but they're primitive. They don't go far enough. They lack intelligence.

TOM I'll fix the floor. It'll be fixed. That's intelligent enough.

ELIZABETH I could fix the floor. If I thought it was important I could fix the floor, design a new floor, make the floor do things.

TOM Whatya mean make the floor do things. A floor doesn't have to do anything except be there. And be level.

ELIZABETH I could design a floor that did things. A floor that cleaned itself. A self-cleaning floor. Or a floor that provided heat. I could run electric current through the floor that would heat this whole room. I could put burglar alarms in the floor. I could put trap doors in the floor. I could put mirrors in the floor that would reflect light so you could use this room as a greenhouse. I could do anything to that floor. I could take your basic primitive idea of a floor and make something really amazing out of it.

TOM So what.

ELIZABETH So you have to deal with me. I don't have to deal with you.
I know things you'll never know and I know more about the things
you do know. The floor is an example. Do you want another
example.

TOM Sure. Go ahead.

ELIZABETH No. You choose. Choose anything.

TOM The future.

ELIZABETH The future is shit. Just like the present. And the past. The
future is tyranny and chaos and bitterness and suffering with just a
little bit of joy thrown in to make it endurable.

[TOM's *tone changes. Fast. Becomes harder*]

TOM The future is not endurable. You made a mistake. There's nothing
in the future to make it endurable. I know. I've been told. The
future is total shit.

ELIZABETH Nothing is total shit. Only a primitive asshole would think
anything was total shit. Only a half-assed asshole could think that.
Your thinking about the future is like your thinking about
everything else. It doesn't go far enough. It doesn't consider all the
possibilities. It starts something but doesn't see it through. It leaves
big gaping holes. Holes full of disappointment. Watch me stuff
these envelopes. I stuff them better and faster than you ever even
imagined they could be stuffed, because you have no imagination.

TOM I don't need imagination. I've got experience.

ELIZABETH I've got experience and imagination.

TOM I can fix things.

ELIZABETH I can change things into other things.

TOM I can organize.

ELIZABETH I don't need to organize. I can do it all myself.

[TOM *smiles strangely*]

TOM I can kill.

ELIZABETH What.

TOM I can kill.

ELIZABETH Me too. I can kill.

TOM I can kill. With my bare hands. I can rip flesh. I can take a knife
and cut throats. I can put it in bellies. When the total shit of the
future comes, I can look it in the eye and keep it out of this
fucking house. I can take anyone who tries to invade this house
and rip his eyes out. I can cheat. I can lie. I can steal. I can beg. I

can sneak and grovel and betray and murder and burn things to the ground to protect this family. I am the soldier of the total shit future. I am the provider of the total shit future. I am the basic ingredient for survival.

ELIZABETH You're insane.

TOM I *am* insane. But I love you. I love this family.

ELIZABETH I don't want your love. This family doesn't need you.

TOM The love of an insane man is priceless in the total shit future.

ELIZABETH You can't scare me with that talk.

TOM Sure I can.

ELIZABETH You get power by scaring people with your insane talk.
[*Pause. He smiles. Seems to soften. He approaches her. Gently*]

TOM I am the warning. The warning is here. The warning has to be listened to. Why would I lie, Elizabeth. Won't you give in to me. Listen to the warning.

ELIZABETH No way.

TOM Come on, you want to.

ELIZABETH Why. Why would I want to.

TOM Well, suppose I'm right. Do you want to do the cheating and lying.

ELIZABETH Insane. Nuts. Like talking to someone in a nightmare.

TOM And if I'm right. Do you want to do the killing.

ELIZABETH I'd do it if I had to.

TOM But do you want to, baby doll. When the starving millions come to take away our food. Do you want to kill them.

ELIZABETH No.

TOM Well, I do. I want to kill them. Because I hate them. I hate them already and they're not even here. I hate their weakness. I've seen glimpses of it and it made me sick. That kind of weakness makes me sick.

ELIZABETH Totally incredibly insane. You're a first-rate full-fledged madman.

TOM But a good guy to have on your side in a crisis. Think about it. Stop resisting. Stop competing.

ELIZABETH No.

TOM You can't kill. You're basically gentle. You get it from your mother. They've been asking too much of you. Think about it.

ELIZABETH No.

TOM Come on. No harm in being gentle. Relax. Be gentle. Give in. Leave the rough stuff to me.
[*He strokes her hair*]

ELIZABETH No way. You're just trying to trick me, Dad.
[*Her eyes widen. She breaks away*]
Who the hell are you anyway. What the hell are you doing here!

TOM I'm fixing the floor, honeybunny.

ELIZABETH Don't call me that! Don't call me anything! Don't talk to me!
[*He turns on her. A crazy screaming anger*]

TOM No! You! Don't talk to me! Don't get in my way. Until you get it straight don't mess around with the way of the world. This world. This family. This house. Get it? Stop resisting. You are resisting the way of the world. The truth of the world. The truth of the total shit future. So stop it unless you are ready to do the killing yourself!

ELIZABETH I'm awfully close to being ready to kill you!

TOM Well, until you can manage even that, stop resisting!
[*They stare at each other.* ELIZABETH *uses one arm to sweep all the envelopes off the table. Then looks at him*]
That doesn't kill me.

ELIZABETH You've brought insanity back into this house.

TOM Just in the nick of time, if you ask me.

ELIZABETH [*just above a whisper*] You brought insanity back and I don't know how to fight it. I never did. Insanity was here when I was a little girl and I couldn't fight it then. It just went away. I didn't do anything to make it go away except pray a lot. And I don't pray anymore. [*starts off*]

TOM I am the soldier of the total shit future!

ELIZABETH [*stops*] Won't you please go away again.
[*She leaves*]

TOM I am the warning. The warning doesn't leave.
[*Blackout*]

That evening

JACK *and* TOM. *Sitting across from each other at the table. Drinking whiskey.* TOM *is not as drunk as* JACK. JACK *has his head down on his arms*

JACK You drink a lot.

TOM I enjoy it. I've never had any problem with liquor.

JACK Really.

TOM Have another one.

JACK I've had enough.

[TOM *laughs*]

TOM Then say what it is you've got to say. They'll be home soon.

JACK You laugh because I can't drink. Well, I can't think either. And I'm losing the ability to understand things. I can't understand the things that are going on here for example. Do you find that funny.

[TOM *goes to sink. Adds some water to his drink*]

TOM Well, a family is a mysterious thing. It has its own natural laws. Stop trying to figure it out. It's beyond the realm of your experience.

JACK They're traumatized. Operating on impulses from the past. Memory. Sentiment. And fear.

TOM You probably think they need psychiatric help.

JACK Actually I think you need psychiatric help.

TOM I used to. Then I got a plan.

JACK Tell me about it. It might help you.

TOM It won't help me. It might help you.

JACK Tell me about it.

TOM It was a great plan. I came here as their father. They had a problem with that. So we started again. That was the plan. They let me stay because they thought my intentions were good. That I was just making up for all the bad things their father had done. That was the plan. Time passed. That was the plan. I became a family member. That was the plan. I saw their problems. I helped them live better. That was the plan. I assumed control. I became the father. The original Tom in all the ways that matter to this family. That was the plan. And it's working. Tom is Tim is Tom.

Always and forever. It's weird I know, but it's better. Life improves. It's a great goddamn plan.

JACK It's psychopathic, Tom.

TOM Call me Tim.

JACK Your name is not the issue. I know who you are. I recognize you. And I'm getting tired of pretending I don't recognize you.

TOM Tom's a new man. He's Tim. Really I am.

JACK You're twisted right out of shape.

TOM You don't think I'm insane, Jackie. You're just afraid of my vision of the world.

JACK [*stands*] This world here would be better off without you!
[TOM *clenches his fists. Advances. Then turns suddenly. Begins to wander around madly*]

TOM But it's better! It's better, you stupid bastard. Sure there are problems. Problems abound in any new world. Elizabeth is a bitch. She's trying to neutralize my influence but she can be changed. A little trickery. A little force. Can't you see that a little force won't kill anyone. Can't you see that a little scare is good for these people. The stove is working. The goddamn stove is working. I left here ten years ago and the goddamn stove was broken and it took my coming back to fix it. And did Nora do anything about my car. I told her. I told her to sell that goddamn car for scrap. Ten fucking years it sat there. Sat there till I sold it. Pitiful. This family is pitiful without me. They need discipline. They need toughness. Can't you see that. Jesus, man. I told you this years ago!
[*With both hands* TOM *grabs* JACK's *clothing just below the neck.* GAIL *appears outside the screen door. She is laughing*]

GAIL Barbed wire. Way to go! No little white picket fence for this family!
[*She comes in. New clothes. A shoulder bag. Laughing. Confident.* TOM *lets go of* JACK]
Hey, I'm back. Or am I. I mean listen, I could be somebody else. Life is strange like that. Especially around here.
[*She takes off her coat*]

JACK Where have you been.
[*She starts to make a sandwich*]

GAIL Out there in the real world. You know it's really different out there. Hardly anybody pretends to be someone else. It took some getting used to. [*to* TOM] You looked like you were about to do something really violent.

TOM I can explain.

GAIL In the real world there are no explanations for certain things. [*to* JACK] Junior was wrong. You don't have to stand out. The real world is dull and stupid. You get by just fine if you don't try too hard. I rented a room. I got a job. I made a friend. I got relaxed. Then, guess what. My mind let go. And something that happened to me when I was a little girl came back. Does anyone want a sandwich.

TOM No thanks.

JACK No.

GAIL Anyway I saw a face. It belonged to a man I knew. I recognized his voice, and the way it gurgled and spat out things that weren't real words. And I recognized his shape. Stooped over. His arms making circles in the air. And I knew this man was really mad. Then I saw me with the man and I knew it was me he was mad at. And I got so scared I couldn't believe how scared I was.

[*She laughs.* TOM *looks uneasy. He sits in the rocker. Pretends to read a newspaper*]

JACK Gail. Don't worry, it's—

GAIL Don't say it's all right. I'll let you know when it's all right.

TOM But it's better! [*to* JACK] Tell her about the stove.

GAIL Shut up! I'm not finished. [*takes a bite of her sandwich*] When I saw my father's face, at first I thought he'd raped me—

TOM There was no rape. Don't start with that rape stuff.

GAIL The look in his eyes! Excited. It was confusing. Then I remembered the beating. I remembered hearing my arm break. Hearing it crack. I remembered being kicked. I remembered bleeding. Was he drunk.

JACK Crazy drunk. Crazy sober. Sometimes you couldn't tell the difference.

GAIL Does anyone want a bite of my sandwich.

JACK No.

TOM No ... I said no. Why are you staring at me.

GAIL [*to* JACK] Didn't anyone try to punish him.

JACK Your mother and I wired his car and tried to electrocute him.

GAIL Thanks.

JACK Actually it was just a low voltage charge. We were only trying to scare him.

GAIL Why didn't you just call the police.

JACK Your mother wouldn't let me. I ... think she felt sorry for him. Anyway he disappeared.

GAIL But beating me up was the crime, eh. The secret all these years. And I finally figured it out. Good for me! I feel great!

[*She grabs* JACK]

How do you feel.

[*She takes another bite of her sandwich.* JACK *stands. Advances on* TOM. *Becoming agitated*]

JACK He came back three weeks later. A month after that he stole everyone's clothes and gave them to the Salvation Army.

TOM They didn't appreciate those clothes. They didn't even need those clothes. Who bought those goddamn clothes. The poor son of a bitch who paid for them could give them to anyone he goddamn wanted. And that's the goddamn law.

JACK & GAIL Shut up!

JACK We retaliated by locking him in a bedroom and starving him for a week. After that there was a temporary cease-fire. War broke out again when he chased your mother out of the house waving his police revolver at her. We arranged a disciplinary action with him tied naked to a tree, hopefully perishing from exposure, just outside the city.

TOM Talk about abuse. Talk about victimization. A poor hard-working son of a bitch under a lot of mental stress and does he get compassion and understanding from his family. No. He gets assaulted, abducted, stripped naked, terrified out of his goddamn mind, and tied like a dog to a fucking tree. Is that justice. Is that tit for tat. Or is that going just a bit beyond the fucking limit. Shouldn't it have ended there. Bygones being bygones. I mean the guy *paid*! It's that simple. I've got nothing else to say on the subject. I declare the issue closed. Let's move on to nicer things.

JACK He got free. Made his way back here. And prepared for the cataclysm. It came one night while you were all asleep. He tried to burn the house down. The 'poor son of a bitch' tried to burn the house down while his whole family was asleep in their beds! Fortunately Elizabeth woke up and not too much damage was done. But we knew then it was time to get serious about self-defence. We ... put out a contract on him.

GAIL Junior Dawson's dad? [*takes a drink of whiskey*]

JACK Who else is there. Anyway there was an attempt on your father's life. It failed miserably. And your father disappeared for good.

TOM Okay. Okay. But if you're gonna be fair, you can't really blame me ... him. Why are you looking at me like that. I said *him*. You know, Tim ... I mean Tom.

GAIL It could happen again. Mary Ann might bring her baby here. I'm not taking any chances.

[*She takes a revolver out of her shoulder bag. Points it at* TOM]

TOM What do you think you're doing.

GAIL I have a healthy unhealthy need to kill my father.

TOM I'm not your father. I was just pretending, remember.

GAIL That's all right. I'm just pretending you're my father too.

TOM This is a mistake.

JACK A family is a mysterious thing, Tim. You gotta take the bad with the good.

TOM [*stands*] Ah Jesus, can't a guy—

[*She fires the gun into the air.* TOM *staggers back onto one knee*]

Ah, shit. What's the good of this. This doesn't help. You're just living in the goddamn past. I'm telling you the future is gonna be worse.

JACK Not for you, asshole.

[JACK *goes to* GAIL. *Staring at* TOM *he reaches out his hand to* GAIL *for the gun. She looks at him oddly. Hands him the sandwich.* JACK *looks at* GAIL. *Throws the sandwich down. Reaches for the gun. After a bit of a struggle* GAIL *lets go. Slowly* JACK *advances on* TOM. *Pointing the gun at* TOM*'s head*]

TOM Ah, Jesus. Am I the only person in the world who reads the newspapers carefully?!

[*Blackout*]

SCENE TEN

JACK *is sitting in the rocker. Rocking slowly*
ELIZABETH *and* MARY ANN *come in carrying a four-by-four wood beam.* ELIZABETH *is wearing one of* MARY ANN*'s dresses and smiling a bit stupidly.* MARY ANN *is angry*

MARY ANN [*to* JACK] Heavy as hell. And we couldn't have it delivered. It's not in the budget. We had to take it on a bus and a subway. I can't tell you how much fun that was.

ELIZABETH Those were the orders.

MARY ANN And we obey orders gladly. Some of us are becoming good little citizens of the consumer socialist republic. Some of us are undergoing personality changes.

ELIZABETH The beams were needed. He explained it to me. It seemed to make sense.

MARY ANN You were supposed to resist.

ELIZABETH [*smiles*] I tried. It was hard. This is easier.

MARY ANN Until we're murdered in our sleep. Until we accidentally break a rule, fail to meet our work quota, eat more than our share of canned pears. Then we'll see. Punishment will come. Death will come. The tyrant will come. The commissar. The dictator. The chairman. In our sleep. Slit our throats.

ELIZABETH Oh, that's scary. What are we going to do about that. Anyone got a plan. I sure hope so.

MARY ANN I want you to knock it off! Stop doing that ... that thing you're doing. I want you to stop smiling.

ELIZABETH [*stops smiling*] Okay.

MARY ANN And I want you to do something about this situation here. I want you to do something about the crazy man who is living in our house and getting us to do crazy stupid things because he's got these crazy stupid evil ideas!

ELIZABETH How about we try an alternative to that. *You* do something.

MARY ANN What can I do.

ELIZABETH I don't know. Starve him to death with your cooking. Tell him about your dreams and fry his brains. Sharpen a knitting needle. Put it through his eyes. Drop a sewing machine on his head.

MARY ANN Sure. Try to scare me. That's easy isn't it. Scare me with that violence stuff. Violence is only one possible solution. There are others.

ELIZABETH Well, consider them all. Think of every possibility and every ramification of every possibility and how it affects this family. That's what I've had to do my whole *fucking* life. And if you need help I'll get you started. Here's your first possibility. What if Tom's right. What if they are coming to get us.

MARY ANN Who are they.

ELIZABETH Could be anyone. There are lots of angry people out there. People who need what we've got. Who believe they deserve what we've got. And they're probably right if you really think about it. Try to think about that, Mary Ann! Genuinely needy people are coming to get this family. And rob and hurt this family. And it's your *duty* and your *responsibility* to stop them!

MARY ANN All right! I give up. Forget it.

ELIZABETH It can't be forgotten. It's already thought about. It's in the head. It's an idea. It's a possibility. They have to be stopped. *You* have to stop them. For Mom, for Gail, for me, for yourself. Come on, Mary Ann. Come on, it's up to you, Mary Ann. Please Mary Ann!

MARY ANN No, I can't! It hurts! Just thinking about it makes me hurt. Physically. Here. On my elbows. And my collarbone. I've got a pain in my collarbone. The skin is stretching and breaking. My collarbone feels exposed. So I want you to forget it. Because it's scary! Just ... Just ... pick up the other end of this ... this beam thing. It can't stay here. It can't! We have to take it somewhere!

ELIZABETH The orders were to take it into the basement.

MARY ANN We'll take it to the attic.

ELIZABETH It's not needed in the attic.

MARY ANN *I* need it in the attic!

ELIZABETH You're disobeying orders!

MARY ANN I know! I can't help it. It's scary. And it hurts. But I can't help it. Now pick it up.

ELIZABETH [*obeys, smiling*] Yes, sir. Honeybunny.

MARY ANN Knock it off! Follow me.

[*They go upstairs.* NORA *and* JUNIOR *enter with a beam*]

JUNIOR [*to* JACK] I could have carried this myself, you know. I could have carried them both. But it's good for a family to work together. [*to* NORA] Here Mom, let me take it downstairs. You just sit down. [*He goes downstairs*]

NORA He's started to call me Mom. I don't mind. It's a bit strange but I feel under the circumstances I should be generous. The circumstances are that he seems to have lost his identity. I think he might be in transition. Do you have any thoughts about any of this?

[JACK *shakes his head.* NORA *smiles and sits down*]

Well, the beams are here. Just two of them. Two less than I thought we'd need. That's progress. That's economy. There's happiness in economy. I think you should look for happiness anywhere you might find it.

[ELIZABETH *and* MARY ANN *come in.* JACK *looks at all of them*]

JACK Gail's home.

ELIZABETH & MARY ANN Is she all right.

[*They look at each other.* ELIZABETH *looks away first*]

JACK Yes. She's all right.

MARY ANN Where is she.

JACK Upstairs. Resting.

ELIZABETH Is she tired.

MARY ANN Why would she be resting if she wasn't tired. [*to* JACK] Why's she tired. I mean she comes home. She goes to bed. What's going on.

JACK She's just a bit tired. Don't worry about her.

MARY ANN Who's worried about her?! I'm just getting really annoyed at the behaviour around here. When you come home you're supposed to say hello to everyone. You know. [*to* JACK] Hello. [*to* NORA] Hello. [*to* ELIZABETH] Hello! … I mean it's a basic thing.

JACK What's wrong with you.

MARY ANN What's wrong with me. What's wrong with me! It's so easy, isn't it. So easy. What's wrong with me. Well, listen to this. [*to* JACK] What's wrong with you! [*to* ELIZABETH] What's wrong with you! [*to* NORA] What's wrong with you!

ELIZABETH Nothing is wrong with her!

MARY ANN Oh. That got a bit of a rise, didn't it. Knee-jerk response probably. She couldn't help herself. Always protect Mom. Protect Mom no matter what.

ELIZABETH Leave her out of this!

MARY ANN Sorry. That's what you do. I don't do that. I figure we're all in this together. Maybe we're all in this because of her.

[ELIZABETH *and* MARY ANN *are face to face. Very close*]

ELIZABETH Shut up! You owe her everything. You owe your life to her!

MARY ANN Wrong! That's what you think. I love her. But I don't *owe* her anything!

NORA So Gail is home. That's a good thing isn't it. That means all the girls are home. Safe and sound. Together. There's safety in numbers. Now there's a theory I actually understand.

[JUNIOR *comes up*]

JUNIOR Where's Tim.

JACK Gone.

MARY ANN Gone where.

JACK Just gone.

NORA Gone for good?

JACK Yes.

MARY ANN Not coming back?

JACK No.

NORA Are you sure.

JACK Yes.

[*They all sit. In a daze. Except* JUNIOR. ELIZABETH *puts her head down on the table. Pause*]

JUNIOR Should I go too.

[*Pause*]

JACK Nora. That's up to you.

NORA What.

JACK Should Junior go.

NORA Where would he go. He has no identity. Do you, Junior.

JUNIOR No. And I have no ambition either. I just want to sleep and work in the basement.

NORA I thought so. [*to* JACK] Besides he's part of the family. Somehow he became part of the family. He has to stay.

JUNIOR Yes. I have to stay. But I won't get in the way. I'll spend a lot of time in the basement. I'll go there right now.

[*He goes downstairs.* ELIZABETH *lifts her head. The old* ELIZABETH *is back*]

ELIZABETH What the hell do you mean Tim's gone. Come on, come on, come on, whatya mean he's gone?!

JACK He had to go. Something came up.

MARY ANN Well, good. I'm glad. I'm just very very thankful. And ... glad.

ELIZABETH [*standing*] Whatya mean something came up. What the fuck could come up?! What the ... What the ... What the ...
[*She goes out the back*]

MARY ANN [*to* JACK] I'm a little worried here. Can I tell you why. It's because I thought I was glad. But really ... I feel disappointed. Why. Is it because he didn't stick around and prove I was wrong about him. Is it because I hate to think we went through all this for nothing. Or is it just because it's a change. And I can't deal with any kind of change. My God. Am I that far gone.
[ELIZABETH *storms back in*]

ELIZABETH Coward! He was a goddamn coward. I gave in to him. I never give in to anyone. I gave in to his system and his lunatic vision of the world and his lunatic vision of a family. And he left. I came a long way towards him and he just left. Jesus Christ!

MARY ANN I'm going upstairs to lie down. [*to* ELIZABETH] Is that all right. I mean is there something I should do instead.

ELIZABETH Why are you asking me! Don't ask me what you should do.

MARY ANN I need to ask someone.

ELIZABETH Well don't ask me! I'm just going to stand here. Don't anyone talk to me.
[ELIZABETH *wraps her arms around herself. Closes her eyes.* MARY ANN *starts off*]

JACK Mary Ann, maybe now would be a good time to bring the baby here.

MARY ANN Ah, leave me alone with this baby stuff!
[MARY ANN *leaves*]

ELIZABETH I think she's deserted that baby. It's a disease. It runs in the family.
[ELIZABETH *leaves*]

JACK What's wrong with them.

NORA A pattern was being established. It seemed familiar. Maybe they were beginning to rely on it.

JACK Nora. He was dangerous. I don't want you to miss him.

NORA He didn't like me. I won't miss him anymore than I missed someone else who didn't like me. I'm worried about some of the things he said though. You know the things he said about ... out there. Maybe I shouldn't have listened.

JACK He forced you to listen.

NORA Yes. Force. He had that in common with the other Tom. Maybe it's hard for them to do without it. Maybe it's biological ... Now that's a terrifying thought.

JACK Yes, it is.

NORA Is there anyone I could talk to ... to verify that thought, Jack.

JACK Military men, professional athletes ... zookeepers.

NORA Did you get rid of him, Jack.

[*Pause*]

JACK Something came up. He had to go. He had to ... catch a bus.

[*He puts his hand out for* NORA]

NORA How did he find out he had to go.

JACK I don't know. He was convinced he had to go. Someone ... convinced him. I don't want to talk about it ... Come here.

[*She goes to him. They hug*]

NORA You haven't done something you can't live with, have you. I mean officially ... I only ask because you look so sad.

JACK Nora, I've come to believe in a certain kind of justice. But I had to stretch myself ... I'm stretched a bit too much, I think.

NORA What does that mean, Jack.

JACK It means I'm retiring.

NORA Shush. Don't tell me that. Tell me something else. Here's an idea. Tell me you just need a rest.

JACK Nora. I love you. I love the girls. I can connect myself to your family and that's about it ... Tom's craziness is the craziness of the world, maybe. I don't want to believe that craziness even exists. And that makes it almost impossible for me to deal with it ... Come on. Let me retire ... Okay?

[*Pause*]

NORA Okay ...

JACK ... Okay.

[*Pause.* NORA *lowers her head*]

NORA We tried to deal with it by making it into a second chance, I guess. A new Tom. A new way of talking. New things to talk about. Some of them crazy. A more positive kind of crazy though. I took it all as a kind of atonement. A gesture. Things occurred. Systems. Ideas. Rehabilitation. Intimacy occurred. Looking back maybe it wasn't all that good. But it was better ... than the first time ... In the overall scheme of things that's probably not even true.

[*She is crying lightly. She stands. Goes to sink. Turns on the tap. Picks up the kettle. Looks off*]

[*trying to get mad*] But it's my job to help this family by keeping a positive outlook on life.

[GAIL *comes in. Smiles.* NORA *turns. Looks out the window.*

ELIZABETH *comes back in. Looks around. Shrugs*]

ELIZABETH Something has happened to me here. And I think ... maybe ... I'm going to need some help figuring out what it was.

[*She sits. Starts to rock slowly in her chair. Looking curiously at the others.* MARY ANN *comes on from hallway. Putting on a coat*]

MARY ANN Bye. See you in a while.

GAIL Where are you going.

MARY ANN To get Samantha Melinda.

GAIL Who is she.

MARY ANN My daughter.

GAIL That's a very courageous decision. To give her a name I mean.

MARY ANN I know.

[MARY ANN *leaves. Pause*]

GAIL Samantha Melinda?

[GAIL *puts two fingers in her mouth. Make retching sounds. Laughs. Looks around at everyone. Shrugs. Sits on the counter. Takes a carrot out of her pocket. Bites into it hard. Chews*]

NORA Is that an apple you're eating.

GAIL No. A carrot.

[NORA *turns around*]

NORA How long have you been eating carrots.

GAIL Just a while.

NORA What's that in your pocket.

[GAIL *takes out another carrot*]

GAIL Another carrot.

NORA How many carrots a day do you eat.

GAIL Ten. Fifteen.

NORA Licorice, candy, mints?

GAIL Butterscotch.

[NORA *smiles. Goes to* GAIL. *Hugs her. Kisses her face a half dozen times*]

NORA [*to* JACK] She's pregnant.

[JACK *looks at* GAIL. *Smiles*]

JACK Are you pregnant.

GAIL Probably. Yeah.

NORA [*to* ELIZABETH] We'll have to hunt down the father and make sure he waives his rights ... It happened when she was wandering around out there at will, I guess.

GAIL No. Earlier. With Junior.

NORA I don't know if that's good or bad, considering our present circumstances.

GAIL You don't have to worry. I'll move out.

NORA That won't be necessary, dear. There's plenty of room. If you look out the window you'll see what I mean. If you look out the window you'll see nothing. No evidence of our room below the backyard. What's to stop us building other rooms below other backyards. To the left. To the right. Across the lane. No one can tell. It's possible. An infinite amount of room. An entire life's work.

GAIL I'm not bringing my kid up in an underground system of caves.

NORA Yeah, caves are dark. We'll have light. Windows. Lawn windows. You know, in the grass. We'll find ways of disguising them so no one knows they're there. We'll develop a prototype. We'll start here. [*points to the floor*] A round one. No, a square one. We'll try both. See which one is better. [*making little circles and squares in the air*] You know ... for some reason, all of this has made me think about wallpaper. Here's a helpful hint I read somewhere. When putting up wallpaper, old shower curtains make a handy dropcloth or furniture cover. Now that could be a problem. Do we want furniture in the new world down below. And if so, what kind. Or do we build our own. Someone has to keep that question in mind. I'll do it. The rest of you just concentrate on becoming happy. [*She goes to* ELIZABETH. *Hugs her*] I've decided happiness is the thing we should all work towards. Why not. What's wrong with happiness. I bet some of you haven't even tried it out. There are books about how to be happy too. Lots of them. Someone should go buy them all. I'll do it. In the

meantime here's a helpful hint. No, here's two helpful hints. One about happiness. And another one about wallpaper ...
[*Music. Lights fade.* NORA *is still talking but the audience can't hear her. And* TOM *appears at the screen door holding an large old portable TV*]
[*Blackout*]
[*End*]

ESCAPE FROM HAPPINESS

Escape from Happiness was first produced by New York Stage and Film Company in association with the Powerhouse Theater at Vassar College, Poughkeepsie, New York, in July 1991 with the following cast:

NORA Suzanne Shepard
ELIZABETH Jane Kaczmarek
MARY ANN Alexandra Gersten
GAIL Ilana Levine
JUNIOR Joseph Maselli
TOM Mark Hammer
DIAN BLACK Deborah Hedwall
MIKE DIXON Victor Arnold
ROLLY MOORE Dan Moran
STEVIE MOORE James Villemaire

Director: Max Mayer
Set Designer: Tom Lynch
Lighting Designer: Donald Holder
Costume Designer: Paul Tazewell
Production Stage Manager: Ruth Kreshka

Escape from Happiness was first produced in Canada by the Factory Theatre, Toronto, in February 1992 with the following cast:

NORA Frances Hyland
ELIZABETH Barbara Gordon
MARY ANN Nancy Beatty
GAIL Jane Spidell
JUNIOR Greg Spottiswood
TOM Ken James
DIAN BLACK Susan Hogan
MIKE DIXON J.W. Carroll
ROLLY MOORE Eric Peterson
STEVIE MOORE Oliver Dennis

Director: George F. Walker
Production Designer: Peter Blais
Lighting Designer: Michel Charbonneau
Stage Manager: Paul Mark

Persons

NORA
ELIZABETH, *Nora's oldest daughter*
MARY ANN, *Nora's middle daughter*
GAIL, *Nora's youngest daughter*
JUNIOR, *Gail's husband*
TOM, *the father of Nora's daughters*
DIAN BLACK, *a police detective*
MIKE DIXON, *a police detective*
ROLLY MOORE, *a criminal*
STEVIE MOORE, *a criminal*

Place

The east end of a large city.

Set

The worn-down kitchen of an old house. A screen door leading to the backyard. A door leading to the basement. A doorway to the rest of the house. An old fridge and stove, a table, four or five chairs, a broom closet, and a pantry. And all the rest of the usual kitchen stuff.

Note

There is an intermission between Scenes Four and Five.

SCENE ONE

Lights up very fast
JUNIOR *has been beaten up. His clothing is torn. He is bloody. He is on his back on the floor.* GAIL *has his head in her lap.* NORA *and* GAIL *are wearing coats. There are bags full of groceries on the counter and the floor. A couple of chairs have been turned over.* NORA *is holding a baby wrapped in a blanket in one of her arms. And she is on the telephone*

GAIL Tell them to hurry, dammit!

NORA [*into the phone*] Hurry, dammit! [*hangs up*]

GAIL Junior, what happened. Who did this to you. God Mom, look at him. It looks serious.

NORA He's not hurt badly. If he was hurt badly there'd be a certain kind of smell in the air. Sure he looks weak and torn up, but that's just the way he looks. Can he talk. Ask him if he can talk.

GAIL Can you talk.

[JUNIOR *groans*]

NORA Did he say something.

GAIL He made a sound.

NORA That could be a good thing. That could be his way of letting us know he's alive.

GAIL What are you talking about. He's alive. He's breathing, isn't he.

NORA I meant alive in a deeper way. Sure he's breathing. But inside has he given up. Is there hope and lightness in his heart. I'm nervous. I'm not sure I'm saying exactly what I mean.

GAIL I can't believe this. We were only gone an hour. My first time out of the house in weeks. We come home and find this. Shit ... Junior, who did this to you?! [*to* NORA] Call 911 again.

NORA No, you can't do that. It annoys them. Also, they get confused and suspicious. I've heard terrible stories about their confusion. We'll just have to hope and pray a reliable person took my call. Ask him to make another sound. Ask him if he feels alive.

GAIL Junior. Can you hear me. Can you say something.

JUNIOR [*groans*] What. [*mumbles*]

[GAIL *has her ear to* JUNIOR*'s mouth*]

NORA What's he saying.

GAIL He's saved.

NORA That's what he said? He said, 'I'm saved'?

[GAIL *puts her ear to* JUNIOR*'s mouth again*]

GAIL No. Not saved. Afraid. He said he's afraid.

NORA That's different than saying, 'I'm saved.' Emotionally. There's a whole world of difference between those two statements, Gail. Try to be more specific. How can I help if you don't translate properly.

GAIL Is that what you're doing. Helping?! How. How are you helping.

NORA I'm ready to help. It depends on him. On his state of mind. If he wants or needs a change in his state of mind to sustain life, I'm ready. Ask him if he thinks he's dying.

GAIL No.

NORA Ask him. Make it clear. Don't mumble. Separate every word. Make sure he understands. Do it. It's important.

GAIL You do it. I can't!

NORA He might lie to me. I'm his mother-in-law. We have an interesting relationship, but I'm not sure it's built entirely on the truth. Ask him if he thinks he's dying. Do it before it's too late, Gail.

GAIL Junior. Are you dying ... Are you dying?!

JUNIOR [*weakly*] Yes.

[NORA *grabs* GAIL *and pulls her away. She kneels beside* JUNIOR]

NORA Junior! Junior! Can you hear me. This is Nora. This is your wife's mother. This is your child's grandmother. I want you to do something for your wife and your child. Junior! You have something to do. If you don't do it the people you love will be destroyed. You'll be destroying your young, innocent family. Junior! Here's what you have to do. You have to get up.

GAIL Mom!

NORA Don't distract me, dear. Get off that floor, Junior! Get off that floor!

GAIL Mom, please. He's bleeding to death. He's probably got internal injuries. He's—

NORA Get up, Junior! You're killing us here! You're killing us with your misery. We need you to get up. Your baby wants you on your feet.

Hear her crying for her daddy? [*pinches the baby. The baby cries*]

GAIL What did you just do.

NORA [*whispers*] I pinched her. [*pinches the baby again*]

GAIL Stop that! Stop doing that. What's wrong with you.

NORA Junior, do you hear your baby crying! She's crying because she
wants you to get up. She's saying, 'Daddy, Daddy please get up.
Daddy, please, please don't die on that floor!'

GAIL Stop it.

NORA Junior! Daddy! Junior!

[JUNIOR *groans loudly. He tries to sit up*]

GAIL No. Don't make him do this. Junior, lie down.

JUNIOR I gotta get up! [*sits up*]

NORA That's not good enough. Look at yourself. You're on the floor.
We need you *off* the floor.

[JUNIOR *is struggling to his feet*]

JUNIOR Gotta get off the floor. Why? Why off the floor.

NORA Because you're alive. You're not dead. The floor is for dying. You
have to avoid that floor. Defeat that floor. Rise above that floor!
Get up!

JUNIOR Okay. [*staggers to his feet. Weakly*] Okay. I'm up. What now.

GAIL The ambulance is on the way.

JUNIOR I'm dizzy.

GAIL Here. Lean on me.

NORA Stay away from him. He's on his own. Talk to him if you want.
Ask him questions he can answer. Simple ones.

GAIL Junior. What time is it.

JUNIOR What? What's wrong with you. Look at me. I'm dying!

NORA Junior! Dance!

JUNIOR What?

NORA Dance. Do a slow dance ... Gail, turn on the radio. Turn it on
now!

[GAIL *turns on the radio. She begins to search for appropriate music*]
Find some nice music. Be patient, Junior. Music is coming. There.
That's good. Now dance, Junior!

[JUNIOR *is moving slowly. An ambulance siren sounds in the distance*]
Ambulance is coming, Junior. Help is on the way. The police, too.

Fire department. Everyone is coming to help. We're not alone, Junior. Life goes on ... [*to* GAIL] He's going to be all right.
[*The ambulance is getting closer. Closer.* GAIL *takes the baby from* NORA. NORA *starts to unpack the groceries.* JUNIOR *is still dancing. Lights flashing outside*]
[*Blackout*]

NORA *is sitting across the table from* DIAN BLACK. DIAN *is a police detective, neatly, pleasantly dressed. She is about thirty-five.* MIKE DIXON, *her partner, is standing a few feet away, hands in his pockets. He is older, tougher looking. At this moment, he doesn't appear interested in what* DIAN *and* NORA *are saying. He is casually looking around the kitchen*

NORA This is irregular procedure. I'm not an expert in these matters. But I have some knowledge of police procedure, and this is irregular. I'm a citizen who reported a crime. Maybe you're just being innovative, but it appears I am being questioned as if I were suspected of something.

DIAN You said you have some knowledge of police procedure.
[*Long pause*]
Well?

NORA I'm sorry. Was that actually a question, dear.

DIAN Yes.

NORA Well dear, were you actually asking me how I got such knowledge.

DIAN Yes. How did you get such knowledge.

NORA My husband was a policeman.
[DIAN *looks at* MIKE. MIKE *nods*]
[*to* MIKE] You knew my husband?

MIKE Yeah. Worked the fraud squad with him.

NORA That's nice. I think his two years on the fraud squad were the happiest years of his life. I don't know why exactly. Wasn't for any reason a normal person could understand. He's dead now, of course. Has been for several years. I'm sorry if this comes as a shock to you.

MIKE I saw him on the street last week.

NORA That's a man who looks remarkably like him. He lives here in my house. He behaves like my husband, and to some degree like the father of my children. But my husband is dead. Don't get me wrong. This man isn't really an imposter. He's just dangerously confused. Does any of this help you with your investigation.

MIKE No.

DIAN [*looks at* MIKE. *To* NORA] It's too early to say.

NORA It wasn't too early for him to say. He said 'no'.

DIAN [*smiles*] Well, he's wrong.

[DIAN *and* MIKE *look at each other.* MIKE *shrugs. He begins to look around the kitchen again*]

NORA Well, here we are again. In a state of irregularity. All I've done is call the police to report a crime. My son-in-law is lying in a hospital bed because he was viciously beaten.

DIAN By two men.

NORA Two men. White. One young. One ... older.

MIKE [*has obviously been only half-listening*] Black guys?

NORA No.

MIKE Oriental guys.

NORA No.

[DIAN *looks at* MIKE. *She frowns*]

MIKE Asian guys. Guys in turbans. [*gives* DIAN *a 'what's your problem?' look*]

NORA No. White men. I suppose they could have been wearing turbans. But that would have been odd. Odd enough that he certainly would have mentioned it.

MIKE He said they were white? He actually described them as 'white'.

NORA No. I know them.

DIAN You know them?

NORA Sort of.

DIAN Sort of?

NORA I know them sort of only as white.

MIKE What does that mean. You know them only as white. Sort of. Is there a possibility they could be something else.

NORA I don't think so. Are there criminals running around out there, white criminals who sometimes appear black. Or black criminals who sometimes appear white.

DIAN We think that drugs are involved. Your son-in-law has a history of drugs, doesn't he.

NORA You must be talking about someone else's son-in-law. My son-in-law was a car thief. He has no involvement with drugs. He has a child. And up to the very moment he had his child he was a child himself. I believe I should call a lawyer. My oldest daughter is a lawyer. I could call her. You'd like her. Well, perhaps you wouldn't like her, but you'd respect her. She'd insist on that.

DIAN You don't need a lawyer, Nora. You're not being charged with any crime.

NORA Well, that clears that up. You've been so vague. Intentionally vague. Almost arrogant. I know you probably don't think so. I've had police people in my house for dinner. In their hearts they're normal people, most of them. But they have an arrogant manner. You serve them a good meal. They just look at you in a funny way. You try to understand what that look means. Does it mean the food's cold. That there's not enough of it. That they expect you to put it directly into their mouths. I don't know. Maybe you could explain that look to me right now. I mean, it all ties together with our conversation here. And your attitude towards my son-in-law. And perhaps even your attitude towards visible minorities and the way they dress.

MIKE [approaches slowly] You were hospitalized once, weren't you. I remember Tom mentioning something. That was a few years back ... So how'd that go. How are you doing these days. Do you ever go back to that hospital.

NORA [to DIAN] My husband had me committed once, dear. [to MIKE] She didn't know what you were talking about.

MIKE So ... how are you.

NORA I'm fine. I've learned a lot since that happened. First, I learned that I wasn't insane. The doctors in that hospital told me that right away. They talked to Tom. They thought *he* was insane. They were right. I'm a grandmother now. I got to be a grandmother by bringing my children up to the point where they could have children. It wasn't easy after your good friend Tom deserted us. But that's another story. This is the story of my son-in-law's vicious beating.

DIAN On the surface, Nora. At first glance. To the uniformed police officers who came here to your house earlier, that's what it probably appeared to be about.

MIKE But we're different. Our job is to go farther.

NORA Farther than what. I mean, how far ... can you go.

MIKE As far as we want.

DIAN He means ... we have information those policemen in uniform don't have. We specialize in taking that information and applying it in various ways to find possible connections, patterns ... an ... organization of events ... Organizations ... That's the area of our expertise.

NORA I'm fond of experts, usually. What's your official name. The outline you gave is impressive. At first. But you could be anything. You need a name.

MIKE O.C.S.

DIAN Organized Crime Squad ... And in this house, Nora—the house where you live with your youngest daughter and her child, where a man who looks like your husband also lives—your son-in-law is possibly—make that probably—performing and arranging to be performed, a variety of criminal activities.

MIKE These are drug-related activities. These are prostitution-related activities, pornography-related activities, money-laundering-related activities ...

NORA Distantly?

MIKE What was that.

NORA Distantly related? Or ... closely related. Distantly related could be just a product of rumour. Neighbourhood gossip. There are dozens of religious fanatics on this street. They report people all the time. They reported me once for abusing my daughters. My daughters had a virus that made their eyes swell up. The fanatics told the police I'd been poking them in the eyes with heated knitting needles. I had to get a letter from a doctor. Show it to the police. Circulate it in the neighbourhood. When they're wrong about people, the fanatics just smile and say, 'Better safe than sorry.' Of course they're in for a very large surprise. Because they're all going to rot in hell.

[*Pause.* MIKE *and* DIAN *look at each other*]

DIAN Yes. Well, we don't rely on rumours. We use investigation. Surveillance ... [*looks at* MIKE] Good judgement. You see, Nora,

Junior's a ... a ... a ...

MIKE He's a crook. He keeps company with other crooks. The beating he received was a payback. A deal went wrong. Money was owed. Junior was to blame. At this moment I'm assuming you know nothing about this. Call it a hunch.

DIAN [to MIKE] A hunch? ... Oh yeah, I forgot. You get ... hunches.

MIKE Something wrong?

DIAN [smiles] No ... No, I agree. I think Nora doesn't really know much about Junior. Even if she believes deep in her heart that she does.

[GAIL comes in from the hallway. She sees MIKE and DIAN]

GAIL Ah, shit.

NORA Something wrong, dear.

GAIL Yeah. They're still here. Can't you get rid of them. Can't you tell them to just get the hell out. Don't they have something else they could be doing. You know, maybe something useful for a change ... Shit.

[She leaves]

MIKE Who was that.

NORA My youngest daughter. Gail.

MIKE So, what's her problem.

DIAN She hates cops, obviously. Right, Nora?

NORA Yes.

DIAN Any particular reason.

NORA Lots of particular reasons. For one thing, she believes being a policeman is what turned her father into a monster.

MIKE Well, that's just stupid. Get her back in here. I'll straighten her out.

DIAN That won't be necessary.

MIKE Says who. Besides, we should question her. Just because I've got a hunch about the mother here doesn't mean I've got the same hunch about her kid.

DIAN I'm afraid he's right, Nora. Gail's involvement will have to be determined at some point. We can assume only so much.

MIKE Listen, we don't have to tell you any of this. What we assume. Or don't assume. We're doing it because you're Tom's wife. And Tom was a good cop.

NORA Tom's dead! And he was a good cop but a lousy father. A neglectful, bitter parent. I'm a good parent, relative to him, anyway. You'll have to remember that if you bring trouble to my family. If you remember that, you'll understand my anger and why I'll be trying to destroy you ... I'm sorry I said that. That wasn't me talking. Not really. That must have been some dark part of my soul talking. Forget what I said. You just do your police work and everything will be fine. That's what we have to believe. That the positive will win out. That the dark parts of a mother's soul won't be awakened. [*stands*] In the meantime I'll just go upstairs. I have something productive to do up there. I'm wallpapering the bathroom.

[*She leaves. Pause*]

DIAN So?

MIKE So? What.

DIAN What do you make of her.

MIKE She's a fuckin' flake. They'll be putting a net around her any day. When she talks, my skin crawls. I get a headache. If we have to interrogate her again, you do it alone.

DIAN What's your problem. Does she remind you of someone in your past or something.

MIKE Did I say that. You're out of line.

DIAN Just curious. Is it common for you to have such an emotional personal response to people.

MIKE You're way out of line. They've told me about you. I think we should keep our relationship professional.

DIAN I'm a professional. Don't worry. Didn't I handle that interrogation in a professional manner.

MIKE Not really. No. I thought you were kind of weird with her. Kind of friendly or something. Like you were trying some ... new approach. Maybe it's the approach I've been told to watch out for. No one knows exactly what it is. But it's new. And no one likes it.

DIAN I have degrees in sociology and urban planning. Could that be what you're talking about.

MIKE I don't know. Maybe. Why'd you tell me that. What's that prove. It's like you're always trying to impress me or something.

DIAN I think police work is just an expression of my need to participate. A way to use my education to interact fully in the human experience.

MIKE I don't want you interacting with me. Let's get that straight. First of all, I'm married.

DIAN You think I'm interested in you sexually. You're old enough to be my father. Actually, you remind me a lot of my father. Maybe that's why I have these strange, ambivalent feelings about you. Relax. I'm just thinking out loud now.

MIKE Hey, hey! Come on, I was just saying I get enough interaction. I've got a family that does that all the time. You're just my partner. We're cops looking for crooks. That's it.

DIAN That's part of it. The rest of it is we're human beings. We need a certain degree of self-awareness, or we can't do our jobs properly. For example, when I ask you for an opinion about a suspect, and you launch into an obsessive whine about how that suspect gives you a headache and makes your skin crawl, I feel it's important to find out why. I think maybe she reminds you of your mother.

MIKE You can't talk to me like that. You wanna know why? Because I don't understand what you're saying. Also, it freaks me out. We've got a job to do here. We can't be freaking each other out. I'm freaked already. I'm so freaked I can't stand to be in the same room with you. I'm gonna wait in the car. [*starts off*]

DIAN Hold on a minute. Talking about professionalism, what was all that about black guys, Asian guys, guys in turbans.

MIKE Questions. They were just questions.

DIAN Incredibly insensitive questions. Surely you know that our attitude to racial matters is publicly suspect. You do read the newspapers occasionally, I assume. Because if you don't, if all you do is follow your ... hunches, well you're just not aware enough to do your job properly.

MIKE Look, just shut up. Don't talk to me anymore. All I know is I've got a hunch, yeah that's right, a *hunch* that something's going on in this house. And I'm gonna get a search warrant. A good, old-fashioned search warrant.

[*He leaves*]

DIAN [*throws her arms in the air. She starts off, talking to herself*] Yeah, get a search warrant. Get a couple of attack dogs, too. Hey, why not get the whole fucking army!

[*She is gone.* NORA *sticks her head in. Looks around. Comes in. She is carrying a roll of wallpaper. She goes to the screen door. Then over to the table. Sits. She looks worried. She begins to mumble to herself. Slowly we realize she is replaying her scene with the two cops. We catch the odd key word, recognize a gesture, a movement. After a moment* GAIL *comes back in, holding* TOM *by the arm.* TOM *moves slowly. His head is bowed. He has a blanket around him.* GAIL *helps* TOM *towards a chair*]

GAIL Thanks for getting them out of here. The smell of them was filling the house.

[GAIL *helps* TOM *sit. She gets a box of crackers from a cupboard. Sits next to him. Gives them to him one at a time. He eats slowly*]

NORA They left on their own. In their own good time, I think. They were so irregular. So full of tension. The world out there is getting worse by the minute. And the police are being affected. Their nerves are frayed. Their minds are disintegrating.

GAIL Why'd you let them in. They had no right being here in the first place.

NORA I was just being polite.

GAIL You let people in this house all the time. Total strangers. Derelicts. Crazy people. You have to stop. This is a good time to stop.

NORA Are you saying they weren't actually the police, that they were just crazy people pretending to be the police.

GAIL No. What I'm saying is smarten up. It's time to just stop trusting everyone. Cops included. They're out to get us.

NORA Everyone? Is everyone out to get us.

GAIL No! Yes! Yes. Just assume everyone's out to get us. And if those cops show up again, keep them out. Call someone.

NORA I'll call Elizabeth. She'll know what to do.

TOM Who's Elizabeth.

GAIL Elizabeth is your oldest daughter, Dad. She's a lawyer.

NORA Gail. Please. I've asked you a hundred times not to call this man Dad.

[*She goes to the fridge. Starts to clean it out and rearrange things*]

GAIL   I'm not having this argument with you anymore, Mom. If you don't want to admit he's your husband that's your business. But he's my father. He's Mary Ann's father. And he's Elizabeth's father.

TOM   Mary Ann?

GAIL   Your other daughter. You see, Dad, it goes like this … Try to pay attention, I'm getting sick of telling you. Elizabeth is the oldest, then Mary Ann. Then me. I'm Gail. I'm the youngest.

TOM   Why don't the other two ever come around.

GAIL   They come around when you're asleep, Dad. They don't like you.

TOM   Was I mean to them.

GAIL   Yes, you were.

TOM   Was I mean to you.

GAIL   Yes. You were mean to me, too.

TOM   But you're here all the time.

GAIL   I forgave you.

NORA   Oh sure, you forgave him. You took a total stranger and made him into your flesh and blood. It was an act of incredible imagination and perhaps even generosity. But Gail, I have to ask you, where is it all leading. What good can come from it.

TOM   [*points to* NORA] She'll never forgive me.

GAIL   You got that right.

TOM   Does she know I'm dying. Maybe if we tell her I'm dying she'll forgive me.

NORA   Tell him I know he's dying. And I'm sorry. He's a human being. I feel genuine sadness over the dilemma of death as faced by all human beings. But also tell him that's beside the point.

TOM   There's misery in this house. I can feel it. Is it because of me. It usually is.

GAIL   Junior was hurt, Dad.

TOM   I know Junior. He brings me soup.

GAIL   Junior was beat up by a couple of guys. We don't know why.

TOM   Bastards. Were they bastards.

GAIL   Yeah. And now the cops are on our back. They think Junior is involved with these guys in some criminal gang or something.

TOM   Bastards. Bastard cops. Bastards.

NORA Don't let him get started.

TOM Bastardization! I've had experience with all those bastards. The crooks, and the cops, and their bastardization of the simple, real world that was constructed by simple, real people. I like Junior. He brings me soup, and unsalted crackers. [*stands*] If you see him, send him my best. I've got to go back to bed now. I'm upset. [*starts towards the door to the hall. Stops*] Junior's not here?

GAIL No, Dad. He's in the hospital.

TOM If I need soup, who'll bring it to me.

GAIL I will.

TOM Good. And crackers ... And some juice. The fizzy kind. With a straw, if it's no trouble.

[*He leaves*]

NORA Go watch him. Make sure he doesn't go into my bedroom.

GAIL He knows where his room is.

NORA Go watch.

[GAIL *goes out to the hall*]

He forgets. He *says* he forgets. Sometimes he's in my bed. Under the covers. Naked. I have to sleep down here in the living room. I'm getting scared. Do you think he wants a sexual experience.

GAIL Well, not tonight. He's in his own room.

[MARY ANN *and* ELIZABETH *appear at the screen door*]

MARY ANN Is he gone.

GAIL Yes.

ELIZABETH Go check.

GAIL I just did. He's gone to his room. For the night.

ELIZABETH Go make sure.

MARY ANN Go make sure he's not listening at his door. That he's actually going to bed.

GAIL No.

ELIZABETH Go check, Gail.

MARY ANN We're not coming in until someone goes up there and tells us he's in his bed.

NORA Please, Gail. We need them to come inside. We can't talk about the things we need to talk about through the screen door.

ELIZABETH Look, we're not staying out here indefinitely. We're leaving.

MARY ANN She's right. We're leaving. Or we're coming in. But we're only coming in if someone actually goes up there and checks him out.

NORA [to GAIL] Please, dear.

GAIL Unbelievable.

[She goes out]

NORA This should only take a second. How are you both.

ELIZABETH Fine.

MARY ANN I'm okay, Mom.

NORA How's your daughter, Mary Ann.

MARY ANN She's great, Mom. She misses you. She said to give you a kiss. She said, 'Give gwamma a beeeg kiss-kiss.' She said, 'I miss gwamma. I want gwamma.'

ELIZABETH Shut up!

MARY ANN That's what she said.

ELIZABETH She said 'gwamma'?

MARY ANN Yeah.

ELIZABETH Well, she's four years old. Teach her how to say it properly.

[GAIL comes back]

GAIL He's in bed. He wants split pea.

ELIZABETH He wants what?

GAIL Soup. He likes soup. That's basically all he likes.

NORA You can come in now.

[They come in. ELIZABETH heads for the telephone. Takes a pad from her briefcase. Punches in her code. Writes down her messages]

Will you make his soup for him, Gail.

GAIL That's what I'm doing, Mom. That's why I opened the cupboard. That's why I took out this can.

NORA [to ELIZABETH] Junior usually makes his soup. But Junior— But, well, Junior ... You better tell them, Gail.

GAIL I told them already, Mom. I called them and told them. That's why they're here.

MARY ANN Where's your daughter.

GAIL Upstairs. Asleep. Where's yours.

MARY ANN At home. What do you mean. She's at home, of course. She's asleep, too. What do you mean, Gail. What were you getting at.

GAIL Nothing. Relax. You asked about mine. I asked about yours.

NORA That's what sisters do. They ask each other things.

ELIZABETH How come Dad only eats soup. Is he getting worse.

GAIL Yeah.

MARY ANN Has he seen a doctor lately.

NORA Now, why would Gail want to talk about that. Talk about a man who, to be kind about it, may or may not be her actual father, when her actual husband is lying in the hospital fighting for his life.

MARY ANN His life?

[ELIZABETH *hangs up the phone*]

GAIL No. He's going to be all right. Broken arm. Ribs. Cuts and stuff. Mom, why do you do that. Say outrageous exaggerations like that.

NORA To get attention, perhaps. To bring the truth into focus. To provide a topic for discussion. To get things rolling. Something like that. Tea anyone? Sit down. Everyone sit down. Except you, Gail. You just continue making the man upstairs his soup. And make sure you serve it at just the right temperature. I know you will, though. I know you deeply respect his needs. [*to* MARY ANN] She deeply, deeply respects his needs ... for some reason.

MARY ANN She feels sorry for him, Mom.

ELIZABETH Yeah, Mom. She's like you that way. She has sympathy for the diseased and dying.

GAIL He's my father.

ELIZABETH So what. He's my father, too. And do you see me taking care of him. I'd like to throw him off the fucking roof.

MARY ANN You see, Mom, we all feel our own way about him. Elizabeth hates him. I'm afraid of him, and Gail feels sorry for him. And that's okay. It has nothing to do with you. It's not directed at you. Any of it.

NORA He's in my house. He eats my food. Uses my furniture. And my bathroom. Occasionally sleeps in my bed.

GAIL By accident.

NORA So *she* says. But, well, I'll give her that one. That one is too distressing to discuss in detail. We'd have to explore the darkest part of human sexuality.

ELIZABETH Mom, please.

NORA I know. I know. That man upstairs says he is your father. And you all have a tremendous inner need to believe him.

ELIZABETH And you have a need not to believe him. We respect that, Mom.

MARY ANN We agreed to that, Mom. We agreed to let you not believe. And you agreed to let us believe.

NORA But from an historical perspective, Mary Ann—it's hard. Historically, your actual father deserted us and left us in a wretched hole of poverty and debt. And then ten years later a man just ... shows up. The man upstairs. *Why?* It's a simple question. But the answer could be historically terrifying. It scares me. I can't sleep. I'm thinking of taking pills. Lots of pills.

GAIL Oh, stop it. You're fine. You don't see him much. You never talk to him. You can deal with it. He stays. I want my kid to know her grandfather. I want her to have roots.

NORA Okay. Forget it. I'm *fine* ... if she says so—

ELIZABETH [*to* GAIL] Whatya mean roots. She doesn't need roots from that jerk. He's her grandfather, but he's slime.

MARY ANN Anyway, she's got us. We're her roots.

GAIL You're never here.

MARY ANN We're here.

GAIL You sneak in at night for a few minutes. Give Mom a hug, then piss off. When's the last time you saw Gwen.

MARY ANN Who's Gwen.

GAIL Gwen's my daughter's name, you asshole.

MARY ANN Please be nice to me. I've made so much progress in the last few months. I'm a much stronger, more independent person. But I believe my strength and independence are entirely dependent on people being nice to me. So does Clare.

GAIL Who's Clare.

ELIZABETH Her therapist.

MARY ANN My friend ... My therapist and my friend. Mom. I have something to tell you.

GAIL Not now. [*to* ELIZABETH] Please don't let her get started.

MARY ANN I have knowledge. It's important knowledge, and I want to share it with my mother. With you too, Gail.

GAIL No. Look. I guess you guys have forgotten why I called you. You know. Junior. The crooks. The cops.

ELIZABETH Don't worry. I'm looking into it. I've called my contacts on the police force.

NORA I thought everyone on the police force hated you, dear.

ELIZABETH Ignorant, neanderthal bastards can't take a little constructive criticism.

NORA [to GAIL] Elizabeth has recently been publicly critical of the of the police in several sensitive areas.

MARY ANN We're all real proud of her.

GAIL Right. But now we've got to—

ELIZABETH Don't worry. When I've got time I'll call my contacts back. See what they found out.

MARY ANN Mom. Gail.

GAIL When you've got time?

MARY ANN Gail. Mom. Listen. I have to share this knowledge with you. I've always shared my knowledge with you. All of you.

ELIZABETH And that's what's made us the people we are today.

MARY ANN Elizabeth is a lesbian.

ELIZABETH What.

MARY ANN You're a lesbian. And you're proud of it. And I'm proud of you for being proud. And now Mom and Gail can be proud of you, too.

ELIZABETH Mary Ann, what are you doing.

MARY ANN I'm outing you.

NORA What, dear.

MARY ANN I'm outing her. She's been in the closet. I'm helping her get out. She's a lesbian. Say it loud and clear. She's a lesbian. She's a lesbian! Clare told me to do it. Someone did it to Clare, and it was the best day of her life. So I'm doing it to you Elizabeth. You're a lesbian. You have sex with women. Lots and lots of women. Right?!

ELIZABETH [to NORA and GAIL] Let's talk about Junior.

NORA We went to see him in the hospital.

GAIL There were two cops guarding his door. I mean, come on—they think he's some kind of criminal mastermind.

NORA I'm worried, Elizabeth. The beating was unprovoked. Junior was alone here. They broke in and beat him for a reason Junior doesn't know.

ELIZABETH Or isn't telling.

GAIL He doesn't fucking know. Okay? We got that straight? We can move on from that?

ELIZABETH Yeah. Okay. He doesn't know.

MARY ANN [*pointing at* ELIZABETH] Lesbian!

ELIZABETH Look, what's your problem.

MARY ANN It won't work unless you admit it. Admit it, and let us all hug you and love you. Lots and lots and lots.

ELIZABETH If I admit it, do you promise not to hug and love me lots and lots and lots.

MARY ANN Whatever.

ELIZABETH Okay.

MARY ANN Say it.

ELIZABETH I'm a lesbian.

MARY ANN Tell Mother.

ELIZABETH Hey, Mom. I'm a lesbian.

NORA I know, dear.

ELIZABETH She knows.

MARY ANN She knows? For how long.

ELIZABETH Forever, you silly cow. You're the only one in this family who didn't know.

MARY ANN Why. Why am I the only one who didn't know. Why. Tell me.

ELIZABETH Guess.

MARY ANN No. Tell me. Why didn't you tell me. How come Clare had to tell me.

ELIZABETH *Your* therapist told you I was a lesbian?

MARY ANN Yes. Clare told me. She says you're famous in lesbian circles. You're a famous lesbian. She told me to be proud of you. So I am. Not that I wasn't before. But now I am, too. But more so.

ELIZABETH Why? Why more so?

MARY ANN Because it was hard.

ELIZABETH What was hard.

MARY ANN Being a lesbian.

ELIZABETH Get another therapist.

MARY ANN Wasn't it hard.

ELIZABETH Your life's falling apart. You've been a basket case for almost twenty years, and you sit around talking to your therapist about me ... Amazing ... Now tell them. Stop talking about me, and tell them what's new with *you*.

MARY ANN Not yet.

ELIZABETH Tell them. Or I will. And I won't make it all sad and gooey like you will.

MARY ANN I'm leaving my husband.

GAIL Again?

MARY ANN I have to. I'm at a crossroads. How many times does a person come to a crossroads.

GAIL If they're like you, about every three months.

NORA What about your daughter. Is she with Barry.

MARY ANN Larry. Yeah. He loves her. He'll be good to her. He understands my needs. He understands me.

GAIL Great. Maybe he could explain you to us.

ELIZABETH I asked him once. Actually, I begged him to explain to me what makes her tick. He just shook his head and whistled. And then he made the sound of a loon.

MARY ANN You should talk to Clare. She could explain me to you. She explained me to me ... Okay. This is the thing. I'm a kindred spirit of all the victims of the women's holocaust. A once powerful gender-species decimated by the religious patriarchy because they were terrified of their feminine strength.

GAIL What the hell is she talking about. And why is she talking about it now!

ELIZABETH [*smiles. To* MARY ANN] A witch. Are you saying you're a witch.

MARY ANN I would have been a witch if the witches hadn't been decimated. [*to* NORA] The way it is now, I don't belong anywhere. I'm at a crossroads, though. I'm ready to belong somewhere. And the thing is, I've always admired Elizabeth so much. Elizabeth has always been my strength. So I'm thinking maybe I'll become a lesbian, too.

ELIZABETH You see, that's why I never told you. I knew you'd pull some kind of wacky shit like this. This is not something you choose.

MARY ANN I think you might be wrong. Clare showed me some statistics.

ELIZABETH All right. It's something *you* shouldn't choose. I made a choice. But all your choices are wrong.

MARY ANN That's not fair!

GAIL [*suddenly bangs the pot of soup down on the stove, hard*] Okay! That's it. That's enough! I mean, come on. Junior's in the frigging hospital. And there are cops swarming all over our lives here.

NORA Mary Ann. I don't like saying this, but you leave me no choice. You could go to hell and rot there for eternity if you don't stop deserting that child of yours.

MARY ANN I'm not deserting her. I'm at a crossroads!

GAIL [*bangs the pot*] Hey! Shut up! Shut the fuck up! I didn't call you here to listen to this garbage!

MARY ANN It's my life!

GAIL Your life is a joke! [*starts to bang the pot over and over again*]

ELIZABETH Okay! Okay! That's enough! I haven't got much time. I've got two ex parte restraining orders in chambers, a gender bias submission that was due yesterday and a poor sick bastard I'm trying to get committed! I'm very, very busy! Let's deal with this Junior thing, whatever it is.

GAIL You're always very, very busy. If you can't spare the time to help your family, get the hell out!

ELIZABETH Listen, kid. Watch your attitude. I'm here, aren't I?!

MARY ANN And so am I!

NORA But that could be a mistake, Mary Ann. You're here. But is there somewhere else you should be instead. Perhaps somewhere in the vicinity of the innocent, little child you brought into this world.

MARY ANN Please, Mom. Don't keep doing this.

[GAIL *throws her arms up. She goes to the table. Sits. Puts her head down*]

ELIZABETH She's your mother. She's just expressing an opinion.

MARY ANN But it's so morally loaded. Isn't it. It's so dense with ... guilt. And stuff. Guilt and remorse. She can say whatever she wants, but she can't—

[TOM *appears at the doorway*]

TOM Hey, where's my soup.

MARY ANN Oh my God.

[*She runs into the basement*]

TOM Where's she going. Who is she.

ELIZABETH Get him out of here.

TOM Who are you.

ELIZABETH Get him out of here. Or I'm history.

GAIL [*looking up*] Go back to bed, Dad. The soup is coming.

TOM Is this woman one of mine. She looks like me, I think. Shouldn't
we be introduced.

GAIL This is Elizabeth, Dad. Your oldest daughter. You know her.
You've just forgotten.

TOM Sure. I remember now. I've forgotten. [*to* ELIZABETH] Hi. How
you doin'. Come here. Give me a hug.

ELIZABETH Okay. That's it. I'll be out back. Let me know when this
clown's back in his bed. You've got five minutes.

[*She goes out back*]

NORA Tell him to leave, Gail. Tell him he's causing turmoil.

TOM Well, that's obvious! I forget things but I'm not, you know ...

GAIL I'll be right up, Dad.

TOM The thing about soup is the temperature. You know, just like the
porridge in 'Goldilocks.' Think of me as Baby Bear. That's what I
always tell Junior. Any word about Junior.

GAIL He's going to be fine. Thanks for asking.

TOM Well, as long as he dresses warmly and puts his wages in the bank.
If he does that, Alaska can be a friendly, profitable place. Besides,
the world needs that pipeline. You should be proud of Junior for
helping to build it. When his plane gets in send him upstairs and
we'll have a little chat.

[*He leaves*]

NORA Everything he says has a purpose. Don't ever let him convince
you otherwise. That man has a reason for being here, and a reason
for everything that comes out of his mouth.

[GAIL *has a small tray prepared. She goes to the counter. Pours the soup
into a bowl on the tray*]

GAIL He's sick. He's got a disease that's done something to his mind.

That's all there is to it. I'll take him his soup. Tell his other loving daughters it's safe to come back.

[GAIL *leaves.* NORA *goes to the basement door*]

NORA Mary Ann. You can come up now. [*goes to the screen door*] Elizabeth. It's all right. He's upstairs. [*goes to the table. Sits. Pours herself some tea*] Mary Ann! ... Elizabeth!

[*A moment's pause. From the basement,* MARY ANN *appears. Behind her, with a hand over* MARY ANN*'s mouth, is* STEVIE MOORE. *He is holding a gun*]

STEVIE Okay, lady. Stay real calm. Stay calm, and I don't hurt her.

[*He takes* MARY ANN *to the screen door. Yells out*]

You out there? Okay. Come in ... Come on, come on. [*to* NORA] Okay, stay calm.

[*The screen door opens.* ELIZABETH *appears. Behind her is* ROLLY MOORE. *He has his arm around her throat. A gun to her head*]

ROLLY Did you tell everyone to stay calm.

STEVIE Yeah.

ROLLY Are they. Are they calm.

[MARY ANN *passes out in* STEVIE*'s arms*]

STEVIE I don't know for sure. But I think so. I think they're calm. Look at them ... What do you think.

[STEVIE *lays* MARY ANN *against a cupboard*]

ROLLY Yeah. I guess. Okay. [*to* NORA] You're the mother, right. We know you. [*to* STEVIE] Did you tell her the thing.

STEVIE Yeah ... No.

[ROLLY *cuffs* STEVIE]

ROLLY [*to* NORA] Okay, this is the thing. You've got something of ours. We want it back. That's the thing.

STEVIE The thing is, also, we're ready to kill.

ROLLY Yeah. That's part of the thing, too. We're ready to kill. You understand us so far.

NORA Yes.

ROLLY Okay. So far so good. [*to* STEVIE] What do you say.

STEVIE Yeah. I say that, too. So far so good.

ROLLY Okay.

[STEVIE *and* ROLLY *look at each other. Nod.* GAIL *comes in, breast-feeding the baby who is wrapped in a blanket. A long pause]*

GAIL Great. Just great.

STEVIE Oh, man. Dad, she's got a baby.

ROLLY I can see that.

STEVIE I can't do bad things to a baby. No way.

ROLLY Yeah. Okay. No one ever asked you to hurt a baby. Stay calm. Everyone! Stay calm.

GAIL I know you guys. You're the guys who put my husband in the hospital.

NORA Gail. We don't have any opinion about the identity of these two men. These two men could leave now, and it would be like they were never here.

ROLLY Except we need something you've got. And the thing is— The thing is—

STEVIE I can't, Dad. Not in front of a baby. We might have to use maximum force here. And I don't know. I just don't know.

ROLLY Hey, stay relaxed. You know. Calm down. Okay. Okay. This is the thing … We're … leaving. [*to* NORA] Like you said. We were never here.

STEVIE Yeah. We were never here. But we'll be back.

ROLLY We'll have to come back. Because the thing you've got, we need it. I don't know. Maybe you don't even know you've got it. It's a … strange thing.

STEVIE Yeah. But we can't get into that now.

ROLLY Right. Now we're leaving.

[*They look at each other. Nod. Let the women go. Back up. Go out the screen door.* ELIZABETH *goes to the sink. Fills a glass with water]*

GAIL Did you see that. Those assholes had guns. Didn't I tell you. This is a serious situation we've got here. Maybe next time I call a family meeting to discuss this situation we can stick to the fucking point! [ELIZABETH *walks past* MARY ANN *without stopping. She throws the water in* MARY ANN'*s face.* MARY ANN *wakes up suddenly.* ELIZABETH *continues to the telephone. Picks up the receiver]*

What are you doing.

ELIZABETH Calling the police.

GAIL No.

MARY ANN Yes.

GAIL No!

ELIZABETH Yes!

GAIL Mom?

NORA I have mixed feelings. Give me a minute to think about it.

[*They are all looking at her.* GAIL *hands the baby to* MARY ANN]

GAIL Mom, we don't need the police. They're all pricks. I don't trust
them. No fucking way do I trust them. We can handle this
ourselves. If we just put our heads together, and forget all that
other shit, and try to concentrate on this one fucking problem
here, we can do it on our own. We can, Mom! Goddammit!

NORA I'm thinking. In the meantime, Gail, if you don't mind a bit of
advice. Now that you're a young mother with an innocent child
you should try to watch your language. Every time we run into a
bit of trouble your language deteriorates and eventually winds up
in the gutter. It's not the words themselves that bother me. But
they show that inside you've given up. That you feel trapped. Had
a failure of the imagination. And that's no state of mind a young
mother should be in. A young mother should be positive at all costs.
No matter what the world throws at you, remain positive, remain
buoyant, light … light as a feather. In fact, that's good advice for all
of you. Remain light as feathers and everything will be fine.

[*Pause*]

GAIL [*looks at* ELIZABETH. *Gestures feebly*] You better call the police.

ELIZABETH Okay.

[ELIZABETH *is dialling.* MARY ANN *is trying to get the baby's attention,
making little noises for her.* NORA *is looking around at all her
daughters. Smiling.* GAIL *is shaking her head, sadly*]

[*Blackout*]

DIAN *and* MARY ANN. DIAN *is sitting at the table, nibbling on a* *sandwich that* MARY ANN *has made for her.* MARY ANN *is busy icing a* *chocolate cake and occasionally rearranging the condiments in front* *of* DIAN

MARY ANN Is this family doomed. I used to ask myself that question all the time. Are we forever doomed. Forever on the brink of destruction. Under some enormous shadow. Has God constructed a gigantic, mean-spirited shadow full of noxious, evil vibrations emanating poisonous, soul-killing rays, that has one job and one job only. To hover over this family and keep us doomed. And then one day I asked myself, why would God single out this family. And I knew right away that God wouldn't. God just made the shadow. And like everything else that God made, the shadow has a mind of its own. The shadow picked this family to hover over. I figured all this out a while ago, and it came as a great relief. You see, I didn't have to wonder anymore how we'd displeased God. I could forget about God for a while—which is always a great relief for me, seeing how I feel basically that God hates me— Mustard?

DIAN No thanks.

MARY ANN Anyway, I could forget about God, and concentrate on the shadow, and what possibly motivated it. You see, the shadow is fate. And our fate, the fate of this family, has some enormous grudge against us. So I figure we have to appease it, make amends, make some kind of huge, almost mythic, apology. We have to find a way of apologizing for something we don't know we did. So it has to be symbolic. It has to symbolize in some way everything bad each one of us has ever done as an individual or as part of a group. It's an almost impossible task. But we have to do it soon. Because we're doomed. Unless we make the shadow, you know, go away. Events are unfolding here that prove we're running out of time. Right now I'm making a chocolate cake, but inside what I'm really doing is apologizing. This cake is an apology for all the times I know that people I loved or people I hardly knew needed some special little treat, and I didn't have the energy to make them one. Just a little thing. But you see this huge, symbolic apology will actually be made from thousands and thousands of little things just like this ... This cake ... This chocolate cake, and oatmeal cookies, and blueberry pancakes, fudge, a nicely pressed pair of slacks, a bit of change to someone in need, taking care of a friend's cat, smiling on the subway. These are the things that are going to save this family.

DIAN You're an awful lot like your mother.

MARY ANN A chip off the old block. Yeah. Sort of. What do you mean.

[NORA *comes in from upstairs*]

NORA [*to* DIAN] Your partner said to tell you he'll be right down. He searched the entire upstairs. He has a search warrant.

DIAN Yes, I know.

NORA Right now he's in that man's room. Talking. He thinks he knows him, of course. What can I do about it.

MARY ANN Bake a cake. Fix a chair. Give someone a hug. The little things.

NORA That's right, dear. The little things.

[*They hug each other*]

Did you call your daughter yet, Mary Ann.

MARY ANN Yes, Mom. She's fine. She misses me.

NORA I'm sure she misses you. But it's also possible she's beginning to question your reliability.

MARY ANN That's a chance I'll have to take.

[MIKE *comes in, laughing*]

MIKE Same old Tom. The same basic guy. Still breaks me up. Don't know why ... [*to* DIAN] Upstairs is clear.

DIAN What about the basement.

MIKE I know, the basement. [*to* NORA] Where's the basement.

[NORA *points*]

I suppose you want to come with me. [*laughs*] You know, to make sure I don't plant anything.

NORA If it's all right.

DIAN Go ahead.

MIKE I was talking to her. But *you're* giving her permission.

DIAN She doesn't actually need permission.

MIKE You're saying that in front of *her?* Okay. If you say so.

DIAN I do.

MIKE [*to* NORA] Come on. To the basement.

[MIKE *goes downstairs.* NORA *waves at* DIAN. *Goes downstairs*]

MARY ANN Would you like a piece of chocolate cake.

DIAN No, thank you. Would you mind answering a few questions for me.

MARY ANN I don't like questions. I'd rather just give you things. If you don't want any cake, maybe I could make you another sandwich … or a casserole …

DIAN They're not hard questions. I'm just looking for a little clarification.

MARY ANN Oh my God. Clarification. I'm no good at that at all. Maybe in a year or two. Right now I'm just working on saying anything that comes into my mind. You know, unblocking myself. Maybe you could wait till my sister Elizabeth gets here. She's an expert on clarification.

DIAN Elizabeth. She's the lawyer?

MARY ANN Yes. A lesbian lawyer. We're very proud of her. She overcame so much to be what she is. Well, look around. This family has nothing. We used to have a bit. The usual amount a family like ours has. But our father took it all away when he left. Of course he came back eventually, but he didn't bring anything with him. And now, well, he's a vegetable, sort of. That's what they tell me. I don't know for sure, though, because I never see him. He scares me. It's odd about my father. When he deserted us, everything just fell apart. Who would have thought he had that kind of power. Not me. Before he deserted us, I barely gave him a second thought … Except when he was doing something loud and horrible. But we were talking about Elizabeth … Why.

DIAN Elizabeth seems to be a very important part of this family.

MARY ANN She's our weapon. She's the thing that protects us. I mean, if we're threatened.

DIAN Like now.

MARY ANN Like now. And then. Whenever.

DIAN That's a heavy responsibility to take on.

MARY ANN She can handle it.

DIAN Mary Ann. Here's the problem I have. The men who broke in here, the men who beat up Junior ... Your mother seems to know these men ...

MARY ANN That's actually a question, isn't it. I'm supposed to answer that, I can tell.

DIAN Just try to make that clear for me. And then maybe I'll have a piece of cake or something.

MARY ANN Okay. My mother hires people. Men mostly. Derelicts. Fallen men. Criminals even. She hires them to do handiwork around the house. She just finds them, we don't know how. They come here and work. She talks to them. Pays them. Talks to them some more.

DIAN So she wouldn't really know much about them. Their names, or ... how to find them ...

MARY ANN No. She doesn't ask them questions like that. She just talks to them. Would you like that cake now.

DIAN Sure. You know, Mary Ann, this is one rough neighbourhood here. This is a dangerous world you live in. Perhaps your family should try a more realistic approach to dealing with it.

MARY ANN [cuts a piece of cake. Puts it on a plate] Realistic? Oh. I think I know what you mean. We've tried that. It doesn't seem to work for us. It was very real when I was a kid. My dad was here. There was anger and violence. Hopelessness. I think what we do now is better. It's more like Mom than Dad. And Mom's way is more ... well ...

DIAN Innocent.

MARY ANN [laughs] Innocent? No ... Hopeful.

[NORA comes up]

NORA He found something. I'm a little worried.

[MIKE comes up. Carrying two large garbage bags. Each about half full]

MIKE [to DIAN] They were hidden in a hole in the wall. Behind a work bench.

[MIKE puts the bags down. DIAN goes over. Looks in them]

DIAN Did you know about these bags, Nora.

NORA No.

DIAN So you don't know what's in them.

NORA No. I mean, I suspect it's something of substance. Some substantially evil thing. I picked that up from the substantially evil way your partner smiled at me.

MIKE Hey!

NORA [to MARY ANN] I'm a little worried about the neighbourhood fanatics. Break-ins. Police cars. I bet they're passing around a petition.

DIAN Drugs.

MARY ANN Oh my God.

[MARY ANN goes to NORA. Puts her arms around her neck. Hangs on]

DIAN Hundreds of thousands of dollars worth of drugs. I think you'll have to come with us, Nora, so we can straighten this out. I'm sorry.

MIKE You're sorry. You're telling her you're sorry.

DIAN That's right. Come on, she didn't know they were there.

MIKE [goes to DIAN] You're saying that right in front of her. Where the fuck were you trained. Disneyland?

DIAN I'll deal with you later!

MIKE I'll deal with you later! [to NORA] Turn around. Put your hands behind your back.

[MIKE is trying to handcuff NORA. But MARY ANN still has her arms around NORA and is turning her around. MIKE is turning with them]

DIAN No cuffs.

[DIAN is trying to restrain MIKE]

MIKE We're in a war here. You ever hear about it. It's called the war on drugs. Drugs are the main thing now. It's what we're all about. It's our reason for fucking living, and she's a suspected *drug dealer*.

[All four of them are tangled and turning]

DIAN No fucking cuffs! If you don't get your hands off her right now I'll have your head!

[DIAN groans and pulls MIKE away from NORA and MARY ANN. She is poking him in the chest and backing him up. MIKE is trying to resist. Trying to control his temper]

I've got friends. Friends high up. [poke]

MIKE Back off.

DIAN You know, the ones you resent. The ones you talk about behind my back. [*poke*]

MIKE Get your hands off me. Back off.

DIAN The ones you say gave me my job because I screwed their brains out. [*poke*]

MIKE Back off. I'm warning you.

DIAN I think you should assume these friends will do anything for me! [*poke*]

MIKE Hey, you were warned. Now back the fuck off!

[*He pokes her. She grabs him by the collar. He grabs her by the collar*]

DIAN If I ask them, my friends will take your badge and shove it so far up your ass your spleen will think it's under arrest!

MIKE You talk to me like that?! In front of them?! I gotta say fuck you! I really do! [*shakes himself free. To* DIAN] Fuck you. [*to* NORA *and* MARY ANN] Fuck you, too. [*picks up the garbage bags. To* NORA *and* MARY ANN] No, to you I'm sorry. [*to* DIAN] But to you, definitely, fuck you!

[*He leaves*]

DIAN [*trembling slightly. Searches her purse. Finds a small plastic tube*] Lip balm. Do you mind.

NORA No.

DIAN [*applies the lip balm, strenuously*] That was ugly, wasn't it. Sorry you had to witness that. Obviously my partner and I are having problems maintaining a relationship. There are just so many co-factors involved. Differences. Age, sex, levels of intelligence. The conflicts are very deep. The relationship is deteriorating rapidly.

NORA Would you like a cup of tea, dear.

DIAN No.

MARY ANN Cake?

DIAN No. Thank you … We should go now, Nora. Back to the office. Talk this thing through in detail. You'll be back in no time.

MARY ANN I want to come, too.

NORA No you don't, dear.

MARY ANN You're right. I *want* to want to come. But I don't really want to come at all.

DIAN [*to* NORA] Do you need a coat ... or a sweater.

NORA No ... Should I call my daughter Elizabeth, though. She's a lawyer.

MARY ANN She's the lesbian, remember. You'd like her. Not that I think you're a lesbian. Not that there's anything wrong with being a lesbian. I'm thinking about it myself. I just meant she was ... well, you know what I meant.

DIAN No. But it's all right. Come on, Nora. You can call Elizabeth from my office.

NORA [*goes to* MARY ANN] Maybe you could cook supper.

MARY ANN I would anyway. That's what I do when I run away from home, remember. I come here and cook things.

NORA I've been thinking, Mary Ann. It's possible you aren't a good mother. It's possible you're just average. Maybe you could go home and just be a good, average mother. Think about that while you're cooking. I'll see you soon.

[NORA *and* DIAN *leave.* MARY ANN *looks around. Lost. She goes to the table. Sits in a chair. Puts her head in her palms*]

MARY ANN [*looks up suddenly, a puzzled look on her face*] When I said she'd like Elizabeth because Elizabeth is a lesbian what *did* I mean. Really. I think I meant Elizabeth is *great*. She'd like her because she's great. Why do I say lesbian instead of great ... I don't know. But maybe I don't really want to be a lesbian. Maybe I just want to be ... great ... Do I have to be a lesbian to be great ... I'll ask Elizabeth. She wasn't always a lesbian. She wasn't always great, either. What came first. The lesbianism or the greatness. When did she become lesbianistic. Is that a word. Use it in a sentence. Never mind. It's beside the point. Just ask her. Okay. Yeah. Of course, she hardly ever listens to me. Unless I cry. When I cry she listens. Okay. Yeah. I'll cry. It's demeaning. But I'll do it. Because I need to know. I mean, I'm working things out here. Important things. Yeah.

[TOM *appears at the hallway door*]

TOM I'm starving to death.

MARY ANN Oh dear.

[*She stands. Hurries towards the basement door. Leaves. Reappears*]

No. No. I can do better than this. I can. [*looks at* TOM. *Smiles weakly*] Hi.

TOM Hi.

MARY ANN You're hungry?

TOM [*lowers his head*] I'm starving to death.

MARY ANN Would you like some chocolate cake.

TOM Not soup?

MARY ANN I can do soup. Soup is all right, too. I'll … make you some. From scratch. I'm good at soups. It'll take some time. Can you wait.

TOM No.

MARY ANN Okay. Have the cake now. Here. I'll cut you a piece. No. Here, take it all. Here's a fork. Take it.

TOM [*takes the cake*] It's big.

MARY ANN Yeah.

TOM But there's a piece missing.

MARY ANN Is that okay.

TOM I don't know. Why shouldn't it be. Can you think of a reason. Who are you, anyway.

MARY ANN Mary Ann.

TOM My daughter?

MARY ANN Yeah.

TOM I've got to ask you a question.

MARY ANN Oh … okay … I guess.

TOM How you doin'. How's your life. Are you having a good life. Have you recovered.

MARY ANN Ah … From what.

TOM Me … I guess. Recovered from me. The things I did. I did some bad things to this family. I think I had a … I had a … I had a—

MARY ANN Problem. You had a problem.

TOM Drinking.

MARY ANN Drinking. Yeah. And a vicious temper. And awful impatience. But, well … I'm okay. Sure, I'm fine now. That was your question? So … I'm basically … well, I've got some things to work on … some choices I have to … but basically—

TOM I'm tired.

[*He leaves.* MARY ANN *sits down. Lowers her head on to the table. Keeps it there a moment. Sits up*]

MARY ANN Soup.

[*She stands. Goes to the cupboard, the fridge. Hunting up ingredients for vegetable soup.* GAIL *and* JUNIOR *come in through the screen door.* GAIL *is helping* JUNIOR, *who has a slight limp, an arm in a cast and sling, and various cuts and bruises on his face.* ELIZABETH *is right behind them carrying a small suitcase*]

GAIL Hi ... Well, here he is. Look at him. Disgusting, isn't it. If I get my hands on those creeps I'm going to rip their faces off.

ELIZABETH What good will that do.

[*She heads for the telephone. Punches in her code. Takes out a pad*]

GAIL It will make me feel terrific. That's what. You know, sometimes you just have to lash out, Elizabeth. You just have to lash out to keep yourself from going nuts. I learned that from you, Elizabeth. That's how you used to be before you became so ... busy.

ELIZABETH What's your problem. You've been sniping at me all day. You were taking shots all the way home in the car.

JUNIOR Can I sit down.

MARY ANN Let me help you.

JUNIOR Hi, Mary Ann. Why are you looking at me like that. I look pretty bad, eh.

MARY ANN You probably just need some food. [*makes herself busy*] Lots and lots of food.

JUNIOR Could I have a glass of water.

GAIL Sure, honey. I'll get it.

MARY ANN I'll get it.

GAIL I said I'd get it! ... Look at him. Pathetic or what. He's probably going to lose his job, too.

JUNIOR Ah, no. You think so?

GAIL Your foreman called. He said the police were by the plant. They told him some bad stuff about you. I'm going to go talk to him later. Maybe I can fix it.

JUNIOR Maybe I should talk to him.

GAIL Yeah? What would you say.

JUNIOR Ah, I don't really—

GAIL Well, until you can think of something, leave it to me. [*to* MARY ANN] Where's my baby.

MARY ANN Still asleep, I think.

GAIL What do you mean you think. Haven't you been checking on her.

MARY ANN I checked her a while ago.

GAIL When.

MARY ANN I don't know.

GAIL Well, was it ten minutes, an hour, two hours.

MARY ANN I don't know!

GAIL Too much. I feel like I'm in one of those science-fiction movies where I'm the only human being, and everyone else is some kind of plant life.

MARY ANN I feel that way sometimes, too. Only the opposite.

GAIL There. That's an example of what I mean. Nothing you say makes any sense to me. In fact nothing makes much sense to me these days. I'm married to a guy who has bad luck following him around like it's a close friend. And my oldest sister here, who I used to trust more than anyone, has turned out to be the biggest disappointment in my life.

[GAIL *grabs the phone from* ELIZABETH. *Hangs up*]

ELIZABETH Ah, come off it. I'm not responsible for all your problems. Where the hell do you get off blaming me.

GAIL I'm not blaming you for the problems, Elizabeth. I'm blaming you for not helping to solve them. Are you a member of this family or not.

MARY ANN She's changed, Gail. She's a changed person and she's trying to deal with it. It's because she's—

ELIZABETH If you say I'm a lesbian again I'm going to take you upstairs and drown you in the bathtub.

MARY ANN Are you saying you're *not* a lesbian.

ELIZABETH Who I sleep with isn't the issue. It's never the issue. It's always never the issue. Why are you trying to make it so important. I sleep with women *and* men, if you must know. I sleep with anyone I like. I find nice, sexy people and I sleep with them.

GAIL When you can spare the time.

ELIZABETH Ah, fuck off.

GAIL Go ahead. Talk some more about yourself. Talk about your personal life, your love life. Like it's some big deal. Like we really care. I've got to go check on my baby.
[*She leaves*]

ELIZABETH Unbelievable. Why is she on my back like this. What the hell is her problem.

JUNIOR She's upset.

ELIZABETH I'm upset.

MARY ANN I'm upset, too! You were supposed to be a lesbian. You were supposed to have made a choice. But no. You sleep with anyone just because they're nice! What kind of choice is that. That's not courageous. That's not politically … important. Anyone can do that. Even I can do that.

ELIZABETH No! No you can't. You can't even sleep with your husband. So go to hell!

MARY ANN Don't talk to me! I'm busy. I'm cooking. And I'm re-examining my life! [*she is cutting vegetables*]

JUNIOR Where's Mom.

MARY ANN At the police station.

ELIZABETH What's she doing there.

MARY ANN The police took her there.

ELIZABETH Why.

JUNIOR Is she under arrest.

MARY ANN I don't think so.

ELIZABETH [*to* JUNIOR] Get serious. [*to* MARY ANN] What do you mean you don't think so. You don't know for sure?

MARY ANN That's right. Not for sure.

ELIZABETH Could you make a guess.

MARY ANN No. Not really. They said they just wanted to question her. But that could have been a trick. Something they just said so she wouldn't make a fuss.

ELIZABETH They can't do that. If she was under arrest they'd have to tell her.

MARY ANN That's what you say about that now. Who knows what you'll say about it tomorrow. Maybe tomorrow you'll say they can arrest anyone anytime. Men. Women. Anyone who is sexy. And nice!

ELIZABETH Shut up!

JUNIOR Question her about what.

MARY ANN About what they found when they searched the house.

ELIZABETH They searched the house? You let them search the house?

MARY ANN They had a warrant. Mom said it looked official.

JUNIOR What did they find.

MARY ANN Drugs. In the basement.

ELIZABETH What are you talking about?!

MARY ANN Hundreds of thousands of dollars worth of drugs in two garbage bags.

[JUNIOR *groans. Puts his head down on the table*]

ELIZABETH How the hell did they get there.

MARY ANN How am I supposed to know. Questions I can answer are one thing. Questions like that I don't feel bad for ignoring.

ELIZABETH Oh God, you're too much, Mary Ann. And you didn't think any of this was worth mentioning when we first got here. Cops come here with a warrant, search our house, find a bag full of dope, take our mother away, and you just go about your business like usual. You just cook something!

MARY ANN Dad's hungry.

ELIZABETH *Who's* hungry?

MARY ANN Dad. I talked to him. Yes. I know we promised we never would, but I couldn't help it. I was trying to be a better person. Make apologies.

ELIZABETH You're apologizing to him? You've got that kind of ass-backwards, haven't you.

MARY ANN Not in the mythic, larger—

ELIZABETH Shut up. We'll deal with that later. [*starts off*] I'm going after Mom. She's probably scared half to death. [*stops*] Where'd they take her. To the local police station. Or downtown to headquarters? Why am I asking you that. You don't know, do you. You didn't fucking ask, did you. Did you?!

MARY ANN That's right! I didn't! I'm sorry!

[ELIZABETH *grabs* MARY ANN]

ELIZABETH When I get back I'm going to do something to you, Mary Ann. I'm going to change your outlook on life. I'm going to crawl inside your brain and alter your entire personality. The neurotic idiot child you are now is going to cease to exist. Say goodbye to her forever! ... Shit!

[*She goes out the back.* JUNIOR *lifts his head*]

MARY ANN [*kind of thrilled*] That's how she used to talk to me. Remember?

JUNIOR Yeah.

MARY ANN You look worried.

JUNIOR Aren't you.

MARY ANN About Elizabeth? No. I like it sort of when she talks to me like that. I can't explain it. I'm sure it's not healthy, but what can I do.

JUNIOR I meant your mother. Aren't you worried about your mother being in jail.

MARY ANN Oh yeah. But I can't think about that. I'd die.

[GAIL *comes back in*]

GAIL She was hungry. She was lying there ... hungry.

[*to* JUNIOR] You know that sad, hurt little look she gets.

MARY ANN Why didn't she cry.

GAIL She doesn't cry.

MARY ANN Not even when she's hungry. Why not.

GAIL I don't know. Maybe she just trusts us. Maybe she thought, 'Hey, they're all responsible adults. One of them is bound to look in on me before I starve to death.'

MARY ANN Well, if I were you I'd teach her how to cry. Adults can let you down. They aren't perfect ... I think adults are expected to do too much, anyway. Why can't we—

GAIL Why do you do that. I was just being sarcastic. Just trying to make a point. Why can't you just let me make my point without launching into one of those long, complicated ... things. You're getting more like Mom every day.

MARY ANN I know!

GAIL In some ways. Just in some ways. I mean, Mom cares more about kids. Mom would never neglect a kid.

MARY ANN [*starts to cry*] I know! I know!

[*Pause*]

GAIL I looked in on Dad. He says you're making him soup. He's fantasizing, right.

MARY ANN No. I'm doing it.

GAIL Really ... He says you talked to him.

MARY ANN A little.

GAIL Really ... Do you want to talk to him some more. He needs company. I could finish the soup.

MARY ANN It's vegetable. Not out of a can. From scratch.

GAIL I think I can manage that, Mary Ann. Do you want to go up and see him.

MARY ANN I don't know. Maybe I said all I've got to say to him right now.

GAIL You could read to him. He likes that. There's a pile of books beside his bed ... So?

[*Pause.* MARY ANN *is staring at the floor*]

Come on, Mary Ann. What's it going to be. Are you going all the way with this one or not. Are we going to be living in the past forever with this guy, or are we going to make a little progress here. Mary Ann, he's dying. Do it for the same reason I do it. So that when he's dead you won't feel so shitty. You'll feel it was basically okay with him for a while at least. Not great. But okay.

[*Pause*]

MARY ANN Yeah.

[*She leaves*]

GAIL That's a breakthrough. You know, just when you've written her off she surprises you. She's always done that. Sometimes at the last moment ... You know, just when your hands are around her throat, and you're about to apply serious pressure.

JUNIOR I like her. I've always liked her.

GAIL What's wrong. That look on your face. Are you in pain.

JUNIOR Come here. Sit down. Here. On my lap.

GAIL What about your ribs.

JUNIOR Don't worry.

GAIL Nah. I don't want to hurt you, honey. I'll sit next to you. [*she does*]

JUNIOR But you see, I'd kind of like to hold you ...

GAIL Are you going to cry.

JUNIOR No.

GAIL That's what you say when you're going to cry. That you want to hold me.

JUNIOR Yeah. I know. But I'm not. Just sit on my lap.

GAIL Okay. But let's be careful.

[*She sits on his lap. Puts her arm around him*]

What's wrong. Something real terrible I bet. You had another one of those dreams where I meet someone with money and style, and take off with him.

JUNIOR Your mother's in jail.

GAIL Oh. Right. Sure.

JUNIOR The cops found some drugs in the house. I guess they think she's been dealin'.

[GAIL *starts to laugh. Harder. Really hard. Rolls off* JUNIOR. *On to the floor. Sits up. Points at him*]

GAIL I love you. You always know when I need to laugh.

JUNIOR No, seriously. The drugs were in the basement. In green garbage bags. Hundreds of thousands of dollars worth.

[GAIL *pounds the floor. Laughing almost hysterically. Falling back*]

No, seriously ... Gail ... We've got a real problem here. Come on. Really.

[*Lights start to fade.* GAIL's *laughter continues into the ...*]

[*Blackout*]

SCENE FOUR

JUNIOR, MARY ANN *and* TOM *are at the table.* TOM *has a blanket around him, his head is bowed.* JUNIOR *is feeding* TOM *soup. He has to lift* TOM*'s head for each spoonful.* MARY ANN *has her elbows on the table, her head in her hands. She's staring at* TOM, *smiling a little After a while,* GAIL *comes in from the hallway, pushing the baby in a stroller*

GAIL I'm off. I won't be long.

JUNIOR Where are you going.

GAIL I told you. To talk to your foreman.

JUNIOR You can leave the baby here, if you want.

GAIL Are you kidding. This beautiful, little girl is going to save your job. I'm going to pick her up, put her eye level with that foreman, and dare him to fire you. You don't mind me doing this, do you. I mean, it won't make you feel weak, or unmanly, or something stupid like that.

JUNIOR Just save my job. That's the only important thing.

GAIL I love you. Are you coming, Mary Ann.

MARY ANN Where are you going.

GAIL How do you do that, Mary Ann. How can you be in a room and not hear a word that's said.

MARY ANN I don't know. Practice, I guess. Where are you going.

GAIL I've got something to do. And then I thought we'd go shopping.

MARY ANN Grocery shopping?

GAIL Whatever. Do you have any money.

MARY ANN Yeah. I took some of our life savings. Larry always agrees to let me do that when I leave.

GAIL Larry is a very generous, understanding man. Larry might be Jesus Christ come back to earth, did you ever think of that.

MARY ANN He's got faults like everyone else. So you can't make me feel bad saying things like that. I'm beyond guilt anyway. I'm in some other place now.

GAIL Yeah. Where is it.

MARY ANN [*shrugs*] It's in the place where I have to be.

GAIL Let's not talk to each other for a while. Let's just go shopping.

MARY ANN Okay. [*stands*]

JUNIOR Was that Elizabeth again on the phone.

GAIL Yeah.

JUNIOR Something wrong? She got Mom away from those cops, didn't she. They didn't try to take her back or anything.

GAIL No. Elizabeth just wanted me to know they had something to do before they came home. She wouldn't tell me what. She sounded really, really ticked off. Like the old Elizabeth. It's great to hear her like that.

MARY ANN Yeah. It is, isn't it. I wonder why.

GAIL Let's go. [*to* JUNIOR] See ya.

[JUNIOR *waves*]

MARY ANN Do you think we've got a hang-up about Elizabeth. You know, some older-sister-as-a-parent kind of thing.

[GAIL *opens the back door. Pushes* MARY ANN *through. Follows her.* JUNIOR *stands. Limps over to the door. Limps back*]

JUNIOR Great! The cops think someone is dealing dope out of this house. This house right here. People we're supposed to love are living in this house ...

[TOM *mumbles*]

What? I can't hear you. Lift your head. They're gone.

TOM I'm afraid they might come back. If they come back and see me normal they'll make me leave. [*lowers his head*]

JUNIOR They're not coming back. Lift your head. We have to talk. The people in this house are in deep trouble.

TOM [*lifts his head*] Yeah. I know. Did you put drugs in our basement ... for some reason.

JUNIOR No. I thought you did for some reason.

TOM Then it's a mistake. [*lowers his head*]

JUNIOR A mistake? Someone's going to jail. In my bones I feel it. Someone in this house is going to do some time over this. Whatya mean a mistake. That's gotta be the wrong word. Think about it. A mistake is like ... an accident. Those garbage bags didn't get down there by accident. Please lift your fucking head! I need your help!

TOM [*lifts his head*] I mean a mistake in our strategy. Someone figured out what we were doing, and did it to us for some reason.

JUNIOR Who the hell could figure out what we were doing. I mean, I was actually doing it, and I could hardly understand it myself.

TOM Look, you have to stop underestimating these crooks. I warned you about that right from the start.

JUNIOR No, you didn't. You just threw me in. Right into the middle of a bunch of low-life scum.

TOM They're scum. But they've got experience. Experience can make stupid people smart. Experience is a kind of replacement for intelligence.

JUNIOR Not close up. Not when they open their mouths and talk to you. You've put me in a position where I've had to listen to a lot of scum talking right at me. Real close, you know? Guys who mug, steal, break and enter. Guys who rent their sisters out for twelve dollars an hour. They trusted me. They showed their, you know, inner thoughts. And their inner thoughts are stupid! So stupid they make me want to puke. God, man. They're everywhere. And I'm right in the middle of them.

TOM [*pulls himself closer to the table*] That's right! That's my point, goddammit! This neighbourhood is going down the toilet. And no one else seems to be doing anything about it. Fucking cops, social workers, fucking press. I don't know ... Maybe the bastards don't have enough at stake. But this is where my family lives. I owe it to them to fix their neighbourhood. Okay. Let's get to work! [*stands suddenly*]

JUNIOR What? Calm down. Sit down. We're not doing anything. Not until we figure out what we've already done.

TOM I owe my family. You know I owe them! [*he is agitated. Moving around*]

JUNIOR Yeah. I know. But that's not—

[TOM *approaches* JUNIOR *quickly*]

TOM Do you! Do you really know?!

[TOM *grabs* JUNIOR *by the shoulder of his broken arm*]

JUNIOR [*groans*] Yeah. I really do. I do!

TOM I hurt this family. I was a frigging monster. I have to make amends for all the bad things I did to them. I have to apologize in a really major way!

[TOM *is staring into space. Squeezing* JUNIOR's *shoulder*]

JUNIOR Don't get too worked up, man.

TOM Do you know what I did? I tried to burn this house down once. I tried to burn it down while they were all asleep in their beds ... So I guess I tried to kill them. What do you think. Does that sound like attempted murder. Attempted goddamn mass murder!

JUNIOR Yeah. But try to calm down a little.

TOM They didn't even have me arrested. Nora felt sorry for me. God, man. What a lucky bastard I was. I owe them. I've got to fix this part of the world where they live. This little part of the world is theirs. I've got to make it better. I do!

[TOM *starts to move around again.* JUNIOR *stands. Gently approaches* TOM]

JUNIOR Maybe you don't. Maybe it's too much. Maybe there's a limit to what you can do, you know, a line ... and you've crossed it. I've been thinking about this. Maybe you just have to talk to them. Let them see that you're basically all right now. Just be yourself.

[TOM *turns on* JUNIOR]

TOM Myself?! That's not enough!

[*He grabs* JUNIOR]

You know that! That's not enough. Goddammit!

[JUNIOR *loses his balance. Falls. Groans loudly. Grabs his broken arm*]

Ah, shit! Are you all right.

JUNIOR Holy fuck. I can't believe what's happening to my life.

TOM I'm sorry ... You see, I can't be myself. This is the self I can't be. They'd never trust me. And who could blame them. They'd toss me out in a minute. [*sits. Puts the blanket around himself*] I'm here because I don't look threatening to them. [*lowers his head*] And that's the way it has to stay.

JUNIOR [*getting up slowly*] So that's it? You've only got two speeds? You're either gonna rant and rave or sit there like a zombie. Can't we get you somewhere in between those two things. And can't we get you out of the past. Sort of here and now. And sort of normal. Because these people here are in deep shit right now. That's the *real* thing you've got to come to grips with. Not that other stuff.

The house thing. The drinking. That's yesterday's shit. Today we're in this new shit. I mean, come on, I'm probably going to lose my job. I'm the only person in this house with a real job. Mom still stuffs envelopes, but there's no real money there. She won't take anything from Elizabeth. Why. I don't know. And there's the baby now, and Mary Ann's here. Probably for good this time. I figure her husband won't let her go back. I don't think he likes her much, anyway. I think he just liked her cooking. Which is a plus for us. I mean, if she concentrates on it, and doesn't leave out important ingredients, her cooking can be really good. And she hardly eats anything herself. So, overall Mary Ann is a plus. But it's still dire. Overall, it's a really dire thing we're in—and—and—

TOM Look, I'm sorry to interrupt. But what the fuck are you talking about. What's Mary Ann's cooking got to do with this. I thought you wanted to work out a solution here. This is no time to go haywire. You can't let your mind run around in circles like that.
[JUNIOR *puts his head down on the table*]
Okay. You're upset. We're both upset. And scared. Being scared is a hard thing for a, you know ... a man to admit. Okay, maybe not for you. But for me it is. It's the pressure. A ... you know ... a *man* has all this pressure to prove things. So he gets worked up. It's the pressure of self-imposed leadership. Okay, it's bullshit. But it's genetic.

JUNIOR Someone's coming.
[*Noises outside*]

TOM Meet me here tonight. When they're all asleep. Together we'll work out a plan to save these people.

JUNIOR Okay. But it's got to be a plan that makes sense. Something I can understand.

TOM And something that won't put too much pressure on us.
[TOM *lowers his head.* JUNIOR *lowers his head, too.* NORA *and* ELIZABETH *come in. They are pushing a shopping cart, with something large inside it, covered with a blanket*]

ELIZABETH What's he doing down here. Tell him to go away.

JUNIOR He was just leaving. Tom ... Go ... upstairs. Upstairs, Tom. I'll bring your soup up in a minute.

[TOM *nods, rises slowly, leaves*]

[*to* ELIZABETH] I'm sorry about that. I was just ... I mean he ... asked me to ... tell him a story.

NORA Really. What kind of story. A war story?

JUNIOR No. Just a story ... I made one up. I'm not very good at that stuff. What's in the cart.

ELIZABETH I decided to go on the offensive.

[ELIZABETH *pulls the blanket away. She and* NORA *tip the cart and* ROLLY *falls out on to the floor.* ROLLY'S *feet and hands are bound. And he has an old rag stuffed in his mouth*]

You should recognize this man, Junior. He's one of the guys who beat you up.

JUNIOR [*stands*] Excuse me. I've got to go to the bathroom.

[*He leaves*]

NORA Was that an unusual response for Junior to have, Elizabeth.

ELIZABETH Seeing his assailant again can't be the easiest thing in the world. Help me get this guy in a chair.

[*They are getting* ROLLY *settled in a chair*]

Okay, asshole. We're going to make you comfortable. Then I'm going to ungag you and ask you a few questions. The same questions I asked you in that alley. If you answer them this time I won't have to use this again. [*points to a can of mace strung around her neck*]

NORA [*to* ROLLY] Please don't make her use that ... that ... What's it called again, Elizabeth.

ELIZABETH It's mace, Mom.

NORA Please don't make her use the mace again, mister. It was so upsetting to watch you writhe around like that.

ELIZABETH Don't worry, Mom. He's going to be a good little asshole this time, aren't you fuck-face.

NORA You're the expert on these things, Elizabeth. But do you really think calling him names like that is helpful.

ELIZABETH It helps *me*, Mom. It makes me feel good. Don't worry. I'm sure he's been called worse. Right, ass-wipe?

[ROLLY *nods.* ELIZABETH *takes some rope from her pocket. Ties* ROLLY *to the chair*]

Good little asshole. Here, let me take this piss-soaked rag away. How did such a disgusting, piss-soaked rag come to be the only thing in the vicinity suitable for sticking in your mouth. Well that's life, eh. That's what some of my friends might call karma. Karma can be a really ugly experience for dirt-bags like you ... There. Feel better?

[ROLLY *is making gagging sounds. Wiping his lips with his tongue. Groaning*]

NORA Can I take that rag away, Elizabeth. Or will you be needing it later.

ELIZABETH Depends. Just leave it on the floor for now ... [*to* ROLLY] Okay, stay calm! [*smiles*] Are you ready for that first question, shithead.

ROLLY Yeah.

ELIZABETH What's your name.

ROLLY Rolly. Rolly Moore.

ELIZABETH You're a crook, aren't you, Rolly.

ROLLY Whatya mean.

ELIZABETH You found that question difficult to understand?

ROLLY Come on. You ask if I'm a crook. What am I supposed to say. 'Yeah?' What good can come to me for saying 'yeah' to a question like that.

ELIZABETH I have to know who you are, Rolly. What you're up to. So I'm asking about how you make your living. You make your living by breaking the law. Right?

ROLLY Sometimes.

ELIZABETH Sometimes. So what are you saying here, Rolly. You occasionally do straight work.

ROLLY I'm not a young man. I can't always take the tension of doing crime. I need calmer things to do every once in a while. Ask her. I worked for her once.

NORA Yes. He helped me make my garden.

ROLLY I carried rocks. It was hard. But I didn't complain.

NORA Yes. You did. You complained a lot. And I think you stole my wheelbarrow.

ROLLY Come on. Hey. [*to* ELIZABETH] Is that what this is about. Jesus, you people gotta be kidding—a wheelbarrow. What's that cost, twenty bucks, I mean—

ELIZABETH Hey! Take a good look at me. I'm a busy woman. If I have to keep listening to your bullshit you're going to get hurt!

ROLLY She brought it up. She was the one who brought up the thing about the wheelbarrow.

NORA That's true, Elizabeth. I did. [*to* ROLLY] She's upset. I'll tell you why. She believes the police are making plans to charge me with a very serious crime.

ROLLY That's too bad.

ELIZABETH All right! All right! Mom, why don't you go see how Junior's doing.

ROLLY Why does she have to leave. I'm a little nervous to be left alone with you. I'm sorry to offend you. But I'd feel a lot better if she stayed.

NORA Is that good, Elizabeth. Is it good or bad if he feels less nervous. You're the expert.

ELIZABETH Go ahead, Mom. We'll be fine.

NORA Please, Elizabeth. Just don't do anything you can't live with later. [*She leaves*]

ELIZABETH [*looks at* ROLLY. *Smiles*] I can live with a lot. By most people's standards that is. An awful lot. [*leans into him. Close*] Now, you're probably going to try to dance around this for a while. Buy some time to help your little brain find its way out of this mess. I'm a very, very busy woman. I've got a law practice to keep going, and an apartment I've been trying to finish painting for six months. But I'm going to have to stay here and listen to some extreme amounts of bullshit from you unless we find a way to cut right to the issue here ... Now, where's that piss-soaked rag. Ah, there it is.

[ELIZABETH *picks up the rag. Sprays it with mace. Grabs* ROLLY's *nose, and when he opens his mouth, she shoves the rag in.* ROLLY *gags*] Believe it or not, a part of me hates doing this to you. You're a pathetic bastard. I see guys like you every day. Messed up. Stupid. Defenceless. Beaten up by everything and everyone. You even get beaten up by the police. And that pisses me off. They have no right, no right at all to punish you physically ... But this is different. I'm not the police. I'm not a representative of the state. I'm just a member of a family. A family you've fucked with! You see, this is personal. This is a deeply personal thing. This is not sanctioned by the government. And therefore there's a limit, a restriction on the damage that can be done here. The only thing that can be damaged here is you. And basically, I think that's okay. Because really, all I'm doing is ... defending my family.

[ELIZABETH *removes the rag.* ROLLY *gags. Coughs. Licks his lips. Starts to cry*]

ROLLY Ah, Jesus.

ELIZABETH Why did you beat Junior up.

ROLLY Ah, Jesus. That was awful. I can't ... breathe ...

ELIZABETH Why did you break in here and beat Junior up. Why?!

[*She holds the rag close to his mouth*]

ROLLY He ripped me off!

ELIZABETH Bullshit.

ROLLY Honest. We had a deal. We made a deal. Then we made a time for a meeting. He was supposed to bring his man to the meeting. His suit man. It was a simple thing. The usual thing. Except when they showed up they were armed. They had serious weapons in their possession. I was not prepared. I don't do crimes with weapons. I'm against it, you know, on principle.

ELIZABETH I told you I don't want to hear this bullshit!

ROLLY They ripped me off! They took my merchandise. That's the simple truth, man. Two big bags full of top-grade stuff. Beautiful stuff. Explicit. You know, *real* explicit.

ELIZABETH [*backs away. Lowers her head*] Ah, shit.

[*She goes to the hallway door. Yells upstairs*]

Junior! Junior get down here. Now!

[ELIZABETH *starts to pace. Stops. Looks at* ROLLY. *Shakes her head*]

The word is illicit by the way. Not explicit. *Il-lic-it.*

ROLLY Ah, no. I'm sorry. But I think it's explicit.

ELIZABETH Listen, I know the word, asshole. The word to describe your drugs is illicit.

ROLLY Drugs? It wasn't drugs. I don't touch drugs on principle. Also, that's for younger guys. I'm talking porn. Pornography. Real first-rate stuff. You know—explicit.

ELIZABETH What are you talking about.

ROLLY My business is pornography. I'm the king of it. Ask anyone. Been doin' it for years. Some good years, a few bad years. But that's what I do. I sell pictures of naked people doing things to other naked people. And videos. Videos you can't get in any store. The market is huge. And it's growing. I don't know why. There must be a reason for it, you know, a need. I'm just helping people with a need they've got. I don't know, it's a strange—

ELIZABETH Okay. Shut up. Keep your mouth closed.

ROLLY Okay.

[*Long pause*]

ELIZABETH I believe you. I think you're telling the truth, you disgusting little pile of vomit.

ROLLY Thank you.

ELIZABETH Not that it helps me one stinking little bit. Not that I understand how pornography turned into drugs and wound up in—

[NORA *comes in*]

Where's Junior.

NORA Gone. I think he went out through a window. And he took the man upstairs with him. What's going on here, Elizabeth. Has this Rolly person implicated Junior in some crime. You can tell me. I know you probably don't want to worry me. You're generous like that. But—

ELIZABETH You're going to have to be quiet for a while, Mom. I'm thinking.

ROLLY Can I go now.

ELIZABETH No.

ROLLY Can I go later.

ELIZABETH No. Probably not.

ROLLY Well, I have to go sometime. You're not making any sense. Sooner or later I gotta go. I mean, what else can I do. I can't just stay. What's the point in that.

ELIZABETH I might need you.

ROLLY Why. I told you all I know. He did that to me. So I did that to him.

ELIZABETH I might need you! If all this comes together in the worst possible way. You know, in a meaningless, arbitrary, pathetic, ugly, destructive way with no true purpose, and nothing but sad and wretched consequences—well, I might need an outlet for that! I might need to kill someone. That might be you! I mean, why the fuck not, eh! Why the fuck not you! I mean, why the fuck is this happening to my family. So why the fuck shouldn't you die! [*She is shaking* ROLLY]

ROLLY [*to* NORA] Could you help me out here. Maybe calm her down a bit.

NORA Not when she's like this. Maybe later. Maybe when she's had a little sleep.

ELIZABETH Good idea. Sleep. Just a little nap. To clear my head. Wake me in thirty-five minutes. [*starts off*]

NORA I will, dear.

ELIZABETH [*stops*] Gag him, Mom. You have to gag him. And don't let him go. I know in your heart you've already forgiven him for whatever he's done. But if you let him go, I'll just have to go get him again.

NORA I know, dear.

ELIZABETH And could you call my office for me, Mom. Tell them I won't be in for a couple of days.

NORA I'll say you're ill.

ELIZABETH I *am* ill, Mom. I'm really, really ill.
[*She leaves*]

ROLLY You could let me go. I think that'd be okay.

NORA I have to trust Elizabeth on this. Elizabeth is sometimes the only thing this family has going for it in the struggle.

ROLLY What struggle.

NORA *The* struggle. You know. The one out there. [*standing at the counter looking for something in a drawer*]

ROLLY Oh yeah. The struggle out there is ... really something. [*starts to cry*] That's my struggle, too. The one out there. That's the one where everyone and everything doesn't make sense. And everything you do is wrong. And they find out. And—

NORA You can't talk anymore. Talking doesn't help you anyway. I've noticed that. Talking just makes you wallow and cast blame. I found some tape in the drawer. I'm going to put a piece over your mouth. It's better than the rag. I'm sorry about the rag, I really am. But this tape is better.

[*She rips off a piece. Puts it across his mouth. She gets a chair to put next to him*]

I'm going to talk to you now. Talk to you for a long time. Until I get tired and have to go to bed. You have to listen closely and try to understand what I'm saying to you. There's a little trick you can use. When I'm talking don't pretend I'm not really talking about you. Don't let yourself believe I'm saying these things about someone else. Someone neither of us knows. For example. If I say you feel worthless and afraid, you can't say to yourself that's not true. And then not listen when I suggest all the reasons you feel worthless and afraid. Because if you do, you won't understand when I get to the part when I talk about all the ways you can maybe stop feeling worthless and afraid. So that's the trick. Try to understand. And don't pretend. All right. Get ready. Are you ready.

[ROLLY *nods*]

Good for you.

[*Lights start to fade*]

First. You were born. Right away you shared some experience with everyone else in the world. Everyone in the past, everyone rich and poor, and smart and average. That's a fact. You were born. You were alive in the world. So far so good ...

[*Lights fade.* NORA *is still talking, but the audience can't hear her*]

[*Blackout*]

[*Intermission*]

ROLLY *alone. Still tied up. Eyes wide*
TOM *and* JUNIOR *come in from the screen door*

TOM Okay. Go make sure they're all asleep.

JUNIOR Are you sure this is a good plan.

TOM Well, it's better than doing nothing.

JUNIOR Are you sure. Maybe doing nothing is better. Maybe it's the best we can do right now ... Okay. So let's do that instead.

TOM Get a hold of yourself. Try to act like a ... you know ...

JUNIOR A what. Try to act like a what.

TOM Forget it. Go check on them.

[JUNIOR *starts off. And passes* ROLLY]

JUNIOR [*to* ROLLY] Look what you did to my arm, asshole.

[*He leaves*]

TOM [*goes to* ROLLY] Okay, listen to this, insect. I'm going to untie you. If you make a move to escape I'll be forced to hurt you. The ugly part of me wants to hurt you anyway, so I won't need much of an excuse to cause you grievous bodily harm. Understand?

[ROLLY *nods*]

Good.

[TOM *starts to untie* ROLLY]

We heard you talking to Elizabeth, insect. We were hiding outside the window here. We heard you deny knowledge of those drugs. Maybe you were telling the truth, maybe you weren't. We will determine that when we get you to a more secluded place. But someone set us up. If it wasn't you, it was your kid. To save your life, insect, you might have to lead us to your kid. Do you think you'll be able to make that decision when the time comes.

[ROLLY *nods*]

That's what I thought.

[JUNIOR *comes back in*]

JUNIOR They're all asleep. How you doin'.

TOM Getting there.

JUNIOR Elizabeth isn't going to like this. She hunted this guy down.

She went to a lot of trouble. I mean, look at all the rope she bought.

TOM Yeah. She thinks ahead. She's committed to a job well done. God, I admire her. If she's ever talking to me again I'm going to tell her that.

JUNIOR You know what, man. I don't think that's ever gonna happen. We're finished in this house. This guy told Elizabeth we were doing business with him. That means we're *both* outta here. They don't really need us anyway. They'll be fine without us. Better.

TOM Get a hold of yourself. You can't talk that way. We have a part to play in this family. We do.

[TOM *has finished untying* ROLLY]

JUNIOR Yeah? What.

TOM We're working that out. That's part of what we're doing. Look, don't fall apart on me here. Think about all of the good things we've done.

JUNIOR Yeah? What were they.

TOM Come on, get a hold of yourself! We've done plenty. We ripped off that gang of break-and-enter artists, and we made them think they'd been ripped off by that other gang of break-and-enter artists. They had a nice little battle about that. Put a few of them out of action. And that guy with the pit bull ...

JUNIOR The pimp?

[TOM *pulls* ROLLY *up*]

TOM No! The pimp had the Doberman! The guy with the pit bull had the old Dodge van and that crack house. He doesn't have that crack house anymore.

[*They all start off*]

JUNIOR Oh, right. 'Cause of the pimp with the Doberman. We took money away from the break-and-enter artists, and bought some of that pimp's girls away from him and—

TOM Made it look like the guy with the pit bull in the Dodge van was looking to move into the prostitution business. And bingo!

JUNIOR The crack house gets burned to the ground! It was great.

TOM Yeah, it was. Feeling any better?

JUNIOR A little. Someday we gotta get rid of all those fucking dogs around here. I mean, especially with the baby around ...

[*They are gone.* NORA *comes in. Goes to the door. Watches a moment. Turns*]

NORA It's better this way.

[ELIZABETH *comes in. Hair tousled. Blouse outside her skirt. Barefoot*]

ELIZABETH Mom, I said just thirty-five min— Hey! Where is he. Where's my prisoner.

NORA Junior and the man you call Dad took him. It's better this way.

ELIZABETH They had no right! He was mine. I wasn't finished with him. I just left him down here to stew for a while. [*she is agitated. Moving around*]

NORA Junior and the man you call Dad know about these things. They both have past lives with criminal content. They've probably made plans that Rolly person that will resolve this whole dilemma. I'm a little worried about Junior. If something bad happens let's pray it happens to the man you call Dad.

ELIZABETH Typical bullshit! I do the hard work. Someone else gets the glory. It's just like at work. This is the same crap the senior partners are always pulling. I work sixty-five hours a week ... I've got a family that's in more or less perpetual crisis, and all I want out of life, I mean *really* all I want, is just a fucking even break!

NORA Maybe you should get some more sleep, Elizabeth.

ELIZABETH Come on, Mom. I had that little rodent on the edge of collapsing. Telling me things he didn't even know he knew. Junior and Dad aren't the only ones who know about guys like that. I've spent my whole life around guys like that. I'm the fucking expert here! They had no right to interfere.

NORA Are you hungry. Thirsty. Do you want to play a game of cards. [*quickly takes a deck of cards from a drawer*]

ELIZABETH I thought he was dying! How could he have gone anywhere or taken anyone anywhere. He's a drooling, mumbling mess!

NORA That was a trick of course, dear. A disguise. I suspected it. This confirms it. If nothing else good comes out of this, we'll all discover the true nature of the man you call Dad.

ELIZABETH [*slams the cards down. Stands*] He *is* my dad! That's why I call him Dad, Mom. Because he *is!*

[MARY ANN *comes in, wearing a bathrobe and slippers. Looking angry*]

NORA Hello, Mary Ann. What's wrong. Trouble sleeping?

MARY ANN Gail sent me down. All this shouting is waking up the baby.

NORA I'm not shouting.

ELIZABETH She means me.

MARY ANN That's right, Elizabeth. I mean you. What's wrong, Elizabeth. Did you have a hard day. Did someone question your right to change your mind about something. Perhaps question your ability to make a choice and stick to it.

ELIZABETH Ah, Jesus Christ.

MARY ANN That's right, Elizabeth. I haven't forgotten. I never forget. And certain things, I never forgive.

ELIZABETH Go back to bed.

MARY ANN You go back to bed. I don't do things because you tell me to anymore. I've discovered recently that you can be very wrong about things. Dad, for example. You were wrong about him. He's nice. I like him. There. What are you going to do about that.

ELIZABETH Didn't I tell you before if you didn't stop acting and talking like an idiot I was going to do something about it.

MARY ANN I remember words to that effect. But so what. I'm not afraid of you anymore. And do you know why. You're inconsistent. Seriously inconsistent. Mom, I have something to tell you. Elizabeth is *not* a lesbian. Elizabeth will sleep with anyone. She hasn't made any hard decisions at all.

[ELIZABETH *has her teeth clenched. She is approaching* MARY ANN]

ELIZABETH Please go back to bed.

MARY ANN No.

ELIZABETH I don't want to hurt you.

MARY ANN I don't care if you want to hurt me or not. I'm on a voyage of self-discovery. I can't be stopped. You're part of that voyage. Getting to the truth about you. There are other things on this voyage, of course, but I'm dealing with you right now. Dealing with things is all I care about.

ELIZABETH Really. You don't care about the police, and the drug charges, or any of that.

MARY ANN Those aren't my problems. I can only deal with myself. My personal self. My unconscious self. Clare taught me that.

ELIZABETH Then Clare should be killed. I'll do it. Give me her address. Give it to me! Now!

[ELIZABETH *makes a wild grab for* MARY ANN. MARY ANN *backs away*]

NORA Who is Clare.

ELIZABETH The devil!

MARY ANN My therapist!

[ELIZABETH *grabs* MARY ANN. *Puts her over her shoulder*]

Okay, okay. Clare also taught me the value of the apology.

[ELIZABETH *puts* MARY ANN *inside the broom closet. Closes the door*]

[*from inside the closet*] I know I've hurt people and disappointed people myself. The two of you, for example. So, as well as taking care of myself in an inner way, I'm taking care of others in an outer way. That's why I cook for you. That's why I fixed the strap on your briefcase, Elizabeth. Before I went to sleep I fixed it and put it back beside your bed. You don't have to thank me. I didn't do it for thanks! I did it for mythic reasons! Symbolic reasons! The reasons of dreams!

ELIZABETH You're nuts! You're out of your goddamn mind!

[MARY ANN *comes out of the closet holding a box of Bisquick and a muffin pan*]

MARY ANN Says who?!

ELIZABETH Me! Me! And her. [*points to* NORA] She'd say it too, if she wasn't so nice, and if she wasn't your mother. Everyone would say it. Everyone on the planet who had to listen to you for more than five seconds!

[GAIL *comes rushing in*]

GAIL Hey, hey come on! The baby! Your voice is bouncing off the walls.

MARY ANN Sorry.

ELIZABETH She means me!

GAIL Yeah. What's wrong with you, anyway.

ELIZABETH What makes you think something is wrong with me. I mean, you were on my back before for not getting involved in this family's problems like I should. So now I'm involved. And ... this ... is ... what ... I'm ... like ... when I'm involved!

GAIL Keep your voice down!

MARY ANN Yeah. There's no reason to shout. I express very personal, upsetting feelings without shouting. You can do the same.

ELIZABETH [*throws her arms up in the air*] I need a drink. [*starts searching through the cupboards*]

GAIL Hey. Where's that guy who was tied up here before.

MARY ANN Oh, yeah. I didn't notice.

ELIZABETH [*mocking*] 'Oh yeah. I didn't notice.' I'm a good person, but I didn't notice. I cook for people, do things for people, tell people what their problems are, but I don't notice anything … My name is Mary Ann, and I'm looking for a job. Do you have anything a semi-conscious idiot with a lot of opinions could do … Where's that bottle of scotch. It used to be under the sink.

GAIL [*to* NORA] So where is he. The guy.

NORA Junior took him.

GAIL To the police?

ELIZABETH We don't think so. That would not be our first guess.

GAIL Yeah. So where did he take him.

ELIZABETH Our first guess would be some unpopulated and heavily wooded area just outside the city. Somewhere the ground isn't too hard for digging. Where's my scotch. Who took my scotch. I left it under the sink. It's not there.

MARY ANN Are you that messed up, Elizabeth. You leave bottles in places. Do you leave them everywhere you visit.

ELIZABETH No. Just anywhere you might be.

NORA I took it, Elizabeth. I threw it out. I thought it belonged to someone else. You know … [*points upstairs*]

MARY ANN The baby?

NORA The man.

GAIL What's she talking about, Mom. She's saying Junior took that guy out to the country to kill him. Is that right.

NORA Is that what you were saying, Elizabeth.

ELIZABETH [*looking in other cupboards now*] It was just a guess. You wouldn't have any other alcohol in the house would you, Mom. Of course not. Not since Dad got drunk that last time and tried to kill us all. That was a stupid question. I'm sorry for asking, Mom. How about rubbing alcohol, lighter fluid, glue.

[GAIL *goes to* ELIZABETH. *Starts to follow her around*]

GAIL So, why would Junior want to kill that guy.

ELIZABETH He's one of the guys who beat him up.

GAIL Yeah. I know that. But that wouldn't be enough of a reason. What are you getting at.

ELIZABETH Relax. It was just a guess. I could be wrong. I'm wrong sometimes. Right, Mary Ann? Hey Mom, where's that stuff you spray on frying pans. I hear you can get a buzz off that.

MARY ANN Stop her, Mom. She's doing that thing she does. When she's overloading. I don't like it.

NORA Elizabeth, you're scaring your sisters.

GAIL Elizabeth. I want you to stop for a moment.

ELIZABETH In a moment. In a moment I'll stop for a moment. Right now I need something. A little something.

MARY ANN You better stop her, Gail.

ELIZABETH [*mocking*] 'You better stop her, Gail.' [*searching frantically now. Pulling things out of the cupboards*] Stop her before she says something, does something, finds something. She's doing that thing she does, Mom. What thing, dear. The thing she does when she's falling apart, Mom. Had it up to here, Mom. Right up to the fucking nose. Right here. Almost full. Filled right up. Just can't take much more …

[GAIL *grabs her.* ELIZABETH *shakes her off*]

Get off! Get the fuck off! I'm on a mission here. A mission of self-fulfilment. This one's for me, Mom. I'm enjoying this. I'm going to rip this home apart, Mom. I think it's time you moved, anyway. Moved everyone, the whole family. My family. The one I'm responsible for!

[GAIL *grabs her.* MARY ANN *is moving closer to them*]

GAIL [*to* MARY ANN] Help me!

ELIZABETH Let me go! You have to let me go. I gotta go. Let me go you little bitch before I rip your scalp off!

GAIL [*to* MARY ANN] Help me!

MARY ANN Okay.

[MARY ANN *grabs* ELIZABETH. *They are both trying to put her on the floor*]

ELIZABETH Ah, shit. This won't work. This will only make me mad. Jesus. Get away from me. Get off me. You're trying to kill me. Aren't you. You want to kill me. I know you do. Ah, here's some hair. What happens if I just pull a little.

[MARY ANN *screams*]

I like that sound. I like that sound a lot.

[MARY ANN *screams*]

MARY ANN Let go!

ELIZABETH You let go!

GAIL Don't! Don't let go. We've almost got her down.

[ELIZABETH *grabs* GAIL'*s hair. Now she has them both by the hair*]

ELIZABETH You've got miles to go before I'm down, kid. I'm absolutely indestructible. Right, Mom. I'm a rock. Aren't I, Mom. A rock. A rock doesn't go down.

GAIL Trip her!

MARY ANN How?!

GAIL Just trip her. Put your foot out!

ELIZABETH How about another little pull on the hair, sis!

[MARY ANN *screams*. GAIL *screams*]

MARY ANN I hate you! Stop that!

GAIL Ouch! Shit! Trip her!

MARY ANN I'm trying!

[*The three of them are swaying back and forth.* ELIZABETH *in the middle. A tangle of arms and hands*]

ELIZABETH They're weak, Mom! Very weak. Gail talks tough, but she's really a pussycat. And Mary Ann's, well ... Mary Ann's a shadow. My shadow. And my pussycat. Look at them. Mom. I'm still up. I'm still standing. If you need a daughter to rely on, Mom, I'm the one. Call me anytime. Call me night or day. [*sings*] 'Call me. Don't be afraid to just call me.' But you do, don't you. You all call me. You all call me, and call me, and call me ... !

[*Finally* MARY ANN *succeeds in putting a foot behind* ELIZABETH. GAIL *pushes.* ELIZABETH *falls. They fall on top of her*]

GAIL Okay! We've got her. Don't let go.

MARY ANN Don't you let go!

GAIL Okay, Mom. Do it!

MARY ANN Hurry, Mom. We can't hold her much longer.

[NORA *is nodding. She gets down on her knees beside them*]

GAIL Quick, Mom!

[NORA *opens up the bottom two buttons of* ELIZABETH's *blouse. Leans over. And starts to blow on* ELIZABETH's *stomach, giving her a huge raspberry.* ELIZABETH's *groaning and yelling gradually subside and slowly turn into laughter. The laughter grows.* MARY ANN *and* GAIL *sit back on the floor.* NORA *continues to blow on* ELIZABETH's *stomach.* ELIZABETH *is laughing hysterically*]

It still works.

MARY ANN Thank God.

NORA [*stands*] Are you all right now, dear.

ELIZABETH I'm fine, Mom. [*giggles*] I love that. Do that again.

NORA Maybe later ... I'm going to put the kettle on.

MARY ANN [*getting up*] I'll make toast.

[*Pause.* ELIZABETH *is sighing happily*]

GAIL Elizabeth.

ELIZABETH What, honey.

GAIL I'm really worried about Junior.

ELIZABETH Oh. [*sits up. Hugs* GAIL] He's all right. He's fine. I was just being pissy. They probably took that guy and handed him over to the cops.

GAIL Really. You really think so.

ELIZABETH Yeah. I really do. [*hugs her tight*] I love you.

GAIL I love you, too. I'm sorry you're such a frigging mess.

ELIZABETH So am I.

GAIL Maybe you should stop practising law. Stop doing all that political stuff you do. Take a vacation or something.

ELIZABETH Yeah. Maybe you could come with me. Take a little break from young motherhood. We'll go away together. Some place soft and warm.

MARY ANN Can I come too.

ELIZABETH & GAIL No.

MARY ANN I know you don't mean that.

GAIL Yes—

ELIZABETH We do.

MARY ANN No, you don't. I know you don't. I'm coming. Wherever you go. I'm coming. You love each other. But you love me, too. I know that. I'm confident about that. They love me, don't they, Mom.

NORA Of course they love you. They were taught to love you. I paid special attention to that part of their education. I knew there would be times it would be easier not to love you. Because of your ... well, because of your—

MARY ANN Gee, Mom. I was only kidding. When I asked you if they loved me it was just a joke. I feel like crying.

NORA Why.

MARY ANN Well, because of what you just said. That's sad. That you had to teach them to love me. That's so very sad.

ELIZABETH [*getting up*] She's going to tell Clare about that, Mom. Clare is going to have a lot to say about what that means.

MARY ANN Clare loves me.

[ELIZABETH *goes over. Puts her arms around* MARY ANN]

ELIZABETH No, Mary Ann. We love you. Clare just thinks you're very interesting.

MARY ANN What do you want on your toast.

ELIZABETH Cocoa.

MARY ANN No way. I hate that. That's disgusting.

[ELIZABETH *grabs* MARY ANN *by the hair*]

ELIZABETH It's my toast, Mary Ann. You asked me. I told you. Put cocoa on my toast. Lots of cocoa. Okay?

MARY ANN Sure ... Gail? ... Jam? Marmalade?

GAIL I've got to go back to bed.

MARY ANN You can't. We're all here. The four of us. We're never together anymore just the four of us. It's the family.

GAIL The family has grown a bit since you last looked in on it, Mary Ann. I've got to get up with the baby. [*starts off*] Goodnight. [*stops. Looks at* ELIZABETH] Is there something you're not telling me about Junior.

ELIZABETH No. Junior's fine. Don't worry about him.

GAIL Because he's my life, you know. A large part of it. If he's going down the drain, so am I.

ELIZABETH Trust me. Go upstairs. Get your daughter. Get in bed. Hug her. Go to sleep.

[ELIZABETH *hugs* GAIL. GAIL *leaves*]

NORA [*to* MARY ANN] You're sad, aren't you. Feeling guilty about leaving your daughter. Gail is going up to sleep with her daughter, and this makes you feel empty, hollow, hard ... Doesn't it, Mary Ann.

MARY ANN Yeah, Mom. A bit. I guess. So?

NORA So what, dear.

MARY ANN So, what should I do.

NORA I wouldn't give you advice about that, dear. You're the expert about your own life. Besides, you have so many things on your mind. Things I could barely understand even if I had the desire to listen to them. Things more important than your only child, the child you brought into this world. Things you've recently found out at ... at that place where you said you are ... Where was that place again, dear.

MARY ANN Crossroads. I'm at a crossroads. Your toast is in the ... thing. I'm going to bed. [*starts off. Stops*] I am, though. I really am at a crossroads ... Dammit.

[*She leaves*]

ELIZABETH She'll go home to her daughter, Mom. She always does.

NORA But why does she leave in the first place.

ELIZABETH Her father deserted *her*. Maybe she's just repeating a pattern.

NORA Why. Why is she repeating a pattern ...

ELIZABETH You have to stop worrying about her, Mom. She just basically has a difficult time living. The only solution would be to put her out of her misery ... Harden your heart, put her in a sack and drown her like a kitten ... That was just a joke, Mom.

NORA I know, dear ... And I know Mary Ann could never actually be happy. She'll never be ... light-hearted.

ELIZABETH Anyway, I don't think Mary Ann's in any worse shape than the rest of us.

NORA She deserts her child! There's nothing worse a mother can do. Don't be stupid!

[*Pause*]

I'm sorry.

ELIZABETH That's okay.

NORA I have to tell you something, Elizabeth. It's about that man you call Dad ... Guess what. I know he really is your dad. I'm not insane about that. That's good news isn't it, Elizabeth. So far so good. And I actually had a very good reason for not acknowledging him. For the first time in years I had something he needed. Needed badly ... Do you want to know what it was. Recognition! The power of simple recognition ... Of course, I just stumbled across this power. But once I had it I used it without remorse. You see, when he first came back after what ... ten years?

ELIZABETH Yes.

NORA Yes. Ten. Anyway, when he came back a terrible thing happened. I saw him. And right away I wanted to kill myself. I thought I'd rather be dead than go through any more awful experiences with him. Of course, I couldn't do that because of you and your sisters. I couldn't leave you alone with him. So I came up with another way. I just pretended he was a total stranger. I don't know where I got the idea, but it seemed to work all right. I didn't have to have anything to do with him. And you girls could have a father if you needed one.

ELIZABETH Why are you telling me this, Mom.

NORA Circumstances change. The needs of people change. What this family needs now is something more clear. Clearer roles. Lighter burdens for ... some of us. [*starts off. Stops*] You know, Elizabeth, I have a theory about why bad things keep happening to this family. Do you want to hear it.

ELIZABETH [*sighs*] Sure, Mom.

NORA I think we believe that we don't deserve to be happy. We're running away from happiness. We think we need to struggle, and suffer, and work really hard before we can just stay still, and let happiness catch up and surround us. What do you think about that theory, Elizabeth.

ELIZABETH It scares me, Mom.

NORA Oh. Then just forget about it. I could be wrong ...

[NORA *gestures, shrugs. She wants to say something soothing.*

ELIZABETH *turns away*]

NORA Goodnight, Elizabeth.

ELIZABETH Goodnight, Mom.

[NORA *hesitates. Then leaves.* ELIZABETH *wraps her arms around herself. Shudders. Looks around. Begins to clean up some of the mess she made earlier*]

[*Blackout*]

SCENE SIX

Later

ELIZABETH *is at the table, her head down*

TOM, JUNIOR *and* ROLLY *come in.* TOM *has* ROLLY *by the scruff of the neck. They are all dirty and wet*

ROLLY Please, please let me go. I did what you asked. I tried to help you find my kid Stevie. I took you to all our special places. Why won't you let me go.

JUNIOR [*whispering*] Shut up. [*to* TOM] Who is that over there. Oh no. Is that Elizabeth.

TOM It's okay. She's asleep. If we're quiet we won't—

ROLLY She's waiting! She's been waiting for me! She can't wait to get her hands on me. Let me go!

JUNIOR Shush!

[TOM *whacks* ROLLY *on the head*]

ROLLY Geez! That hurt!

JUNIOR Shut up. Shut your mouth!

ROLLY He hurt me. Geez! He hit me with his knuckles. I'm dizzy.

TOM [*calmly*] Look. I'm trying not to really hurt you. I'm trying to control a really ugly, violent urge I've got to take away your face.

ROLLY Take away my face? What's that mean.

JUNIOR What should we do.

TOM Tie him up again.

JUNIOR What good will that do.

TOM We didn't accomplish anything by taking him so the least we can do is put him back where he was.

[*They start to tie him up*]

ROLLY Oh no, don't do this. There's no purpose in this. Look, the truth is the women in this house are kinda spooky. The mother—she's a nice lady, I guess, but she just wants to talk to me all the time. She talked to me for hours. She said things that really bothered me. Really personal things about me. Like she knows me or something. Knows all about my life. It's spooky. And this one here. The one you call Elizabeth. She's something else. She's like a monster of some kind. She comes across as some kind of evil thing from some other planet. No offence. I know you're related. But she's worse than guys I've met in prison who kill people with saws. You can't give me back to her! You keep me!

TOM She hunted you down. You belong to her.

JUNIOR We just borrowed you.

ROLLY [*crying*] I can't stay. It's spooky here! While I was sitting here before, these two other women came in, with a baby in a stroller. Just came in, saw me all tied up. And they just smiled at each other and went upstairs. Like having a frigging prisoner in the kitchen, some guy tied up like a frigging dead pig, was a normal thing. I can't stay here. I can't, I can't, I can't!

[TOM *whacks* ROLLY *hard.* ROLLY *is unconscious. They continue to tie him up*]

JUNIOR Did you have to do that.

TOM Yeah. That's the least I had to do. I've told you, I've still got these ugly things inside me. Things that get stirred up by stuff like this. By scum like this. I'm trying hard to change, but sometimes—

JUNIOR Can we talk about this later. Let's just get out of here before Elizabeth wakes up.

TOM She must be a tired person to sleep through all of that. Do you think she works too hard. I've heard them talking about her. Nora and Gail. They say she's working herself to death.

JUNIOR Look. We have to talk about this later. I'm depressed. This whole thing is really depressing.

TOM And confusing. Why aren't things working out better for us. Why wasn't his kid at any of those places.

JUNIOR And why were those places so disgusting. Do you think they really live in that sewer. Who can live in a sewer, man. Or that bush by the railway tracks. I mean a bush, man. They had a little clearing inside a bush. Talk about depressing.

TOM Get a hold of yourself.

JUNIOR Stop telling me to get a hold of myself. That doesn't help. Try to say something that helps. Anything.

TOM Okay. He's all tied up. Just the way he was. Let's get out of here.

JUNIOR Okay.

[*Their backs are to* ELIZABETH. *She sits up suddenly. Eyes wild*]

ELIZABETH Stay exactly where you are!

[JUNIOR *and* TOM *jump.* ELIZABETH *stands. Walks around them. Looking at them. Hard*]

JUNIOR [*to* TOM] We should explain to her. She looks like she definitely wants an explanation.

ELIZABETH Be quiet, Junior. I want this man here to talk. This man here who's not supposed to be able to talk. This man here who is supposed to be sick. Dying.

JUNIOR [*to* TOM] She wants to hear it from you. [*to* ELIZABETH] Can I go upstairs, then.

ELIZABETH Stay where you are. [*to* TOM] Go ahead.

TOM I ... don't know where to start. How much did you hear. I mean, when did you wake up.

ELIZABETH I wasn't asleep.

JUNIOR [*whimpers*] I'm feeling a little sick to my stomach.

TOM Cut that out. Act like a ... you know.

ELIZABETH A what?

TOM Let Junior go upstairs, Elizabeth. You and I can work this out. Junior is nervous. Aren't you.

JUNIOR Yeah.

TOM And he's making me nervous.

ELIZABETH He stays. If anyone is leaving it's you. And I don't mean upstairs to your cozy room. Now what in God's name are you up to! Speak!

TOM Okay. So first, you're probably wondering why I seem better all of a sudden.

ELIZABETH No. I've figured that out. Skip to the part where you explain everything bad that's happened to this family lately, and how you're responsible.

JUNIOR See that look in her eyes. I've seen that look before. Tell her before she does something!

TOM Okay! Okay, yeah ... [*to* ELIZABETH] I had a plan.

JUNIOR I just want to make that part clear. *He* had a plan. Okay?

TOM It was a plan I got all of a sudden. It was a good plan, but it came from a bad place in me, I think. From guilt. From all the bad—

ELIZABETH   Yeah, I got it. What was the plan.

TOM   At first it wasn't a plan. It was just a feeling. I heard about what was going on in this part of the city. I read about it in the newspapers. I saw how things were deteriorating. The crime, the awful victimization—

ELIZABETH   Okay. Be quiet. That's enough.

TOM   No, but I haven't—!

ELIZABETH   I said that's enough! I got it. I know what you did.

JUNIOR   She's amazing. You didn't tell her, really. But she knows. She's unbelievable.

ELIZABETH   No. I just know him. Know how his mind works. He went into his protector mode. He hatched some plan to clean up the neighbourhood.

JUNIOR   Amazing.

ELIZABETH   And he sucked you right into the middle of it.

JUNIOR   Right. Right into the middle. I got sucked in.

ELIZABETH   You idiot!

JUNIOR   Right again!

TOM   We infiltrated. We developed a complex and daring plan to make contact with all the criminal elements in this neighbourhood. And then by trickery and theft make them think they were being double-crossed by each other.

JUNIOR   And that would start a war.

TOM   A crime war. A war in which they would all be destroyed or made totally ineffective. Like I said, it was a complex plan.

JUNIOR   I never really understood it.

TOM   It was beyond understanding. It was designed to operate on momentum. It was a plan that came from deep inside me. From my experience and my heart.

JUNIOR   A plan of love, really.

TOM   And anger and regret.

JUNIOR   And fear. At least for me. Fear was a big part of the plan.

ELIZABETH   But that old standby 'stupid' was the biggest part, right?

TOM   We each had a part to play. I was the money man. The suit man.

JUNIOR   I worked the streets.

TOM   He did pretty good. I'm proud of him in many ways. [*to* JUNIOR]

I haven't told you that till now.

JUNIOR Thanks.

ELIZABETH But something went wrong! What was it!

JUNIOR We don't know.

TOM We think we were set up. I know we can find out who did it. But it will take time.

ELIZABETH You've got six hours. Is that time enough.

JUNIOR I don't think so. It usually takes us a few hours just to talk about what we're going to do, and then the first thing we do is usually wrong, so we have to—

TOM Elizabeth. Why do we only have six hours.

ELIZABETH [*stares at* TOM. *Speaks very clearly*] When I went to get Mom away from those cops I cut a deal. They gave me until eight o'clock this morning to come up with the person or persons who put those drugs in our basement. Failing that they are going to arrest my mother, God bless her, and charge her with possession for the purpose of trafficking.

JUNIOR Really?

ELIZABETH Really.

JUNIOR [*to* TOM] We can't let that happen.

ELIZABETH [*turns to* JUNIOR] Don't look at him when you say that. He can't help you. He's a total fuck up. [*to* TOM] Aren't you. Aren't you?!

TOM I ... just wanted—

ELIZABETH What, what did you want?!

TOM To help! But I was isolated. Wasn't allowed to be in the family. Had to pretend to be sick ... All that made me not think straight.

ELIZABETH Sad ... Jesus. [*to* JUNIOR] That's his excuse. He wasn't allowed in the family so his mind got cloudy. What's yours.

JUNIOR I don't know. I didn't know he had a cloudy mind. Maybe having the baby made me extra worried. Maybe it made me cloudy, too.

ELIZABETH [*to* TOM] You're a plague. And a curse. You're a life-long, enormous, black hole of misery to this family.

TOM I'm trying to change. I just ... Well, you see, I ... [*mumbles something*]

ELIZABETH What. What did you say.

[TOM *goes to* JUNIOR. *Whispers in his ear*]

JUNIOR He loves you.

ELIZABETH What?!

[TOM *whispers in* JUNIOR's *ear*]

JUNIOR He loves this family.

ELIZABETH He loves us. He loves us?! Amazing! Can you imagine what he'd do to this family if he hated us. The mind boggles. I don't know, could be anything ... little nuclear devices shoved up all our assholes!

[*A knock at the back door.* DIAN *is standing there*]

DIAN Hi.

[*They all look at each other.* JUNIOR *starts to cry*]

We got a call about a prowler around your house ... Can I come in.

[ELIZABETH *goes to* ROLLY. *Sits on his lap. Puts an arm around his neck*]

ELIZABETH Sure.

[DIAN *comes in*]

DIAN Thanks. I thought it might give me a chance to see how you were getting along with our little problem. Any solutions to that yet.

ELIZABETH What about the prowler.

DIAN I looked around. Seems fine. So ... you didn't answer my question.

ELIZABETH We have till eight o'clock. That was the deal.

DIAN Pretty stupid deal if you ask me. That was my ex-partner's idea ... Deadlines ... That was the last stupid idea I could take. I asked to work alone. I mean, the guy's a throwback.

ELIZABETH What are you doing here. Really.

DIAN You seem hostile, Elizabeth. But notice I haven't even asked you about your hostage here.

[ELIZABETH *gets off* ROLLY's *lap. Goes to* JUNIOR. *Gives him a quick whack.* JUNIOR *stops crying*]

Because I know people need plenty of space to wheel and deal in things like this. This could be a matter entirely within the family. The human interaction in this family is extremely complex. That would be my guess. But you still didn't answer my question. Are you any closer to finding out who put all that illegal substance in your basement.

ELIZABETH We're working on it.

DIAN Hi, Junior. How's the arm.

JUNIOR All right.

DIAN [to TOM] You must be the father. We haven't met. [puts out her hand] I'm Dian Black, O.C.S.

TOM Hi.

[They shake]

DIAN You guys look kind of messed up. And you don't smell so good, either. Been down in the sewers, have you. Searching for a rat? No, no don't answer that. I was just thinking out loud.

ELIZABETH Why don't you just go away. I told you I was working on it.

DIAN Well, I'm glad you're working on it, Elizabeth. But there could be forces at play here beyond your knowledge. I'm about to stick my neck out here, Elizabeth. You have to appreciate that, appreciate all the implications of that vis-à-vis my career, my personal safety.

TOM What's wrong with you. You talk like you're on drugs.

JUNIOR Yeah.

DIAN Shush. I'm talking to the brains in the family now. Right, Elizabeth? Your hostage here is a dead end. He's just a victim of Junior's shenanigans. That's right! We know about the avenging angels here. And we don't care. Not the people I work for anyway ... But hey, wait a minute ... my ex-partner, he might feel different. [to TOM] You know him, don't you Tom. You know Mike Dixon. [takes out her lip balm. Applies it casually]

TOM We worked together for a while. A long time ago.

DIAN You see, this is leading somewhere, Elizabeth. Ever do anything to him that might deserve a payback, Tom. No, don't answer that! Just think about it. You get my drift, Elizabeth. You see how I'm opening up the possibilities here. I mean if a cop, a certain kind of cop, or a number of cops, are very, very annoyed with someone, well ... well, revenge may be too strong a word, but—

ELIZABETH It's me, isn't it. This was a set-up to pressure me. To neutralize me.

DIAN How did you do that. Get into the middle of my thought process like that. No one has ever done that. Wow. Okay. We have to be careful now. Vis-à-vis our personal safety, our careers. Maybe we should talk about this alone, in another room.

ELIZABETH It's me. Shit!

DIAN I can help you with this, Elizabeth. But we have to be discreet.

ELIZABETH I'm not sure I want your help, Dian. So go fuck yourself. I think I owe my family an explanation.

TOM You don't owe me anything, honey. Let's just call it even.

ELIZABETH [to JUNIOR] Did you hear what he just said.

JUNIOR He didn't really mean that, Elizabeth ... [to TOM] How the hell can you be even, man. Did she try to burn the house down and shit like that.

TOM It was just an expression!

ELIZABETH Unbelievable.

JUNIOR I wouldn't mind an explanation, Elizabeth.

ELIZABETH I was just getting really sick and tired of defending people who'd had their brains beaten out in the back seats of cruisers, in the basements of police stations.So I complained. And I tried to organize other people, lawyers mostly, so they could complain.

DIAN Bad timing, Elizabeth. You caught the police force at a particularly sensitive moment, is what I think. They've received so much negative press.

ELIZABETH This is criminal conspiracy we're talking about, Dian.

DIAN Maybe ... Maybe. But is there a possible deal here, Elizabeth. Do you have a message you want me to take downtown vis-à-vis your public campaign against police brutality. Or do we let your mom go to jail. Come on, Elizabeth. You know how it works! Make an offer for chrissake!

[Pause]

ELIZABETH I'm willing to talk about it.

DIAN A settlement which will satisfy all parties.

ELIZABETH We'll talk about it.

DIAN Can I use the phone.

ELIZABETH Sure. Go ahead.

DIAN This has to be a private call, Elizabeth. Is there another one somewhere.

ELIZABETH In the hall upstairs.

DIAN Thank you. This shouldn't take long.

[*She hurries off*]

JUNIOR [*to* ELIZABETH] Do you really think she's trying to help us.

ELIZABETH I don't know. She's hard to read.

TOM She doesn't talk like a cop. Maybe it's a woman thing.

ELIZABETH Jesus. What's that supposed to mean.

TOM Some woman sees some other woman in a tight spot. So she, you know, feels something about that only a woman could feel.

ELIZABETH You mean something human? Like sympathy? Look, don't answer that. I don't want to talk to you anymore. I didn't mean to talk to you in the first place. I forgot.

TOM I'm glad you forgot. I enjoyed talking to you. Whatever happens, I'll always remember these last couple of minutes.

[STEVIE *suddenly appears at the basement door. Holding a gun*]

STEVIE Okay. Hands up. Up high. Really high. Come on!

ELIZABETH How did you get into our basement again. We put bars on that window.

STEVIE So what. You think bars mean anything to me? I do this for a living for chrissake.

[TOM *takes a step towards* STEVIE]

TOM Do you want me to take that weapon away from this insect, Elizabeth.

ELIZABETH Stay out of this. [*to* STEVIE] What do you want.

STEVIE Whatya mean what do I want. I want my dad. You can't just take a guy's dad away like that. Look at him. He's been tortured or something. You rotten bastards … Untie him … Come on, untie him!

ELIZABETH [*to* JUNIOR] Do it.

[JUNIOR *starts to untie* ROLLY]

STEVIE Hey, not the guy with the broken arm, man. That'll take hours. You think I'm stupid? I want someone with two arms to untie him. You rotten bastards. Look at him. I hate the way he looks. Wake him up. Slap him or something.

TOM My pleasure.

STEVIE Hey, I heard that, you pig. Okay, I changed my mind. Splash him with water. Come on. You. The woman. Get water. Splash him. You. The guy with two arms. Untie him. Well, what are you waiting for. Do it. Do it, you pigs!

[TOM *is approaching* STEVIE. STEVIE *is backing away*]

TOM Okay. Look, I'm going to do what you ask. But I'm warning you, for your own safety, to be careful how you talk to us.

STEVIE Jesus! He's threatening me. I've got a gun. But he doesn't care. He wants to hurt someone so bad he doesn't care about guns or anything. What's wrong with you people. You're all crazy-mean. Jesus!

ELIZABETH [*moving to get a pot, which is sitting on the stove beside a burner. To* STEVIE] You're getting yourself all worked up here. Why don't you just put that gun away. We'll give you back your dad. And the two of you can just ... leave.

[*She throws a pot of liquid on* ROLLY. *He starts to stir.* ELIZABETH *begins to untie him*]

STEVIE Oh right. I'll put the gun away. Like I trust you or something. I saw you kidnap my dad. I saw you spray him with that stuff. That was horrible, man. Seeing your own dad roll around and puke like that.

ELIZABETH Really. So why didn't you try to help him.

STEVIE Well I'm here now, eh. I had some business to take care of, but I'm here now.

ROLLY [*opens his eyes. Sees* ELIZABETH. *Screams*] Keep away from me! Keep her away! What's this. What'd she put on me. Some kind of oil. She's gonna burn me up! Help me!

STEVIE Relax, Dad. Stay calm.

ROLLY Don't let her burn me up.

[STEVIE *moves to* ROLLY's *side*]

STEVIE Don't worry, Dad. It was just ... soup. [*to* ELIZABETH] You poured soup on him. Why. I ask you to splash him with water, and you pour a pot of soup on him. You're a pig!

TOM Look, didn't I warn you about that kind of talk.

[TOM *takes one step towards* STEVIE]

STEVIE I'm sorry, okay?! [*starts to cry*] Ah, man. You're just lookin' for an excuse to hurt me, aren't you.

ROLLY Hey. Stevie. It's you. [*he is free. Stands*]

STEVIE Yeah, Dad. I'm here.

[ROLLY *cuffs* STEVIE *on the head*]

ROLLY So what took you so long. Eh?! You know what I wish. I wish you were a girl. In my older years I wish I had a daughter instead of you. A daughter would have been here earlier. A daughter would take care of me in my older years. Look at her. She's a daughter. Look at all the shit she goes through for her loved ones. Why can't you be like that you little bastard.

[ROLLY *cuffs* STEVIE *repeatedly*]

STEVIE Come on, Dad. Watch it. Watch out. I've got a gun I'm trying to aim at these people. This gun is the only thing that's keeping these crazy people away, Dad. You're going to make me drop it.

ROLLY Hey that's real! Who said you could have a real gun. Since when is a real gun a thing we use. Why didn't you bring one of the toy guns we usually use.

[ROLLY *starts to cuff* STEVIE *again*]

STEVIE I mean it, Dad! Watch out. Okay. Okay. Fuck it. I'll just drop the gun. Then you'll see what happens to us here!

[DIAN *comes in*]

Hey, it's you. What are you doing here.

DIAN [*takes a gun from inside her coat*] Put that gun down, Stevie.

STEVIE I'm confused by this. Why are you here.

ELIZABETH You know her?

STEVIE Yeah. I know her.

DIAN Put the gun down. And you can go. Both of you. You can just walk away.

ROLLY She's talkin' like a cop. Is she a cop.

STEVIE She's—

DIAN Hey! Shut up! Put the gun down and leave. Or I'll use my weapon.

ELIZABETH Who is she, Stevie. Who do you think she is.

STEVIE I feel like I'm in an awkward situation here. I just came to get my dad.

DIAN And now you've got him. So leave.

ELIZABETH I want to know how you know her, Stevie.

DIAN If you make him tell you that, Elizabeth, you'll be putting us all in a very unfortunate position. [*to* ROLLY *and* STEVIE] Get the hell out of here!

[MIKE *swings around the basement door. Gun up*]

MIKE Everyone stay very still. [*to* STEVIE] Drop your weapon. Do it now!

ROLLY Now, he's a cop for sure. Drop it, Stevie.

[STEVIE *drops his gun.* MIKE *turns to* DIAN. *Points gun at her. She points her gun at him*]

MIKE Dian ... I want you to drop your gun, too.

DIAN That's not going to happen, Mike.

JUNIOR Oh, this looks bad. This is weird. Two cops pointing guns at each other. [*starts to sob*]

TOM What's going on here, Mike.

MIKE Can't talk now, buddy ... I think my ex-partner here wants to kill me.

ELIZABETH Is that right, Dian.

DIAN It crossed my mind ... Look, Mike, I think I know why you're here. But for the good of the force we better work together on this.

STEVIE Can me and my dad leave.

MIKE & DIAN Yes!

STEVIE We can go, Dad.

MIKE That's right, Dad. You can go. You can disappear back into your hole. But you have to forget everything you saw here.

DIAN And every*one* you saw here.

MIKE [*to* ROLLY] You got that?

ROLLY What about our merchandise. I'm sorry to bring it up. But it's all I've got in life. I don't have a pension, or anything.

STEVIE It's okay, Dad. You mean the videos, right? I've got them.

ROLLY Yeah? So they were right about you. You pulled a switcheroo. You brought drugs to that meeting in the alley. You sneaky little bastard. Who said you could sell drugs?!

[*He cuffs* STEVIE]

STEVIE I didn't bring drugs to that meeting, Dad. I was given the drugs later.

ELIZABETH Who gave you the drugs, Stevie.

DIAN He can't answer that question. People might get hurt if he answers that question. The best thing right now is for him and his dad to leave!

MIKE [*to* ROLLY] Did you hear that.

ROLLY Yeah.

MIKE So why the fuck are you still here?!

[MIKE *is advancing on* ROLLY *and* STEVIE. ELIZABETH *puts herself in front of* ROLLY *and* STEVIE]

ELIZABETH Stay away from them. They belong to me. Stevie, I want you and your dad to stay a little longer. I'll make it worth your while.

STEVIE Is that an offer.

DIAN [*pointing her gun at* ELIZABETH] Back away, Elizabeth.

ELIZABETH You're aiming your weapon at me. What malfunctioning part of your brain is telling you to do something like that, Dian.

DIAN You're interfering in police business.

ELIZABETH You're in my mother's kitchen you demented bitch!

[MIKE *suddenly cuffs* ROLLY]

MIKE Why the fuck are you still here.

[*He cuffs* STEVIE]

How many fucking times do I have to ask you that question.

[*He cuffs them both. Fast*]

How fucking stupid are you, anyway. Are you so stupid you like pain.

TOM Hey, Mike. Not in front of my kids. Not in my house.

MIKE Can't be helped, buddy.

[*He grabs* ROLLY *with one arm.* STEVIE *with the other*]

ROLLY Okay, okay, we're leaving.

STEVIE But she made me an offer, Dad. It could be a good one. What's a little beating. A little pain. Fuck you, cop. I'm going to tell this lady the truth about those drugs.

MIKE Sure you are.

[*He knees* STEVIE *in the groin.* STEVIE *doubles up.* MIKE *grabs* STEVIE'*s hair. Smashes his head into the refrigerator.* STEVIE *crumples to the floor*]

ELIZABETH Ah, Jesus. I told you he belongs to me. Leave him alone!

[TOM *grabs* MIKE'*s shoulder*]

TOM Okay, that's enough, Mike.

MIKE I told you to stay out of this.

[MIKE *swings at* TOM. TOM *ducks. Grabs* MIKE's *arm and twists it behind his back. Pushes* MIKE *face first over the kitchen table. Takes his gun away.* ELIZABETH *is moving towards* DIAN. *And what happens next happens very, very fast*]

ELIZABETH Junior.

JUNIOR What.

ELIZABETH Attack!

JUNIOR What.

ELIZABETH Attack, Junior. Kill!

JUNIOR What?! Who?!

ELIZABETH Her. Now, boy. Attack. Kill. Go for the throat.

JUNIOR Come on, Elizabeth. Give me a break here.

ELIZABETH Look, I'm telling you to kill her or suffer the consequences!

JUNIOR Okay, okay!

[JUNIOR *drops to his knees and moves towards* DIAN, *growling wildly.* DIAN *turns to face* JUNIOR]

DIAN All right, that's far enough. I'll use my weapon.

[ELIZABETH *has moved quietly and quickly behind* DIAN. *She grabs her in a bear hug, trapping* DIAN's *arms. Lifts her off the ground*]

ELIZABETH Junior, get her gun!

[JUNIOR *grabs* DIAN's *gun*]

DIAN Elizabeth, it's still not too late to make a deal.

ELIZABETH Sure.

[ELIZABETH *throws* DIAN *to the floor. Grabs the gun from* JUNIOR. *Puts her foot on* DIAN's *head, pressing it to the floor. Points the gun at* DIAN's *head*]

JUNIOR Good trick, Elizabeth. All that Junior attack and kill stuff. I was supposed to be like a mad dog, right. I didn't get it at first. Where did that come from, Elizabeth.

ELIZABETH I don't know. My subconscious, I guess. Don't worry about it.

JUNIOR Sure. But if that's how you really feel about me I'm a little—

ELIZABETH [*points gun at him*] I said don't worry about it!

JUNIOR Okay, okay …

TOM What now.

ELIZABETH Well, now we find out which one of these cops has set us up. And which one is just trying to cover up the set-up. Rolly, why aren't you picking your son off the floor.

ROLLY Fuck him.

ELIZABETH [*points gun at him*] Do it!

MIKE I'm cooled down now, Tom. You can let me up.

ELIZABETH [*points gun at him*] Keep him where he is.

DIAN You people are in over your heads. You people have crossed the line.

[ELIZABETH *stamps the floor near* DIAN*'s head.* DIAN *curls up in fear.* ROLLY *has* STEVIE *on his feet*]

ELIZABETH How you doin', Stevie.

STEVIE You know something? I don't give a fuck how I'm doing! That's how I'm doing!

ELIZABETH You were going to tell us something.

STEVIE You were gonna make me an offer. I wanna hear what it was.

ELIZABETH [*points gun at him*] Your life.

ROLLY Tricked again. I coulda told ya.

STEVIE [*to* ELIZABETH] You won't use that.

ROLLY Sure she will. She's meaner than any of them. And we're nothing to her. We're sewage. [*to* ELIZABETH] Aren't we. Shit floating in the dark. Big, fat, floating turds!

STEVIE Come on, Dad. Calm down. Have a little, you know, self-respect. I say let her shoot. Fuck her. Fuck them all. How about it.

ROLLY Yeah. Yeah, okay. Fuck you. We've been abused one too many times. We're gonna show you something here. We're gonna show you some class. Kill my kid. Go ahead. Kill him.

STEVIE [*starts to cry*] And you too, Dad. Tell her to kill you, too. Come on, Dad.

ROLLY Yeah, okay. The hell with it. Kill us both. [*starts to cry*] Come on. Whatya waiting for you big, mean, spooky woman!

[*They are approaching* ELIZABETH *arm in arm. Crying*]

STEVIE Yeah. Come on!

ROLLY Come on!

ELIZABETH [*lowers the gun*] A thousand dollars.

ROLLY What.

ELIZABETH I'll give you a thousand dollars. All Stevie has to do is tell me which one of these cops hired him to plant those drugs.

STEVIE Okay, that's more like it. That's an offer we can live with.

ROLLY Where's the money.

ELIZABETH I don't have it on me. I'll get it to you.

STEVIE Yeah. Like we trust you or somethin'.

ELIZABETH [*mocking*] Yeah. Like you got a choice or somethin'.

ROLLY Tell her. Fuck it.

STEVIE Should I.

ROLLY If I didn't think you should, would I tell you you should.

[*He cuffs* STEVIE]

STEVIE Okay, okay. It was her. The lady cop.

DIAN You're making a big mistake.

[ELIZABETH *stamps the floor.* DIAN *curls up in fear*]

STEVIE But I didn't know she was a lady cop. I thought she was a lady crook. She told me she was connected to the big-time. She contacted me. Told me she wanted a favour. [*to* ROLLY] This was after we broke in here, but had to leave 'cause of the baby—

ELIZABETH Get on with it!

STEVIE Okay, she told me she wanted me to break in here again. Find our merchandise, and put the drugs there instead. If I did this I would be given things. Money. Good references. Future business dealings. Things like that. I could give you the details.

ELIZABETH That's not necessary. You can go now.

STEVIE That's it?

ROLLY We can go?

ELIZABETH Yeah.

ROLLY And you'll get that thousand dollars to us.

ELIZABETH Yes, I will.

STEVIE Oh, sure you will. But you know what. I don't care. Fuck you! And everyone here! And fuck the things you're all doin'! Whatever they are! That's what I say. [*to* ROLLY] Right?

ROLLY Sure. I say that, too. But I'd still like the money.

STEVIE If we get the money, that's a good thing, I agree. But you still gotta say fuck them.

ROLLY Okay. Yeah … Fuck you! And the things you're doin'! 'Specially to us!

STEVIE Now all we gotta do is leave with some class.

ROLLY Come on.

[*They leave*]

ELIZABETH Okay. Everyone up.

[ELIZABETH *and* TOM *back away.* MIKE *and* DIAN *get up.* TOM *hands* MIKE*'s gun to* ELIZABETH]

TOM Here. You gotta excuse me. I'm not feeling very well. [*starts off*]

ELIZABETH Are you faking illness again.

TOM No … This stuff reminds me too much of other stuff. And the other stuff reminds me of … other stuff … Bastards.

[*He leaves.* ELIZABETH *hands guns to* JUNIOR]

ELIZABETH Here. Take the bullets out of these for me, will you.

[JUNIOR *sits at the table*]

Why did you do this to my family, Dian. Is it because you're insane.

DIAN You were planning to do serious damage to something to which I owe a high degree of loyalty. You understand loyalty. Think of the police force as my family and you'll understand better.

ELIZABETH My family is made up of human beings. You're loyal to an institution. I'll visit you in the asylum some day and explain the difference.

JUNIOR These are unloaded. Can I go upstairs now, Elizabeth. I want to see my wife and daughter.

ELIZABETH Sure. Go on. Give them both a kiss from me.

[*He leaves*]

DIAN [*takes out her lip balm*] Isn't that lovely. Everyone's all cozy and tucked in their beds. But who's out there protecting them while they sleep. Who stands guard and keeps the scum from the door.

ELIZABETH Who are you, Dian. What are you.

DIAN A committed social servant. Look, you had to be stopped. I'm truly, truly sorry I had to involve your mother. But a police force damaged and soiled in the public's eye is not going to be an effective player in the ongoing societal conflict! [*begins to apply her lip balm furiously*]

ELIZABETH [*to* MIKE] Are you listening to all this.

MIKE Yeah.

ELIZABETH So what do you make of it.

DIAN What are you asking him for?! I'm the only one with vision! With imagination. I see the big picture. I see the big picture with details. Details that contradict what *you* see in the big picture. You think that's easy?! It's scary! It makes you do scary things sometimes!

MIKE You're nuttier than a fruitcake.

DIAN This woman here was out to destroy the force!

MIKE I don't know what force you're talking about. The one I work for just gives you a book full of laws and tells you to arrest anyone who breaks them. It's simple, really.

DIAN [*mocking*] 'It's simple, really.' It's not simple. You think it's simple because you're rigid and stupid. I know it's not simple because I'm flexible and extremely intelligent.

MIKE Why do you think I followed you here. I mean, if you're so smart how come a bozo like me could figure out what you were up to. You know how? Hunches.

[DIAN *screams. Turns away.* MIKE *pursues her*]

DIAN Walk away, Mike. Let me cut a deal with Elizabeth. She'll back off to keep her mom out of jail. The police force will be saved any more unfortunate publicity.

MIKE No!

DIAN It's the best solution.

MIKE No. No can do.

DIAN 'No!' 'No can do.' ... Why not, asshole?! Why the fuck not?! [*she is very mobile. Very agitated. Much lip balm is being applied*]

MIKE Because I've got a better plan! I got it while I was listening to you talk like a fruitcake. I came here to try and cover up your crazy scheme. But now what I want is for you to leave these people alone. Let Elizabeth make all the fuss she wants. And let the police force deal with her any way, any goddamn *legal* way it can.

DIAN Damn you! Damn you guys. Cut me some slack here. I'm the kind of cop this city needs now. I'm creative. I can arrange solutions to difficult problems in non-linear ways. I am the future!

You big, dumb jerk. And I'm tough. I'm tough, too. I'm that rarest of human beings. A caring, sensitive, intelligent adult who also happens to love law and order!

MIKE Go home, Dian. Have a bath. Take a pill. Write a letter of resignation.

DIAN I'm not quitting. I don't care what you say. In fact, I'm asking to be made your permanent partner. We're engaged in something here, Mike! It's big, this thing we're engaged in! Big and contradictory. It's new and old. Woman and man. Daughter and father. Smart and dumb. Really, really smart! And really, really dumb!
[*She grabs his cheeks. Gives him a long hard kiss*]
See you tomorrow, partner.
[*She rushes off. Out the screen door. Pause*]

MIKE [*sighs. Gestures feebly*] Ah, I'm really sorry about all—

ELIZABETH I only need to hear an official confirmation that all charges against my mother, or any other member of this family, pertaining to those drugs are dropped. Can you give that to me.

MIKE Yes. I can.

ELIZABETH Thank you. And now pay attention, Mr. Policeman. I'm going to continue my campaign against police brutality. I'm going to bring your beloved police force to its knees. I'm going to start with that insane bitch. And then I'm going to destroy anyone who was even remotely involved in what she was doing to me and my family, and if that includes you, tough fucking luck!

MIKE Did you say something about police brutality? Well, you just keep right on complaining. I hate it when those awful police get brutal. I mean, who the hell are they to get brutal. All the nice people they get to deal with. All that love and affection they get from that wonderful scum out there. Why the fuck would anyone want to get brutal with that fucking, wonderful, goddamn scum. So you just make a stink about that. I'm right behind you. Goddamn right I am!
[*He leaves. Slams the door behind him.* ELIZABETH *watches him leave.* JUNIOR, *then* GAIL, *nursing the baby, then* MARY ANN, *come in behind* ELIZABETH]

ELIZABETH [*turns*] What are you doing down here.

GAIL Junior woke us up.

JUNIOR I started thinking you might need some help. I thought we should all face it together. Whatever happened.

MARY ANN What did happen.

ELIZABETH We found out who set us up.

JUNIOR It was that lady cop.

GAIL We were set up by a cop? All my worst fears are coming true. We should think about moving to the country.

MARY ANN What. Set us up? How. Why. I don't get it. Will someone explain it to me sometime. Or will it be just another one of those things I'm sort of aware of, but I don't really understand.

[NORA *comes in. They all look at her*]

NORA Is everything okay now, Elizabeth.

ELIZABETH Yes, Mom.

NORA I'm not going to jail.

ELIZABETH No, Mom.

NORA Good. That's good … Tom and I have been talking. I decided to talk to him. Don't make a fuss about that. I had my reasons. He told me what he'd tried to do and why. He wanted to help. I believe him. I decided to believe him. I've got my reasons, don't worry. Anyway. He wants to ask you all something. He's right out there in the hall. Come on in, Tom.

[TOM *comes in*]

Go ahead, Tom. Just ask right out loud.

[ELIZABETH *turns away*]

TOM [*quietly*] Can I stay.

[*Pause*]

NORA I don't think they heard you.

JUNIOR I heard him.

MARY ANN So did I.

GAIL She means Elizabeth.

[ELIZABETH *turns to face* TOM]

TOM [*to* ELIZABETH] Can I stay.

ELIZABETH Would that accomplish anything.

TOM We'd be together. We'd be a family.

ELIZABETH And you think that would be a good thing. You think something positive would grow out of that. I mean, what kind of family do you think we'd be with you ... that we weren't without you. Stronger? Meaner? Better prepared to deal with the shit of the world? We know how you feel about that world full of shit out there. You've been telling us about it since we were kids. Obviously you haven't changed your mind. You still think we need protection. You still think that's your job.

TOM I can't help that.

ELIZABETH You still think we're weak.

TOM No. I don't.

ELIZABETH Sure you do. You make all your decisions about us based on a feeling of superiority.

TOM I don't think you're weak. I just think you've got a different kind of strength.

ELIZABETH Yeah? So what kind is it.

TOM The kind that keeps you together. It's ... [*mumbles something*]

NORA Love. He said love. I heard him.

GAIL So did I.

TOM The strength of love ... I need that. I want some of that, is all I'm saying. I want to be able to give over to it.

ELIZABETH So how do you plan to do that.

TOM I don't really have a plan. I just want to stay. If I stay here with you I figure there's a chance for me. If I go out there alone again I won't last. The shit in my brain will meet the shit in the world and there'll be an explosion.

ELIZABETH So we're supposed to keep you here to keep you safe from the world. To keep the world safe from you.

TOM Yeah. I guess so ... But also ... so I can love you. Get loved by you. I need you all to love me so bad I can taste it. Really. I can taste the need.

ELIZABETH Where do you think love comes from.

MARY ANN Maybe that's enough for now, Elizabeth. Who can answer questions like that.

GAIL Leave her alone. She has to do this. This is what she does.

ELIZABETH [*to* TOM] The kind of love you're talking about. Do you think it's going to rub off on you.

TOM If I let it ... yeah.

ELIZABETH You think it's what ... hugging, kissing ... being nice?

TOM That'd be a good start.

ELIZABETH You think it's just hanging around together. Maybe going on a picnic. Maybe going skating like we used to when we were kids. We don't need you to go skating with us anymore. That would just be a luxury. At best, that would be ... a good time. We don't need you to show us a good time. We don't need you to be nice to us. If you stay we only need one thing from you ... respect. [*Long pause. They are staring at each other*]

GAIL Use another word. Respect is such a sucky word, Elizabeth. It just embarrasses everyone.

ELIZABETH I don't care. It applies. Do you know what I mean, Dad. Do you have any idea what that word means. Why I used it.

TOM I do respect you. All of you. Look what you've made of yourself, Elizabeth. You're a lawyer.

ELIZABETH You're proud! We've survived. We've done better than survive. We're your women and we're chips off the old block ... Well, I don't need you to be proud of me ... You've got to do better that that. A lot better.
[*She leaves. Pause*]

MARY ANN Dad? [*waves*] I could make you a list. I agree with most of what Elizabeth said. But I think what you really need is a list. Something you can carry around. Something that's ... real. You know, a list of things like ... no lying, no pretending, no using your 'man voice' just to get your way. Stuff like that. Do you think that would help.

TOM Maybe.

MARY ANN A list of things you can't do, and a list of things you can. Just suggestions, maybe. Nothing too strict. There's some paper upstairs, I'll bet. I'll go do it now.

TOM That's very nice of you, Mary Ann.

MARY ANN Oh no, I have to help. I have to do what I can. That's usually not much, but I still have to do it.
[*She leaves*]

GAIL Dad?

TOM Yes, honey.

GAIL I love Elizabeth and Mary Ann a lot. But it would be okay with
me if you ignored them. And just tried your best ... Come on
Junior, let's go to bed.

JUNIOR Great. I want to sleep for a week.

GAIL You can't. You've got to go talk to your foreman tomorrow
morning.

JUNIOR You saved my job.

GAIL Unless you do something else really stupid. What *have* you been
doing, anyway. Are you going to tell me about that. Tell me what
ridiculous things you and my dad have been up to.

JUNIOR Sure. But you won't like it. You might get really mad.

GAIL Or I might just laugh.

[*They start off. Arms around each other.* GAIL *stops*]

Something else, Dad ... If you ever want to go skating with me
and Gwen, that would be great. Anytime. I mean it.

[*They leave.* NORA *is sitting at the table.* TOM *joins her*]

NORA They're all different. They grew up to be different people. They
never really agree about anything. That's just the way it is ... You
look a little sad. And confused. Look on the bright side ... You're
still here. There's still a possibility that you could stay here, and
make something positive out of the experience ... Excuse me.

[*She goes out to the back porch. Shouts*]

Attention! Attention fanatics! You can stop watching now. Nobody
in this house is going to prison. The problems in this house are
being resolved ... I'll keep you posted!

[*She comes back in*]

TOM I'm going to get a job.

NORA Don't do anything rash.

TOM I want to make some money. Help out.

NORA We get by. And money isn't very important around here
anymore. Compared to ... other things, I mean. But if it's
something you need to do ... Well, all right. But ... [*sits across
from him*] Here's some advice about that. Here's what I have to tell
you about that idea. You shouldn't take a job with a lot of tension.

Take a job that makes you happy. Even if it only pays a little.
[*Lights start to fade*]
We can't have you working at something that makes you tense, and angry, and resentful. We can't afford the chance that you'll bring tension, anger and resentment home. Maybe you could get a job making things. Little things that are useful. And pleasant to look at. Or a job taking care of things. Or fixing things. Fixing things is useful and rewarding. Filled with satisfaction. Or a job outdoors. Outdoors is the best environment. A job outdoors fixing and taking care of things would be the best. Maybe you could get one of those jobs taking care of a golf course. That could be very nice. Of course that's seasonal work. But maybe seasonal work is good. You wouldn't be overdoing it that way. You wouldn't get too tense. You'd have over half a year to recover.
[TOM *is nodding. Lights are fading*]
What do you think. I think we should investigate the golf course idea. It's up to you, though. There can't be pressure. These are only ideas. ... Suggestions. You know ... hints.
[*Blackout*]
[*End*]

TOUGH!

Tough! was commissioned and first produced by Green Thumb Threatre for Young People and received its premiere at the Vancouver East Cultural Centre on February 4, 1993 with the following cast:

TINA Robyn Stevan
BOBBY Frank Zotter
JILL Leslie Jones

Director: Patrick McDonald
Set & Costume Designer: Phillip Tidd
Lighting Designer: Gerald King
Stage Manger: Cynthia Burtinshaw

Persons

TINA, *nineteen*
BOBBY, *nineteen*
JILL, *nineteen*

Place

A city park.

Time

Now.

Early evening. Late summer
A small city park. A picnic table. A trash can
BOBBY *is sitting on the picnic table, watching* TINA *move around in a very agitated way.* JILL *is lying on the grass a few feet away, writing something on a thick pad.*
BOBBY *is wearing a work shirt, jeans, and boots.* JILL *is wearing a t-shirt and jeans.* TINA *is wearing slacks and a nice blouse. She is carrying her shoes*

TINA It's all lies. Everything you ever told me was a fucking lie. You said I could trust you. That's a lie. You let me think I knew you. What did I know about you. Lies. I knew your lies. Ah shit, aren't you going to say anything. Are you just gonna sit there like a dog. A lying dog.

BOBBY So what do you want me—

TINA Shut the fuck up. Anything you say now is gonna be a lie.

BOBBY No, it's not.

TINA No? You're gonna say something truthful? Why? Why start now. Cause you're under pressure?

BOBBY I'm not under pressure. There's no pressure. I could leave, you know. I don't have to stay here and listen to this stuff.

TINA You could leave and I'd follow you. You could run and hide and I'd track you down like the sad animal you are. And grab you by your fucking ears. And yell the truth into your sad stupid lying face. And I will, you know. I will. So you know you gotta sit there and take it. Because you deserve it. You're a shit. A real shit. And you know what else you are? You're a coward. What. What?! You wanna say something now? You getting mad? You don't like being called a coward, coward. Well what?! What?!

BOBBY You want me to talk?

TINA You wanna talk? Talk. Who's stopping you.

BOBBY Ah ... Listen ... Okay. All I want ... I mean the only thing now is that maybe you're making too much out of what—

TINA Jesus! You had your hand up her shirt. You had your hand up her fucking shirt.

BOBBY Yeah, that's the story. That's what's going round. But—
[JILL *sits up*]

JILL Hey! I saw you, asshole.

BOBBY This is a set-up. I was brought here under false circumstances.

JILL False circumstances. What the hell does that mean. Talk English.

BOBBY It's like a trial. You never liked me.

JILL You're right. But what's that got to do with anything. I still saw you take that bimbo slut into the kitchen.

BOBBY [to TINA] See? Okay, that's not true. Not really. She took me. Really. I was—

TINA Look, be careful. You're gonna lie. You're gonna lie and then I'm gonna kill you.

BOBBY Fuck it. It's a trial. You've got a witness who never liked me. She's the only one giving testimony so I'm fucked ... It's like you've set a trap for me or something. Like you think I'm an animal or something.

TINA I *do* think you're an animal. I've already told you that.

BOBBY Well, I'm not.

TINA Prove it. Explain to me that you've got some human reason for what you did. Because a human would have a reason and an animal would just have done it because it's what an animal does.

BOBBY Come on. I've been working all day. I can't deal with this now. My mind's all fuzzy.

TINA I've been working all day too and my mind's sharp as a tack.

BOBBY Yeah well, that's one of the ways we're different.

TINA Breasts.

BOBBY What.

TINA Tits. That's what it's about. Nothing else.

BOBBY Ah, come on.

TINA Tits, man. You're like a kid. You're ... you know ... What's the word.

JILL Obsessed.

TINA Yeah. Right. Obsessed. You're obsessed with tits. It doesn't even matter what they're attached to. They could be attached to a fence and you'd still go after them. Tits just glued to a fence and you'd be in there rubbing against them. Feeling up that fence, man. People would be stopping and watching. 'What's that guy doin' to that fence.' You wouldn't care. You'd be drooling away, whispering to that fence, 'Can I suck them. I really wanna suck them.'

BOBBY Look, it was a party. I was drinking. I wasn't clear in my head.

JILL Oh, right. Excuse me while I lie down and ignore this. [*she does*]

BOBBY [*to* JILL] You had to tell her, eh.

JILL Well, I thought about it all weekend. I weighed the pros and the cons. But then, yeah, I had to tell her.

TINA [*to* BOBBY] Betrayal. Do you know what that word means.

BOBBY I was trying to tell you how drunk I was. I was ... really drunk.

TINA No, you have to shut up. You can't go down that road. It's not gonna work. Suppose I told you I was drunk when I agreed to go out with you that first time.

BOBBY Were you.

TINA Jesus. It was an example ... A thing you use. What's wrong with you. Are you stupid. Did I make that mistake about you too. I thought you had a brain in your head.

BOBBY What's the deal. You just get to insult me until you feel better, or what.

TINA You were planning to do it with that mindless slut. Don't deny it. Just tell me why. I just want to know why.

BOBBY I was—

TINA You can't say you were drunk. I'll kill you if you say that.

JILL I'll help her.

BOBBY I want her to leave.

JILL Tough.

TINA Yeah, that's right. Tough.

BOBBY She's done her thing. She's given her testimony. Why can't she just ... go away ... I can't deal with this in front of her.

TINA She's here for me. I don't care how you feel about it.

BOBBY [*stands*] Okay. So *I'll* leave.

TINA You leave, we're finished. Got it? You leave, fuck you.

BOBBY Why are you swearing so much. You hardly ever swear. You have a bad day at work? Look, I told you that job could be rough. Selling jewellery is dicey. What do you know about jewellery. I warned you.

TINA [*to* JILL] Are you listening to this.

JILL Unbelievable.

BOBBY [*to* JILL] Hey, I know she's upset with me. I'm just saying she's so upset it's gotta maybe be a combination of things. I mean, swearing and threatening my life, it's outta whack with the ... you know, the thing I did ... So I'm just saying—

TINA You ripped out my heart! You diseased brain-damaged sewer rat!

453

You killed me! I thought we were in this for life. That was one of
your lies. You said forever.

BOBBY Forever. Jesus.

TINA What.

BOBBY Forever. I mean, come on.

[*She moves to him*]

TINA What.

BOBBY Forever is … What's that mean. I mean, come on. I'm really
very young. I've got a whole life to live.

TINA Wrong!

[*She swings really hard and hits him on the side of the head. He howls.
Rolls off the table*]

[*to* JILL] I'm outta here.

JILL I'm right behind you.

[TINA *leaves.* JILL *gets up. Brushes herself off. Looks at* BOBBY *who is
now on one knee. Rubbing his head*]

BOBBY What. You wanna hit me too?

JILL Hit you? No. I was thinking I should have brought my knife. I
told Tina. Let's bring a knife and cut off his balls.

BOBBY Wow. What's your problem. How come you hate me so much.
What did I ever do to you. It's weird the way you hate me so
much. It really bothers me.

JILL You've been messing around for months haven't you. This was just
the first time you were caught. Right?

BOBBY I'm not saying anything. What can I say. This is a trap. You're
setting me up. Ah, this sucks. I've been working like a dog all day.
My life isn't exactly great, you know. I've got problems no one
knows about. Heavy ones. Confusing too. Confusing heavy
problems about … life. I'm not an animal to be trapped. I'm a guy
with problems. Jesus.

JILL Stop whining. I've got something to tell you.

BOBBY I've got enough to deal with without you telling me anything.

JILL She's pregnant, asshole. Deal with that.

[*Pause*]

BOBBY Tina? Pregnant? … Pregnant … Pregnant … Pregnant?

JILL What. You tryin' to figure out how to spell it or something.

BOBBY Pregnant?

JILL Yes. Yes! Pregnant. Carrying a baby.

BOBBY No way. No sir.

JILL Carrying your baby.

BOBBY No way. No no no no no. Hey, come on. Me? No way. No.

JILL You little insect. Are you denying it. Are you gonna try and weasel out of this.

[TINA *comes running on*]

TINA [*to* BOBBY] You fucking coward. [*to* JILL] I heard him. I was hiding behind a tree. I knew he'd deny it. And he did. [*to* BOBBY] Coward! If I had a gun I'd shoot you. What's happened to you, Bobby. You used to be a human being.

JILL He was never human. He was always an insect in disguise. You were just blinded by love.

TINA Killed by love. Run over and flattened by love. I'm dead. Really. my life's over. Ah, what am I gonna do.
[*She starts to cry.* JILL *hugs her. Sound of a siren going by on the street near them. This immediately takes* BOBBY'*s attention*]

JILL Don't cry in front of him. Don't let him see this.

TINA I can't help it. It's the way I feel.

JILL Try to feel something else. Think about getting revenge or something. I liked it better when you talked about getting a gun. Say something else like that.

TINA No! I just wanna be sad. Can't I be sad here. Aren't you my friend. Can't you just let me be whatever way I have to be. Can't you.

JILL Yeah. I guess. Yeah, go ahead. Cry. [*to* BOBBY] Are you happy now. Look at her. Hey! Try to pay attention. What's wrong with you. [*to* TINA] God I can't believe you've let a guy like this into your life. I really don't think crying in front of a guy like this is a good idea.

TINA I can't help it … He denied it. I really … never thought he'd deny it. I said I thought he would … But I didn't really think he would.

BOBBY [*stands suddenly*] I use condoms! Always! Condoms are my thing. I was using them before anyone. I use them all the time. Ask … anyone.

TINA I can't talk to him until he admits it's his. Can't he see what he's saying about me by not admitting it's his.

JILL Sure he's saying you're as much of a betraying cowardly whore as he is. He knows that.

BOBBY But I use condoms! She knows I use condoms.

JILL You have to stop saying that.

[*She pats* TINA. *Walks over to* BOBBY]

You have to stop talking about condoms.

[*She grabs* BOBBY *with both her hands by his shirt*]

Get it?! Because you're talking about them like they're some kind of gift from God or something. Some powerful thing that God gave you to make you immune. God didn't give you the condoms, asshole. You bought them in a store. The store bought them from a company that's got a factory. The factory makes them. And sometimes the factory fucks up ... Everyone else on the planet knows this. I gotta think you know this too and you're just looking for a way out of this mess. But there isn't one. There's no way out. You're the father of this baby and if you don't just admit it pretty damn soon we're going to kill you. We're going to kick you to death. Okay?! ... Okay?!

BOBBY Yeah, but—

JILL But nothing! You're the father of this child. My friend Tina does not sleep around. *She only sleeps with you!* Because she *loves you*. Don't ask me why. I don't know. No one knows. None of her friends know. Her mother doesn't know. I bet God doesn't even know. It's a mystery of the universe that even God doesn't fucking understand!

BOBBY I'm ... not feeling very well. Please let me go. You've said your thing. I ... just need to be let go now.

JILL You gonna run away? Running won't work, I'm telling you.

BOBBY No. I'm not running. I can't run. I'm sick. I just need some ... You're too close. I can't breathe. Please let me go. Please.

TINA Let him go. He's pretty pale. He passes out when he's that pale. I've seen it.

JILL I don't like you, Bobby.

BOBBY I know ... Please, just let me go. Okay? ... Okay?

JILL Yeah ... Okay.

[*She lets go of him. He goes to the picnic table. Sits*]

BOBBY [*to* JILL] Thanks.

TINA Put your head down. Between your legs.

BOBBY Yeah. [*he does*]

TINA [*to* JILL] He's got a condition. A kind of anemia. Had it since he
was a kid. He's got to take shots.

JILL I didn't know that.

TINA I think I told you once.

JILL I never listened when you were talking about him. I pretended to.
Just to be polite, you know.

TINA Oh.

JILL I mean I listened when it had to do with you. Your feelings and
stuff. But things that were just about him, I zoned out. You gotta
remember I've known this guy just about all my life. Longer than
you. Since kindergarten. And I've never seen anything in him that I
like.

TINA Not even a little?

JILL No.

TINA Come on. There must have been something. A little thing.

JILL No, not really.

TINA That's strange, eh. Because usually we like the same things. I
mean more than usually, really. Almost always.

JILL I remember when I found out you were going together. I
remember saying to myself, 'You gotta warn her about him.'

TINA Why didn't you.

JILL I did. I told you every selfish rotten thing I could remember him
doing.

TINA Love is blind.

JILL And deaf.

TINA And stupid. And you know what else love is? Love is dangerous.
I'll never love again. It's too dangerous. If I live through this I'm
going into seclusion. Even at work. I'll ask them to take me off the
counter and move me into the store room. I can do inventory. You
hardly have to see anyone doing inventory ... How you feeling,
Bobby.

BOBBY Who cares.

TINA Keep your head down. You look awful.

BOBBY I never understood why she didn't like me.

TINA Who.

BOBBY Her. Jill. I mean, what's so bad about me. Compared to other
people. She's hated me since we were five years old. It's ... just ...
weird.

TINA Keep your head down.

BOBBY Well, she said she wanted to kick me to death. I think it's weird. I don't know ...

TINA She just wants you to take responsibility.

BOBBY Everything's in my face ... and rushing into my head. You know? All of a sudden I'm a rotten shit. Some rotten little shitty thing that people want to kick to death ... I'm just trying to tie things together for myself. I'm really very young and things— [*shrugs. Gestures. Shakes his head and lowers it*]

TINA What.

BOBBY I've got things to say. But I can't say them in front of her. What's she doing here anyway. And what's she writing. I mean is she taking notes or something.

TINA What are you writing, Jill.

JILL It's an essay.

BOBBY Yeah, right. School hasn't even started.

JILL It's a multi-purpose essay. I know what courses I'm taking. It'll fit in somewhere. Maybe twice, even.

BOBBY Well, great. I've got all these hard things to say to you and your friend the university student is just gonna lie there and write an essay.

TINA What kind of things.

BOBBY Things to ... things to just say to you, I guess. You're pregnant. So ... well ... okay. Right. Okay. So I ... need to ... what I need to say about that ... I don't know. Ah, fuck it. She can stay. What's the difference.

TINA No, she'll go. You can go, Jill. Is that okay.

JILL Is it okay with you.

TINA Yeah. I guess.

JILL You're sure?

TINA Yeah. You can go ... But ...

JILL What.

TINA Not home. Can you just go for a walk. Don't leave altogether I mean. I don't know. Maybe ... you could just wait over by that tree.

JILL Ah. No. Bad idea. Hookers hang around trees. Some guy will take me for a hooker. Come up to me. Piss me off. I'll have to kill him ... How about I go over to the store. Get something. A Coke or something.

TINA Yeah. And then come back.

BOBBY She doesn't have to come back. I'll walk you home if that's what you're worried about.

TINA Maybe I won't want you to walk me home, Bobby. There's no guarantee.

JILL You want a Coke?

TINA Sure.

JILL What about him. Should I get him a Coke.

TINA You want a Coke, Bobby?

BOBBY She doesn't want to get me one.

TINA She offered.

BOBBY Yeah, but she doesn't really want to. I don't know why she offered. Probably so she could say something crappy to me if I said yes. Something like 'Get it yourself.'

JILL Ah, for chrissake. You want a Coke or not?

BOBBY Diet Coke.

JILL Diet Coke. [*laughs*] Jesus ... See ya.

[JILL *leaves*]

BOBBY See? Just cause I wanted a Diet Coke, she makes a thing about it. She laughs that way she does. She's been laughing at me like that since we were five years old. Shit, I'm haunted by her. It's like she knows something about me even I don't know. Something really rotten, I guess ... What is it. Do you know what it is she knows that I ... don't.

TINA Bobby. This isn't—

BOBBY No, it's all tied together. I think it is. It's a feeling I've got. Her attitude towards me has something to do with my attitude towards myself or something. And that's gotta have something to do with why I'm not ... you know, myself really. I mean my better self. I mean myself really about you and ... you know ... it ... if it, you know, the ... I mean I'm not saying you're lying but are you sure you're ...

TINA I'm sure. I went to a doctor.

BOBBY And he was sure.

TINA She. Yes. It's due in February.

BOBBY Ah, Jesus ... Ahhh ... Jesus ... [*puts his head between his legs*]

TINA Are you all right.

BOBBY Am I all right … Am I all right … No. No, I'm not all right.
Definitely not. I'm scared shitless. [*gets up. Starts to pace*] Come on.
Come on, get a hold of yourself, Bobby. Come on, man. [*stops
suddenly*] Shit. That's right. You're right. I'm a coward. Holy fuck.
How'd you know that. She told you, didn't she. Jill told you. That's
the thing she knows. And she told you. And she's right. I'm a
fucking coward. Holy fuck. I don't even care about you I'm so
scared. I want to, I want to care about you. But really I don't. Holy
fuck. I'm scum!

TINA Is this a trick.

BOBBY What.

TINA What are you pulling. Am I supposed to feel sorry for you.

BOBBY Hey, look. I'm scum. I'm just telling you.

TINA I think it's a trick.

BOBBY It just came to me. Whatya mean a trick.

TINA If it's not a trick what is it.

BOBBY It's … nothing. It's what I am. I'm just telling you.

TINA Why.

BOBBY Whatya mean why. It just came to me.

TINA I think you think it's a way out. You tell me you're scum,
cowardly scum, and I just write you off. Let you off the hook. Is
that what you're doing.

BOBBY I … don't think so.

TINA Whatya mean you don't think so.

BOBBY Well, if I'm real scum I'd pull anything wouldn't I. I might not
even know what I was pulling. I'd just be doing it because that's the
way a scum works. I mean a scum would want off the hook, there's
no doubt about that.

TINA You prick! I can't believe I'm even listening to this. What is this
garbage. We're not going down this road. Forget it. What do you
think I am. Some martyr or something. You think I'll just write
you off and take it all on my shoulders. Say to myself 'Bad choice,
Tina. He was just a mistake. Well, live and learn. On with my life.'
No way. What kind of scum would pretend to be a scum. Jesus …

BOBBY Look. I'm under pressure. I'm not sure I'm saying what … my
head isn't— Look, okay. I had plans. I was going to go back to
school. I didn't tell you that, I know. But I was talking to my dad.

TINA Shut up. The hell with you. What about me. And the baby.

What about the baby.

BOBBY The baby?

TINA The baby. The baby!

BOBBY Wow. It's not a baby yet. Don't call it a baby. You'll get attached to it.

TINA Whatya mean by that. I said whatya mean.

BOBBY Nothing. I don't know.

TINA Abortion. You're thinking abortion.

BOBBY I'm not thinking anything.

TINA Liar. You are.

BOBBY I'm not. I'm not thinking anything. And anything I'm thinking I'm not understanding. Come on. Give me a break.

TINA Go to hell. Go away. I've changed my mind and I want you out of my sight. That's what you wanted. You got it. Piss off.

BOBBY Wait a minute.

TINA Wait for what.

BOBBY A minute. I never said—

TINA All that cowardly scum talk. That's what you wanted.

BOBBY I was thinking out loud. You know, trying to ... trying to understand my ... you know, feelings. I've got ... you know, feelings too. I was just trying to understand them.

TINA Yeah, right.

BOBBY No, really. I felt like scum so I started thinking I *was* scum. I mean I was feeling bad anyway. Feeling bad about ...

TINA What.

BOBBY The thing. The thing that happened at the party ... in Jill's kitchen. I mean we never really talked about that.

TINA You wanna talk about it now?

BOBBY Not really. But I was feeling bad about that. And you and Jill were in my face about that. I'm not blaming you but ... Anyway. So I felt like scum. And then I thought if you feel like scum, maybe you *are* scum. And then she tells me you're pregnant. Wham! [*he hits himself on the head*] Wham wham wham! But anyway ... Well, I don't want to go. I want to ... you know stay here with you. Look, I just want to sit down for a minute. And figure out what I want to say to you. I know I want to say something. I just need to figure out what it is.

[*He looks at her. She shrugs. Sits next to him. Pause*]

My jacket.

TINA What?

BOBBY Where's my jacket. I thought I brought it.

TINA I don't think so.

BOBBY I need a smoke. I think they're in my jacket.

TINA Are you gonna say you want to go home and get your jacket.

BOBBY That wouldn't be a good idea?

TINA Not really.

BOBBY Okay. Well ... But I need a smoke.

TINA Yeah, you need a smoke. Maybe you need a drink too. Maybe you need to take some heavy drugs. Maybe you need to meet a rich girl with big breasts and live in a condo in Hawaii for the rest of your life. Tough. You're here. What you've got is what you've got. Now if you've got something to say to me say it.

BOBBY I'm going to.

TINA When.

BOBBY Now.

[*Pause*]

TINA Hey, Bobby. Now is like ... now. Now isn't soon. It's right away.

BOBBY Yeah but—

TINA Speak!

BOBBY Speak? Speak ... Speak.

TINA Speak! Tell me about us. And the baby. How it's going to be. What we're going to do! What do you want to do!

BOBBY I don't know what I want to do. I only know what I was going to do! I was ... going to break up with you.

[*They are just looking at each other*]

TINA Yeah?

BOBBY I ... was going to break up with you. I had that in my mind. It's been coming. It was in the back of my mind and then ... it was in the front.

TINA Yeah?

BOBBY For a few weeks.

TINA For a few weeks? Really.

BOBBY Because ... because, well, I've been looking around, you know. I found myself looking around at ... others ... and thinking, hey, they look nice. Why can't I be ... with them too. I mean look at the way they dress, it's nice.

TINA I can't believe you're telling me this.

BOBBY Me either.

TINA I mean you're making me sick.

BOBBY Sure. Me too. It's sickening. I was sick about it. I've been sick about it for months.

TINA Months? Now it's months.

BOBBY Maybe not months. Weeks. A month ... and a half maybe.

TINA You've wanted to be with other people for a month and a half?

BOBBY But I was sick about it. Because I was with you. And because I was with you and I wanted them I started thinking maybe we shouldn't ... you and I shouldn't ... maybe I should just ... You see, that's why I went into the kitchen with what's-her-name.

TINA What's-her-name?

BOBBY Yeah ... What's ... her name.

[TINA *gets up*]

TINA You don't know her name? You don't even know her fucking name.

BOBBY Who cares about her name. I went into the kitchen with her because I was trying to let loose, I think. I didn't care ... about you and me. I just wanted to see if I could let loose. So I—

TINA Her name is Leah. Leeeee ... ahhhhhhh!

BOBBY Look, don't lose it. Try to stay calm. I'm trying to explain.

TINA Leeeee! Ahhhhh! Say it!

BOBBY Yeah. Okay. Leah. Okay? I said it. Okay?

TINA Sure. What else.

BOBBY What.

[*She moves really close to his face*]

TINA Do you ... have ... something else ... to ... say ... to ... me.

BOBBY Look, you're gonna hit me or something. I know that's what you're leading up to ... But it won't do any good because—

TINA I'm fine. I'm not planning to do anything to you.

BOBBY Sure you are. I know you.

TINA Yeah? You know me. Really? Well, maybe you know me like I know you. And right now I'm thinking I know nothing about you.

BOBBY You know lots about me. I'm basically still me. The guy you know.

TINA You're a child. I thought you were a man.

BOBBY Please don't start on that child-man stuff. That just drives me

463

nuts. I was talking to a guy at work. A guy in shipping. He's got a girlfriend who's into that child-man thing. She's always on him about it. 'Don't be a child. Be a man.' What. Did you guys all get counselling on that. Is that a thing you were taught to say. That's what the guy in shipping thinks. We were talking and—

TINA Hey, hey. Whoa! ... I don't know where you're going with this, but it's no place useful. I wanna talk about what happened.

BOBBY Yeah, but you started—

TINA You got bored with the sex. That's what happened.

BOBBY I never said that.

TINA That's basically what you said. How could you get bored with our sex. It was ... I thought it was wonderful. Jesus it was *love* and sex. And you said it was ... well, really you never said anything except great things about it.

BOBBY I was never bored. I mean I was always afraid I'd *get* bored. And I never did. But I couldn't stop being afraid that I would.

TINA Yeah. Afraid. Like a child. You're a child.

BOBBY [*throwing his arms in the air*] Okay, okay! I'm a child! And you're an adult! You're all grown up. I mean, come on. That's the problem. You're a hundred years old to me. You might as well be. You've just got it all figured out.

TINA Oh, right.

BOBBY Sure you do. Compared to me you do. You just attacked me like an adult attacks a kid. And even when you're not attacking, even when you're ... when you're loving me it's like you've got it all in place ... you've got the picture all finished and I'm just a nice part of that picture.

TINA Really. You figured all this out with your friend the shipper?

BOBBY No. Come on.

TINA Look, just tell me what it's supposed to mean. This, I've got the picture and you're just part of the picture stuff.

BOBBY Well, it makes sense of what I'm thinking now.

TINA You're thinking something now?

BOBBY Yeah, I'm thinking ... Listen, I gotta say this. This is what I'm thinking so I gotta say it without you hitting me.

TINA Well, take your chances.

BOBBY Well, I'm gonna have to, aren't I. Because what I'm thinking is important to say.

TINA Really.

BOBBY Yeah. Because what I'm thinking is that basically being, you know, pregnant is ... all right with you.

TINA Really.

BOBBY Because, well, overall it's what you wanted.

TINA You saying I planned it?

BOBBY No. No. I'm not saying you planned it. I'm saying you wanted it.

TINA Oh. Sure. Right. So that's the story you'll tell. The little bitch was so desperate to have a kid with me she poked holes in my rubbers. Your dad will believe that no problem. He's a bigger asshole than you are.

BOBBY Shit! I'm not saying that. I'm saying—well, what else do you want in life. You left school. School was nothing to you. It wasn't life. Not enough of life, anyway.

TINA Well, it wasn't. It was bullshit. For me it was bullshit.

BOBBY I know. For me too. Sort of. I know. But really, not like you thought it was. You knew it was bullshit because you knew there was this ... this fuck ... other thing! Yeah! This other thing. Just ... what did you call it. You had a list. You know, a simple job you liked ... and ... and—

TINA A man to love. Some kids. A few good friends. A nice place to live.

BOBBY Yeah. That's it. That's the list. That's Tina's list!

TINA It's a good list. It's full of real things. What's wrong with it. You got a better one? Oh ... oh you do don't you. You've got a bigger better list all of a sudden. You've got dreams or something. Big ones. Is that what you're telling me. You've got *ambition* all of a sudden?

BOBBY No, I've got no ambition. What's that mean.

TINA Maybe you want to be a lawyer, an architect, a doctor even.

BOBBY No. No, I don't. None of that's for me. I know that. All I'm saying is it's *your* list. It's what *you* want. And it's not just that it's what you want, it's that you can *say* it's what you want.

TINA So say what it is *you* want. Come on. Say it. Try to say it. Maybe you can. Maybe you'll surprise us both. Maybe you're more than a dog in heat. Maybe you're a person. With a person's brain.

BOBBY Ah, what's the point ...

[*Pause*]

TINA I'm waiting. Come on, Bobby. Say something human. Show me you don't have the brain of a dog.

BOBBY [*sighs*] Brain of a dog. Great.

TINA I'm waiting. Seriously. I really am.

BOBBY Yeah ... Yeah, you're waiting. You're very patient. You're very understanding. You're standing there all ... complete or something. Everything's figured out. You've got your first kid already inside you and all you need is for me to get with it here. Just need ol' Bobby to say the right thing, put his name on a piece of paper, sign on board for the rest of his stinking life.

TINA Okay! That's enough. I'm history. [*starts off*]

BOBBY Wait a minute.

[*He grabs her*]

TINA Let me go.

BOBBY We're not finished.

TINA Wrong!

[*She takes a swing at him. He blocks it with his arm*]

BOBBY No. Screw that.

[*He grabs her*]

You're staying. We're going to—

TINA Look, take your hands off me, Bobby. [*struggling to get free*]

BOBBY No way. We've started and we're going to—

TINA Look, don't touch me. You've got your hands on me. I want them off.

BOBBY Come on, Tina.

TINA No! You lied to me! About everything. That's all that matters! You jerk! Everything ... anything I ever said about life or what I wanted in life you agreed with. You lying jerk! You're just weak. And ... and ... [*starts to cry*] Let me go! Let me go!

[JILL *comes running on. Yells. Drops the bag she is carrying. Rushes over. And tackles Bobby. He falls. She lands on top of him*]

BOBBY Hey. What the hell.

JILL You asshole!

[*They are on the ground. She is on top of him. Hitting him.* TINA *is sitting down. Crying. Pulling grass furiously*]

BOBBY Come on. Stop it. Jesus!

JILL You wanna beat someone up? Beat me up. Come on!

BOBBY Hey. I wasn't—

JILL Asshole. Coward!

BOBBY Tina. Tina, get her off.

JILL What's wrong with you. She's pregnant.

[*She is hitting him. He is trying to crawl away*]

BOBBY I wasn't hurting—

JILL You don't hit pregnant girls. You don't hit girls, period.

BOBBY Tina! Tell her! Look. Knock it off. I wasn't doing anything.

JILL Yes, you were!

BOBBY No, I wasn't.

JILL I saw you asshole!

[*Now she is standing. Kicking him as he crawls away*]

BOBBY Ah. Fuck. Knock it off. Leave me alone.

JILL Piece of shit.

BOBBY Jesus. Ouch! Look. Leave me alone. If you don't stop I'm gonna get mad.

JILL Go ahead. Get mad. I can hardly wait.

BOBBY I mean it. Shit! Ouch!

JILL Yeah. How's it feel! How's it feel! I said, how's it feel.

[BOBBY *jumps to his feet*]

BOBBY It hurts! It hurts okay?! Now knock it off or I'll rip your fuckin' face off!

[*Pause*]

JILL You'll what.

[*She is approaching him slowly*]

BOBBY Look. Just stay away from me.

JILL You're gonna rip my face off. Is that what you said.

BOBBY I ... don't want to hurt you.

[JILL *is still moving toward him. He is backing up*]

JILL Do I look scared. Look at me. Do you think I'm afraid of you. Do you!

[*She pushes him*]

BOBBY Ah, Jesus. Okay. I give up. [*sits*] Kick me. Kick me to fucking death. Go ahead. You'll be doing me a favour. [*starts to cry*] Go ahead!

[*He lies back.* JILL *looks at him. Shrugs*]

JILL Piece of shit.

[*She goes over to* TINA]

You okay, Tee?

TINA [*crying*] Great!

[JILL *sits next to* TINA. *Puts her arms around her.* BOBBY *is sobbing quite loudly now*]

JILL Hey. Shut up. You're gonna attract a crowd. Jesus. Listen to him. I've never heard a guy cry like that.

TINA Yeah ... yeah. It's something, eh. He cried like that after the first time we made love.

JILL You're kidding.

TINA No. It's why I fell in love with him. [*starts to cry*]

JILL Come on, honey. He's not worth it.

BOBBY [*sits up*] I am worth it! Shit! I am worth it! I am!

JILL Shut up.

BOBBY I want an apology from you!

JILL Yeah? For what.

BOBBY Whatya mean for what. For attacking me. I didn't do anything. I wasn't hurting her.

JILL I saw you.

BOBBY You saw shit, you crazy bitch.

JILL [*leaps to her feet*] What did you call me.

[*She takes a step towards* BOBBY]

Man, you're a glutton for punishment, aren't you.

BOBBY Tell her! Tell her, Tina. Come on!

TINA Yeah ... Yeah, I just wanted to go. He was trying to stop me. That's all.

JILL He was using force.

BOBBY Come on. I just wanted her to—

JILL You had your hands on her. You were using force!

BOBBY Just a little!

JILL That's too much!

BOBBY But I needed her to stay.

JILL But she wanted to go! If she wanted to go, she should have been able to go. And no one should have tried to stop her! Get it?!

BOBBY But I ... But I ... Ah, forget it. I give up.

JILL You say that but I don't think you mean it. Maybe you should though. Maybe you should just give up and crawl away. Throw yourself off a bridge.

BOBBY You'd like that, wouldn't you.

JILL You know I would.

TINA He can't. He's got big dreams. He's got a big new life he's going to live.

JILL Yeah. [*laughs*] He told you that?

TINA Sure did. He's really very young, you know. But he's got a future. I mean if I don't mess it up.

BOBBY I never said that.

TINA And in this future are all kinds of girls and women who dress nice who he's going to do it with.

BOBBY I never said that either.

JILL I bet you were thinking it.

BOBBY Well, I wasn't.

TINA I don't know. Maybe he's been watching too much television. Maybe he's got us all confused with those kids on those shows who live near a beach. And drive nice cars. And whose parents have big houses. He's pretty ... you know ... impressionable. Did you get me a Coke?

JILL Yeah.

[JILL *goes looking for the bag she dropped*]

TINA Is that it, Bobby. You having TV dreams?

BOBBY I don't know what you're talking about.

TINA Your father drives a cab. You know that, eh. You haven't forgotten.

BOBBY I don't think you understood what I was saying. I think you got it wrong somehow.

TINA Maybe. Maybe not.

[JILL *hands* TINA *a can of Coke*]

Thanks ... Did you get one for him.

JILL You want him to have it?

TINA Sure.

JILL You're a saint.

[JILL *throws* BOBBY *a can of Coke. He catches it*]

Say thanks.

BOBBY Thanks. I ... wanted Diet Coke.

JILL I don't buy Diet Coke. Under any circumstances. For anyone.

BOBBY I can't drink this. I might be borderline diabetic.

JILL Yeah? Drink it anyway. Find out. If you go into shock I'll get you to the hospital real fast. That's a promise.

BOBBY I bet.

[*They all pull back their tabs. Drink.* **BOBBY** *groans*]

TINA What's wrong. You sick?

BOBBY No ... Shit. Look at that. I almost sat on a needle. Shit.

TINA Don't touch it.

BOBBY I'm not touching it. I thought they were supposed to clean this place up. Didn't they hire people to clean this place up.

JILL No.

BOBBY I thought they were supposed to.

JILL Well, they didn't.

BOBBY Shit. It's depressing. Look at it. We can't just leave it there.

TINA Don't touch it.

BOBBY I'm not!

TINA I'll get rid of it.

BOBBY No way.

TINA Well, you're not touching it.

BOBBY Yeah well, neither are you.

JILL Ah, for chrissake.

[**JILL** *gets the bag she brought the Cokes in. Goes over. Puts it around the syringe. Picks it up. Puts it in the trash can*]

BOBBY Thanks.

JILL Yeah.

[*They all drink*]

TINA What was I saying to you, Bobby.

BOBBY When.

TINA Before ... something about ... something.

BOBBY Something I didn't understand the point of ...

TINA Oh, yeah. About what your dad does for a living.

BOBBY Yeah. So what? What's that got to do with anything. I mean if you're saying you can't want stuff because your parents don't have stuff, I don't get it. That's not what I was talking about before, anyway. But I still don't get it. 'Cause really I could be anything I wanted. I could go back to school and ... well, nothing that you needed math for ... but lots of other stuff. I don't know. Jobs even. Just jobs better than the one I've got. Better than any job my dad ever had. I could do that.

TINA So do it. Who's stopping you.

BOBBY But that's not what I was saying. I'm just saying now it's wrong for you to say we can't want more because of who we are or something. What I was saying before was really ... only that I was ... young and I didn't know what I wanted ... or didn't, you know ... want.

TINA Stop wanting anything. That's my advice to you. That's my advice to me too.

BOBBY I'm sorry, but that's bad advice.

TINA It's in the future. Wanting is tomorrow's stuff. I mean until it happens it's not real. It's not useful. Whatever it is. Ah. I can't explain it to you. You're too stupid.

BOBBY No, I'm not.

TINA Listen, all I'm saying ... all I wanted to say to you is ... Jesus, Bobby ... [*starts to cry a little*]

JILL Don't beg him. Whatever you do don't beg.

TINA I just wanted to tell him one thing really. Can I just tell you one thing, Bobby.

BOBBY Yeah.

TINA Just one thing I really mean, I really believe in. Can I Bobby.

BOBBY Yeah ... yeah.

TINA Yeah. Well, it's this ... It'd be okay. You. And me. And the baby. It'd be okay. The three of us. We'd have a life. That would be ... enough. Because really there's nothing else ... better. I believe that.

BOBBY I know you do.

TINA Yeah. I know you know ... But I'm right. I believe that too.

BOBBY You're probably right. I don't know.

TINA Do you love me, Bobby ... I know you do. You weren't thinking about breaking up with me because you don't love me, were you.

BOBBY No. I mean ... I don't know for sure but—

TINA Yes, you do. You don't have to say you don't know when I know you do. I'm not that stupid. It's impossible I could be that stupid. I know when I'm loved and when I'm not loved. So just say you love me, Bobby. What's that gonna cost you.

BOBBY I love you.

TINA Do you mean it.

BOBBY I think I mean it.

TINA Jesus! Come on. You gotta mean it. What's it gonna cost you to mean it. Even if we never see each other again. You love me. We have fun. We have good sex. We have great sex, Jill. I've told you that, haven't I.

JILL I don't remember.

TINA It's true. Isn't it, Bobby. Tell her.

BOBBY I don't want to tell her.

JILL I don't want him to tell me either.

TINA All I'm saying is it won't get better for you, Bobby. I know that. And I know you don't know that. Your head is just full of wondering. Wondering if this. Wondering if that.

BOBBY Wondering can be important. You gotta wonder.

JILL Oh, for God's sake. What are you both going on about. We need decisions here. It's hard facts time. She's not going to get an abortion. We all know that. If anyone here doesn't know that he's an asshole. She's going to keep the kid. She's going to be a single mother. The only question is are you going to help her or is she going to be a single mother on welfare who lives in a rotten little basement apartment and never gets any sleep and who has a life that's basically rat shit and a future that's worse.

TINA Jesus. [*starts to cry*]

JILL I'm sorry. I didn't mean to upset you. I was just making a point.

TINA But you could be right.

JILL Nah. Really I was just making a point. But it had to be made.

TINA No but ... no but ... Remember how hot it was last week. It was really hot. Anyway, one day last week about four in the afternoon, I saw a mother and her kid downtown. She was our age. And the kid was about ... I don't know ... a year. And it was asleep on her. She was waiting for a bus. I guess they'd been out, maybe to the doctor I don't know. But she looked whacked. The kid was just sprawled over her shoulder. It was sticky hot. She had a bag full of stuff she was carrying. She looked like she hadn't slept in weeks maybe. And the kid is all dead weight on her. Asleep. But holding her real tight anyway. She's just standing there like a zombie in that heat holding her kid and waiting and waiting for that fucking bus. And I knew, I just knew they were alone. There was just the two of them. And when they got home there'd still be just the two of them. Having their supper. Their bath. Going to bed. I mean I couldn't take my eyes off her and I was feeling ... well ... There was a great love. A great, great love between them. Jesus. You could just feel it. But also ... well ... sadness, eh. Sadness was in the air too. I mean I don't know if she was sad or if I was sad from watching her. Maybe she wasn't sad, maybe she was just so … tired she wasn't feeling anything. Yeah, I don't know but maybe I was feeling all these things especially the sadness and she was just so tired she wasn't feeling anything … Not even the love. [*gets up. Wipes herself off*] Well, that's life. Take it on the chin and ask for more. That's what my mom says.

JILL Really? She says that?

TINA Almost every day.

BOBBY You told your mom yet? About being pregnant?

TINA I thought I'd tell you first, Bobby.

BOBBY Why.

TINA Well, thinking about it now I haven't got a lousy clue why.

JILL Maybe she thought you could tell her mom together.

BOBBY Yeah … well, we could still do that … Are you gonna tell anyone else.

TINA Yeah, I'm gonna spread it around real fast … Is that what you're worried about.

BOBBY No … I was just asking.

TINA Yeah. Right. Well, I could tell my dad. But I don't know where he is. I might track him down though. Let him know there's still guys like him in the world.

BOBBY You mean me, right?

JILL No, she means the fucking Pope … Jesus.

BOBBY I was … ah, never mind. Look, I meant it when I said we could tell your mother together. Do you want to do that.

TINA I don't think so.

BOBBY Why not.

TINA What'd be the point.

BOBBY I'm the father. I know I've got responsibilities.

JILL Really. What are they.

BOBBY I was talking to her.

JILL So now you're talking to me. Tell me what you think your 'responsibilities' are.

BOBBY Being with her when she told her mom would be one. Giving her money would be another one.

JILL You just heard her talk about that mother and her kid waiting for the bus and *now* you're talking about money. I just stopped hating you, Bobby. You're scaring me now. You're really terrifying me.

BOBBY Yeah, right.

JILL Before I thought you were just a ... guy. Just another young stupid selfish guy.

BOBBY Yeah.

JILL But now you're my worst nightmare. You're the worst part of all the men in the world. And you're terrifying.

[*She goes to the picnic table. Sits*]

BOBBY [*to* TINA] What's she talking about.

TINA Ask her.

BOBBY No way. It's that weird thing she's got against me. And now she's got it against all the men in the world too. You think I'm gonna ask her what it is? You think I'm nuts? It's probably really rotten. I don't want to know what it is. I just want her to be nicer to me for chrissake. I'm trying to be nice here. I'm trying to do something here. I said I'd talk to your mother with you ... Okay. Wait a minute.

[*He walks over to* JILL]

You think I didn't get upset when she talked about that young mother and her kid. You think I didn't see Tina and the ... baby ... didn't see them in my head doing that exact same thing? And living somewhere alone. I did. I saw where they lived even. It was ... shitty. They lived in a shitty place.

TINA I won't live in a shitty place. No way.

JILL So that's what the deal with the money was about.

BOBBY Whatya mean. Sure. I guess. I couldn't let them live in a shitty place.

JILL You'd save them from that, eh.

BOBBY Yeah.

TINA I'm not living in a shitty place.

BOBBY That's what I'm saying.

JILL Terrifying.

BOBBY What's terrifying. How the hell is that terrifying. What the fuck are you talking about!

JILL You think it's your responsibility to save her, is that right.

BOBBY Save her from that. Yeah, I'd save her from that.

JILL You think that's your job here. That's your place in all this. You can just stand back and decide what she needs—money probably—and then throw it at her. You think you've got the final

474

decision about where and how she lives. If she succeeds or fails. If she lives okay or she lives like rat shit. And that's terrifying! What the hell is wrong with you.

BOBBY I'm just trying to be nice!

TINA I'm not going to live in a shitty place!

BOBBY Jesus! I'm not gonna let you live in a shitty place!

JILL It's not up to you if she lives in a shitty place!

[**BOBBY** *starts to move around. Frantically*]

BOBBY Jesus! Christ! What?! What am I supposed to say here. Everything I say is wrong. I can't talk about money or anything. What am I supposed to do. You got something in your head for me to do? Just tell me and I'll do it! Shit! What! What?! What am I supposed to do.

JILL Fuck off and die ... You could do that.

BOBBY You first! You first! Shut up! Shut up. Fuck off. Fall down. Die. And shut up for fucking ever! What is your problem. You're driving me crazy. Don't you think I'm trying here. I've got a big thing here I'm trying to deal with. So just knock it off! Jesus. Ahh. [*starts to shake violently*] Ah shit, look at me, man. I'm outta control. [*to* **JILL**] Look what you're doing to me. I'm outta control here. I'm sick or something. Are you happy now.

JILL A bit.

BOBBY Shit. Look at me. Something's happening to me. And I don't even know what it is. [*to himself*] Brain of a dog ... brain of a ... dog.

JILL [*to* **TINA**] Brain of a what?

TINA Dog. It's something I said to him. Sit down, Bobby.

BOBBY Sit down, Bobby. Say something, Bobby. Go away, Bobby.

TINA Sit down, Bobby. Put your head between your legs. Take deep breaths.

BOBBY Okay. Deep breaths. Yeah.

TINA Do it. Come on.

BOBBY Okay. Okay. [*whimpers, mutters to himself*] Outta control ... outta control ... brain of a dog, outta ... control. [*drops down. Puts his head between his legs. Begins to inhale and exhale deeply*]

JILL This guy's a physical wreck. Even if he did marry you he'd be dead in ten years anyway.

TINA That's kind of cruel.

JILL You think so? I could lay off him if you want.

TINA Nah. I like the way you talk to him. Just don't make fun of his sickness. It's the one thing he can't help.

JILL Sure. Whatever you say. Anything you want. I mean that.

TINA You're a great friend.

[*She goes to* JILL. *Hugs her*]

The best.

JILL You too.

[*They hug again.* BOBBY *is watching them*]

I'll always be there for you. Whatever you need. Ask. I'll do my best.

TINA I know.

[*They hug.* BOBBY *groans*]

JILL What?!

TINA Another needle?

BOBBY No ... No ... that ... [*groans. Gestures toward them. Groans*] I don't want to be the enemy. I mean look at you guys. You're nice to each other. Really nice. And I'm like ... the hated enemy ... Look, you might not believe this but I need something right now. I'm looking at you two and I'm ... well, I guess what I need is *that*.

JILL 'That.' What are you talking about. What's ... 'that.'

BOBBY That ... hug. [*gestures*] Hug.

JILL You need a hug.

BOBBY Yeah well, I'm not totally sure. But I think I do.

TINA Who from.

BOBBY You ... And her.

JILL You need a hug from me.

BOBBY Well, you're hugging her. I see what you're doing. It looks nice. I think I want it done to me. And you're here. So yeah.

JILL Maybe I pushed him too far. I was just trying to shake him up. Get him in touch with reality. Maybe I've pushed him over the edge.

BOBBY There's nowhere else I could go for one. My mother I guess, but ... she's so worried about my dad ... He's not well. Not that you care. I'm not even sure I care. And I don't have a friend I could ask for one. They're not that kind of guy, my friends. They'd think I'd gone you know ... gay ... They're nice guys but they don't ... touch each other.

TINA Bobby, is something wrong. Are you feeling light-headed or something. It's just a hug. Why are you going on about it when our lives are falling apart here.

JILL [*laughs*] No, this is good. He's talking about his tribe. Usually you can't get them to talk about their tribes. It's not allowed. All you can ever hear about them is where they go. To the mall. To the bar. To the track. So this is good. So Bobby, your tribe sounds pretty basic. Nice guys. But no hugging. You can go just about anywhere and do just about anything but you can't touch each other. If you touch another tribe member you're a pussy or a queer and you're out of the tribe. Is that basically it … I mean they don't stomp you or anything. They don't scar your face to leave the mark of an outcast. They just say get outta here you weak little faggot or something like that.

BOBBY God, man. All I was saying was it looked nice. That hug. It seemed warm and you know, cozy. Talking about tribes. Jesus. I saw the hug. I got a longing for the hug. The hug was all I was talking about, man.

JILL Listen to him. He's gone nuts. His brain is soup. He's drowning in his own messed-up thoughts.

BOBBY Yeah well, who's the one who was talking about tribes.

TINA It's easy to hug, Bobby. You're making it sound like it's some huge magical thing beyond your powers.

BOBBY That's not what I meant. I meant it was a thing about women. One of the things you can get from women that I like. The cozy thing. I'd miss that. I guess if I just slept around I'd never really have that. You see, that's the thing. Women offer you one or the other. The hot thing. Or the cozy thing.

JILL Ah. Now he's back on track.

BOBBY But you can't have both. No way! It's not allowed. That's a fact! You can have it hot and sexy or warm and cozy. It's a choice.

JILL Yeah, he's got a hold of his thing again. He's stroking it good now.

BOBBY No sir, you can't have both! Shit!

TINA Sure you can have both.

BOBBY I want to be with you, Tina! That's the truth. It is. But I don't want to be with *just* you, Tina. That's also the truth. Really. It's taking guts to say this, Tina. I'm trying to be a man about this.

JILL Ah, shit.

BOBBY I mean I'm trying to face it. Face to … face.

TINA You know your friend Nicky? That guy you play hockey with.

BOBBY What about him.

TINA Every time I see him I get wet.

JILL Bingo! Bullseye! Ding! A thousand points! [*laughs*]

BOBBY [*to* TINA] You get what.

TINA In my pants. Wet. And hot.

BOBBY Holy fuck.

TINA Really wet and hot.

BOBBY Holy fuck! Don't say that. What are you doing. You don't have to talk like that.

TINA It's a chemistry thing. Sometimes he looks at me and I can't breathe.

BOBBY Jesus, you're gonna keep talking about it.

TINA I mean the guy, there's just something about him. He looks at me. My nipples get hard.

BOBBY [*sort of writhing. Covering his ears*] I'm not listening to this shit. No way.

TINA He looks at me and I go home and think about him. I try not to. I'm guilty at first because he's your friend. He's your left winger. But then I think, what's the harm, I'm just thinking. So you know I just think it all the way through. In my head, I mean. In my head I get him in my bedroom. Take off his clothes.

BOBBY Ah Jesus, Tina. Come on.

JILL Keep going, girl.

TINA I gotta keep going. I'm getting excited just talking about him. No way I can stop now.

BOBBY Jesus.

TINA I get him naked. He's got a great ass. He's really, you know … what's the word.

JILL [*shrugs*] Big?

TINA Really big.

JILL Really big?

TINA The biggest.

BOBBY Oh, yeah. Right. Gotta be the biggest. Great. Well, who cares. I'm not small you know. I know that. I'm okay about that. I may have the brain of a dog, but I don't have, you know, the dick of a dog.

TINA Oh, be quiet.

JILL That brain of a dog comment made a real impression, eh.

BOBBY I'm just saying if you're doing a number on me you can't do it on the dick.

TINA Knock it off! This isn't about you and your dick. It's about me.

JILL It's about you and Nicky's dick.

TINA Right. So where was I. In my head, I mean.

JILL In your head he's naked. In mine too.

TINA Yeah?

JILL So keep going.

TINA So I get naked too. I take off my clothes real slow. And while I'm doing it, he gets hard. I want to hold it. It looks powerful. It's a powerful hard thing he's got. He's gotta put it somewhere. I'm wondering where should I let him put it first.

BOBBY Come on! Come on! Okay, okay okay okay. I get it. Okay? I get the number you're doing. You don't have to make this shit up. You don't think things like that.

TINA Listen. I'm being honest about this. It's taking guts but it's only fair I tell you cause you told me.

BOBBY But you made it up!

TINA Wrong! Your friend Nicky turns me on. And I could name three other guys we both know who turn me on. And once every few weeks or so I see some guy on the street who turns me on. And that's the facts! And now we both know the facts!

[BOBBY *puts his head between his legs*]

JILL Hey, Bob. You wanna hug?

BOBBY I'm gonna puke.

TINA [*shrugs. Looks at* JILL] I guess he really didn't know.

JILL Never entered his head.

TINA Hard to believe ... Come on, Bobby. Didn't it ever occur to you that maybe I could feel the same way you do about that stuff.

BOBBY No.

TINA Never?

BOBBY No.

TINA Well, now that you know, how do you feel.

BOBBY I told you. I wanna puke.

JILL Ah, grow up.

TINA Yeah, she's right. Throw up. Then grow up.

BOBBY Come on. How would you feel if I told you I wanted to do it with Jill.

TINA Do you.

BOBBY No.

TINA Then I'd wonder why you were lying.

BOBBY Suppose I really did want to.

TINA Do you.

BOBBY No!

TINA Then what's the point!

BOBBY You don't get it.

TINA No, you don't get it. I'm trying to deal with real things here. Real feelings. If you've got any real feelings we can talk about them. If you want to screw Jill we'll deal with it. If you want to become a lawyer we'll work out a way you can do that. If you want to be a father to our baby we'll make that happen. But if you think you're the only one in serious confusion here, if you think you're the only one who wants more than one thing, maybe a few things that don't go together, we're not going anywhere useful with this. You might as well just go home.

BOBBY I don't want to go home.

TINA No? Are you sure.

BOBBY Pretty sure.

TINA So what *do* you want to do. Do you have any idea what you want to do.

BOBBY When.

TINA Now.

BOBBY No.

TINA But you don't wanna go home.

BOBBY No.

TINA Do you want us to leave you here alone.

BOBBY I don't know.

TINA Do you wanna keep talking.

BOBBY I don't know.

TINA Do you wanna have sex with Jill. Do you wanna think about having sex with Leee-ahhh! Do you wanna puke. Do you wanna tell me why you don't care if your dad's sick. Do you wanna tell me what you want to do with your life, you know just give me a little hint. Do you wanna know what *I'm* gonna do. Do you, Bobby. Do you wanna know even just a little what I'm gonna do.

BOBBY Yeah. I do.

TINA I'm going to have this baby.

BOBBY I knew that.

TINA Take some time off from the store. Have the baby. Get my mom to help out a bit. Go back to work. Bring up the baby. Hang out with my friends when I get the chance. That's about it.

JILL You left out having great sex.

TINA Yeah. Have some great sex, when I can, with ... whoever.

JILL Great guys. Maybe older guys.

TINA Whoever ...

BOBBY Nicky, probably.

JILL & TINA Ah, grow up!

[**BOBBY** *gets up. Brushes himself off*]

TINA You going somewhere?

BOBBY No.

TINA You look like you wanna go.

BOBBY Yeah. Well ...

TINA Go ahead.

BOBBY I'm not really sure what I—

TINA Look Bobby, you might as well go away. What are you gonna tell me if you stay. I've pretty much got the picture. All you can do now is lie. You can say you wanna marry me or something. And what an enormous stinking lie that'd be. I mean I guess you've come through this. We put a lot of pressure on you here. I was willing to do anything to keep you. Really I was ... But I've come through that. I don't feel that way anymore. I don't know why. But you can go. You can go that way. [*points*] And I'll go that other way. And we don't have to see each other ever again. You can send money if you want. Or not. I don't care.

JILL I do. Your mom will too.

TINA She's right. But I want you to know when you're in court for non-payment it won't be my idea. Because *we* were special to me. And anything less than special is shit. Pressure's off. Go home. Go on.

[*Pause*]

BOBBY Is this a trick.

TINA No. Go. It'll be all right.

BOBBY What'll be all right.

TINA Everything. Don't worry. You can just leave ... See ya. Take care of yourself.

[JILL *walks to* BOBBY. *Puts out her hand*]

JILL No hard feelings.

[BOBBY *just looks at her hand*]

Come on. Put it there.

[BOBBY *looks at them both*]

BOBBY What's goin' on.

TINA Nothing. It's over.

BOBBY What's over.

TINA Everything. You and me. Just forget it.

BOBBY Forget what.

TINA Everything.

[JILL *puts out her hand*]

JILL No hard feelings.

BOBBY What the hell is with you people. Whatya mean, it's over. Just like that, it's supposed to be over. You're fucking me around.

TINA No, I'm not.

JILL She means it. I mean it too.

BOBBY What. What do you mean.

JILL No hard feelings. It's over between us too.

BOBBY What's over. What's between us to be over.

JILL My lifelong hatred and disappointment in you. Fifteen years of bad feelings. You're out of her life. Means you're out of mine finally. Why hold a grudge. Come on. Shake. I'd feel better if you did.

BOBBY Really. Talk about weird shit. I'm supposed to shake your hand to end some weird rotten thing we've had since kindergarten that I never even understood. And then you're just gonna walk out of here with your friend who just happens to be carrying my baby inside her and that's the end of that. You're fucking me around. Aren't you. Aren't you fucking me around. And if you are, why. Why do this to me. I'm willing to reach an agreement here. That's really all I've been trying to do, you know. Reach an agreement. I never wanted an abortion. I never said I wanted an abortion so that must mean something.

TINA It means nothing. If I wanted an abortion. I'd get one. I wouldn't care what you thought about it.

BOBBY You wouldn't?

TINA Why should I.

BOBBY I don't know. But I guess ... well, I wasn't saying you should anyway. I was just trying to say something ... right. Saying I'd agree to whatever you want, whatever you say ... to just, you know, be there in some way. I never said I wouldn't be there for you, in some way, Tina. I never said that. So why are you doing this. Why are you saying it's over. It's like you're giving up.

TINA I told you. It was special. Now it's shit.

BOBBY I don't think it's shit. It might not be as special as it was but it's definitely not shit.

JILL Come on. Shake. Be a man!

BOBBY Put your fucking hand down. Stay away from me. Stop messing with me. Look, I know you're smarter than me. You always were. You go to university.

JILL Community college actually.

BOBBY The point is you're smarter than me.

JILL But who isn't.

BOBBY I just want you to stop messing with me. I'm just trying to be nice here.

TINA Nice doesn't cut it. Nice is shit. I wanted you to be brave and strong and grown up. I need someone strong and grown up.

BOBBY I'm trying to grow up. I wanted to grow up. That was always what I was aiming for. I didn't know I had to do it all of a sudden. I was hoping I'd get some time.

TINA You were braver when I first met you. You're weaker now. And younger too. I think you're going in the wrong direction.

JILL I think that too. If she keeps you around by the time the kid is born she'll be changing diapers for both of you.

BOBBY Look. I told you to shut up.

JILL Did you. When was that. I must have missed it. Tell me again. Come over here. And tell me. Come real close.

BOBBY This is a good thing for you, isn't it, Jill. This has gotta be the high point of your life so far, I bet. Getting to give me the gears. You're a sick person. That's what I think. I'm gonna stop wondering why you've been so rotten to me. I'm gonna stop wondering what's so rotten about me that's made you treat me like garbage and I'm gonna start thinking you did it just because you're mean and sick.

JILL Hey, didn't I offer my hand to you. Didn't I offer you the chance to make up, you asshole. All you had to do was leave.

BOBBY I'm not leaving. You leave.

JILL I'll leave when she leaves.

BOBBY Well, she's not leaving and neither am I.

TINA I think you should leave, Bobby.

BOBBY I'm not going anywhere!

TINA But it's over.

BOBBY Don't say it's over.

TINA But it is.

BOBBY You don't mean that.

TINA Yes, I do.

BOBBY How. How can you mean that. That's cold. That's so fucking cold. You're doing this like you're just closing a door or something. Something simple like closing a door. There, click it's closed. That simple. How can you get so cold, so fast. That's just ... mean. Yeah, it's mean. Don't be mean, Tina. I never was mean to you. Okay, I was selfish and I fucked around a bit. But I wasn't mean. Don't be mean, please. I hate it.

TINA I'm sorry. I'm not trying to be mean. I'm just being practical. You're not going to be any help to me. I can't see you being a useful part of my life, that's all.

BOBBY You're just saying that now. Because of how I am now. But how I am now isn't necessarily me. I mean I'm under pressure and—

TINA You handled the pressure okay. You protected yourself okay. You didn't commit yourself to anything here. You told me about the things you needed. The time. You told me about your dreams.

BOBBY Ah, don't start with the dream stuff. I never said anything about dreams. That was you.

TINA No. It was you. It was all about you. You you you.

BOBBY Ah, Jesus. That's just how it sounded. Come on. I was under attack.

TINA No, that's just how it sounded. I gave you opportunity. You could have said some stuff. You could have gone forward. Made a move. Got involved in the possibilities.

BOBBY What. You saying it was a test or something.

TINA I didn't mean it to be a test. But maybe it was. Maybe it was a test.

BOBBY Yeah. And I failed. Well, no surprise there. Now that you put it that way I get it. Just another failure. Just someone else to let down. Okay. I can live with that. That's no big deal. I've been doing that all my life.

JILL Ah, Jesus. [*to* TINA] You've opened up something pretty ugly here. We're not gonna have any fun with this at all. He's just gonna—

BOBBY Hey, it's just the truth, okay. I'm sorry if it's not entertaining enough for you. All I'm saying is the stinking truth. I'm a failure. Ask my dad, he'll tell you. Ask my foreman at work. But ask him fast because I probably won't last there very long. Ask any of the teachers I had. [*points to* TINA] Ask her mother. Her mother's not gonna be surprised I let her down. I know she expected it. I've felt her expecting disappointment from me ever since I met her. Ah, fuck it. It's just life. Who cares. I don't know. Maybe I didn't take it seriously enough. Or maybe I wasn't good enough to have a life in the first place. Yeah, maybe I'm good enough to live but not good enough to have a life worth living. Now that's confusing. Where's my jacket. Did I bring anything else. Ah, who cares. Okay, I'm outta here. Good luck. Good luck to you, Tina. I give up. So what's new, eh. [*starts off muttering*] I give up. What's new about that. You thought it was sex and good times, Bobby. Well wrong! Okay, live and learn. Live and learn. What. Learn what. I don't know. Grow up. [*stops*] Yeah. Grow up, asshole ... Stupid little asshole.

[BOBBY *is just standing there. Head lowered. Muttering to himself 'stupid little asshole' over and over again.* JILL *and* TINA *are watching him. Occasionally looking at each other. This goes on for a while. Suddenly a siren goes by on the street. And then another ... And another. Pause*]

I ... think I'll go see what's going on ... It ah ... sounded like they were headed the way I was goin' anyway.

[*He shrugs. He leaves.* JILL *and* TINA *watch him silently. He is gone.* TINA *looks at* JILL. JILL *shrugs*]

JILL I guess he just needed a graceful way out.

[TINA *starts to wander around, gesturing*]

You okay?

TINA What.

JILL You okay?

TINA I don't know.

[*Pause*]

JILL I'm just glad he didn't get into any detail about his father. I bet that would have been truly ugly. You know, ugly in that boy man son dad boy dad dad son boy boy kind of way.

TINA Yeah ... His dad ... You ever meet his dad?

JILL No. Thank you, God.

TINA An asshole.

JILL And his mom?

TINA Wife of an asshole ... She tries but ... Well, what can she do ...

JILL He drinks, right?

TINA Drinks. Messes around. Spends a lot of time with his buddies ... But mostly he drinks. Bobby never drank. There was that about him.

JILL Yeah, there was.

TINA I mean he couldn't anyway. Because of his condition.

JILL Yeah. It's pretty pathetic that he used being drunk as an excuse for messing around. I mean he knew you knew he couldn't drink.

TINA He was desperate. At first, I thought it was good he was desperate. Because maybe being desperate meant he really wanted to keep me ... Wrong again! It's just the way he is. Desperate. But for what. What's he want. He's gotta want something. What is it!

JILL Maybe after what he's been through here, he just wants to go home and put his head in a vice. Get some guy in his tribe to tighten it for him.

TINA We were pretty hard on him I guess.

JILL You think so?

TINA I don't know. Maybe.

JILL You weren't. You were just trying to get to the bottom of something. I was hard on him. But that's only because I hate all men. [*laughs*]

TINA [*sits*] Do you.

JILL Come on.

TINA No. Really. Do you hate them all. I'd understand if you did.

[JILL *is walking over to* TINA]

JILL But I don't ... Well ...

TINA Sometimes?

JILL Yeah, sometimes. But ... sometimes ... other times ... you can be
with one of them and it seems okay ... Some guy, an ordinary guy.
He talks to me like I'm a human being. He seems like one himself.
And I think, this is good. This is all we need. To like each other. I
think, hey yeah, I like this guy. A lot. Kind of ... Well, at least he
doesn't want to kill me or maim me. So I guess ... some of them I
like. A few. This doesn't happen often. I've only met a few I like.
Two actually. But I'm still young. [*sits next to* TINA]

TINA I can't see myself being with anyone for a long time. Being close
to any guy. Talking ... or anything. It's all outta the question ...
because I'm ... you know ...

JILL Yeah, you're pregnant.

TINA Really.

JILL Yeah.

TINA Pregnant with Bobby's child ... But ... he's gone. So I'm, you
know ...

JILL You're not alone.

TINA No. I'm not alone. But I'm pregnant with someone's child ...
who isn't here. Someone who's gone. I mean the father's gone. So
that's different ... There's a different feeling about the whole thing
now.

JILL What is it.

TINA I don't know yet. I mean he just left ... It'll take some time to
understand it.

JILL He was never really involved. He was never a sure bet.

TINA I had hopes. I loved him, you know. I still love him.

JILL Yeah ... Why.

TINA You mean why still.

JILL No. I guess I meant why ever.

TINA Reasons ... You know you might fall in love sometime with some
guy I hate. And the reasons will be ... I mean why you love him
and I hate him ... Well, we'll never know, maybe.

JILL I hated Bobby because I never saw him show any concern for
anyone or anything besides himself.

TINA I loved Bobby because he cried when we made love. And because
... well, because I thought he loved me.

JILL Well, now we know.

TINA I mean more or less that's why.

JILL Well, we know more or less.

[*Pause*]

TINA God. I *am* young. Really. Think about how young I am.

JILL That's not necessarily a bad thing … You mean you're scared?

TINA I'm not giving up this baby. No way am I giving up this baby.

JILL I know that.

TINA I mean not even a little. My mom's not gonna raise it or anything. I mean she can help … But she's gonna be the grandmother. I'm the mother. There's not gonna be any confusion about that. Not like Grace what's-her-name.

JILL Gallagher.

TINA Yeah … Her mother's raising that kid. Her mother's the mother really. Grace is just doin' the stuff she did before. Hanging out with her friends. She goes to bars. Just like nothing happened. What kind of crap is that. That's bullshit. Don't you think that's bullshit.

JILL Well, I don't know what their circumstances are. I mean knowing Grace it's probably better for the kid.

TINA I'm not gonna do it that way.

JILL Well, you're not Grace Gallagher.

TINA No way am I Grace Gallagher. Not even a little. Not even one little stinking piece of my brain is like her. You ever hear anyone saying we're the same, you gotta straighten them out.

JILL I will.

TINA Because, Jesus, well, the only thing that's the same is … well, you know …

JILL What.

TINA Well, who's the father of Grace's kid.

JILL Beats me.

TINA Yeah. That's my point. He's gone. So it's the same. The father thing for my kid is gonna be the same as it is for Grace Gallagher's.

JILL That's not necessarily bad.

TINA Except it gives me something in common with her, and she's a total fucking idiot … and … also it's different. Different than the way I thought it would be … A bit harder. A lot harder probably.

[*Pause*]

JILL So you're really giving up on him? Bobby.

TINA Yeah … Well, what's the point … I mean I've got to make plans.

I've got to be real about this thing. It's my life. I've got to get it off on the right foot. There can't be any confusion about this. I mean look around this world we live in. All you see is confused people fucking up. And they're fucking up because they're confused about where they stand ... about ... just about everything really ... So you can't have basic stuff like who wants each other and who wants this kid just floating in the air. That's bullshit.

JILL Yeah ... I just meant he might go away and think about it.

TINA He'll miss me. I know. He'll come sniffing around. He'll make it hard and confusing. I'm gonna have to convince him to just leave me alone ... My mom went through this with my dad. My dad sniffed around for a long time. My mom waited for us to come together as a family. Until I was five or six. She tried. Maybe he even tried too. But it finally just fucked up ... I'm not going down that road. I gave Bobby his chance.

JILL Yeah.

TINA Yeah.

[*Pause*]

JILL Yeah. But ...

TINA What.

JILL Maybe not. I'm just thinking now. About guys our age. Maybe we should talk about this some other time. I mean—

TINA No, go ahead. Come on.

JILL Well you're never gonna meet a guy your age who's got as much figured out as you do. Well, a few ... Maybe ...

TINA But not Bobby.

JILL Fucking 'A' not Bobby. Look, I'm gonna try and be fair here. Forget my personal feelings about him for a while. I mean I can't stand the little prick. And I really loved kicking him. I really did. But maybe we should be looking down the road here. Considering all the possibilities ... you know, you being alone with the baby and still having these feelings for Bobby, and finding some way to make him understand that he—

TINA I told you. I can't do that. It's gotta be up to him. And it's gotta be clear.

JILL Yeah. But you see, the thing about most guys is ... It's true someone's gotta kick them when they're acting like a crazy dog. But what I'm saying is after you kick them maybe you gotta give their adolescent brains a chance to focus in on what's happened. 'Hey, I've been kicked like a crazy dog. I wonder why. Gee.' ... Okay. That's hard. That sounds hard ... Ah shit, why don't they just get it ... Why are we always made to feel bad for trying to get them to act like just basic human fucking beings! Sometimes I get the feeling they wanna suck my brains out and tie me naked to the nearest tree and fuck me to death. Because that's what they think I'm for. That's my purpose. To give them pleasure. Even if it kills me! Okay okay, I got that out of my system. So what I'm thinking, I've thought this for a while, is maybe they just need more time and instruction. Time and instruction through those dangerous stupid years between about fourteen and twenty-six. Maybe it's that simple. Maybe we have to help them. Maybe that's part of our purpose here on earth. Not all of it. Not all of it by any shot. But part of it ... So?

TINA I've got a kid due in about eight months. If you want to become some kind of tutor for Bobby that's up to you.

JILL I was thinking of conditioning. You know, lock him in a room. Then show him a thousand pictures of people in situations where they don't get to do what they want to do. No one gets to do what they want to do in any picture. They only get to do what they have to do. You know, like an adult.

TINA How about love.

JILL I think adult love is better. Okay. It's not ... pure or anything. It's mixed up with lots of other things. Responsibility. Guilt even. But overall it's better. It's got a chance of lasting. So?

TINA What.

JILL You wanna work on Bobby a little more? Turn him into an adult human being?

TINA No.

JILL Why not. It might be fun.

TINA No. He's gotta do it on his own. For his own reasons. I mean *really* he does ... I gotta eat something.

JILL Okay ... What.

TINA Anything.

JILL You getting sick yet? You know, in the mornings.

TINA I don't want to talk about that. It comes later anyway. You got any money?

JILL Hey. You're the one with the job. I'm a starving student.

TINA But I'm pregnant. I'm a single-mother-to-be. I'm headed for a life of despair and shiftiness.

[*They start off*]

JILL Over my dead body.

TINA Mine too. Not that I wouldn't take welfare if I had to.

JILL Why the hell shouldn't you if you had to.

TINA And I'd try not to be ashamed.

JILL Why the hell should you be ashamed. It's there. The money's there. And if it's not there, it should be there. What other great things are they doing with it. I mean have they got better things to do with it than give it to mothers ... If you ever have to take welfare and if anyone ever makes you feel ashamed for taking it, you tell me and I'll kick them to death.

TINA It's a deal ... And also if you hear people talking about me that other way, you know, feeling sorry for me and making me sound all sad and pitiful ... kick them to death too. Will you do that.

JILL Definitely.

[**BOBBY** *comes on*]

BOBBY Hey!

[*They turn toward him*]

So ... You leaving?

TINA Yeah.

BOBBY Yeah ... So ... I came back.

TINA Yeah ...

BOBBY You see, I've ... It's just that ... well, I've been ... I've been thinking ...

TINA Good for you. Keep it up.

[**TINA** *walks past* **JILL**, *and leaves*]

JILL She means that.

[**JILL** *winks. Turns and leaves.* **BOBBY** *watches them. Pause*]

BOBBY Hey! ... Hey, I ah ... I ah ... [*to himself*] Hey. Hey ... [*sits down. Gestures a couple of times. Shrugs. Scratches his ear*]

[*Blackout*]

[*End*]

CHRONOLOGY

The following chronology lists premieres, publications and a range of international English language productions of plays by George F. Walker since he began writing. The chronology also notes theatre residencies, artistic directorships and commercial ventures that the playwright has undertaken during this period, as well as the major awards he has received. While a number of Walker's plays have been translated into other languages—notably, German, French, Hebrew, Turkish, Polish and Czech—information about their production remains sketchy.

1970   Walker writes his first play, *Prince of Naples*, in response to a lamp-post bill soliciting scripts for Toronto's newly-founded Factory Theatre Lab.

1971   *Prince of Naples* is produced (directed by Paul Bettis) at the Factory where Walker assumes a five-year term as playwright-in-residence. He receives the first of the five Canada Council grants he will receive, and his second play, *Ambush at Tether's End*, premieres at the Factory.

1972   *Sacktown Rag* premieres at the Factory, directed by Ken Gass.

1973   Walker's first radio play, *The Private Man*, is broadcast by the Canadian Broadcasting Corporation. *Bagdad Saloon*, after premiering at the Factory, travels to the Bush Theatre in London, England.

1974   *Demerit* and *Beyond Mozambique* premiere at the Factory.

1976   Walker directs his first production—his own play, *Ramona and the White Slaves*, at the Factory. His teleplay 'Sam, Grace, Doug and the Dog' is aired by CBC-TV.

1977   Walker begins a three-year affiliation with Toronto Free

Theatre which premieres *Gossip* (directed by John Palmer) and *Zastrozzi* (directed by William Lane) this same year. Two microdramas for television, 'Overlap' and 'Capital Punishment,' are produced by CBC-TV, and 'Quiet Days in Limbo' is aired on CBC Radio. *Zastrozzi* wins the Floyd S. Chalmers Award for best new Canadian play.

1978   *Gossip* is presented at the Williamstown Festival in Massachusetts and is produced by the Empty Space Theater in Seattle, Washington. Walker returns to the Factory Theatre Lab as artistic director and directs a remount of *Beyond Mozambique*. Coach House Press publishes *Bagdad Saloon, Beyond Mozambique* and *Ramona and the White Slaves* in a volume titled *Three Plays by George F. Walker*. 'Curious' is aired on CBC Radio. *Zastrozzi* is produced by the Wakefield Tricycle Club at the King's Head Theatre in London, England.

1979   *Filthy Rich* premieres at Toronto Free Theatre, under the direction of William Lane. Walker resigns as artistic director of the Factory to devote more time to writing and directing. *Gossip* is produced at the Arts Club Theatre (Vancouver), the PAF Playhouse (Long Island, New York) and the Cricket Theater (Minneapolis, Minnesota). *Beyond Mozambique* becomes the first of many of Walker's plays to be produced in Australia when it opens at the National Institute of Dramatic Art in New South Wales.

1980   Walker directs the premiere of his first musical, *Rumours of Our Death*, at the Factory. *Zastrozzi* opens at the Court Theatre in New Zealand.

1981   Walker serves as playwright-in-residence at the New York Shakespeare Festival which presents the New York premiere of *Zastrozzi*, directed by Andrei Serban. Walker returns to Toronto to direct the Factory's premiere of *Theatre of the Film Noir* at Onstage '81, Toronto's international theatre festival. *Theatre of the Film Noir* wins the Floyd S. Chalmers Award.

1982   *The Art of War* is commissioned by Simon Fraser University

as the keynote address to the Conference on Art and
Reality. The Nimrod Theatre in Sydney, Australia, mounts
its first production of many of Walker's plays, *Beyond
Mozambique*. *Theatre of the Film Noir* wins five Dora
Mavor Moore Awards in Toronto, including one for best
new Canadian play; subsequently it tours to Vancouver.

1983 *Science and Madness* opens the season of the Tarragon
Theatre in Toronto. *The Art of War* is produced by the
Factory at Toronto Workshop Productions, directed by the
playwright. The Northern Light Theatre (Edmonton)
production of *Filthy Rich* is directed by Robert Woodruff of
San Francisco.

1984 *Theatre of the Film Noir* tours England. Walker directs *The
Art of War* as the opening play of the Great Canadian
Theatre Company's tenth season in Ottawa before flying to
Australia to direct *Zastrozzi* at the Nimrod Theatre in
Sydney. Coach House Press publishes *Gossip*, *Filthy Rich*
and *The Art of War* as a trilogy under the title *The Power
Plays*. *Criminals in Love* opens the Factory Theatre's new
Toronto space in a production directed by the playwright.

1985 *Criminals in Love* wins the 1984 Floyd S. Chalmers Award
for best new Canadian play and subsequently is published
by the Playwrights Union of Canada.

1986 *Better Living* premieres at the St. Lawrence Centre for the
Performing Arts in Toronto, directed by Bill Glassco.
Walker wins the Governor General's Award for English-
language drama for *Criminals in Love* (1985).

1987 *Beautiful City* premieres at the Factory Theatre, directed by
Bob White. *The Art of War* opens at the New Theater of
Brooklyn in New York.

1988 *Nothing Sacred* premieres at the Mark Taper Forum in Los
Angeles under the direction of Michael Lindsay-Hogg, one
of six American productions it receives this year. The
Canadian premiere of the play soon follows at Toronto's
Bluma Appel Theatre, under the direction of Bill Glassco.
Nothing Sacred wins both the Dora Mavor Moore Award

for best new Canadian play of 1988 and the Floyd S. Chalmers Award. It subsequently is published by Coach House Press. *Better Living, Beautiful City* and *Criminals in Love* are published as *The East End Plays* by the Playwrights Union of Canada.

1989 *Love and Anger* premieres at the Factory Theatre in Toronto, directed by the author. The play is published by Coach House Press and wins the Floyd S. Chalmers Award. *Better Living* opens at the Matrix Theater in Hollywood. Garth Drabinsky's Live Entertainment Corporation of Canada mounts a successful commercial production of *Nothing Sacred* at the Bluma Appel Theatre during the summer. The play also is produced in numerous theatres across the United States and Canada including the National Arts Centre in Ottawa, the American Conservatory Theater in San Francisco, the Arena Stage in Washington, D.C. and the Seattle Repertory Theater. *Nothing Sacred* also wins Walker his second Governor General's Award for English-language drama.

1990 *Nothing Sacred* is produced in Israel, Sweden and Australia. Walker wins the Dora Mavor Moore Award for best new Canadian play with *Love and Anger* (1989-90) which opens at the New York Theater Workshop in November. *Zastrozzi* is produced by the Oxford University Dramatic Society in the UK.

1991 *Escape from Happiness* premieres at Vassar College in a production by New York Film and Stage Co. in association with the Powerhouse Theater in July. *Love and Anger* opens at the Round House Theater in Maryland.

1992 Walker directs the Canadian premiere of *Escape from Happiness* for the Factory Theatre and wins both the Dora Mavor Moore Award for outstanding new Canadian play (1991-92) and the Floyd S. Chalmers Award. *Criminals in Love*, directed by Lee Milinazzo, opens at the TriBeCa Theater in New York. *Nothing Sacred* premieres in New York at the Atlantic Theater Company, directed by Max

Mayer. It later opens at the Hong Kong Repertory Theatre. *Love and Anger* opens at the Actors' Theater of San Francisco. *Zastrozzi* opens at the Shakespeare Institute in Warwickshire, UK. *Gossip* is produced at the Artists Repertory Theater in Portland, Oregon.

1993 *Tough!* premieres at Vancouver's Green Thumb Theatre for Young People and then opens at the New York Stage and Film Company. *Beyond Mozambique* opens in Chicago. *Escape from Happiness* is produced widely in the United States—at, for example, the Center Stage Company in Baltimore and the Yale Repertory Theater in Connecticut. *Criminals in Love* opens at the Round House Theater in Maryland. Walker, along with the cast and crew of *Theatre of the Film Noir* form the Shared Anxiety Cooperative to produce the play in Toronto as a commercial venture.

1994 *Tough!* opens at the Factory Theatre in Toronto, directed by Patrick McDonald. *Escape From Happiness* opens at the Round House Theater in Maryland. Walker forms the Nothing Sacred Corporation along with designer James Plaxton, producer Dian English, stage manager Paul Mark and other investors to produce the play as a commercial venture at the Winter Garden Theatre in Toronto, where it opens in September in a production co-directed by Patrick McDonald and the playwright. Walker wins a Toronto Arts Award. Coach House Press publishes *Shared Anxiety: The Selected Plays of George F. Walker.*

WORKS BY GEORGE F. WALKER

Stage Plays

Ambush at Tether's End. In *The Factory Lab Anthology.* Ed. Connie
  Brissenden. Vancouver: Talonbooks, 1974: 89-183.
The Art of War. In *The Power Plays.* Toronto: Coach House Press,
  1984.
Bagdad Saloon. In *Three Plays by George F. Walker.* Toronto: Coach
  House Press, 1978.
Beautiful City. In *The East End Plays.* Toronto: Playwrights Canada
  Press, 1988.
Better Living. In *The East End Plays.* Toronto: Playwrights Canada
  Press, 1988.
Beyond Mozambique. In *Three Plays by George F. Walker.* Toronto:
  Coach House Press, 1978.
Criminals in Love. In *The East End Plays.* Toronto: Playwrights
  Canada Press, 1988.
Escape From Happiness. Toronto: Coach House Press, 1992.
Filthy Rich. In *The Power Plays.* Toronto: Coach House Press,
  1984.
Gossip. In *The Power Plays.* Toronto: Coach House Press, 1984.
Love and Anger. Toronto: Coach House Press, 1989.
Nothing Sacred. Toronto: Coach House Press, 1988.
Prince of Naples. Toronto: Playwrights Canada Press, 1973.
Ramona and the White Slaves. In *Three Plays by George F. Walker.*
  Toronto: Coach House Press, 1978.
Rumours of Our Death. In *Canadian Theatre Review,* 25 (Winter
  1980): 43-72. Also in *The Canadian Theatre Review Anthology.*
  Ed. Alan Filewod. Toronto: University of Toronto Press, 1993:
  107-131.

Sacktown Rag. Toronto: Playwrights Union of Canada, 1972.

Science and Madness. Toronto: Playwrights Union of Canada, 1982.

Theatre of the Film Noir. Toronto: Playwrights Union of Canada, 1981.

Zastrozzi: The Master of Discipline. Toronto: Playwrights Union of Canada, 1977. Also in *Modern Canadian Plays.* Ed. Jerry Wasserman. British Columbia: Talon Books, 1984: 249-273.

Radio Plays

'Ambush at Tether's End.' TS, CBC Radio, 1974.

'The Desert's Revenge.' TS, CBC Radio, 1983 (Rebroadcast 1990).

'Curious.' TS, CBC Radio, 1978.

'Prince of Naples.' TS, CBC Radio, 1973.

'The Private Man.' TS, CBC Radio, 1973.

'Quiet Days in Limbo.' TS, CBC Radio, 1977.

Television Plays

'Capital Punishment.' TS, CBC-TV, 1977.

'Overlap.' TS, CBC-TV, 1977.

'Sam, Grace, Doug and the Dog.' TS, CBC-TV, 1976.

SELECTED CRITICISM

The following list includes press reviews of premieres, newspaper features, critical commentary from theatre magazines, interviews, dissertations and scholarly discussions of Walker plays published in academic journals.

Bemrose, John. 'Urban Survival: George F. Walker's Black Comedy Attacks Greed.' *Macleans* 102.43: 76-77.

'Best of '88.' *Time* 133.1: 106.

Borkowski, Andrew. 'Theatre of the Improbable: George F. Walker, Canada's Unlikely King of the Boards.' *Canadian Forum* 70.802 (1991): 16-19.

Bruckner, D.J.R. Rev. of *The Art of War* by George F. Walker. *New York Times* 28 April 1987: 13.

—. Rev. of *Criminals in Love* by George F. Walker. *New York Times* 7 October 1992: 16.

—. ''Filthy Rich': a Sleuth Spoof.' Rev. of *Filthy Rich* by George F. Walker. *New York Times* 8 October 1985: 13.

Conlogue, Ray. 'Walker Seeks New Voices.' *Globe and Mail* 21 November 1981: E3.

—. 'Playwright Plies Trade in U.S. but not for Free: Public Taste Catches up with George F. Walker.' *Globe and Mail* 5 November 1988: C3.

Conolly, L.W. 'Modern Canadian Drama: Some Critical Perspectives.' *Canadian Drama* 11.1 (1985): 141-9, 221-5.

—. 'Dramatic Trilogies.' *Canadian Literature* 112 (Spring 1987): 110-112.

Donnelly, Pat. 'Toronto Takes it on Chin from English Canada's Foremost Playwright.' *Gazette* (Montreal) 16 October 1989: F6.

Duchesne, Scott. 'Our Country's Good: The export market favours Walker, Tremblay and Thompson.' *Theatrum* 38 (1994): 19-23.

Fox, Terry Curtis. 'Unexaggerated Rumours.' *The Village Voice* 2 April 1979: 90-1.

Gass, Ken. 'Introduction.' *Three Plays by George F. Walker*. Toronto: Coach House Press, 1978: 9-15.

Godfrey, Stephen. 'A Canadian Hit on Three Continents.' *Globe and Mail* 29 January 1985: M7.

Gussow, Mel. 'Turgenev, with License.' Rev. of *Nothing Sacred* by George F. Walker. *The New York Times* 13 January 1989: C5.

Haff, Stephen. 'George F. Walker.' *Yale Repertory Theater Newsletter* January-February 1993: 2.

—. 'Just Say It.' Rev. of *Nothing Sacred* by George F. Walker. *Village Voice* 3 November 1992: 112.

—. 'Slashing the Pleasantly Vague—George F. Walker and the Word.' *Essays in Theatre/Études Théâtrales* 10.1: 59-69.

—. 'Spoken Opera.' Rev. of *Escape From Happiness* by George F. Walker. *Village Voice* 30 March 1993: 96.

Hallgren, Chris. 'George Walker: the serious and the comic.' *Scene Changes* 4.2 (March-April 1970): 23-25.

Johnson, Chris. 'George F. Walker.' *Post Colonial English Drama*. Ed. Bruce King. New York: St. Martin's, 1992: 82-96.

—. 'George F. Walker: B-Movies Beyond the Absurd.' *Canadian Literature* 85 (Summer 1980): 87-103.

—. 'George F. Walker Directs George F. Walker', *Theatre History in Canada* (Toronto) 9.2 (Fall 1988): 157-172.

Johnston, Denis W. 'George F. Walker: Liberal Idealism and the 'Power Plays'.' *Canadian Drama* 5.2 (1984): 195-206.

Kirchhoff, H.J. 'Money Helps After 20 Years of Freelance Terror.' *Globe and Mail* 3 March 1992: D2.

Knowles, Richard Paul. 'The Dramaturgy of the Perverse.' *Theatre Research International* 17 (Autumn 1992): 226-35.

Lane, William. 'Introduction.' *Zastrozzi: The Master of Discipline*. Toronto: Playwrights Canada Press, 1979: 3-6.

Messenger, Ann. 'Canajun, eh?' *Canadian Literature* 86 (Fall

1980): 89-93.

Milliken, Paul. 'Walker's living theatre ignites the imagination.' *Performing Arts in Canada* 18.3 (Fall 1981): 3-6.

Nunn, Robert. 'Marginality and English-Canadian Theatre.' *Theatre Research International* 17 (Autumn 1992): 217-25.

Parker, Brian. 'The Power Plays.' *Canadian Theatre Review* 43 (Summer 1985): 190-192.

Pressley, Nelson. 'Defeating the Floor.' *American Theatre* 10.4 (April 1993): 8-9.

Prokosh, Kevin. 'Housing Crunch Inspires Playwright.' *Winnipeg Free Press* 14 June 1989: 36.

Riley, Pauline. 'Theatre and Community Development.' *Links* 1989: 6.

Sinclair, Gregory J. 'Live from Off-Stage.' *The Canadian Forum* 66 (August/September 1986): 6-11.

Smith, Catherine Mary. 'Parody in the Plays and Productions of George F. Walker.' Diss. University of Toronto, 1991.

Smith, Colin. 'Tough! Act to Follow.' *Vancouver Sun* 6 February 1993: C6.

Taylor, Kate. 'Theatre for Theatre's Take.' *Globe and Mail* 18 June 1993: D9.

Uncredited. 'Biographical Checklist: George F. Walker.' *Canadian Theatre Review* 25 (Winter 1980): 39-41.

Van Gelder, Lawrence. 'Turgenev Adaptation With a Lot To Say.' Rev. of *Nothing Sacred* by George F. Walker. *New York Times* 27 October 1992: C17.

Wallace, Robert. 'George F. Walker.' *Profiles in Canadian Literature No.6.* Ed. Jeffrey M. Heath. Toronto: Dundurn Press, 1986: 105-112.

—. 'Moving Towards the Light.' *Canadian Drama* 14.1: 22-33.

Wallace, Robert, and Cynthia Zimmerman. 'George F. Walker.' *The Work: Conversations with English-Canadian Playwrights.* Toronto: Coach House Press, 1982: 212-225.

Wagner, Vit. 'Playwright Escapes his Russian Runaway.' *Toronto Star* 7 October 1989: J1,J8.

—. 'Toronto Playwright Cited in 'Powerful People' List.' *Toronto*

Star 8 September 1993: C3.

—. 'Walker Comedy a Hit Because it Hits a Nerve.' *Toronto Star* 13 January 1990: G3.

—. 'Walker Goes Back to the Family.' *Toronto Star* 15 February 1992: J1,J6.

Wasserman, Jerry. 'Making Things Clear: The film noir Plays of George F. Walker.' *Canadian Drama* 8.1 (1982): 99-101.

Wynne-Jones, Tim. 'Acts of Darkness.' *Books in Canada* 14.3 (April 1985): 11-14.

Editor for the Press; Robert Wallace
Cover Design: Malcolm Brown
Cover Photograph: D. Loek, *The Toronto Star*

COACH HOUSE PRESS
50 Prince Arthur Ave. #107
Toronto, Canada
M5R 1B5